THE GREAT WAR
AND AMERICAN
FOREIGN POLICY,
1914–24

THE GREAT WAR AND AMERICAN FOREIGN POLICY, 1914–24

ROBERT E. HANNIGAN

PENN

UNIVERSITY OF PENNSYLVANIA PRESS

PHILADELPHIA

A volume in the Haney Foundation Series, established in 1961 with the generous support of Dr. John Louis Haney

Published by
University of Pennsylvania Press
Philadelphia, Pennsylvania 19104-4112
www.upenn.edu/pennpress

Printed in the United States of America
on acid-free paper

10 9 8 7 6 5 4 3 2 1

Library of Congress Cataloging-in-Publication Data
ISBN 978-0-8122-4859-3

*Dedicated to the memory of J. Garry Clifford
and to the spirit of "the foreign policy seminar"*

CONTENTS

The Great War constituted a milestone in the development of the United States as a world power, a matter of immense importance to both American and world history. The United States—or at least elements thereof—grew rich as the European powers exhausted themselves during the conflict, while Washington deployed its growing economic leverage, its military might, and its diplomatic activity in numerous efforts both to shape the outcome of the war and to influence the future of international relations. It can indeed be suggested that the episode constituted a kind of first comprehensive rehearsal for Washington's subsequent engagement with other major powers, the underdeveloped world, and the foreign policy sentiments of the American people in the twentieth century.

As with most topics associated with what after 1939 would frequently be referred to as the First World War, this one has attracted the interest of historians before. Yet, I think it is hard to come away either from the general literature on the war or from the—on their own terms often quite excellent—studies of America's role feeling that the subject has been given its full due. This is perhaps because general studies of the Great War have largely been written by historians whose principal background, understandably, is in European history. But I would argue that it is also because those historians have had to rely on an American historical literature that cries out for a broader and more long-range view.

This book delineates the meaning and nature of American policy during the World War I era. Before all else, I would argue, it is a task requiring that U.S. activity be put in proper context. The subject of America and the Great War is usually treated as if it had little to do with events before August 1914, or even May 1915, when the *Lusitania* was sunk. But that approach makes all but impossible a clear appreciation of what American policy in the era of the Great War was about, this because it simply ignores all-important issues having to do with Washington's preexisting attitudes toward the world (and not just Europe). Likewise, and far more troubling from the standpoint of the ostensible mission of professional history, the Wilson administration's planning for the peace is still too often written as if its goals can be discerned by simply taking at face value the rhetoric of America's wartime president. Well before 1914, the United States (albeit without the strong support—or even knowledge—of most Americans) had begun to emerge as a player with its own aspirations on the global stage. And, not surprisingly, this powerfully conditioned its reaction to the European war. Washington's response to the Great War is fundamentally the story of how the United States sought to protect and then put on more stable foundations an international order to which American leaders, well before 1914, had already become strongly attached.

The study is divided into five parts. The first, consisting of one chapter, provides a discussion of American world policy as it had developed before 1914, the year war in Europe broke out. In part a distillation of my book *The New World Power*, on U.S. policy in the very late nineteenth and early twentieth centuries, it argues that, regardless of changes in administration, Washington had, well before 1914, adopted a basic approach to the world that was inherited and adhered to by the Wilson presidency (please note I am not suggesting that each administration in this period did not have its own distinctive qualities and style).[1] Part II, consisting of three chapters, treats the period of what the Wilson administration insisted was American neutrality. It explains the U.S. reaction to the war against the backdrop of Washington's commitment to a particular international order. And it traces how that administration was guided by the desire to protect and, if possible, reform that order so as to put it on firmer foundations. Ideally, the Wilson administration hoped to achieve its goals without U.S. military involvement in Europe, but its pursuit of a particular set of arrangements and, related, of a particular place for the United States in the coming twentieth-century world, in the end mattered more.

The entire course of U.S. belligerency was dominated by the Wilson administration's desire to play a major role in the settlement of the conflict, this so as to reconstruct and stabilize the world along the lines that it wanted. That story is related in the three chapters of Part III. These focus on the mobilization of U.S. power, on the public diplomacy conducted by Wilson in the period up to and after the Fourteen Points Address, and on the negotiations for an armistice.

The six chapters of Part IV discuss the American policy makers' agenda and activities at the Paris Peace Conference in service of the same aims, including U.S. participation in the design of the League of Nations and in the framing of the Treaty of Versailles. Also examined is the president's losing battle for the ratification of that treaty after his return home. Finally, in Part V, the book adumbrates the continuities between Wilson and the Republicans who succeeded him. It describes how, under circumstances that were considerably more constrained, the policy makers of the Harding-Coolidge administration sought to realize fundamentally similar international objectives. Insofar as the Great War is concerned, these culminated in the adoption of the Dawes Plan in 1924.

Absolutely central to this study of course is Woodrow Wilson, an activist president who played a pivotal role in the formulation of U.S. foreign policy for most of the years that are the principal focus of this book. It will quickly be noted that this study takes sharp issue with a view of the twenty-eighth president that remains pervasive not only in popular discourse but even in the writings of many biographers and historians (despite numerous specialized studies in recent decades that point in a different direction).

The notion that still dominates is that Wilson was essentially unique. While other great-power statesmen in history were driven by the readily identifiable motives of greed, power, and national self-interest, Wilson, it is asserted, was actuated by disinterested altruism. With a missionary's zeal and an unwavering commitment to principle, he sought to promote global peace, self-determination, and democracy. Befitting a figure propelled by such goals, he was supposedly dismissive of traditional considerations of strategy, power, and geopolitics.

This portrayal of Wilson first came broadly to be accepted in popular culture during his presidency. Perhaps that explains why it has been so easy for people to repeat it ever since. But it should never have gained the kind of authority it has, above all because its origins lay precisely in how the president advertised himself. Students of Wilson regularly comment on the care he lavished on his speeches, on the emphasis he placed on language and rhetoric. Yet, after all these years, this has not stopped many scholars from continuing to take largely at face value the president's own depictions of his actions.[2]

Perhaps the explanation rests in Wilson's exceptionally persuasive way with words. I do not wish merely to argue though that he consciously sought to put a particular gloss, especially an idealistic gloss, on his diplomacy. Not

unlike many statesmen, the twenty-eighth president had little trouble convincing himself that the policies he wanted to pursue were noble and in the
interests of all. (If he differed from others, it was rather in the degree to
which he also believed that he, and only he, could be entrusted with those
interests.)

Too many scholars have also failed to explore the meaning of the terms
and concepts Wilson employed in his writings and speeches. Wilson's rhetoric begs to be compared with his practice. Likewise, historians and biographers have no justification for saying that he was committed, for instance,
to peace—which he most definitely thought he was—without exploring
what Wilson implicitly meant by that. The same is true of his commitments
to democracy and self-determination.

Woodrow Wilson has excited strong feelings among those who have
written about him, but many critics *and* devotees have taken only a surface
measure of the man. Supporters have hailed Wilson as a kind of secular
martyr—given the president's physical collapse and the Senate's rejection
of the Versailles Treaty—on behalf of peace, freedom, and American minis-
trations to the world. Critics meanwhile have held that his foreign policies
were inattentive to considerations of self-interest, to the realities of the
world scene, and to diplomatic factors based on considerations of strategy
and power. Both of these views proceed from the president's own description of himself.

The flesh-and-blood Wilson was, however, much less consistent than
he has often been (and wanted to be) portrayed, and he most certainly did
not preside over a disinterested diplomacy. Nor did Wilson pursue a foreign policy in which geopolitical and strategic factors were absent. Whether
he was a successful diplomatist is of course a separate matter.

Woodrow Wilson is a more complex, and at least in some ways more
sophisticated, figure than the abstraction of him that has survived in far too
much public discourse and scholarship, but he may also be a more important figure—especially for Americans—to grapple with. For it is tempting
to venture that there is another reason why the abstraction—often held to
be the template of a "Wilsonianism" running through much subsequent
U.S. diplomacy—has persisted so long.[3] And that is that it has offered
Americans the comparatively happy (if misdirected) task of debating
whether it is good or bad for the United States that its policy in the world
has been so idealistic.

PART I

Background (1890s–1914)

[Americans are] part of one great English-speaking family whose proud destiny it is to lead and control the world.
　　—Former Secretary of State Richard Olney, 1897

I think the twentieth century will still be the century of the men who speak English.
　　—Vice President Theodore Roosevelt, 1901

If the existence of the British Empire should be called in question there is no knowing what constellation might then make its appearance among the powers.
　　—Secretary of State John Hay, c. 1900

[Should Britain suffer a serious disaster] in five years it will mean a war between us and some one of the great continental European nations, unless we are content to abandon the Monroe Doctrine for South America.
　　—New York Governor Theodore Roosevelt, 1900

The Anglo-Saxon people have undertaken to reconstruct the affairs of the world, and it would be a shame upon them to withdraw their hand.
　　—President of Princeton University, Woodrow Wilson, 1904

It is confidently expected that the initiative of the United States will lead to the early establishment at The Hague of a permanent court of arbitration. Such an eventuality will be the realization of one of the aspirations of all the centuries. The ideal is as old as the Roman altar of peace.
　　—Secretary of State Philander C. Knox, 1910

CHAPTER 1

The United States Steps Out

Washington had a definite world policy in 1914, the year the Great War broke out in Europe. Understanding what it was is critical for grasping the nature of the U.S. response to that conflict. While the members of the Wilson administration, which had come to power in early 1913, had certainly brought with them their own particular ideas and emphases, they operated broadly within a set of fundamental tenets most of whose origins dated back to the end of the nineteenth century. This chapter provides a summary overview of this all-important background.

Foreign policy activism was not something new for the republic at the turn of the century. Indeed, Massachusetts senator Henry Cabot Lodge was on fairly safe ground when he asserted in 1895 that the United States had "a record of conquest, colonization, and territorial expansion unequalled by any people of the nineteenth century."[1] But earlier activity had been focused overwhelmingly on the acquisition, occupation, and development of the most valuable portions of North America. What was different, starting in the late nineteenth century, was that a growing number of influential political, military, and business figures, taking stock of the U.S. rapid industrial expansion and growing might, were now focused outward on the world beyond that continent.[2]

In many ways the model was England, this particularly insofar as prominent Americans, following the lead of the naval strategist Alfred Thayer Mahan, were now coming to think of their home continent as a kind of gigantic analog of the British Isles. America here was reconceptualized as a kind of oversized island whose future destiny was to be shaped by its ability to expand its economic activity and project its influence out across the surrounding seas. In widely read books and articles, Mahan, the celebrator of sea power of the sort that Britain historically had practiced, encouraged the American national elite to pursue what he called its future "wealth and greatness" via comparable naval and maritime means.[3]

The way this subsequently was pursued owed yet more to the British example. In the broadest terms, influential U.S. political, business, and military leaders had, by the end of the nineteenth century, come strongly to identify with key elements of an international order that had taken shape over the course of the previous fifty to one hundred years, largely under the aegis of the policy and power of Britain, "the first industrial nation." They were convinced that if essential elements of that international order—as they saw it, that *natural* international order—could be sustained, America would in the coming century ascend to a rightful global position of leadership, responsibility, and influence comparable to, if not exceeding, that of its "mother country."

As was the case with the other large industrial and industrializing powers at this time (including England), which it saw as its rivals, the policy of the United States was driven by the idea that America's future depended on its standing in the broader world.[4] In turn, this was seen to depend on the success with which it could assert its leadership and expand its economic activity in less industrial regions in competition with those other powers. (Such extensive activity had of course become possible only over the course of the nineteenth century because the industrial revolution had given rise to new forms of power, especially military power, and to new methods of transport, communications, and protection from disease for people from northern climes who were sent to undertake tasks in other parts of the globe.)[5]

At this point, American leaders looked in particular to the rest of the Americas and to China as lands that were valuable and in which they had a strong chance to fare well, this partly because of what they felt were geographic advantages they had relative to their European (British and continental) rivals in accessing those areas. The United States also had a greater domestic resource base than any of the other industrial states and growing supplies of capital. Its manufacturing output was in the 1890s already exceeding that of England. So long as this growing economic competitiveness, stemming from these factors, could be brought to bear, U.S. leaders felt every reason to be optimistic that American trade and influence would ultimately come to dominate in both regions.[6]

Yet, there was the rub. The future that American leaders envisioned for other lands was not necessarily that desired by the leaders of other, rival states (or by the people who lived in those lands themselves). If the earlier expansion of the United States across North America had led many Europeans (starting at least as early as Alexis de Tocqueville) to sit up and take notice, turn-of-the-century American leaders took alarm at the rapid European partition of Africa in the 1880s and 1890s. To them it was axiomatic that the whole world would benefit by American leadership in the twentieth century. But if such dividing up of the less industrialized world continued elsewhere, the prospect of that would be diminished.

American leaders wanted to discourage that trend in general. But they were especially anxious to prevent any interference with the expansion of American activity in the Americas and in China. To avoid that they sought to shore up and make permanent the existing political boundaries and open door (equal access) commercial framework in both regions. To a large degree, those arrangements had been set up and upheld by London during the nineteenth century. They dated back to Britain's efforts (in the post-Napoleonic era) to undermine the control over South America exercised by Spain and Portugal and (in the era of the Opium War and after) to break the Qing Empire's resistance to the involvement of others in China. Now they were to become the hallmark of Washington's two most fundamental turn-of-the-century foreign policies, known in shorthand as the Monroe Doctrine and the "open door policy."

These aspirations carried obvious implications for U.S. policy toward its neighbors in North America. If Washington was going to enter into rivalry with the other major powers of the world, it seemed increasingly important that its strategic priorities also become those of the Dominion of Canada to the north and the (after 1910) increasingly nationalistic Republic of Mexico to the south. The former was largely achieved as a consequence of a major confrontation (with both Ottawa and London) over the boundary between Alaska and British Columbia in 1903. As shall be seen, Mexican-American relations were, by contrast, to be in considerable turmoil throughout the period of the Great War. For both Canada and Mexico, relations with Washington were also impacted by the latter's desire to see their food and raw materials become an extension of the resource base of the United States.

Of especial pertinence to this story, America's extracontinental aspirations ultimately seemed also to require greater attention to affairs in Europe. The possibility of war there, among intensely rivalrous, increasingly globally oriented major powers, many of whom shared common boundaries, seemed to American leaders to be something they should not ignore. Not only might such conflict jeopardize a very important trade, mostly in farm products, that the United States continued to conduct with that continent. It also might bring about rearrangements of power that could affect adversely a broader international order that American leaders wished to maintain. As noted, throughout the early to mid-nineteenth century the U.S. posture had repeatedly been that of a state testing existing boundaries and challenging the status quo. Perhaps ironically, as the United States emerged as a rising power on the world stage, it did so in important ways as a defender of the status quo.

American leaders were particularly anxious that Britain's predominant influence in the eastern hemisphere not be overturned (this by contrast with the western hemisphere where they were eager to see Britain's role reduced). Washington saw itself as a rival of London. At the same time, it believed that Britain's posture and key policies were often aligned with those the United States desired. Such policies included relatively equal trade access for all nations to British markets. "[T]hrough what agency," former Secretary of State Richard Olney asked an audience at Harvard rhetorically in 1898, "are we so likely to gain new outlets for our products as through that of a Power whose possessions girdle the earth and in whose ports equal privileges and facilities of trade are accorded to the flags of all nations?" (For this among other reasons, Olney described Americans as "part of one great English-speaking family whose proud destiny it is to lead and control the world.") They included as well London's avowed support for existing political boundaries and for the open door policy in China and South America.[7]

U.S. leaders did not want to face a situation where the power of Britain and its fleet in the eastern hemisphere was eclipsed by that of one or more rivals who might be less attached to a global order seen to work to America's advantage. Anxious to head off the turmoil and possible rearrangements of power that might accompany a European war, Washington, beginning at the turn of the century, gradually began to promote better relations with England and, when called for, to bolster that power's position in the eastern hemisphere. Simultaneously, American leaders sought, often in conjunction with their British counterparts, to promote reforms in the conduct of international affairs, particularly mechanisms for the settlement of disagreements that would diminish the prospects for wars and upheavals.

In the late nineteenth and early twentieth centuries, U.S. leaders commonly explained their overseas activities and ambitions, both to themselves and to anyone else who would listen, by recourse to social evolutionary thought.[8] Variants of such thought had become popular in both Europe and America in the wake of the rise to prominence of theories of evolution in the field of biology in the nineteenth century. At bottom they involved the misapplication of those scientific ideas to society.

Such thought initially gained currency in the United States as much for reasons of domestic as foreign policy. In a society that was coming increasingly to be marked by inequality during the Gilded Age and after, social evolutionary ideas became especially popular among those who wished to defend from criticism what they saw as the fundamental fairness of the way the social and economic system was organized. In this telling, huge disparities of wealth and power in America were principally to be explained by the fact that the country was filling up with more and more people who were not of old-stock, Protestant, Northwestern European background. Such latter folk were the ones who largely controlled wealth and power in America, it was maintained, because they had evolved further than other people beyond the nasty, brutish creatures that all humans originally had been. Above all they were endowed with a superior character, specifically a self-mastery, that fitted them for accomplishments and responsibilities that others were incapable of. (In this view, the idea that "all men are created equal" was simply seen as quaint and naive.)

Such conceits, dressed up as science, were easily transferred to the global scene. Seemingly without exception, every American policy maker in the late nineteenth and early twentieth centuries accepted a social evolutionary view that presented the world as a place composed of an enormous array of differently endowed "races," each of which, it was held, occupied a specific evolutionary position somewhere back down the "path of progress" behind the elements who led the United States. In this view, America was the seat of the most mature and civilized men in the world. It was axiomatic that they had an obligation to exercise leadership and, most importantly, prevent "irresponsible" or "selfish" people, who lacked their self-controlled wisdom, from interfering with the world as it should be.

Strikingly, U.S. policy makers found one of the biggest threats to such international custodianship to actually be the American people. For—"irresponsibly" or perhaps "selfishly"—sizable numbers of them often voiced objections to the overseas activities American statesmen wanted U.S. resources to be used for. Indeed, these views were often articulated in Congress. Many Americans felt that the new activities inappropriately broke with tradition. A still quite widely shared sentiment, dating back to the early republic, held in suspicion a large military establishment, an executive branch with wide latitude in foreign affairs, or any other of what were seen as the trappings associated with empire. These were considered counter to the ideals the country had been founded on and were seen as a potential threat to citizens' liberties.

Large numbers of Americans were particularly opposed to any "entanglement" by the United States in European affairs. Political or military involvement in Europe, or alliances with European powers, was held to be contrary to sage advice that Washington had given in his Farewell Address. More to the point, such activity was thought dangerous. It could draw the United States into costly conflicts among the seemingly always quarreling Old World powers.

Still others incorporated foreign policy into a critique of corporate power that was widely held in turn-of-the-century America. Many argued that the new "trusts" were coming to exercise a dangerous degree of power over the economy and the political system of the country. A move toward a more active overseas policy, they thought, represented an effort by those same business and financial entities to get the nation to promote and protect their economic interests abroad. Such criticism was voiced in Congress by numerous southern Democrats and, after 1909, by insurgent midwestern Republicans.[9]

Proponents of a more active overseas policy sought to counter such opposition in a variety of ways. They employed nationalism and tried to rouse support within society around such symbols as the flag and the navy. They spoke, as Theodore Roosevelt among others did, of manhood and racial strength, of the importance of an active foreign policy to the maintenance of American virility. And, more successfully, they spoke—increasingly over time—in terms of duty, uplift, and service to civilization. Woodrow Wilson was hardly the first to define U.S. overseas activity in such terms, although he was unusually effective.[10]

*   *   *

For the period from the late nineteenth century up until the outbreak of the war in Europe, the unfolding of American policy on the world stage can best be traced and understood by examining it regionally. This is true despite the fact that (as shall be noted in several instances below) concepts and practices that first emerged in one area often inspired—or at least ran parallel—to those applied elsewhere. (Indeed, many of Washington's efforts to establish order overseas in these years bear comparison with certain reforms—part of a "search for order"—at home that were endorsed by self-styled "progressives" such as Roosevelt and Wilson.)

U.S. Latin American policy at the turn of the century is best comprehended if a distinction is made between the region around the Caribbean and South America.[11] Unlike the countries to the south, the lands of the Caribbean, with the one exception of Cuba, were not held to be of great economic potential by American policy makers. On the other hand, from the standpoint of the broader role in the world Washington was envisaging, the region was assigned enormous strategic importance. This derived above all from the desire of American policy makers to build and control a canal across Central America. Such a canal was seen as having immense commercial value. It would provide a shortcut for the transport of goods from eastern, industrial America to all of the markets bordering the Pacific. It was also seen as possessing great military value. Once built, strategists pointed out, it would greatly facilitate the movement of vessels in America's expanding navy between the Atlantic, across which the greatest U.S. rivals lay, and the Pacific, across which Washington hoped to develop its influence in the coming century. The canal would double the utility of each warship the bicoastal United States built and allow it to mass power in either ocean.

In order for it to serve, economically and militarily, as desired, however, the United States would have to control access to the canal. Subsequent American policy toward the Caribbean largely flowed from this requirement. Such control seemed to necessitate, first of all, naval bases in the region. The United States was able to begin acquiring these in the aftermath of its war with Spain over Cuba in 1898. It also obliged Washington to prevent any potential enemies from building up such facilities for themselves.

Initially, policy makers saw this as a matter of convincing other great powers that the United States could, and successfully would, go to war to prevent any of them from expanding their political-military influence in the region (the threat, embodied in the Monroe Doctrine, first announced in 1823 but emphatically reasserted in the mid-1890s, as discussed below).

During the opening years of the new century, however, this task resolved itself into something more complex. Rather than it being challenged overtly, American leaders began to fear that there was a greater likelihood of their prohibition being undermined obliquely. States in the Caribbean might "invite" political-military involvement on the part of U.S. rivals. In particular, such intervention might be the upshot of issues related to claims, debts, or disorders in these weak and impoverished countries. These in turn could lead, under prevailing international law, to legal occupations of territory by European states. Such were the lessons American policy makers took away from a confrontation between Venezuela and several European powers in late 1902.

In the aftermath of that—successfully contained—crisis, the Roosevelt administration articulated a "corollary" to the Monroe Doctrine. The objective was to eliminate any occasion or pretext for other powers to play a political-military role in the Caribbean. Intent upon showing "those Dagos," as he privately referred to the people of the region, that they had to behave as the great powers wished, TR issued a warning. "[W]rong-doing," or disorder, he announced, might call forth "intervention" by a "civilized" nation. But if such was called for, it would be undertaken by the United States. Washington could not ignore what TR called "this duty."[12]

From this point forward, it was Washington's policy to make sure that a pro-American stability and financial order prevailed among all of the small nations of the Caribbean. Policy makers endeavored to bring to power, to cultivate, to tutor, and to support individuals and groups they felt they could depend on. Generally, they looked for these purposes to rich landed elements or the military. They looked down on the vast majority of the people of the region, seeing them as "weak" and "irresponsible." Indeed, their "race" was held to be the cause of the corruption, widespread poverty, and political turmoil in the region.

Where necessary, Washington pursued greater oversight. Drawing on ideas popular in "progressive era" America for dealing with immigrant "misrule" in U.S. cities, policy makers tried in a number of instances to take "out of politics" the key financial levers of power in Caribbean states. Purportedly disinterested Americans would then provide from behind the scenes the management of these countries that "civilization" demanded and under which they might be "uplifted." The hope also was that banking and business ties with the United States would grow, displacing European interests and solidifying the American connection. Customs, or financial, receiverships, or "guardianships," were pursued with a number of the island and Central American countries of the Caribbean with these ends in view.

But policy makers hardly ruled out military force. In fact, the navy constantly patrolled the region and marine contingents were landed on numerous occasions. The navy was used to intimidate uncooperative nationalist politicians and to influence the outcome of local revolutions. Cuba was occupied for a second time between 1906 and 1909 (the first had occurred immediately following the U.S. war with Spain). An oversized American legation guard lent support to a regime set up during the administration of William Howard Taft in Nicaragua. And these events established a precedent for the establishment of military occupations by the United States in Haiti and in the Dominican Republic in 1915 and 1916.

By contrast with most of the countries of the Caribbean, the nations of South America were felt to hold considerable economic value and political weight. Policy makers prized the markets and resources of this vast region (described by policy influential James G. Blaine as early as the 1880s as a "commercial empire that legitimately belongs to us").[13] They also hoped to align the entire continent behind the United States in international affairs. But there were threats to this future. Here too, these were seen to lie both in the "selfishness" of other powers and in local "irresponsibility."

American leaders worried that rivals might try to become major political-military players in the region, likewise that they might assert influence in such a way as would make less secure U.S. access to its markets. Against the backdrop of the partition of Africa, policy makers were nervous that that "scramble" might move on to South America. Fears of that sort led the Cleveland administration in 1895–96 to make an issue of what it perceived as London's ambitions along the frontier between British Guiana and Venezuela. It accused Britain of trying to grab valuable land to which it had no legitimate claim. And it used the occasion to broadcast to the world that the United States still took seriously the Monroe Doctrine. One breach of its prohibition of further European expansion in the Americas would lead to others, argued the American secretary of state. Soon the United States would have to arm on land as well as sea to preserve what he called the "predominance of the Great Republic in this hemisphere."[14] The dispute was ultimately settled amicably between the powers, and Washington came to accept that Britain too opposed "any disturbance of the existing territorial distribution" in the western hemisphere.[15] But the same confidence was not expressed about other powers, especially Germany.[16]

Concerned about "selfishness" on the part of its rivals, Washington maintained that it would, if necessary, forcibly uphold the Monroe Doctrine. At the same time, it disavowed any interest in territory for itself in South America, promised U.S. support for the open door there ("save," said TR, "as the individual countries enter into individual treaties with one another"), and pledged that European nationals and investments would not be without protection.[17] The hope was that the other powers would accept these ground rules.

Policy makers also fretted over behavior and attitudes in the region itself. In many ways, the oligarchic, export-oriented governments that had come into being in much of South America by the late nineteenth century exemplified what Washington was after. They were seen to be progressive, as American leaders defined that, in terms of their general attitudes toward order and property. And their leaders, generally of European ancestry, were seen as a bulwark against the allegedly inferior mestizo, Native American, and African-descended masses of those countries. TR's secretary of state, Elihu Root, lavishly praised the governments of the region in these terms during a trip to the principal coastal cities of South America in 1906.[18]

At the same time, Washington still worried that the conduct of South America's governments might be such as to open the way for U.S. rivals to intervene and play a greater role. Given ongoing boundary disputes throughout the interior of the continent, policy makers worried that disorder arising from interstate conflict might create an opportunity for such involvement. They were also uneasy because many Latin American statesmen took a different view than the great powers as to the "rights" possessed by outsiders doing business in their countries. International law—largely the product of the great powers—recognized a state's right to intervene diplomatically on behalf of its nationals to ensure that they and their interests were treated in accordance with "internationally recognized" standards when operating in a foreign land. However, in Latin America this principle was viewed as affording special privileges to the big powers and their citizens and as an affront to the sovereignty of small states. Argentine publicist Carlos Calvo insisted that foreigners should have to conduct their business in Latin American countries on the same terms that citizens of those countries did.[19] This hesitancy by the region to accept its "international obligations" not only constituted, from Washington's perspective, a challenge to the conditions desired for Americans interested in doing business there, but also "invited" confrontations with Europe.

In addition, culturally and economically, all of these nations had historically closer ties to Europe than to North America. And the Spanish-American states, in particular, had, since the U.S. annexations in the era of the Mexican-American War, viewed Washington with suspicion. They worried less about European than American domination.

American policy makers sought to address these challenges in a variety of ways. Root argued that American political figures had to try to overcome the strong cultural and other traditional ties to Europe by being more solicitous of their Latin American counterparts ("The South Americans now hate us," he lamented upon becoming secretary of state, "largely because they think we despise them and try to bully them").[20] During his tour of the southern continent, he sought to dampen fears of the United States by pledging Washington's commitment to the "independence and equal rights" of all states. Upon his return, he tried to stimulate a major trade offensive toward the region by American exporters. He also worked to get the government to promote the expansion of American banking and shipping ties with the region.

Root, however, had no patience with the philosophy associated with Calvo. Despite his public professions of respect for the sovereignty of all states, he in fact believed that sovereignty was something "held upon the condition" of a country performing its "obligations" to outsiders.[21] The crucial challenge, as he saw it, was to find a way to pressure the South Americans to "behave" in accordance with the desires of the great powers without further alienating them from the United States.

The issue arose most dramatically in connection with widespread Latin American support for the Calvo-inspired Drago Doctrine, named for the Argentine foreign minister Luis Maria Drago. It involved opposition to the idea that force was an acceptable means of big countries collecting public debts owed by small countries. Root implored the Latin American states not to make a regional stand on the principle and instead agreed to raise the question at the Second Hague Conference, of 1907. However, the resolution that passed there—with the support of the European powers—actually condoned force in certain instances. Force would be ruled out if, but only if, a debtor state did not refuse a request for the dispute to be submitted to an outside arbitral tribunal (upholding, it was expected, great-power standards) for assessment and disposition.

The Taft administration tried to sustain the South American offensive of its predecessor. This was assisted by the new interest Wall Street was exhibiting in foreign business in this period. But political relations with most of the region deteriorated badly over the course of its tenure. At least in part, this was a reflection of the poor diplomatic skills, and sometimes openly bullying tone, of Philander C. Knox, Taft's secretary of state. When Wilson entered the presidency, he tried to revive the emphasis on what a later age would term "soft power" that had been Root's hallmark.[22]

Washington's most comprehensive response to the challenges it faced in South America came in the form of the Pan-American movement. It was designed to build closer ties between the United States and Latin America at the expense of Europe. One of its key objectives was to promote the peaceful settlement of disputes among states in the Americas. The U.S. position was that it was the only great power that should be involved in such efforts. More broadly, American leaders pushed for regularly held conferences and the creation of the Bureau of the American Republics (later the Pan-American Union). The Bureau, sponsored and directed by the United States, focused on the promotion of hemispheric commerce and on cultural and educational exchanges. Patent, copyright, and trademark protection, as well as sanitation, were additional topics taken up at the conferences, whose agendas were also largely developed in Washington.

*   *   *

Across the Pacific, policy makers saw China as a land of potentially even greater economic and political significance in the coming century. To them it seemed inevitable that this large and populous country would develop into a huge market for industrial products. Leadership over China seemed likely to flow to whichever outside power played the biggest role in such development. And that in turn seemed certain greatly to enhance the influence that that power would be able to exert in international affairs. The United States was seen to have key advantages by virtue of its rising economic might and the greater proximity it enjoyed relative to its most formidable industrial rivals, in Western Europe. Policy makers were convinced that America would achieve ascendance if the open door framework, promoted by Britain in the nineteenth century, was maintained.

But they were confronted with formidable issues. At the turn of the century, Russia seemed disposed to challenge the open door, at least throughout northern China. It was feared that might set off a "scramble" detrimental to the open door's continuance throughout the empire. In this part of the world, American leaders were reluctant to threaten other major states with force. Washington had taken advantage of its victory over Spain to acquire a chain of base sites across the Pacific. In 1898, it obtained Guam and the Philippines from that power, while it simultaneously formalized its control over Hawaii. But the United States did not have the ability to match the land forces that an adjoining power like Russia could bring to bear on the mainland of Asia. Nor was it likely that such a course would anytime soon have the support of the American public.

China's behavior also posed a problem. By comparison with those in South America, its government appeared weak and less capable of maintaining the kind of order the great powers wanted. Popular resentment of foreign involvement was growing. Washington worried that this could not, perhaps would not, be checked by Beijing. The government's deficiencies, as American policy makers saw it, threatened to "invite" more in the way of great-power involvement there.

Unable to ban the participation of other great powers in the region, Washington sought instead to limit its rivals' freedom of unilateral action. In his famous open door notes of 1899, William McKinley's secretary of state, John Hay, tried to put Russia on the spot by asking all of the interested powers to reiterate that they had no intention of interfering with the open door.[23] Simultaneously, American policy makers hoped to involve all of the powers in the collective promotion of a Chinese government that would be both strong and cooperative, that could and would "behave."

In 1900, with the so-called Boxer Rebellion, antiforeignism assumed unprecedented dimensions in northern China. The United States participated in a combined great-power military expedition sent to put down the hostilities. It also sought to maintain the principle of collective action during the negotiations with Beijing that followed the suppression of the rebellion. Hay said that Washington's objective was to protect American interests and prevent "a recurrence of such disasters." In accomplishing that last result, the United States would seek "a solution which may preserve Chinese territorial and administrative entity, protect all rights guaranteed to friendly powers . . . , and safeguard for the world the principle of equal and impartial trade with" all of the empire.[24]

Saint Petersburg tried now to solidify its control over the northernmost provinces. Hay was ultimately prepared to concede that, providing Russia did not close the area off to other powers' trade. But Tokyo was not. It was uncomfortable with Russia's growing political-military presence in Northeast Asia. And it was in a position to act, by virtue of the fact that over the course of the late nineteenth-century Japan had ultimately been able to sidestep integration as a subordinate into the new global order being created by the industrializing states. It had been able to develop its military and economy by adapting the methods of the other powers and was now emerging as their rival in this region. Entering into an alliance in 1902 with Britain helped. In 1904, London's new ally launched a surprise attack aimed at clearing both southern Manchuria and Korea of Russian influence.

The Roosevelt administration was initially exultant. Japan, TR said, was "playing our game."[25] It was not long, however, before Tokyo's victories began to give rise to a concern that Japan might now become a threat to American ambitions in the region. TR subsequently worked to ensure that the war did not result in Russia being removed altogether as a force Tokyo would have to worry about.

Chinese "behavior" had again become an issue by mid-1905. Beginning in July, the United States was confronted with the organization of a popular boycott of American trade. The dispute had its origins in decades of American discrimination against, and harassment of, immigrants and visitors to the United States from China. The boycott was an early manifestation of a new national spirit that had begun to take root there. But it hardly represented the kind of cooperative "regeneration" American policy makers had been envisioning. The protest activity was viewed as a threat not only to U.S. trade, but also to Washington's prestige in China and its standing among the other powers. The Roosevelt administration tried to defuse the issue by pushing the U.S. Bureau of Immigration to show less "insolence" toward Chinese "gentlemen" and students. But it simultaneously pressed Beijing to suppress the popular movement and made preparations for a major demonstration of U.S. military force if it could, or would, not do that (it did). The eruption of a similar dispute with Tokyo beginning in 1906 led Washington officials to conclude that issues involving immigration or the organization of China might someday bring a confrontation between the United States and the Japanese Empire.

After 1908, policy makers hoped that Wall Street's new interest in overseas business might finally give them the leverage necessary to address the "greed" of rivals as well as Chinese "weakness" and "irresponsibility." The Taft administration sought to gain American participation in Chinese development projects, and Knox also wanted to establish the principle that every major project there be handled collectively by the powers. The substitution of an interlocked, "harmonious" approach in place of unilateral action, as he saw it, would shore up the open door, counter Japan's efforts to create a sphere of influence in southern Manchuria, and promote stability in the region. It would also strengthen the powers in their efforts, directly and through their banks, both to supervise China and to transform its economic and political practices. (Years later, Knox would depict what he was trying to promote as a "league of nations" for China.)[26]

Little came of this activity. But Knox supported the principle of cooperative action even more firmly after China began to undergo a major revolution at the end of 1911. Under such circumstances, "harmonious action" seemed vital, both as a means by which the powers could coordinate the protection of their interests in China and as a mechanism that would inhibit forms of unilateralism threatening to U.S. policy.

Anxious about its strength and inclinations, the United States and the other outside powers withheld recognition of the new republic declared in 1912. They and their banking groups, now comprising an international financial consortium, also responded sternly when approached by the new regime about a loan. They sought foreign financial oversight and the reorganization of China's tax system and public administration. The new government resisted such a "guardianship" and sought better terms. Woodrow Wilson gambled that the United States could gain more by breaking with the other powers and recognizing the republic. But, as shall be seen, he was no less interested in promoting American leadership over China and propping up the open door (and that would eventually lead him back toward the cooperative approach pursued by his predecessors).

There was an overarching thrust to U.S. policy toward Latin America and China as the twentieth century opened. In both places, Washington strove to shore up and stabilize political boundaries and frameworks for trade that had been established earlier, to a considerable extent by Britain. The worry was that these might be challenged by other powers.

The approach taken depended largely on the influence Washington was capable of bringing to bear. European powers were warned off of the Americas, while they were at the same time given assurances (not always adhered to in the Caribbean) as to the open door. The United States also assumed responsibility for "policing" Latin America's behavior on behalf of "civilization." The hope was that the other powers would all come to accept the arrangements Washington wanted to see prevail. By contrast, in China, policy makers were not in a position to declare the United States the sole superintendent of "civilization." Their activity was directed instead toward the absorption of all of the other powers there into a unified "community of interests," a collective supervision of that state premised on its existing political boundaries and the open door. In both cases, policy makers envisioned themselves as rescuing these areas from "selfishness" and taking them "out of politics."

Simultaneously, Washington sought to address what it saw as "weakness" and "irresponsibility" on the part of the governments and peoples of these regions. Policy makers tried by various means to promote friendly regimes that, by the standards of the powers, could and would "behave." This would help to shore up existing political boundaries and frameworks for trade and to pave the way for the growth of U.S. influence and commerce.

*   *   *

In economic as well as political-military terms, North America as a whole was coming to be thought of as the U.S. home base. During the early twentieth century, Washington warned other powers, especially Great Britain, against any interference with this agenda, but the challenges it faced came principally from within Canada and Mexico themselves.

Canada and the United States had oftentimes quarreled over land and resources, and such disagreements continued to dominate their relationship at the turn of the century. The most serious dispute was over the boundary of Alaska. Convinced that Ottawa dared challenge the United States over such questions only because of the dominion's continued connection to London, the Roosevelt administration decided to use this occasion to give both governments a powerful lesson. The vigor of its subsequent response—including the threat to use force if necessary to settle the matter—was designed not only to win this argument. It was meant to teach Britain that a drastic curtailment of its role in North America was the price of good relations with the United States. And it was intended to show the "spoiled child" Canada that it had no choice but to accept a subordinate position.[27]

After the Alaska boundary dispute was settled on its terms, Washington adopted a friendlier attitude toward Canada. Employing many of the techniques of Pan-Americanism, policy makers worked to line Canada up behind U.S. global policy and to present Washington as that country's natural protector. Policy makers encouraged the creation of bilateral commissions to regularize the settlement of future disputes. The objective was to smooth over Canadian-American relations and to integrate the dominion into a framework of U.S. continental leadership. Unsuccessfully, the Taft administration, via a reciprocal trade treaty, tried in one fell swoop to ensure that Canada continued to develop as a resource adjunct of the U.S. economy.[28]

At the very start of the twentieth century policy makers were, by contrast, immensely pleased with the situation in Mexico. Porfirio Díaz, that country's authoritarian president since the 1880s, presided over a government that could and did "behave," that ensured order, and that cooperated with the United States. At one point, TR proclaimed him "the greatest statesman now living."[29] Díaz worked with Washington on several occasions in Central America and in hemispheric affairs, acting as a bridge between the United States and rest of the countries of Latin America. He also encouraged Mexican-U.S. trade and extensive American investment, particularly in mining and oil (though the extent of Mexico's dependence on America eventually came to frighten Díaz). Americans owned so much property in Mexico, and its economy had come to be so integrated into that of the United States, that State Department officials in 1910 described Mexico as an economic "extension of the [U.S.] southwest."[30]

All of this seemed in jeopardy after a revolution toppled Díaz in 1911. The Taft administration hoped it could promote similarly favorable conditions and relations under new leadership. It worked to uphold Díaz's successor, Francisco Madero, while at the same time pushing him to maintain the kind of order that Washington wanted. Massive social and political tensions had built up in the country however.

The U.S. ambassador ultimately lost patience with the new president and abetted a bloody seizure of power by one of Madero's generals, Victoriano Huerta. But the horrified reaction to this event throughout much of Mexico raised questions as to its impact on stability. From the standpoint of the incoming Wilson presidency, an even more important issue was what impact recognition of the new government would have on American objectives in the Caribbean. This concern added yet another dimension to U.S. engagement with its southern neighbor.

*   *   *

While they looked southward from their continent-island toward Latin America and westward across the Pacific toward China, American policy makers also felt compelled to pay attention to broader questions of great-power politics, especially to the balance of power in the Old World and to rivalries within the European state system from which Washington histori-cally had tried to remain detached.[31] American policy makers did not want to become enmeshed in European politics. They also knew that there was immense opposition to "entanglement" on the part of the American public. But, anxious to stabilize the existing international order, they began to take steps to influence affairs across the Atlantic.

The United States worked to diminish Britain's political-military role in the Americas, and the two powers clashed over other matters as well (particularly the influence to be allowed Japan in northern China). But Washington valued and supported London's continued preeminence in the eastern hemisphere. Policy makers appreciated Britain's general commit-ment to the open door for trade. The Royal Navy was seen as an important prop of the Monroe Doctrine. And London and Washington were seen as sharing a common stake in the essentials of the status quo.

A strong Britain was a hedge against the emergence in Europe of a state that was capable of challenging the existing international order. Despite its own preference to avoid "entanglement," London historically had in-tervened in continental affairs to prevent a single state from becoming predominant. A number of American policy makers came to see such a balancing role by Britain as working in the U.S. interest.

Although Washington would drive a hard bargain, it was receptive when London sought to improve relations beginning in the late 1890s. These had been testy ever since the American Revolution. The two states settled many outstanding issues, and Washington came to adopt a generally more

positive and cooperative attitude toward Britain. At times, this was manifested in diplomacy that was meant to prop up London's position relative
to its rivals. The United States provided valuable diplomatic assistance to
Britain during the Boer War (1899–1902), at a time when London was
faltering militarily in South Africa and absorbing considerable criticism
from continental Europe. Washington also tilted in favor of Britain and
France, versus Germany, at the Algeciras conference in Spain in 1906. "If
the existence of the British Empire should be called in question," commented Hay on the former occasion, "there is no knowing what constellation might then make its appearance among the powers."[32] Should Britain
suffer a disaster, TR predicted, "in five years it will mean a war between us
and some one of the great continental European nations, unless we are
content to abandon the Monroe Doctrine for South America."[33] Despite a
desire to maintain friendly relations with Germany, Root told America's
chief delegate to the Spanish conference on Morocco several years later, the
Entente Cordiale (between London and Paris) "is useful to us as well as
agreeable."[34] Such thinking was becoming more common among policy
makers.

On another level, U.S. leaders also sought to promote arbitration and
other schemes for the peaceful settlement of disputes among the powers.
Wars not only disrupted commerce, they could lead to rearrangements of
power and to the creation of a formidable challenger to the Anglo-
American-oriented status quo. Here again the objective was to stabilize the
prevailing international order.

The United States, quite often in collaboration with Britain, took a leading role in promoting means (beyond bilateral negotiations) by which disputes between countries might be settled short of war. This included
encouragement of mediation, commissions of inquiry, treaties of arbitration, the development of international law, and regular conferences at The
Hague to take up such questions. Alongside Britain, the United States
played a key role in establishing a Permanent Court of Arbitration at the
First Hague Peace Conference, in 1899. Eight years later, in connection with
a second Hague Conference, the Roosevelt administration inaugurated a
campaign, continued under Taft, for another court that would be more
truly judicial. Joseph Hodges Choate, Washington's chief representative,
praised this as an institution that would "build up a system of international
law" to "regulate the conduct of nations."[35] Smaller states raised sharp

objection, however, to the big powers' idea that they should control the court's bench (and, thereby, the law it produced).

There were issues that American leaders were themselves unwilling to arbitrate. Likewise, occasions arose when Washington was itself prepared to use force. But this simply underscores the fact that policy makers were not after just any peace.[36]

*   *   *

Each prewar presidency had its distinctive qualities and style. Nevertheless, a basic world policy was adhered to throughout the entire period from the end of the nineteenth century on. To the limited extent that foreign policy was even discussed, Woodrow Wilson ran for the presidency in 1912 as one who would reverse the policies of his predecessors, but such rhetoric is belied by his administration's actual behavior. Wilson voiced criticism of "dollar diplomacy" and promised to improve the image of the United States in Latin America left by the Republicans. But, referring to recent political turmoil in the Caribbean, the candidate also bluntly told publisher Oswald Garrison Villard that this was a time when the "big nations" were "not going to put up with misbehavior by the small ones." Lest his comments during the campaign be misunderstood south of the border, Wilson, within a week of taking office, publicly declared his antipathy to further revolutions there.[37]

Though subsequent generations of historians would repeat uncritically Wilson's own description of his goals in Latin America, these in practice often diverged quite a bit from democracy and self-determination. The new president claimed to break with what he described as his predecessor's policy in the Caribbean—asserting that that was driven simply by the narrow self-interest of Wall Street banks—while in fact continuing the Republicans' quest for stability and control.[38] Like those who came before him, Wilson was convinced that the soon-to-be-completed canal was going to shift the "center of gravity of the world."[39] That made it imperative, as he saw it, that the surrounding countries have governments that were close to the United States and that would behave as it wanted. Within his first year in office, this meant that the new administration was following up on plans that had been pushed by Taft's secretary of state for an even more intimate relationship between the United States and Nicaragua. It was also moving to place Haiti under the kind of financial protectorate that had earlier, under TR, been established next door in the Dominican Republic.

Wilson's efforts to improve America's standing in South America represented in many respects a reprise of Root's efforts to undo the damage caused by Roosevelt's announcement of his "corollary" to the Monroe Doctrine.[40] During the 1912 campaign, Wilson told gatherings of political figures and businessmen that the United States was primed for the "commercial conquest of the world."[41] Upon taking office, his administration immediately pushed measures meant to promote that goal. Tariff policy was reformed, in part in the hope that lower rates would open up foreign markets, give manufacturers cheaper raw materials, and lead American business to be more efficient. The Federal Reserve Act (1913) included provisions meant to help American banks expand their international operations. And the Department of Commerce was revamped, under Secretary William C. Redfield, a former president of the American Manufacturers Export Association, so as to encourage the growth of American trade. South America was a central focus of the administration's planning. Far more attuned than Knox had been to the competitive challenge the United States faced there from Europeans, the Wilson administration tried to diminish the southern continent's resentment. An ultimately unsuccessful effort was made to repair relations with Colombia, still troubled as a result of TR's intervention to secure the separation of Panama from that country in 1903. The legations of Chile and Argentina were raised to embassy status (as Brazil's had been in 1905). Wilson tried to be responsive to the suggestion of John Barrett, the director of the Bureau of the American Republics, that he give a "Pan-American tone" to his efforts to affect events in Mexico.[42] The president's most important (though unofficial) foreign policy advisor, Colonel Edward M. House, likewise pushed the idea that Argentina, Brazil, and Chile could be enlisted to help the United States in "policing" the hemisphere.[43] Among other things, it was hoped this would reduce Latin American antipathy toward the United States. But, ultimately, every step the administration took in this direction was undermined by its obvious intention to make sure that the hemisphere was "policed" in accordance with Washington's wishes.

The new administration was no less desirous than its predecessors had been to shore up the existing political boundaries and framework for trade in China.[44] Nor was its policy there driven by a commitment to democracy.

As a political split developed in the new republic, the Wilson administration accommodated itself to military strongman Yuan Shikai's dictatorial consolidation of power. In fact, it tilted in his direction (over the movement led by Sun Yat-sen).

The new Underwood tariff (1913) largely addressed what had been the goals of Taft's reciprocity treaty with Canada, namely the admission at lower rates into the United States of Canadian food products, as well as lumber, coal, and other raw materials.[45] Meanwhile, with regard to Mexico, the biggest difference between the new administration and its predecessors lay in the degree to which Wilson looked at events there in terms of their effect on developments throughout the entire region surrounding the canal.[46] He not only wanted a government in Mexico City that would carry out its "international obligations." Wilson worried that acceptance of a revolutionary overturn of power in Mexico would encourage revolt in the Caribbean.

An instructive comparison can be found in the administration's treatment of Yuan Shikai, of China, and of Huerta, of Mexico. It was acquiescing in the former's consolidation of dictatorial power at the very same time that it was challenging the undemocratic Mexican general. It was not democracy that was driving Wilson's diplomacy. The underlying connection between these policies was a quest for order and influence. Support of Yuan was viewed as contributing to the advancement of those objectives in China, while the Mexican general was seen as a threat to the achievement of the same goals in upper Latin America.

When Huerta resisted Wilson's political prescription for the restoration of order and constitutionalism, Washington decided to isolate him and then to confront powers, like Britain, suspected of propping him up. In a speech in Mobile, Alabama, on October 27, 1913, Wilson cast the United States as a defender of Latin American countries against such selfish Europeans.[47] Wilson and Bryan had been more blunt (and less diplomatic) earlier, in the draft of a note to the powers that ultimately was not sent. It read, "This government . . . is and must continue to be of paramount influence in the Western Hemisphere."[48] London quickly gestured its acceptance of whatever policy Washington wished to pursue. Foreign Secretary Sir Edward Grey's private secretary, Sir William Tyrrell, met with Wilson in the White House. Afterward, he wrote his chief that the president was a strong partisan of a "sympathetic alliance" with Britain. This was the right "psychological moment" for solidifying that feeling.[49]

Huerta was subsequently chased from power. Revolutionary armies had mobilized against him. Then, in April 1914, the United States seized the country's principal gulf port, Veracruz. But, by the time the Great War was enveloping Europe, Wilson was already quarreling with Huerta's successors.

Finally, the new administration also demonstrated an interest in global stabilization comparable to its predecessors.[50] Early on it negotiated the renewal of arbitration treaties that had been signed under TR. And it issued a call for a third Hague Conference, to be held in 1915. It paid still more attention to possible political arrangements that might serve to promote such stabilization. Under the guidance of House, the administration explored the prospects for composing the differences between England and Germany that appeared to threaten war. Its ultimate objective, as shall be discussed, was then to forge an arrangement among these and other powers to oversee world affairs on behalf, fundamentally, of the status quo.

PART II

American "Neutrality" (1914–1917)

We discussed what might be the final distribution of power some centuries hence. He [President Wilson] thought it quite possible that eventually there might be but two great nations in the world, - Russia, on the one hand, and this country [the United States] on the other.
  —Colonel Edward M. House, August 30, 1914

Whichever of these two powers [Britain or Germany] is successful will find itself confronted by the certainty that sooner or later its supremacy will be challenged by the United States.
  —Austin Knight, Rear Admiral, United States Navy, July 1915

England, the President pointed out, very seriously infringed on America's rights before we became a belligerent through the improper use of her blockade, in fact did the same thing on the seas as Germany did to Belgium, and on the same grounds – necessity.
  —Cary T. Grayson, December 8, 1918

CHAPTER 2

Washington Reacts (1914–15)

For years there had been worry that a generalized great-power war might break out in Europe. In the summer of 1914, such occurred. The precipitant was the assassination on June 28, in Bosnia, of the heir to the Austro-Hungarian throne. To Austria-Hungary's leaders, this was but the most recent, but also most unsettling, manifestation of the threat that rising nationalist aspirations posed to their large multiethnic empire's survival. Tracing the epicenter of South Slav nationalism to neighboring Serbia, imperial officials grew eager after the assassination to bring affairs there under their control.

Right from the start, however, that project was understood by most observers to carry the risk of more than a local war. It was not just that Russia saw itself as having interests in the Balkans. Intense rivalry and mutual suspicion on the part of all of the European great powers had led them in recent years to form alliances and understandings that they hoped would act as a check on their most feared competitors. Overstretched and nervous about the rise of Germany, Britain had worked to improve relations with its principal late nineteenth-century rivals in Africa (France) and Asia (Russia). These were two powers that, in the 1890s, had already entered into the Dual Alliance largely to counterbalance the growing might of their mutual German neighbor. For its part, Germany had become increasingly committed to the survival of its principal ally, Austria-Hungary. Any appreciable gain or loss experienced by a single participant in these alignments had by 1914 come to be seen as something that would constitute a gain or loss for all of the other powers, creating the prospect that a conflict in the Balkans could easily be gauged as of consequence to many more than just those two states. This situation was, in turn, made more dangerous by the time-sensitive mobilization plans that all of the powers had devised to ensure that they would not be found unready if a serious matter did arise. Historians continue to debate which power or powers deserve most responsibility for this crisis eventuating in a Europe-wide great-power conflict, but it seems hard to deny that all of them bore some onus for the state of affairs that had been created. By early August, a state of war had come to exist between Germany and Austria-Hungary, on the one hand, and the Triple Entente, or Allies, composed of Britain, France, and Russia, on the other.[1]

The Wilson administration's response to the outbreak of this war was shaped from the outset by its desire to protect an already established set of foreign policy objectives tied to what it hoped would be America's standing in the coming twentieth-century world. In particular, an urge to prop up, reconstruct, and, through reform, stabilize the essentials of the preexisting international order guided the approach of the president and his chief for-eign policy adviser, House. President Wilson very much wanted to avoid U.S. military involvement. But that was never his highest priority. Over and again, he took steps designed to promote what, well before 1914, had become Washington's fundamental foreign policy goals, and these increas-ingly carried the risk of military conflict.

*   *   *

In 1914, American policy makers neither wanted nor envisioned belligerency for the United States. They were also keenly aware that the vast majority of Americans—even if disposed by their immigrant heritage to root for one side or the other—had no desire for such involvement.[2] Yet its most important priorities led the Wilson administration early on to take actions that were pro-Allied and partisan. The president asserted American neutrality on August 4. He then told his fellow citizens two weeks later that all who truly loved America "must be neutral in fact as well as in name."[3] Wilson, though not always House, would persist in describing the United States as neutral, and indeed he was anxious for it to be seen as such, particularly by the American public. But by early 1915, at the latest, the United States had assumed a posture that cannot accurately be described by that term.

The pro-Allied attitudes and actions of the administration were by no means a simple function of Anglophilia. Wilson had great regard for British history and culture. But that had not, for instance, prevented him from sharply confronting London in 1913 over what he saw as its challenge to American predominance in Mexico (and, more broadly, the western hemisphere). Nor would it prevent Wilson at later points from taking a critical and confrontational posture toward that power. Washington's orientation had much more to do with what by 1914 had become the customary attitude of American leaders toward Britain and its role. British power was reflexively identified with the existing world order.

In late August, both Wilson and House voiced the worry that if Germany should win the United States would have to build up a bigger military machine to guard its interests.[4] Three months later, as the nature of America's "neutrality" began to take concrete form, House told the president "that Germany would never forgive us for the attitude we have taken in the war, and if she is successful, she will hold us to account. I told him that I had it on fairly good authority that the Kaiser had it in mind to suggest to us that the Monroe Doctrine should extend only to the Equator." To this, Wilson "replied that the war was perhaps a Godsend . . . , for if it had not come we might have been embroiled in war ourselves."[5]

Not only did Wilson and House not want to see British power undermined relative to Germany. They were also anxious to see the settlement of the conflict accompanied by such safeguards as might prevent a long feared destabilizing event like this from occurring again. This was another reason why the administration took measures that were pro-Allied. The assumption was that the Allies would win. American policy makers expected England to be central to the making of the peace, and they hoped that by maintaining good relations with London they could pave the way for Anglo-American collaboration on behalf of the broad contours of the peace and of postwar stabilization.

Albeit invested now with a much greater urgency, the latter effort was at least broadly in line with reforms that the United States had been pushing since the turn of the century. House took the leading role in this area, as he did with the administration's policy toward Europe generally until at least late 1916 (and then again after the United States became a belligerent). But Wilson warmed to the task. Almost twenty years earlier he had in fact spoken of England and America, if united, as holding in their hands "the future destinies of the world."[6] In 1914, House held out to him the appealing prospect of playing a world historical role.[7] With the end of exercising such influence in view, the administration, as shall be seen, almost immediately sought to position itself as the one and only possible mediator of the conflict.

A key step taken early on, reflective of its orientation, involved the administration's acquiescence in the measures of commercial warfare adopted by London, measures that were in fact not unlike those that had brought war between Britain and the United States during the Napoleonic era a century before.[8] An understanding between the two powers was not reached without some disagreement. Britain's leaders, certain of the nobility of their cause, were impatient with any resistance to the measures they implemented. American officials meanwhile did not want to be seen as acting in a fashion that was unneutral, nor formally to surrender American rights. Nevertheless, go along they did. On the surface, the administration would continue to present itself as committed to the traditional American doctrine of "freedom of the seas." But, in practice, it took the attitude that, just this once, fundamental exceptions would be made. The United States possessed ample leverage with which to challenge London's infringements. And British leaders later conceded that they would have bent before such a challenge.[9] But, eager to influence the war's outcome and to play a mediatory role, the Wilson administration accommodated itself to the Royal Navy's measures.

Though the term "blockade" is often used to describe its course, London never in fact tried to impose a legal blockade on Germany. Factors such as geography and the likelihood that Berlin would effectively be able to counter a formal blockade with modern submarines and mines were viewed as making that course prohibitively complicated and expensive.[10] Instead, Britain sought, in steps, to accomplish comparable results by the creative use of the concepts of contraband and continuous voyage. London progressively expanded what it considered the former and simultaneously applied the doctrine of continuous voyage (the right to confiscate commerce on the basis of an assessment about its final destination) to conditional as well as absolute contraband (goods that *might* be used by the military as opposed to arms and ammunition). The distinctions traditionally made were eventually erased, as the ultimate objective was to intercept at sea (if not forestall altogether) any and all trade with Germany.[11]

The issue of this "blockade" underscores a certain naïveté on the part of Berlin's military strategists. Well aware that a European great-power conflict might be long, they had intentionally shaped their war plans with an eye to preserving the neutrality of the Netherlands. Worried about the British navy, they had been anxious to have a "windpipe" that would enable Germany "to breathe," to import some foreign goods and supplies from overseas.[12] This reflected wishful thinking, however, as to the policies London would pursue (as well perhaps as to what the most powerful neutral, the United States, would allow Britain to do).

Both German and British planners had been entertaining steps that would violate international norms and agreements. Insofar as Germany was concerned, its attitude toward the neutrality of Holland's southern neighbor, Belgium, was the most notable example. Like all of the European powers, Germany was pledged to respect that under a treaty dating back to the era of Belgium's independence in the 1830s. But Berlin had decided well before 1914 that unless Brussels allowed its troops free passage, the country's borders would be forced. Moving by way of the quickest route possible against France—through Belgium—at the outset of hostilities, as German troops began to do at the beginning of August 1914, was held to be the only way that Germany could prevail in a war against the Dual Alliance.[13]

Meanwhile, key British strategists had been discussing maritime measures that would aim to keep not only arms and ammunition from the German army, but also food from Germany's civilian population. And to do that, they proposed to violate other neutrals' rights to trade. These measures had their origins in plans that had taken shape in the minds of such navalists as First Sea Lord Sir John Fisher and Maurice Hankey of the Committee for Imperial Defense. While army leaders focused on the dispatch of ground troops to the continent, as a way of keeping France in the war and of quickly defeating Germany, these men continued to think of sea power as Britain's greatest asset. Particularly in the event of a long war—which many of them also predicted—it was counted on to ensure the volume of food and supplies that England and its army would require from overseas while simultaneously denying as much of such trade as possible to Germany.[14]

State Department legal advisers were immediately taken aback by the drift of British policy. They noted that there was no international court of prize that might rule on Britain's assessments, and they pronounced portions of the British Orders in Council of August 22 "wholly unacceptable." Accession to them "would be to make neutral trade between neutral ports dependent upon the pleasure of belligerents, and give to the latter the advantage of an established blockade without the necessity of maintaining it with an adequate naval force." That hearkened back to the practice of "paper blockades" that had long been discredited. They also worried that acceptance of London's position would compromise the United States before Germany.[15] One consultant, Harvard law professor Eugene Wambaugh, asserted that the Orders were "so injurious . . . and so inconsistent with general International Law as to bring it wholly within the legal rights of a neutral . . . to protect its commerce by war."[16] A note of formal protest was prepared and presented to the president at the end of September. Wilson, however, balked at going further. He immediately summoned House, who deemed the tenor of the note "exceedingly undiplomatic," and they instead insisted that an effort be made to try to reach an accommodation with London through informal discussions.[17]

Over the next month, Robert Lansing, the State Department counselor, encouraged Britain to proclaim that it would adhere to the Declaration of London of 1909. This was an agreement on maritime practices during war that had been signed, though not ratified, by all of the major powers. Berlin had said earlier that it would abide by those rules if its enemies did. From Lansing's perspective, a similar announcement by London would protect the administration from charges that it was abandoning American rights or acting in an unneutral fashion. It would also diminish the possibility of friction with either power. He told the British ambassador that such a step would nevertheless still allow Britain to accomplish most of its objectives. And Lansing actually offered advice as to how that might be done. London could continue to expand the contraband list and it could pressure the small European neutrals to embargo trade with Germany. Washington, he said, was even likely to go along if Britain asserted a sweeping new belligerent right under which a neutral's port might be declared an enemy base (Britain was already moving to apply such pressure on the European neutrals).[18]

London rejected acceptance of the Declaration without drastic modifications, but Grey simultaneously proposed the basic course that the administration would henceforth follow. The foreign secretary suggested to the American ambassador, Walter Hines Page, that the United States neither accept nor protest against Britain's measures, but rather "be content to declare that we reserve all rights under international law" and "take up cases of damage if any occur as they arise."[19] After this, for at least the next year and a half, Anglo-American dealings over the blockade were diverted in practice away from confrontation over general practices and instead toward discussion of particular cases and the postwar settlement of claims. Some general protests were lodged, but these were meant principally for public consumption. In some cases, Britain sought to mitigate the impact of its "blockade" on the American economy and to reward Washington for, in essence, not performing its obligations as a neutral.

On November 3, London declared the entire North Sea a military zone. All merchantmen headed to ports around it were advised to stop first in Great Britain for directions. In fact, this was the only real choice they had, given that those international waters were now to be laced with mines. The step was meant to make the "blockade" both more economical and effective, but it constituted a bold new assertion of belligerent rights. Some of the European neutrals protested immediately and forcefully. But Washington held off. Eventually, as criticism mounted on the part of some affected American businesses and shippers, and on the part of some in Congress and the press, the administration, on December 26, lodged a formal protest containing a broad indictment of British measures. But it neither threatened nor was followed up with any action.[20]

*   *   *

The Wilson administration's efforts to compose Europe's differences actually preceded the outbreak of war in August 1914. Of particular note, House, with Wilson's support, undertook to improve Anglo-German relations and pursued that objective during two trips that he took across the Atlantic, one to England in mid-1913 and the other to England and Germany the following spring.[21] Early in 1912, House had written and published anonymously (some took it to be the work of TR) a novel titled *Philip Dru, Administrator: A Story of Tomorrow.*[22] In it, the protagonist successfully forged a close relationship between Britain and the United States and then used that to create a broader concert of power dedicated to upholding the kind of international order that those two nations wanted. Passages in House's book roughly anticipated the project he embarked upon a year and a half later.

House prized the Anglo-American rapprochement that had been developing since the late 1890s and supported the initiatives that had been pursued at The Hague since the turn of the century. But he thought that more had to be done to promote stabilization. Specifically, he hoped that Germany could be turned from a discontented potential challenger into a supporter of the status quo. He envisioned a "pact" among those three powers, and perhaps others who might subsequently be brought in. This would ensure a peace among the participants premised upon the acceptance of existing territorial boundaries and the open door. And those powers would then agree among themselves as to the political superintendence of the underdeveloped world. Collectively they would use their power to isolate and contain any powers not prepared to go along.

These ideas were not without precedents in the diplomacy of Wilson's predecessors. They clearly shared kinship with Washington's long-standing promotion of a great-power-dominated world court. All of the powers were offered a privileged position in that body, which was principally designed to stabilize the status quo. Meanwhile, House's "pact" for the preservation of peace—above all among the powers in Europe—envisioned its utilization of peaceful settlement mechanisms that had been promoted by the United States for years. These included arbitration, which had been encouraged, among other things, as a way of preserving order in another continent, South America. House's project also bears comparison with the efforts of the Taft administration to promote the notion of commonly held interests among the great powers in China and to substitute cooperation and "harmonious action" there for competition among them.[23]

Nor was House the first prominent American policy figure to contemplate the creation of a great-power political association as a way of securing international order. In 1910, ex-President Roosevelt had suggested that it "would be a master stroke if those great powers honestly bent on peace would form a League of Peace, not only to keep the peace among themselves, but to prevent, by force if necessary, its being broken by others." And his successor, Taft, subsequently had also offered that the way "to bring about peace" was "to enforce it" if an arrangement to do that could be brought about "between England, Germany and the United States, and possibly two or three more Powers."[24]

The way to bring Berlin into such an arrangement was to offer it more scope for expansion and to convince its leaders that they had more to gain by joining up with Britain and America than they did by pursuing an independent course (which, they were warned, was likely to lead to war and their defeat). In the spring of 1913, House suggested to Count Johann von Bernstorff, Germany's ambassador, "that it would be a great thing if there was a sympathetic understanding between England, Germany, Japan, and the United States." Together, "[t]hey could ensure peace and the proper development of" what he called "the waste places, besides maintaining an open door and equal opportunity to every one everywhere."[25]

House set out to assure Germany that the door for emigration and trade (though not political influence) would remain open to it in South America. Meanwhile, he hoped to get Britain (which he felt had been too "intolerant of Germany's aspirations for expansion") to agree to concede Berlin a "zone of influence" in the Middle East (particularly abutting Russia, the country House felt was least likely to join a great-power understanding and the country he was most anxious to see contained).[26]

For its part, Germany would have to abandon its naval aspirations. When he met the kaiser in 1914, House told him that the British "were very much concerned over his ever-growing navy, which taken together with his enormous army constituted a menace." "[T]here might come a time when they would have to decide whether they ran more danger from him . . . than they did from Russia." "[W]hen that point was reached," he said, "the decision would be against Germany."[27] Indeed, House was convinced that such a "cataclysm" was on its way. As he saw it, writing to Wilson on May 29, "Whenever England consents, France and Russia will close in on Germany and Austria."[28]

*   *   *

Once the war began, at the initiative they believed of Germany, Wilson and House put the United States forward as the one and only mediator of the conflict. They were eager to play a central role in determining under what terms the war would end. And their motivation stemmed from their desire to protect and put on more solid footing the international order to which they were attached. In this regard, their efforts constituted a direct continuation of House's prewar missions. House and Wilson wanted an outcome that would be favorable from the standpoint of the distribution of world power. And they hoped to see provisions instituted that would guard against such an upheaval happening again.

Wilson's first secretary of state, William Jennings Bryan, sought to assume a leading role in bringing an end to the conflict, but the president reined him in. Not only was he not seen as having sufficient diplomatic skill. As historian Ernest May puts it, the secretary seemed principally motivated by a desire to "bring the bloodshed to an end."[29] By contrast, for Wilson and House it very much mattered what the peace looked like.

Wilson and House worried about the war's disruptive effects on American trade and business, even on U.S. politics. They believed that the world order they wanted would be placed in greater jeopardy the longer the struggle went on. These concerns led them to want the war to come to an end quickly. But, they were at the same time eager that Germany first be denied any gains and taught a lesson. Moreover, they accepted the idea that England had to be ready to settle, for the maintenance of harmonious relations with London was seen to be important to the achievement of Washington's plans for long-term stabilization.

The hope initially was that these conditions would be met within a matter of a few months. The administration pressed the idea of mediation on London on several occasions in late 1914 and early 1915, but time and again it drew back, sometimes in the face of battlefield conditions, at others in the face of British resistance.

Wilson and House discussed the impact of the war on the distribution of world power from the conflict's inception. House wrote the president on August 22 that "Germany's success will ultimately mean trouble for us." But he also voiced the worry that an Allied victory might mean "the domination of Russia on the Continent of Europe." Neither was a "good outcome." Wilson, in his reply, concurred.[30]

The best scenario, both came to feel, would be for Berlin swiftly to learn that it could not prevail and for peace discussions to begin before Germany was decisively defeated. A lopsided defeat could undermine hopes for stabilizing Europe, since that might only lead Berlin to prepare for a war of revenge. Such an outcome might also strengthen Russia, a power they saw as antagonistic to the Anglo-American international order. France and, especially, Japan (which entered the war on August 23)—Britain's other principal allies—were also sources of concern. Both might become stronger as the result of a resounding Allied victory, and Tokyo, in particular, like Saint Petersburg, was viewed as a threat to U.S. aspirations in China. House meanwhile retained the hope that Germany, once shown the error of its ways, might still become a valuable buttress of the world order American leaders wanted.

At the end of the month, the two men met in New Hampshire, where the president was trying to recover from the recent death of his wife. Wilson was briefed in greater detail about House's May to early July mission and, according to the latter, "said my knowledge of these men and of the situation in Europe would be of great value to him." The president condemned Germany as "essentially selfish."

Discussion of the war stimulated broader, still more long-term speculation about the distribution of power in the world. House recorded in his diary that Wilson thought "eventually there might be but two great nations . . . Russia, on the one hand, and this country [the United States] on the other." For his part, the president's adviser thought there would be three, with China eventually emerging to dominate Asia, "Russia dominating Europe, and a part of Asia, and America dominating the Western World and perhaps the English speaking colonies." In the musings of both men about this "final distribution of power," it will be noted that the United States was destined for an expansive, central role while England (as well as Germany) went unmentioned.[31]

Germany's hopes for a quick victory were dealt a sharp setback in September. Not far to the northeast of Paris, its army's forward movement was checked at the River Marne. House expected that many German leaders—especially the kaiser's civilian advisers—would now view the war as a failure. Talks might commence. Bernstorff encouraged this idea. Indicative of House's grasp of London's maritime objectives, the president's adviser was also convinced that the Germans had a "great fear" of the British policy of "starvation." House was anxious, meanwhile, to get negotiations going while London still "dominates her allies," because he believed that those other powers treasured territorial objectives that could over time make concluding the war, and achieving the kind of peace the administration wanted, more difficult.[32]

British officials, however, put House off, and he deferred broaching the topic of mediation again for over two months. He believed that the Allies "would consider it an unfriendly act" until they were more successful. House also began to wonder whether "Germany was sufficiently beaten to cause her to consent to a fundamental change in her military policy."[33]

A new opening seemed to appear in mid-December. Bernstorff suggested that talks might begin even on the basis of "drastic disarmament" and the evacuation and indemnification of Belgium. House told the British ambassador, Sir Cecil Arthur Spring Rice, that "the Allies would be placed in a bad light if they refused to consider peace" on such terms. He was soon off to Europe again.[34]

But, in fact, at the beginning of 1915 neither side was ready to settle on terms that the other would have been willing to accept. Such confusion as existed on that score was largely a reflection of the desire both had not to be seen as responsible for the conflict's continuation.

Germany's bid to knock France out quickly had failed. Berlin's colonies and bases in Africa, the Far East, and the Pacific were either in others' hands or under siege, this as the result of campaigns mounted by Allied colonial forces, the British dominions, and Japan. Its navy and merchant marine had been swept from the seas, and it was confronted with an increasingly more thoroughgoing "blockade." Austria-Hungary had yet to defeat Serbia, and its northeastern region of Galicia was under Russian control.

However, Germany was firmly entrenched in northern France and it occupied most of strategically vital Belgium. It had repulsed an invasion of East Prussia by the tsar's forces, and it now dominated much of Russian Poland. The Ottoman Empire had joined the war on the side of the Central Powers during the fall and its forces were battling the Russians in the Black Sea region and in the Caucasus. Berlin's leaders did not accept that Germany had been defeated. And they were resolved to hold out for changes in Germany's favor, at the very least in the form of a pro-German economic and political realignment of areas of Northern and Northwestern Europe.[35]

For its part, as both Wilson and his principal adviser had begun to comprehend during the fall, London was determined, in House's words, "to make a complete job of it while they are in it." Its leaders wanted to put an end to any potential German challenge once and for all and to eliminate Germany as a power capable of contending on the world scene. Britain had to hold together and, if possible, expand its coalition so that this goal could be achieved. Anything short of that, James Bryce—Britain's former ambassador to the United States—told Wilson, would only lead to a "truce rather than peace."[36]

House's hope that the time had come for negotiations was dampened even before he arrived in London. Though anxious not to alienate Washington, British officials had made it clear that they did not believe Germany was sincere and that such overtures were premature. And Berlin failed to provide confirmation of Bernstorff's assurances.

*   *   *

House thus shifted his focus. The mission became an effort to bolster the likelihood that the United States would be the eventual mediator and to lay out a framework for peace that, before too many more months of fighting, both sides might be willing to explore.[37]

After his first discussion with Grey, House reported to Wilson that the situation at the front was not as favorable for the Allies as he had hoped. He assured the foreign secretary that he had "no intention of pushing the question of peace" because it could not be achieved before the middle of the year. He could "see the necessity for Germany not to be in such an advantageous position as now, for the reason she would be less likely to make terms that would insure permanent peace."[38]

In the meantime he wanted to talk about postwar stability. Since the fall, House had been arguing that every nation in Europe should guarantee "the territorial integrity of every other nation." He also felt there should be restrictions, or a verifiable moratorium, on the production of armaments and munitions. And—an idea that reflected his view of how the war had been ignited in the Balkans the previous summer—he now added that "all sources of national irritation should be removed so what at first may be a sore spot cannot grow into a malignant disease."

Grey expressed interest in seeing the United States play a role in guaranteeing the peace. Without that, he maintained, it was "difficult to see how a durable peace can be secured without complete exhaustion of one side or the other." House believed that the American tradition of nonentanglement prevented the administration from participating in the specifics of a settlement among the European powers. But in England he said that Washington could sign on to a second, more general treaty aimed at enforcing limits on the conduct of war in the future and at preventing the violation of neutral territory. This takes on added significance in light of House's suggestion that all of the territory between Germany and France—including Alsace and Lorraine—ought to be neutralized. However, Grey continued to press for a more explicit American commitment. House, in fact, came away from his meetings with the misimpression that this was all that kept the foreign secretary from endorsing a conclusion to the war that would not entail Germany's decisive defeat.[39]

By the middle of February, House was flirting with the thought that the United States might call for a conference "of all neutral and belligerent nations" later in 1915, over which Wilson would preside. It could meet "concurrently with the peace conference," if an end of the war was then in sight, or "it might be used as a medium of bringing about peace." It would deal with "the rules of future warfare and the rights of neutrals." The convention "would be of far reaching consequence," he wrote the president, "more far reaching in fact than the peace conference itself."[40]

House left London believing that British leaders were concerned about the long-range implications of the submarine. He concluded that London would be ready after this conflict to reverse itself. It would become a supporter of "freedom of the seas" so as, in any future wars, to ensure access to the supplies it was dependent on. This suggested a strategy for promoting U.S. mediation, along with the kind of settlement Washington wanted, in Berlin. After arriving there, House did not share with German leaders his (quite exaggerated) sense of British movement on this issue. Instead, he presented the "freedom of the seas" as something that, with U.S. help, London could be compelled to accept. Berlin, House told Chancellor Theobald von Bethmann-Hollweg in March, could then say to its people that "Belgium was no longer needed as a base for German naval activity, since England was being brought to terms." In the spirit of his prewar mission, House "endeavored to make it clear" to the Germans "that their best interests could be served by working along harmoniously with us."[41]

House wrote Wilson that peace talks would have to await new developments on the battlefield. But he was hopeful that he was putting "us on a good footing" and that these were still only a matter of a few months away. "If nothing arises to disturb the relations we are establishing in these several belligerent countries," he told the president, "I feel hopeful that your influence will dominate to a larger degree than it ever seemed possible."[42] House left Germany at the end of March, returned to London, via Paris, and decided there to wait. He abandoned that course and returned to the United States only in June, after German-American relations were plunged into a crisis over the question of Berlin's use of the submarine.

*   *   *

By the beginning of 1915, the war had reached a condition of stalemate. In reaction, both sides intensified efforts to organize their societies into military machines. The Allies sought an expansion of their ground forces, hoping eventually to be able to sweep Germany from its entrenched positions in northern France and Belgium. More immediately it was determined that the British navy should try to rush the Dardanelles and seize Constantinople. London's hope was that it could thereby undermine the Ottoman Empire, relieve pressure on Russia, and bring Italy and the Balkan neutrals into the war on the Allied side.

Germany's principal focus was to its east where it hoped Russia might soon be pressured to leave the war. So far as the land war in the west was concerned, it went on the defensive. But in the waters around Britain, Berlin announced its own illegal maritime campaign, hoping seriously to interfere with British imports. Unable to contend with the Royal Navy on the surface of those waters, it stated on February 4 that it would use submarines to try to destroy "every enemy merchant ship" found in the area. Such ships would be subject to attack without warning. It would therefore not always be possible to avert peril to "persons and cargoes." Neutral vessels were advised not to sail there, owing to the fact that British ships often engaged in the ruse of flying other countries' flags (House had in fact witnessed this firsthand when, on his trip over to England, the American flag had been employed in this way on the *Lusitania*).[43]

Berlin justified this campaign as a reprisal for British violations of the law. It claimed it was also warranted because of Britain's efforts to starve the German population. Noting that neutral nations—read the United States—had acquiesced in Allied measures, Germany expressed the hope that they would accept the same defense from Berlin, on grounds of necessity, that London had given.

The Wilson administration was brought up short by the announcement and responded sharply. It had in fact been indulgent of London's transgressions. This was because it identified Britain with the world it wanted. The president had remarked to his secretary late in 1914 that "England is fighting our fight." For that reason, he was not going to "place obstacles in her way." Indeed, Wilson said that Britain was fighting for the "life of the world." By extension, Germany constituted in the eyes of the president a threat to that "life," one that he had no intention of indulging.[44]

Washington rejected Berlin's allegation. And in its response, dated February 10, the United States said it would hold Germany to a "strict accountability" if any American ships or lives were lost in the declared zone.[45] It told Berlin that it intended to secure for American citizens the "full enjoyment" of their rights at sea and declared that a "critical situation" would be created if any of them were violated.[46] American citizens and vessels could not "be molested by the naval forces of Germany other than by visit and search" (the procedure by which a belligerent had the right to stop and examine a vessel to determine its true character as well as the status of the cargo it was carrying). Moreover, Germany would run afoul of the United States, the note could be read to suggest, not only if it harmed American vessels, but also if Americans were harmed while sailing on Allied ships. This was a novel position (not adopted by any of the other neutrals), open to the interpretation that the United States was offering up an umbrella of protection both to Allied shipping and to the growing volume of American goods flowing by means of it across the Atlantic.

Threatening Germany in the hope that there would be no execution of its announced policy, the administration was almost certainly guided too by its strong desire to play a central role in arranging the postwar world. Policy makers wanted to convince London that the United States was a world power, that it would not shrink from challenges, and that it could and would play a part in establishing and keeping "the peace" (and not just in "its" hemisphere). But of course, for precisely this reason, Washington's response carried the risk of military conflict if Germany was undeterred and U.S. credibility—which meant so much to Wilson and had now been put on the line—subsequently was subject to serious question.

The topic was openly addressed in a memorandum of February 15 written by Lansing. He suggested that Berlin might no longer see the disadvantages of war with the United States outweighing the advantages.[47] Fearing that this might be the case, Wilson seized on an idea of Bryan's. The secretary received the president's permission to propose a modus vivendi: "we should see whether Great Britain will withdraw her objection to food entering Germany—the same to be distributed there through American instrumentalities, in return for the withdrawal of the German order in regard to the war zone."[48] Berlin, in other words, might be induced to forego its measures if London—which presumably saw them as threatening—would modify its own.

Wilson demonstrated that he was still not prepared to apply pressure on England, however, when this hope was quickly disappointed. Berlin wanted to negotiate for access to many of the raw materials that had been reclassified as contraband too. But Britain rejected Bryan's proposal out of hand. Because it knew that Germany had in fact only a handful of U-boats, London did not view Berlin's war zone as a serious threat and felt that all the benefits of such an agreement would be on its enemy's side. Cecil Hurst, of the Foreign Office, notably opined that it made no sense to "purchase the safety of a few tramp steamers at the price of . . . prolongation of the war."[49]

The administration's indulgence of the Allies continued. Wilson was amenable to exploring means by which a confrontation with Germany might be avoided, but he remained unwilling to take action that might undermine the Allies' efforts or eliminate his chances of playing a world role.

Britain actually saw Germany's new policy announcement as possessing distinctly positive features. London welcomed the prospect that it might generate German-American friction. It was also seen as affording a perfect opportunity for Britain to unveil more maritime measures that it had been considering. Justifying it as in reprisal for Berlin's declaration of early February, London unveiled a new Order in Council at the beginning of March. This dispensed altogether with the issue of what was or was not contraband. Britain now openly announced it as its intention to prevent any goods at all from getting into, or out of, Germany (directly, or via neighboring neutrals). Neutral ships "carrying goods of presumed enemy destination, ownership or origin" would be stopped on the high seas by the Royal Navy and taken into port.[50]

U.S. exports to Germany (never as large before the war as those to Britain) had already largely been cut off. And Page reported that London would buy up the most important—to Wilson, quite politically important—commodity still being traded, cotton.[51] But questions were raised relative to America's rights and its standing as a neutral, these stemming especially from the fact that what Britain was proposing was patently illegal.

A strenuous debate as to the appropriate response took place within the American government. As historian John W. Coogan notes, "Even such dedicated Anglophiles as Robert Lansing and James Brown Scott"—both international lawyers—". . . believed that Wilson, in the wake of his 'Strict Accountability' stand against Germany, could no longer postpone a confrontation with the British blockade." The interdepartmental Joint Neutrality Board characterized Britain's accumulated measures as a "lapse into barbarism." The General Board of the Navy asserted that Britain's measures "might readily be interpreted into a claim of universal sovereignty of the sea." And Wilson's secretary of war, Lindley Garrison, worried that if the United States acquiesced it would forgo its status as a neutral. Germany, he admonished, would legally have the right to regard the United States as an enemy.

Wilson, nevertheless, whatever the risks, rejected such counsel. He was not prepared at this time to pressure Britain. The president dispatched a response to London that largely followed the position Washington had adopted in the fall. It voiced confidence that Britain would not actually act in a way that violated American rights and warned that if it did it would ultimately be held accountable for reparations. As State Department special assistant, and prominent Republican lawyer, Chandler P. Anderson commented to Elihu Root, the note was "stern on the face of it," but had a "twinkle in the eye."[52]

*   *   *

In late spring, Berlin's use of its U-boats became a source of major tension in German-American relations. Wilson still very much wanted to stay clear of military complications with that power. But he was also determined not to surrender the basic stance his administration had adopted in February. The two governments tussled throughout the middle of 1915. Remarkably, they did so almost exclusively over the question of the safety of Americans traveling on Allied vessels. Berlin disavowed any intention of sinking American ships sailing to Britain (in this period, that policy stood in stark contrast to what awaited American vessels if they tried to run the gauntlet of mines that had been laid by the Allies in the North Sea). But Germany insisted that the possibility of Americans being on board could not give immunity to British or French shipping.

The issue became especially dangerous after the sinking of the *Lusitania* on May 7.[53] The giant British luxury liner, which was carrying below deck millions of rounds of ammunition for the Allies, was on its way back to England from America. Before its departure, the German Embassy had placed notices in New York papers informing potential passengers of Berlin's intentions. But no warning came from American authorities, and Cunard Line officials pointedly insisted that there was no way a submarine could possibly catch up with their speedy vessel. Few passengers seized the opportunity to transfer to a slower ship sailing under the American flag scheduled to leave for Britain the very same day. One hundred twenty-eight

Americans were among those who perished when the liner was torpedoed off Ireland. There was great upset in the United States at the loss of American life, while the president interpreted the event as a blatant challenge to the position that his administration had outlined three months before.[54]

Wilson took the position that Germany should be threatened with serious repercussions unless it disavowed the sinking, made reparations, and ensured against its recurrence. In the future Berlin would have to adhere to the rules of cruiser warfare under existing international law in dealing with such vessels. The "usual precaution of visit and search" would have to be followed, and no ship could be sunk without provision first being made for the safety of noncombatants. A stern note along these lines was dispatched to Berlin on May 13. In it, doubt was also voiced that submarines could in fact be used without an "inevitable violation" of these rules.[55]

The note went out over Bryan's signature, but he was uneasy with Wilson's stance. The secretary thought that any protest to Germany should be paired with one to Britain over its violations of American rights. He likewise worried about a condemnation of submarine warfare as inhuman if it was not paired with a condemnation of Britain's starvation policy on the same grounds. Balance in its treatment of the two sides was necessary if America was to retain the trust of both. This was necessary if the United States was going to be of eventual service in bringing the conflict to an end. Still more important to Bryan, it was critical if the United States was going to avoid becoming involved in the fighting itself. Berlin was already upset with America because of its ballooning sales of munitions to Britain. The secretary did not see that trade as unneutral, but Germany asserted that it was at least against "the true spirit of neutrality."[56] He likewise worried that war would come if the United States insisted on an immediate settlement of the *Lusitania* case. There was no reason why that could not be deferred as had been the case in the maritime disputes that had arisen with Britain.

Bryan also thought that the government should warn Americans about the dangers of traveling on board Allied vessels. Otherwise more deaths would occur. They would further inflame public opinion and heighten the chances of war. Americans who continued to take passage on such ships would be guilty of "contributory negligence." The secretary was outraged that Britain, as he saw it, had tried to use the presence of American passengers as a way of protecting the shipment of ammunition that the *Lusitania* had been carrying. It was, he asserted, "like putting women and children in front of an army."[57] Wilson, however, rejected the idea. Lansing counseled that to issue a warning at this point would constitute an admission of negligence on the part of the administration. The president worried that it would also deflect responsibility from Germany and weaken Washington's protest.[58]

Perhaps the principal considerations weighing on Wilson were those urged by both House and Page, from England, in the days following the sinking. "Our action in this crisis will determine the part we will play when peace is made," House cabled on the ninth. "We are being weighed in the balance, and our position amongst the nations is being assessed by mankind."[59] Page reported that in Britain the feeling was "that the United States must declare war or forfeit European respect."[60] "It is a very serious thing to have such things thought," the president told Bryan, "because everything that affects the opinion of the world regarding us affects our influence for good."[61]

Yet Wilson, and House, still hoped, as the latter put it, that "Germany may give the United States necessary assurances so that some way out [of a rupture in relations or military conflict] may yet be found."[62] Toward this end, the president urged his key advisor to pursue again the modus vivendi suggested by Bryan back in February.

With House continuing to claim British interest in his arguments about freedom of the seas, Wilson told the German ambassador two weeks later that if Berlin gave up its submarine campaign he would push for a peace based on that idea and on the prewar territorial status quo—essentially the grounds for settlement of the war that House had been floating earlier in the year.[63]

Worried about the domestic political scene, as well as German relations, the president in this period began for the first time to complain—privately—of Britain's interference with neutral trade. "It would be a great stroke on England's part," he wrote House, "if she would of her own accord relieve this situation and so put Germany alone in the wrong." If it did not, the United States would at some point have to lodge another protest.[64]

But if Berlin was not "alone in the wrong," it was nevertheless the only power that Washington confronted. Wilson's emissary raised the issue with Grey, but when it was clear he would get nowhere, House reminded the president of what he thought were the controlling considerations. "[O]ur position with the Allies is somewhat different," he cabled Wilson, "for we are bound up more or less in their success, and I do not think we should do anything that can possibly be avoided to alienate the good feeling that they now have for us. If we lost their good will we will not be able to figure at all in peace negotiations, and we will be sacrificing too much in order to maintain all our commercial rights."[65] Only in October would a comprehensive protest of British measures be made, and this, like previous documents, was accompanied by no real threat of American action.[66]

*   *   *

Neither Germany nor Britain was interested in renouncing measures that might bring victory. But neither Washington nor Berlin wanted a rupture in German-American relations. Germany delayed answering Wilson's note, believing, correctly, that public opinion in America would calm down over time. When Berlin did reply at the end of May, it expressed a desire to postpone a final response, asking Washington first to consider its contention that the *Lusitania* had essentially been converted into a warship. It insisted simultaneously that it was not German policy to attack neutral ships and pledged that it would pay compensation if any American vessels were damaged.[67]

Washington dispatched a second note, on June 9, basically restating its demands. Bryan concluded, correctly, that staying clear of military involvement was not the president's highest priority, and he now tendered his resignation. But Wilson did continue to hope that he might both effect a change in Berlin's policy and avoid military involvement.[68]

Toward that end, he slightly altered his stance. While Germany's reply to the June 9 note again refused to concede Washington's demands (indeed, it pointedly insisted that American citizens could not "protect an enemy ship through the mere fact of their presence on board"), it also expressed interest in devising means by which Americans might cross the Atlantic in assured safety.[69] In addition, House now noted, "Since your [the president's] first note the German Government has not committed any act against either the letter or the spirit of it." "[I]t may be," he continued, that "even though they protest that they are unable to meet your demands, they may continue to observe them."[70] Such continued observation, combined with an apology and reparations for the *Lusitania*, rather than a repudiation of the submarine campaign, now became the administration's irreducible bottom line.

"Apparently the Germans are modifying their methods," Wilson told House. "[T]hey must be made to feel that they must continue in their new way unless they deliberately wish to prove to us that they are unfriendly and wish war." That message was incorporated into another note, dispatched on July 21, which was meant to finish off the correspondence.[71]

At first it appeared that this might end the crisis. Eager to avoid military conflict with America, Germany had, in secret, modified its submarine campaign. U-boat commanders had been ordered in June to avoid attacking large passenger ships.[72] Tensions rose again, however, when on August 19, the British liner *Arabic* was sunk (again, off southern Ireland) and two Americans on board died.

Wilson had many reasons for wanting to avoid military involvement. He was acutely aware that Americans, despite being upset by such incidents, "were still demanding . . . that I take no risk of war." He feared that Washington would lose the possibility of playing a mediatory role, and with that the ability to bring about a settlement of the war along the lines it wanted.[73] And, the costs of the conflict to those militarily involved in it were, by this point, abundantly clear. House had just passed on to the president an article that suggested how the war was likely to prove suicidal for Europe from the standpoint of its position in the world. The United States was likely to be the "heir to the influence and power hitherto possessed and exercised by England and her continental neighbors and rivals." The president thought this was a "pretty safe prediction," but commented that it was "always supposing we succeed in keeping out of the deadly maelstrom ourselves."[74]

But to Wilson the sinking of the *Arabic* was an act of "brutal defiance of the opinion and power" of the United States.[75] And both House and Lansing, the new secretary of state, took the same view. In House's opinion, "Unless Germany disavows the act and promises not to repeat it, some decisive action upon our part is inevitable, otherwise, we will have no influence when peace is made or afterwards."[76]

A rupture in relations might very well have followed. However, the U.S. ambassador in Berlin was at this time informed of the change in instructions that had been issued to U-boat commanders in June. And Berlin now pledged formally that no liners would be sunk "without warning and without safety of the lives of non-combatants" provided that they did not resist or try to escape.[77]

Tempers flared again several weeks later when Berlin asserted that it would not disavow the sinking of the *Arabic*, arguing that evidence showed it had tried to ram the U-boat. Viewing this as a sign that Germany might say one thing and do another, the president became considerably more belligerent. Ambassador Bernstorff, acting on his own, offered to negotiate an indemnity, fearing the alternative was war. Berlin was left with little choice but to go along.[78] While troublesome issues remained between the two powers, above all a settlement in the case of the *Lusitania*, the administration, by mid-October, was hopeful that it had achieved a favorable, if perhaps not permanent, resolution of the question of how submarine war would henceforth be conducted.

*   *   *

In the wake of the *Arabic* crisis, House decided to again try to mediate. And, once more, he endeavored to pursue that goal on the basis of a close consultation and collaboration with Britain. When he had left England in early June, neither side was ready to talk and there had also seemed a distinct possibility that the United States and Germany would be "drifting into war."[79] But, during the summer, Germany had appeared anxious to avoid adding the United States to its list of military opponents. More importantly, Britain seemed further than ever away from achieving its objective of making "a complete job" of eliminating Germany as a rival world power. Although the Allies had expanded their coalition to include Italy (in late April), the war had not gone well for them. Frustration continued to meet British and French efforts on the Western Front, Rome's offensives against Austria-Hungary had been disappointing, and the campaign at the Dardanelles had turned into a disaster. German and Austrian troops were pushing into White Russia and the Ukraine, and Bulgaria had just joined the Central Powers.[80] Indeed, both House and Wilson were worried about the direction the war was taking, and the president's expression of that concern may have been pivotal in emboldening his adviser to believe that a new opportunity had arrived. In late September, Wilson told him that "he had never been sure that we ought not to take part in the conflict and if it seemed evident that Germany and her militaristic ideas were to win, the obligation upon us was greater than ever."[81] On October 11, House told Frank Polk, the new State Department counselor, that "[i]t will not do for the United States to let the Allies go down and leave Germany the dominant military factor in the world."[82]

It also seemed likely that the United States had more leverage now, particularly if Wilson was willing to discuss the possibility of military involvement. A threat of such might be employed against Berlin if it held out against the kind of peace America wanted. And the Allies might be lured to the table by a promise that the United States would take up arms if Germany did not go along. House also hoped that Britain might be swayed if Washington made a more explicit and definitive commitment to a postwar role.

America might still, of course, become embroiled militarily over Germany's use of submarines. Or an impasse could develop over the details of the *Lusitania* settlement. But, from House's perspective, this was probably an additional reason why Washington should not wait to resume its mediation efforts. He wanted military involvement, or the suggestion of it, to more effectively be harnessed to the administration's broader diplomatic objectives. These included ending the war without a major redistribution of power and establishing mechanisms that would militate against such a disruption of the international order occurring again.

The American public was still staunchly opposed to military participation, and Wilson was clearly more nervous about taking that step than House, but both men may have thought that raising the prospect would suffice to achieve their ends. If not, House seems to have been convinced that the president—in whose rhetorical and leadership skills he had great confidence—would have an easier time rallying the country around a cause that might be depicted as everlasting peace than around the issue of submarine warfare.

Early in October, House proposed to Wilson that the Allies be asked unofficially to let him know "whether or not it would be agreeable . . . to have us demand that hostilities cease." The demand could be put "upon the high ground" that belligerents and neutrals alike were suffering, "and that peace parlays should begin upon the broad basis of both military and naval disarmament." It would be "understood that the word 'militarism' referred to the Continental Powers and the word 'navalism' referred to Great Britain." If the Allies understood Washington's purpose, "we could be as severe in our language concerning them as we were with the Central Powers, the Allies, after some hesitation, could accept our offer or demand, and if the Central Powers accepted, we would then have accomplished a master stroke. . . . If the Central Powers refused . . . we could then push our insistence to a point where diplomatic relations would first be broken off, and later the whole force of our Government, and perhaps the force of every neutral, might be brought against them."[83] With the president's encouragement, House wrote in this vein to Grey on October 17. He said that after conferring with London he would go to Berlin and "tell them that it was the President's purpose to intervene and stop this destructive war, provided the weight of the United States thrown on the side that accepted our proposal could do it." He would not "let Berlin know . . . of any understanding had with the Allies, but would rather lead them to think that our proposal would be rejected by the Allies. This might induce Berlin to accept . . . , but if they did not . . . it would nevertheless be the purpose to intervene. If the Central Powers were still obdurate, it would probably be necessary for us to join the Allies and force the issue." House admonished Grey not to wait too long to act on this proposal.[84]

The British foreign secretary inquired as to whether what House meant by eliminating militarism and navalism amounted to an American commitment to join a "League of Nations" that would enforce the peace.[85] After consulting with Wilson, House replied in the affirmative. Promoting such a plan, he told the president, "is the part I think you are destined to play in this world tragedy, and it is the noblest part that has ever come to a son of man. This country will follow you along such a path, no matter what the cost may be."[86]

CHAPTER 3

Pursuing a Seat at the Table (1916–17)

From the beginning of the war, the Wilson administration had sought to protect and then have set up on more secure foundations the kind of international order Washington desired. Toward those ends, it had been anxious not to see British power undermined by Germany, and it had sought to convince London that it should look to the United States as a partner in arranging a settlement. Washington had been extremely indulgent of British maritime measures. And it had displayed forbearance with and deference toward London over the question of when making a bid for peace would be appropriate.

During 1916, however, that patience began to fray. As the Wilson administration saw it, Britain's continued determination to end any prospect of Germany playing a political or military role in the extra-European world threatened not only endless prolongation of the conflict, with its attendant turmoil. It endangered Washington's hopes for postwar stabilization. The longer the war went on, moreover, the more chance there was that Berlin would opt to cross the "red lines" (in today's parlance) that Wilson had set down over the use of its submarines. The advantages of that course might appear to outweigh the prospect of American belligerency. Wilson still strongly preferred to avoid military involvement, because of its expense, because he feared it would cost the United States a mediatory role, and (something repeatedly driven home to him in 1916) because it was quite evident that American opinion strongly opposed it. As a consequence, during the latter half of 1916, U.S.-British relations became more adversarial. And, when it appeared that there might be a chance of Germany settling on satisfactory terms, the president, late in the year, finally launched a peace bid on his own.

However, not only did it become clear within weeks that neither the Allies nor the Central Powers were ready to discuss terms that the other would consider. At the end of January 1917, Germany announced that it was no longer willing to restrict the use of its U-boats to within Wilson's "red lines."

*   *   *

House had made the complaint more than once in the fall of 1915 that the British did not appreciate all that Washington was doing for them. "We have given the Allies our sympathy and we have given them, too, the more substantial help that we could not offer Germany even were we so disposed—and that is an unrestricted amount of munitions and money. In addition to that," he wrote Page on October 6, "we have forced Germany to discontinue her submarine warfare."[1]

At least in part, Wilson's adviser chose to view his proposal for American assistance in the convening of peace talks (conveyed in his letter to Grey of October 17) as yet another gift. As he saw it, his plan offered London a way of coming away whole from a war that did not seem to be going its way. House was therefore surprised and disappointed at the cautious and skeptical response he received from the British foreign secretary in late November. "[T]he offer which I made in my letter," House recorded in his diary, "which was practically to ensure victory to the Allies—should have met a warmer reception."[2] Traveling back to England in January, a key task he set himself was persuading the principal figures in that government that they should sign on to his idea.

The Allies would be offered a chance, if they wanted, to make one last push. Then, with U.S. help—ideally limited to the convening of talks (rather than military involvement)—they would achieve a settlement that (in House's view) would adequately meet their needs. The United States would subsequently participate in the keeping of that peace.

Such were the inducements that Wilson's adviser saw himself as bringing across the sea. But he had failed accurately to gauge the mood of Britain's leaders. As he immediately wrote back to Wilson, "I find all with whom I have talked so far of the same opinion. Their confidence seems greater now than it did when I was here before."[3] The war had not been going well for the Allies, but they had been making immense preparations for a great push in 1916 (one which would include the ultimately disappointing Somme offensive of July and after). House's reaction was to try to shake that confidence, in part by making the argument that an embattled Russia was likely to pursue a separate peace.[4]

House told Grey and Arthur Balfour (now first lord of the admiralty) that the United States could "safely lead an isolated life of our own" but it was willing to consider how it could "serve civilization." Wilson would make a commitment to preservation of the peace by coming "to an agreement with the civilized world upon the broad questions touching the interests and future of every nation."[5] (This marked a reprise of House's suggestion in his conversations with Grey of the previous year.)

As to Germany, House's proposals during this trip continued to echo the idea he had put forward previously, that it should if possible be transformed into a buttress of the postwar international order. To that end, he in midmonth suggested to David Lloyd George (the minister of munitions) "that England might give Germany a freer hand in Asia and look to Africa as her sphere of influence."[6] To Balfour, who was "unalterably distrustful of Germany," House commented, "What should be done was to get all nations in league together, and at least a majority of them would play fairly *under the lead of Great Britain and the United States*; and Germany would be the loser if she failed to keep her agreement" (emphasis added).[7]

Upon arriving there at the end of January, House did not find Berlin any more enthusiastic about the kind of settlement he wanted. Here too he sought to shake an air of self-confidence. Among other arguments, Wilson's emissary admonished the German chancellor as to the dangers the war was creating globally for the powers. "I told him [Chancellor Bethmann Hollweg] western civilization had broken down, and there was not a marketplace or a mosque in the East where the West of to-day was not derided." "He admitted this," House noted, "but said the fault was not Germany's."[8]

Indeed, House expressed to Wilson his concern that the time might soon be coming when Berlin would remove the restrictions it had been placing on the use of its submarines—even if the result of that was likely to be U.S. military intervention. House thought that the blockade was starting to bite and that the adherents of submarine warfare were gaining political and popular support for the idea that using them was the way to win the war. "They think war with us would not be so disastrous as England's blockade," he wrote the president on the thirtieth.[9]

House subsequently stopped in Paris. As in London, he sought to impress upon officials "the precariousness of the situation and the gamble that a continuance of the war involves."[10] He sought to undermine their confidence while impressing upon them the idea that they could count on the United States. He also went to La Panne to speak with King Albert. House ventured that Belgium should be paid an indemnity by all the belligerents after the war, but also that Germany should be allowed to purchase the Congo as compensation for the territory that it would relinquish in Europe.[11]

While British leaders were not inclined at this time to engage in peace talks, they were also anxious not to alienate Washington, and some, like Grey, were interested in the possibility that the United States might participate after the war in keeping the peace. It was in this spirit, and in the face of House's persistence, that the foreign secretary finally signed a memorandum of understanding with Wilson's emissary in England in late February. "Colonel House," it read,

> told me that President Wilson was ready, on hearing from France and England that the moment was opportune, to propose that a Conference should be summoned to put an end to the war. Should the Allies accept this proposal, and should Germany refuse it, the United States would probably enter the war against Germany.
>
> Colonel House expressed the opinion that, if such a Conference met, it would secure peace on terms not unfavorable to the Allies; and, if it failed to secure peace, the United States would leave the Conference as a belligerent on the side of the Allies, if Germany was unreasonable. Colonel House expressed an opinion decidedly favourable to the restoration of Belgium, the transfer of Alsace and Lorraine to France, and the acquisition by Russia of an outlet to the sea, though he thought that the loss of territory incurred by Germany in one place would have to be compensated to her by concessions to her in other places outside Europe. If the Allies delayed accepting the offer of President Wilson, and if, later on, the course of the war was so unfavorable to them that the intervention of the United States would not be effective, the United States would probably disinterest themselves in Europe and look to their own protection in their own way.[12]

It should go without saying that the undertaking discussed in this "House-Grey memorandum" was totally incompatible with any pretense to neutrality on the part of the Wilson administration.

House came back from England confidently expecting, quite incorrectly as it turned out, that his plan would be implemented by no later than midsummer. He believed that the British would worry that they would lose the help he was holding out to them if they didn't move by then. And the president, after being briefed, came to share this hope. For both men, the plan was valued as a way by which the war might be settled soon and as the United States wanted. It was the hope, and at this point expectation, of the two that the memorandum had secured (in House's words) "an active working arrangement between Great Britain and the United States in the settlement of the world's affairs."[13] That the House-Grey memorandum mentioned the possibility of direct American military involvement was largely left to one side, because both saw a greater likelihood of that happening in the absence of the plan. Yet, the prospect of such involvement was certainly something that Wilson was worrying about much more than House. This was no doubt in part why the president insisted on modifying the understanding so it read that the United States "would *probably* leave the Conference as a belligerent."[14]

*   *   *

Wilson's concerns about congressional and public opinion had been heightened considerably as the result of his experiences with the preparedness and the armed merchant ship issues, most of this while House had been gone. These certainly reinforced the president in his desire to try to achieve his foreign policy objectives without U.S. military involvement in the Great War.

In late 1914, the president had rebuffed the notion that the administration should press for dramatic new naval building and a substantial enlargement of the small American army. House encouraged such expansion as a way of boosting Wilson's diplomatic leverage. But the president expressed concern that it would (in House's words) "shock the country."[15] Wilson knew a buildup would not be popular among southern Democrats and many midwesterners and westerners of both parties. He resented criticism from northeastern Republicans, who pressed for such expansion, and rejoined that they had lost their "self-possession."[16]

This attitude changed in the wake of the *Lusitania* sinking. Wilson not only became more convinced of the value of "preparedness," he wanted to equip the United States for what might be a changed framework of rivalry in the postwar world. The hope was that public and congressional opinion would be more receptive now. House assured Wilson that the administration would be able to outflank the former secretary of state, Bryan, who was a staunch opponent of a buildup. In the end, Wilson was largely able to do that, capitalizing especially on the unwillingness of Democrats to abandon the first president their party had elected in twenty years, but he had to fight a bigger battle than expected.[17]

Opposition to preparedness was extensive, so extensive that the president was compelled to lean heavily on the votes of regular Republicans to achieve his objectives.[18] Clergymen, peace activists, and journalist-reformers, like Oswald Garrison Villard, disapproved, as did many farm and labor groups. Insurgent Republican figures, like Senators Robert La Follette (Wis.) and Asle Gronna (N.Dak.) were critical, but still more unsettling to the president was the size of the "Bryanite" southern and western opposition that materialized in his own party. This was particularly prominent in the House, where it was led by the majority leader, Claude Kitchin of North Carolina.

Critics expressed fear that preparedness would lead to military involvement in Europe. Some also voiced concern that it was a move that would ultimately prove dangerous to the world and to American institutions. Democratic congressman Isaac Sherwood of Ohio opined that the choice was whether America would "continue to endure in the purpose and hope of its founders, or whether we shall enter the devious path of world-power exploitation."[19]

Wilson married his second wife, Edith Bolling Galt, on December 18, 1915, and then left Washington for a two-week honeymoon. But soon after his return he felt compelled to mount a campaign to save preparedness. In late January and early February he undertook a speaking tour that took him from New York westward to Kansas and Missouri. During the trip, the president tried to make the argument that there were some circumstances under which the United States might be compelled to go to war and for which it would need to be prepared. These situations were actually susceptible of fairly elastic definition. They included: if it had to defend its "honor," "to defend the life of this nation against any sort of interference," and, to uphold America's "obligations" under the Monroe Doctrine. "Nobody seriously supposes," Wilson told an audience at the Waldorf-Astoria on January 27, "that the United States needs to fear an invasion of its own territory. What America has to fear, if she has anything to fear, are indirect, roundabout, flank movements upon her regnant position in the western hemisphere."

But the president was again and again compelled to downplay the buildup he was calling for, to reassure voters about his desire to stay clear of military involvement in Europe, and to reject any thought that the United States would expand in the future at the expense of any other country. Indeed, Wilson felt the need to promote preparedness princi- pally as a step that would help the United States to keep out of the Great War.[20]

By spring it was clear that the administration would be able to win much of what it had asked for. But the opposition had exacted a price, not least in the form of the pledges Wilson had felt obliged to make. The regular army was doubled in size (to approximately 220,000 officers and men). But plans to create a much larger new reserve force, called the Continental Army, were jettisoned in favor of a "federalizing" and gradual expansion of the state militias (or National Guard). That controversy cost the presi- dent his secretary of war, Garrison, who was committed to the Continental Army idea. Until the second half of 1916, it also appeared as if the adminis- tration would have to settle for a scaled-down naval expansion that was, moreover, different in emphasis from what it wanted, tilting toward defen- sive capabilities rather than battleships.[21]

The subsequent armed merchant ship controversy gave Wilson a still greater appreciation for how strong the opposition was to military involve- ment in Europe—especially from within the southern and western wings of his party. Ironically, the administration's own actions helped set off the furor.

By early 1916, Lansing had concluded that the United States could not insist that cruiser rules be adhered to by Germany's submarines if, as a consequence, the U-boats stood a strong chance of being destroyed by well- armed Allied merchant ships.[22] Hundreds of British merchantmen were armed. Moreover, they had standing orders to shoot at submarines on sight.[23] "I think that I appreciate the German point of view," the secretary wrote Wilson. No doubt driven, at least in part, by congressional pressure for the United States to pursue an even-handed course, Lansing implied that the United States would have to change its policy. But he preferred to pursue a modus vivendi. The Central Powers would agree "not to torpedo any enemy vessels without putting the people on board in safety" if the Entente Powers disarmed their merchant ships (which otherwise, he thought, should probably be considered auxiliary cruisers). "I am sure the Teutonic Powers would agree to this," he told the president, "and I cannot see how the Entente Powers could reasonably object to such an arrangement."[24]

Wilson thought the idea was "thoroughly worth trying."[25] Its acceptance would enhance the safety of U.S. citizens traveling on Allied merchantmen (provided that those merchantmen stopped). And it would thereby reduce the need for Washington to make good on its threat that a "critical situation" would be created if any such traveler was harmed. It bore comparison with the administration's efforts in 1915 to secure an agreement whereby Berlin would abandon its submarine blockade in exchange for London modifying the blockade in regard to food.

Lansing approached the Allies about his modus vivendi on January 18, and the press was briefed about the proposal at the end of the month. The French government assumed that Washington was right on the legal question at stake, but, contrary to expectations, Britain signaled great hostility. Grey's position was that the United States was suggesting "free play" be given to the submarine.

With striking speed, the administration reversed itself and abandoned the proposal. After learning about the modus vivendi upon his return from the continent to England, House judged that Lansing's efforts were jeopardizing the success of his plan for a settlement of the war through British and American collaboration. He urged that Washington desist from any further consideration of a new policy on armed merchant ships. (Despite growing irritation in America over the blockade, House had similarly been urging Wilson to avoid pressuring London over that.)

Although Lansing had learned of admiralty orders that suggested quite the opposite was the case, the administration in mid-February essentially agreed to accept Britain's contention that its merchant vessels were armed purely for defense. They would therefore not be reclassified, American citizens would not be warned against travel on them, and a serious issue would still be created if any of those citizens were harmed by the actions of a submarine not following cruiser rules.[26]

This about-face set off a congressional firestorm, especially among southern and western members of the president's own party.[27] Representative Jeff McLemore (D-Tex.) introduced a resolution that would ask the president to warn Americans against travel on armed merchantmen. Senator Thomas Gore (D-Okla.) pushed for legislation that would make it difficult for Americans intent on traveling on belligerent vessels to obtain passports. By the last week in February, there were those who thought the McLemore resolution might pass by a ratio of as much as three to one.

Wilson responded with a public letter to Senator William J. Stone (D-Mo.), chairman of the Foreign Relations Committee.[28] It maintained that American rights were at stake. The government could not "consent to any abridgement" of those rights. For that would, in fact, constitute acquiescence "in the violation of the rights of mankind everywhere." More important, the president asserted, any such retreat would constitute a confession of America's "impotency" as a nation.

The executive branch employed every means at its disposal to face down this revolt. And it succeeded, even to the point of getting the House to take up and then vote down the McLemore resolution. Nevertheless, the episode demonstrated to Wilson yet again how much sentiment there was in both Congress and the nation against military intervention in Europe. It also compelled the president to promise once more that he would "do everything" in his power to avoid that. He would opt for such involvement only if the nation's honor or interests were directly attacked.

These were commitments that in fact were quite at odds with the spirit of the proposals that House had just been making to the Allies.

*   *   *

In the wake of the *Arabic* crisis, Germany's "submarine blockade" had largely been suspended. But a new U-boat campaign was launched in mid-March 1916. Although military leaders were eager for far fewer restrictions, commanders were once again directed to torpedo any *enemy* merchant vessels they came upon in the war zone that had been declared around Great Britain. They were also told they could fire without warning on any *armed* enemy merchant ships elsewhere.[29]

Extreme care was still to be taken to avoid harm to passenger vessels. Even so, a French steamer, the *Sussex*, was damaged by a torpedo in the English Channel on March 24, and four Americans onboard were hurt. Either the ship had been misidentified, or the U-boat commander had failed to heed his instructions.

In Washington, the incident was taken to constitute a violation of the *Arabic* pledge. And this raised the prospect that a break with Germany might occur before House's plan had had a chance of being tried.[30] In the event, House and Wilson decided to contact Grey to ask whether he "might wish now to consult with your allies with a view to acting immediately" on that proposal. The war was likely to be "prolonged" further if the United States became a belligerent, they argued.[31] In a follow-up letter, House wrote that there was "another reason [for moving on the plan], and that is that we are not so sure of the support of the American people upon the submarine issue, while we are confident that they would respond to the higher and nobler issue of stopping the war."[32] The foreign secretary responded that the time had not yet come.

House nevertheless told the president that the United States "would lose the respect of the world unless he lived up to the demands that he has made of Germany regarding her undersea warfare."[33] Wilson accepted that advice, and on April 18 Lansing sent a note that threatened severance of relations unless Berlin affirmed that it would avoid sinking "passenger and freight-carrying vessels" without warning (the reference to merchant ships reflecting the secretary of state's long-held insistence as to what the *Arabic* pledge had covered).[34]

Bethmann Hollweg had only narrowly succeeded in heading off demands from the German military for a much broader submarine campaign. Nevertheless, he prevailed with the kaiser again. In early May, Berlin announced that its U-boats would respect Washington's desires (the *Sussex* pledge). It did stipulate though that Germany would reserve the right to abandon such restrictions if the United States did not compel Britain to conduct its maritime measures in conformity with international law.[35]

This response may have encouraged Wilson and House to believe that Berlin might be receptive to peace discussions (its major offensive at Verdun, begun in late winter, had thus far been hugely disappointing). In any event, they now turned their attention back to the Allies, hoping to activate the House plan and end the war along the lines they wanted.

They hoped that Britain would be swayed by the administration boldly committing itself in public to a postwar U.S. role in the enforcement of the peace. Toward that end, Wilson accepted an invitation to speak to a meeting in Washington of an organization, formed in 1915 and led by ex-President Taft, dedicated to the establishment of a postwar League to Enforce Peace. There, on May 27, the president endorsed, in general terms, American membership in a "universal association of nations" for that purpose.[36]

But London was not moved and it again rejected action on the House plan on the grounds that it was untimely. While most British leaders were anxious not to alienate the United States and some were intrigued by the prospect that it might play a role in the enforcement of the peace, they had not abandoned hope of achieving what they envisioned to be a much more advantageous conclusion to the war than could be had at this point. Within government circles there was widespread doubt that Wilson would actually be able to bring America into the war via the House-Grey memorandum (related to this was the suspicion that the president was pushing to make a peace bid largely, in this election year, to win votes). But the controlling factor was that Britain was simply not ready to settle. House's ideas about Germany getting its colonies back and being compensated abroad for the evacuation of territory in Europe were abhorrent. London wanted to remove the possibility of Berlin, as it saw it, becoming a threat to the British Empire again. And to achieve such an outcome it needed to fight on and hold onto its continental allies (an objective bound to be jeopardized by even the mention to them of peace) and the enthusiastic support of the dominions. If the scheme embodied in the House-Grey memorandum had value, it was as an insurance policy that could be of use should the war take a turn for the worse. In any event, the United States might, British leaders thought, eventually join the fighting for free as the result of its ongoing dispute with Germany over the submarine.[37]

House wrote Wilson in mid-May that he saw evidence of "the Allies regaining their self-assurance and not being as yielding to our desires as they were when they were in so much trouble. We have given them everything and they ever demand more."[38] In early June, he cabled Grey that the ungrateful "Allied Governments and press overlook the weight the President has thrown on their side at almost every turn."[39]

Henceforth, Wilson told House, "it will be up to us to judge for ourselves when the time has arrived for us to make an imperative suggestion."[40]

The two men were convinced that the United States was gradually acquiring enormous economic power that it could bring to bear.[41] The Allies appeared to be more and more dependent on the United States for both supplies and credit. The administration was also thinking of how it might, if necessary, bring leverage on the Allied governments via public diplomacy, by trying to capitalize on what it believed was the growing war-weariness of the people of England, France, and Italy.[42]

London's refusal to act on the memorandum brought forth a much harsher view of its policies and intentions. House wrote in May that a "situation may arise, if the Allies defeat Germany, where they may attempt to be dictatorial in Europe and elsewhere."[43] In mid-June, the Allies held an economic conference in Paris. Its principal objective was to promote greater economic coordination during the war, but it also discussed postwar collaboration. Figures in Washington worried that such collaboration might impact negatively on American trade after the war.[44]

Britain's blockade now began to be looked at with a much more critical eye as well, particularly as it began to be expanded further. Over the summer, London started to inspect mail on board ships headed for neutral European ports. And eighty-five U.S. firms were added to Britain's blacklist— a step designed economically to punish those held to being doing business with the Central Powers. Energetic protests of both steps emanated from Washington. More importantly, the administration began to consider retaliatory measures. On July 23, the president wrote House that he was "about at the end of my patience" with Britain. He was thinking about "asking Congress to authorize me to prohibit loans and restrict exportations to the Allies. It is becoming clear to me that there lies latent in this policy the wish to prevent our merchants getting a foothold in markets which Great Britain has hitherto controlled and all but dominated."[45]

Wilson and House also began to deride London's wartime rhetoric. When Ambassador Page was home on leave, they sought to jolt him out of an Anglophilia they felt limited his usefulness. House told him he "resented some of the cant and hypocrisy indulged in by the British," such as the claim they were fighting to free Belgium.[46] Wilson told Page that the war was the consequence of "England's having the earth and of Germany wanting it."[47]

In September, at the administration's behest, Congress gave the president the power to retaliate against British trade and shipping so as to challenge the whole tenor of the blockade. Wilson was reluctant to use this authority, but he hoped that its existence would strengthen his hand with London.[48]

The White House was also coming to view naval expansion with one eye on Great Britain. With the assistance of congressional Republicans, and deftly capitalizing on the dramatic, if brief and inconclusive, encounter between the British and German fleets off Jutland, Denmark, in June, the White House was able to regain the initiative on this issue. In justification of a larger program, proponents of a big navy asserted that Jutland proved the vital importance of sea power to national defense. They also claimed that it demonstrated the importance of an emphasis on battleships. The upshot was that, over the summer, Congress enacted the Naval Act of 1916, which appropriated sufficient funds to make the U.S. Navy, within three years, a close second in size to that of Great Britain. House told Wilson in September that "the real difference with Great Britain now was that the United States had undertaken to build a great navy; that our commerce was expanding beyond all belief, and we were rapidly taking the position Germany occupied before the war." To which the president replied, "Let us build a navy bigger than her's [sic] and do what we please!"[49]

Wilson came to realize that any "imperative suggestion" would have to wait until his campaign for reelection was over. So long as there was any doubt about his future, the president could not be sure what his leverage with foreign nations would be. He was not in a position to commit the United States to a long-term course of action. Moreover, the dynamics of domestic politics would, until November, compel him to avoid any course that could heighten the prospects for American military involvement.

Four years before, Wilson had run against the incumbent Taft, Roosevelt (who had tried to return to the White House as the standard bearer of the Progressive Party), and the Socialist Party candidate, Eugene V. Debs. He had won the presidency with only 42 percent of the popular vote. With the Republicans reunited, victory in 1916 initially appeared to depend on which of the two major-party domestic platforms appeared more appealing to those who had voted Progressive in 1912. The Democrats seemed well placed to succeed at that, perhaps above all because of the positions taken by southern and western Bryanites in Congress.

But campaign strategists eventually felt compelled to acknowledge how important the peace issue was as well. There seemed to be great merit in reassuring voters on that score and worrying them about the consequences of turning foreign policy over to the Republicans. Wilson, in 1916, was put before voters as the man who "kept us out of war," while the Democrats implied that his opponent was someone who would get the United States into the fighting.

Such charges hurt Charles Evans Hughes, the GOP candidate, despite his insistence that he was for strict neutrality. This was perhaps especially due to the noisy campaigning on his behalf engaged in by TR. The former president alleged that the administration's foreign policy was too timid, especially toward Germany (he had made comparable criticisms in the past of the diplomacy of Cleveland, McKinley, and Taft). Given the public mood, at least outside some circles in the Northeast, that was not a line of argument likely to be helpful to the Republican candidate.[50]

*   *   *

But once the election was over, the triumphant Wilson decided to move as quickly as possible toward another bid for peace. He felt considerable pressure because of developments in Germany. Berlin had been indicating since late September that it would respond positively to a proposal for parlays presented as if originating with the United States. It had simultaneously been warning that if such talks were not arranged soon, Bethmann Hollweg would be unable to withstand military and popular sentiment for the unrestricted use of U-boats to cut off British trade. German diplomats reminded Washington of Berlin's conditional commitment to the *Sussex* pledge.[51]

A week after the election Wilson told House that he wanted "to write a note to the belligerents demanding that the war cease." "His argument," according to his alter ego, was "that unless we do this now, we must inevitably drift into war with Germany upon the submarine issue." If Berlin abandoned the *Sussex* pledge, "in order to maintain our position, we must break off diplomatic relations. Before doing this he would like to make a move for peace, hoping there is sufficient peace sentiment in the allied countries to make them consent."[52] House doubted that Berlin was prepared to agree to terms that Washington "could recommend to the Allies."[53] He was also certain that the Allied governments would continue to resist. Wilson's advisor worried that an initiative at this point might not only ruin relations with the Allies, but create greater public acceptance in the United States of a German undersea campaign.[54]

Harking back to the House-Grey memorandum, the president "wondered whether we could not have a separate understanding with the Allies by which we would agree to throw our weight in their favor in any peace settlement brought about by their consent to mediation."[55] But Wilson was no longer content to give the Allies the chance to decide when talks would commence. House doubted this would work. He also believed that Allied public sentiment for peace would have to be developed further.

In the days immediately following, the president's adviser met with the German ambassador and with John Howard Whitehouse, a Liberal member of Parliament traveling in America, whom House considered a keen observer of the British political scene. House was encouraged by his talk with Bernstorff. He reported to the president the latter's assertion that "peace was on the floor waiting to be picked up." But his conversation with the MP only confirmed his misgivings about the Allies. According to Whitehouse, House said that "England was the only obstacle to peace." The United States "had been quite unneutral in its friendliness to England," but this friendliness had not been reciprocated. The president could obtain for London "everything she is fighting for." Whitehouse himself was receptive, but—House subsequently reported to Wilson—the MP did not believe that a peace move at this time would succeed.[56]

For his part, the president may have felt that even an unsuccessful bid could have value, inasmuch as it might improve his ability to mobilize Americans for war. In any event, he was determined to proceed, although—apparently responding to House's misgivings (and a suggestion published by Columbia University president Nicholas Murray Butler)—he now decided he would compose a request for each side to state its terms rather than a demand "that the war cease" (still hoping this would lead in the same direction).[57] Simultaneously he asked House to write Grey, conveying to him America's hostility to "an indefinite continuation of the war."

Wilson was growing more hopeful that Washington could coerce the Allied governments. He urged House to develop ideas as to how the United States might mobilize Allied public opinion behind its efforts.[58] As important, in late November, he discovered, and seized immediately upon, an opportunity to demonstrate how much economic leverage the United States was coming to have over the Allies. This arose in connection with efforts by J. P. Morgan and Co. (the purchasing and financial agent for

Britain in America) to find new means of raising money for the Allied effort.

At the very beginning of the war, the administration had held that loans by American bankers to nations at war were "inconsistent with the true spirit of neutrality."[59] It quickly began to retreat from this position, however, once it became clear how much it would inhibit American trade. By late 1915, the policy had been completely reversed, and over the next year nearly two billion dollars were borrowed by Britain in the United States.

England found, however, that it had to pay high interest rates and put up sizable collateral to attract this money. By late 1916, it was running short of the latter. As a stopgap, J. P. Morgan wanted to sell short-term, unsecured British Treasury bills to American bankers. But this raised concerns on the part of the Federal Reserve Board. And it also offered a means by which Wilson could send London a message. The Fed worried that the scale of the planned sale might have a negative impact on the liquidity of the banking system. It drafted a statement cautioning member banks against investing too heavily in such securities. At Wilson's behind-the-scenes behest, that statement was then dramatically strengthened. Investors were to be told that their purchase was not considered "in the interest of the country."[60]

The publication of this warning on November 27 made pointless any effort to issue the bills. Indeed, it put enormous pressure on the pound. And the signal was read as intended. Ambassador Spring Rice had learned that the purpose, he reported to his government, "is to force us to accept President's mediation."[61]

Wilson finished writing his appeal for a statement of terms in early December. It looked toward a conclusion of the war along the lines his administration had been seeking. It had been striving to restore and put on more solid foundations the basics of the international order that existed up to 1914. Toward that end, the president's note was designed to get both sides to respond in such a way as would allow him to propose a peace conference under his leadership. Wilson hoped they would not want to alienate the United States. He also hoped to capitalize on what he believed was a growing war-weariness on the part of the peoples of the great European powers (in this regard, the note was to be Wilson's first real foray into public diplomacy outside of the western hemisphere). Such pressure would ideally push the contending sides toward the avowal of modest aims and support for a league. The warring parties had asserted that they were fighting to put an end to aggression, the note asserted. They had emphasized their determination to secure guarantees of security and peace. Wilson insisted that such ends were within reach.[62]

Before he could send off his appeal, however, the Berlin government's impatience led it to make a peace bid of its own. On December 12, it issued a call for the Allies to meet to discuss an end to hostilities.[63] Wilson worried that his initiative might now be seen as having been coordinated with Germany. Yet postponement risked the possibility that the Allies would reply to Berlin in such a way as would ruin any chance of his move succeeding. Lest the situation become "even more hopeless," the president sent his note off on December 18, attaching to it a request that it be considered on its own.[64]

Berlin responded on December 26. Noting that Wilson had said that he was "indifferent" as to the exact means by which the two sides set out their terms, the German government simply stated, in the spirit of its own initiative, that it thought this could best be done through a "direct exchange of views" between the two sides. The issue of preventing future wars could best be addressed after this one was settled, in a conference that would include states not parties to the present conflict.[65] Though this fell short of what the president wanted, he continued to be optimistic that Germany would accept what he desired. For weeks he had been receiving reports that it sought peace, that it would evacuate northern France and Belgium, and that it would join a league.[66] Wilson was far less hopeful about the Allies' response and they continued to be his focus.

London had long been determined to resist should it be presented with an American peace move. And the new Lloyd George ministry that came to power in early December was even more united behind this stance than had been its predecessor. Lloyd George himself had tried to preempt Wilson months before when, as secretary of state for war, he told a United Press correspondent of his commitment to a "knock-out" victory over Germany.[67] He, in fact, brought into his coalition government figures such as Lords Curzon and Milner and Leo Amery who were eager to see Britain fight on for territorial prizes in the Middle East and around the rim of the Indian Ocean belonging to the Central Powers. They believed Britain needed a more cohesive empire, as well as the oil of that region, to fend off competition in the postwar world from other powers (including the United States).

It was of course one thing to turn Berlin down flat, as the Allies did on December 29, quite another to incite the United States. British leaders were more acutely aware than Wilson of how economically dependent they had become on America (even though some sought comfort in the thought that the dependency worked both ways). Weeks before the Fed statement of late November, the chancellor of the exchequer reported that Wilson would, if he wanted, be able "to dictate his own terms to us" by mid-1917.[68]

London hoped to disguise the desperateness of its predicament and at the same time respond in such a way as would prevent a confrontation. It quietly reduced the level of its purchases in the United States. Lloyd George told Page that the Allies would not enter into a conference now because Germany still occupied too advantageous a position. But he assured the American ambassador that he saw a major role for the United States in the eventual settlement of the war and in world affairs. He believed there was a special relationship between their two countries and said that the president was the only one who could bring an end to the conflict when the appropriate time came.[69]

Britain also arranged for France to deliver the formal response from the Allies, which Paris did on January 10, 1917. The note praised the league idea, voiced a desire for peace, regretted that such could not be achieved under current conditions, and rejected the notion that the Allies were fighting for "selfish interests." To the extent that their aims were stated, they were cast mostly in terms of an Allied determination to free Europe from "the brutal covetousness of Prussian militarism."[70] Balfour, now foreign minister, followed up with a conciliatory, informal explanation, meant to make the case that reversion to "the *status quo ante bellum* would not be in the interests of the world."[71]

Wilson remained confident that he could coerce the Allies and was eager to apply more pressure before Germany might decide to expand the use of its submarines. On January 3, he and House discussed the notion of the president making a speech once the formal Allied response had been received. The ostensible purpose would be to provide the Senate with information as to what "America would demand if she consents to join a league to enforce peace."[72] The real objective would be to try to arouse Allied public opinion against the Allied governments. Challenging the Allied contention that they had to fight on if they were to achieve a durable peace, Wilson planned to argue that the exact opposite was the case.

Choosing to characterize the replies to his request for terms as more obliging than they were, the president opened his speech on January 22 by asserting that "a definite discussion of the peace" had been brought nearer.

This meant that the time had also come to discuss the "international concert" that would "hold the world at peace." To him it was "inconceivable" that the United States would not participate in such an undertaking—it could not "in honor" shirk such a "service" to the world. Nevertheless, America would feel that it could render that service only under the right conditions. Most importantly, the present war would have to be concluded on the basis of a "peace without victory."[73]

The president hoped that the pressure he was trying to bring to bear on the Allies would allow him to end the conflict on the terms he wanted. The essentials of the pre-1914 international order would be restored. Germany would not replace Britain, but it also would not be crushed. Most, if not all, great powers would agree to act collaboratively as trustees of this system (at least outside of the western hemisphere; there, implicitly, the United States would continue to preside alone), above all by signing on to methods of competition and conflict adjustment that would reduce the likelihood of a war like this occurring again.

Wilson was sufficiently optimistic about his chances of coercing Britain that he felt that all he now needed were concrete terms from Germany. House was urged to press Bernstorff for these. "[T]ell him that this is the time to accomplish something," the president wrote his adviser. "[W]ith something reasonable to suggest . . . I can bring things about."[74] "[T]he time has arrived when Germany should be pushed to declare her terms," agreed House. That would also "make a good impression on the Allies."[75]

On Friday, January 26, Bernstorff visited Wilson's adviser at the latter's apartment in New York. House called his "attention to the danger that lay in postponing peace, and of the probability of their coming in conflict with us on account of their submarine activities." Berlin had to give the president "something definite to work on and immediately." Bernstorff agreed to ask his government to state terms that would "include complete evacuation of Belgium and France" and "offer to go into a peace conference" on the basis of Wilson's recent address.[76]

But they were not only too late. In the following days it became clear that Germany did not share Wilson's conception of a satisfactory peace either (it still harbored the hope of coming away from the war with a stronger strategic position in Europe). Moreover, having concluded that what would constitute such was otherwise not within reach, it was already moving to unleash its submarines.

Berlin's fall peace bid had been launched against the backdrop of a generally frustrating year on the battlefield and, more importantly, out of the belief that Germany would face defeat in 1917 if things continued on as they were. The Allies could draw on more resources and were thus better equipped for a war of attrition. Their blockade of the Central Powers was, meanwhile, having more and more of an effect.

Throughout late 1916, the military (and public opinion, aroused in part by mounting shortages of food) had clamored for the abandonment of restrictions on submarine warfare. Submarines, it was argued, would not only avert defeat but bring victory. Britain, a nation surrounded by water, was highly vulnerable to blockade. Germany could turn the tables and quickly starve England into submission. The United States might go to war over this, but the conflict would be over before that could make a difference (indeed, it was alleged that the United States could not do any more harm than it already was to the Central Powers).

Bethmann Hollweg, as well as foreign ministry and treasury officials, had (correctly) taken the position that such a course carried enormous risk. They worried that the result might not be success, but rather a wider war that could jeopardize the very survival of the regime. The solution was for Berlin first to try to achieve an "acceptable" end to the conflict by capitalizing on the strong position it still occupied on the ground.

The chancellor was given leave to explore this possibility essentially on the understanding that if he did not succeed, Germany would intensify the undersea war. Berlin did not trust the president or see him as an honest broker. It saw him as pro-Ally, and it had no intention of allowing him to participate in the peace talks it envisioned. Nevertheless, in the interest of bringing such talks about, of avoiding the impression that Germany was desperate, and of putting the Allies in disfavor before American and German opinion, Bethmann Hollweg had been eager to get Wilson to make a call for peace. False hopes, as to Berlin's terms, were clearly allowed to be raised in the process.

Advocates of a U-boat campaign maintained that, to have the intended effect, it would have to start by February. Germany dispatched its own call for talks when it appeared that Wilson might not act in time. And the Allied rejection of that led quickly, during the first part of January, to the ascendance of the advocates of the submarine.

Wilson was to be thanked for his efforts, but at the end of the month Bernstorff was instructed to announce the imminent beginning of a new policy. After February 1, much greater latitude would be given to the U-boats. Limited provision would be made for weekly passenger travel to the port of Falmouth, England. But otherwise, any ship of any nationality, sailing into or out of Allied ports, risked being sunk without warning.[77]

*   *   *

Berlin expressed the hope that the United States would accept its measures. But, after the U.S. election in November, Wilson had already accurately forecast what would now happen. In order to maintain its position, Washington would eventually break off relations and the two powers would "drift into war."

Speaking on February 2 in New York, Bryan urged that American vessels be kept out of the war zone declared by Germany (implicitly that the United States respond as it had to Britain's blockade). Differences between the two powers should be deferred and settled after the war in Europe was over. And, he argued, the American public should be consulted via a referendum before there was any question of military intervention.[78] The president still very much hoped to avoid military involvement, but he had no intention of taking his former secretary of state's suggested course, this (quite apart from the large volume of business that would be forfeit) because he did not want to abandon his vision of America's future international role.

At first, Wilson actually wondered aloud about the possible wisdom of not reacting at all immediately. From the standpoint of reconstructing the kind of international order he wanted, military intervention by the United States could be disastrous. Therefore it should be avoided if at all possible. He told House "that it would be a crime for this Government to involve itself in the war to such an extent as to make it impossible to save Europe afterward."[79] Similarly, he told his secretary of state "that he was not yet sure what course we must pursue and must think it over; that he had been more and more impressed with the idea that 'white civilization' and its domination in the world rested largely on our ability to keep this country intact, as we would have to build up the nations ravaged by the war."[80] He shared a related idea with his cabinet, telling it that it might be wise to do nothing if that seemed necessary "to keep the white race or part of it strong to meet the yellow race—Japan, for instance, in alliance with Russia, from dominating China."[81]

But House and Lansing, both of whom had all but abandoned any alternative to intervention, argued that if Washington did not at least break relations right away (following through on the threat it had made during the Sussex crisis) it risked a dramatic reduction in its international influence. And Wilson, as at similar junctures previously, accepted this thinking.

Breaking relations was also made more palatable by the thought that it might help him to achieve his objectives without fighting. Lansing argued that it was unlikely that Berlin would declare war, while House and Wilson mused in conversation about the possibility that resolute action might bring Germany back to its "senses." Once confident that he could command the support of southern and western Democrats, the president, on February 3, went before Congress to make known his decision.[82]

Wilson declared that only "overt acts" by Germany could make him believe that it intended to follow through on its announced campaign. Further action by Washington would depend on Berlin. This stance perfectly captured the president's attitude as he headed into February. He thought there still might be a chance of Germany reversing course (or even, as House suggested, that Germany might "go to pieces" because of the food situation). From the standpoint of public opinion, moreover, it was important to put Berlin in the position of firing the first shot.[83]

Wilson also tried to bring pressure on Germany by other means. He wanted to get the European neutrals to join the United States in severing relations. An appeal for that was included in his address before Congress. However, this bore little fruit, in part because the administration had so often rebuffed other nonbelligerents when they had proposed collective action.[84] Leverage might be applied by way of Austria-Hungary. There were signs that it might be looking to extract itself from the war. Such a development, it was thought, might compel Germany to rethink its course and explore mediation through Wilson. In order to encourage Vienna in that direction, Page was instructed to ask Lloyd George for reassurance that the Allies would not insist on the dismemberment of the multinational empire. It eventually became clear, however, that Austria-Hungary was not prepared to act on its own.[85] Meanwhile, Washington refrained from even a formal protest when Britain announced yet more stringent measures of "blockade" on February 21.[86]

Fearful of sending their vessels into the war zone, American shippers began to explore the prospect of arming them. Lansing argued that Berlin would have achieved its objective if U.S. ships simply did not sail.[87] As a consequence, late in the month, Wilson embraced what he called "armed neutrality," a policy whereby artillery and naval contingents would be put on merchantmen. He ideally wanted congressional endorsement for this move and argued for it on the grounds that the United States needed to protect its rights. Posed this way, very few legislators were inclined to object. Virtually all Democrats rallied around their president, and many no doubt took solace in his pledge—reiterated in his speech before a joint session of Congress—that "[n]o course of my choosing . . . will lead to war."[88] Nevertheless, the administration's armed ship bill was blocked from becoming law, this by a filibuster staged in the Senate mostly by a very small group of Bryanites, including Stone (D-Mo.) (chair of the Foreign Relations Committee), and seven Republican insurgents. They argued that "armed neutrality" would court a war neither desired by nor in the interest of most Americans. The president fumed at what he called this "little group of willful men" who represented "no opinion but their own."[89] Insisting that older statutes gave him the authority to do so, he now simply acted to implement the policy on his own.[90]

Wilson may have thought that this was a way of buying time. Admiral William S. Benson expressed the view that if Germany was informed of the arming of American ships it was just "barely possible" that it would refrain from interfering with them.[91] But the evidence suggests that from late February into early March the president was more and more convinced that Germany was not going to reverse course and that the United States should become a formal participant in the war.

The "Zimmermann telegram" was likely key to this. At the end of February, British intelligence provided Washington with a copy of an intercepted and deciphered cable sent on January 19 by Arthur Zimmermann, the German foreign secretary, to Berlin's minister to Mexico. The latter was informed of Germany's plans for submarine warfare. "We shall endeavor," the cable said, "to keep the United States of America neutral." But if this was not successful, Berlin wanted the minister to then encourage Mexico to join in the fighting on its side. Germany shall give "generous financial support," wrote Zimmermann, and it was understood "that Mexico is to reconquer the lost territory [annexed by the United States in the 1840s] in New Mexico, Texas, and Arizona."[92]

This was an unlikely scenario, to say the least, as war with the United States—at the side of a European power that was cut off from access to the oceans of the world—would have put at risk the very survival of the Mexican government. Nevertheless, the cable fed into Washington's misgivings about Mexico's new president, Venustiano Carranza. Since 1913 he had proven maddeningly resistant to Wilson's efforts to direct the course of that country's politics (see Chapter 4). And, as a result, when war came, the State Department demanded, and received, a Mexican guarantee of strict neutrality.

It also fed into Washington's general anxiety about Germany, or any other major power, possibly becoming a political-military actor in the western hemisphere. Germany's talk of helping an ally to get back territory lost in the era of the Mexican-American War was, of course, not unlike the suggestion made in the House-Grey memorandum, that the United States was likely to look with favor on France recovering Alsace and Lorraine, territories annexed by Germany in another nineteenth-century war. Even had he thought about the parallel, however, it is unlikely that Wilson would have been less incensed.

The telegram appeared in the press on March 1, and that helped the administration to get its armed-ship bill passed by the House. The incident also appears to have generated a sharp, if temporary, upsurge in bellicosity on the part of substantial segments of the American public.

But almost surely the biggest impact of the cable on the president himself lay in the fact that it extinguished any remaining hope that Berlin might turn around. From Wilson's perspective, the telegram confirmed that the Germans were beyond the pale and out of control. A few days after he received the cable, the president told a visiting delegation of activists urging peace, "if you knew what I know at this present moment, and what you will see reported in tomorrow morning's newspapers, you would not ask me to attempt further peaceful dealings with the Germans."[93]

If the president was to achieve his objectives, only force, and formal belligerency, remained. He told his visitors that war had become inevitable. As one of them, the eminent social reformer Jane Addams, recalled, he said that "as head of a nation participating in the war, the President of the United States would have a seat at the Peace Table, but . . . if he remained the representative of a neutral country he could at best only 'call through a crack in the door.' "[94]

Several days later, the famous philosopher Henri Bergson offered up his appraisal of where things stood in America in a report to the French premier, Aristide Briand. He had been asked to go to the United States in the hope that he could put the French cause in an appealing light for the former university professor now occupying the White House. "Here is my impression," he wrote, "They are marching toward war, but, while certain cabinet members wish to enter the war immediately and completely, President Wilson will not take this step until events have made it inevitable, because he still has opinion divided behind him; in the West, many persons still want peace at any price. The President wishes to manage all the transitions."[95] Ten days later word arrived that three American vessels sailing through the German-declared war zone had been sunk. None of them had artillery, but by this point the president had clearly lost interest in "armed neutrality." On the nineteenth, Lansing urged him to call Congress together to "consider declaring war." Wilson "indicated" to him "the fear he had of the queries and investigations of a Congress which could not be depended upon."[96] But he quickly cast those concerns aside, probably after he sounded his cabinet the next day. On the twenty-first, the president summoned Congress into special session set for April 2, "to receive a communication concerning grave matters of national policy."[97]

CHAPTER 4

China and Latin America (1914–17)

While war raged on the other side of the Atlantic, Washington strove to solidify its economic and political position in Latin America. Simultaneously, it tried to limit Japanese challenges to the open door in China that were prompted by the conflict in Europe. Any discussion of the Great War and American foreign policy is incomplete without mention of these engagements. They not only speak to the kind of international order the United States was trying to uphold, stabilize, and expand its trade and influence into. They provide a broader track record by which to evaluate the nature of the Wilson administration's commitment to self-determination, democracy, international cooperation, and other concepts that it was increasingly going to champion on the European and global stage from 1917.

Furthermore, these activities afford additional insight into the administration's thinking with regard to the future of great-power competition in the underdeveloped world and with regard to the problem of postwar European stability. A plan the United States promoted to guarantee order in Latin America was in fact intended to provide a model for the accomplishment of the same objective in Europe.

*   *   *

Though the terms of its alliance with Britain did not require it to do so, Japan entered the Great War on the side of the Entente three weeks after the conflict started in Europe. At a minimum, its government hoped to eliminate Berlin as a rival in the East Asia–Pacific region, to acquire for Japan territorial positions of influence—on the China coast and in the western Pacific—that Germany had obtained during the late nineteenth century, and to make more secure a sphere of influence Tokyo had been trying to develop in southern Manchuria, the latter being driven especially by the greater assertiveness and nationalism coursing, since 1911, through the political scene in China. In the end, the ease with which it prevailed over German forces, combined with the continued absorption of the other powers in events in Europe, led the government of Ōkuma Shigenobu to probe for much more.[1]

By November, Japan had taken all of the German islands north of the equator (those to the south were occupied by the British dominions of Australia and New Zealand) as well as Berlin's leasehold on China's Shandong Peninsula.[2] Its next step, taken at the beginning of 1915, was to present the Chinese government with a list of twenty-one demands. Japan's first priorities were Manchuria and Chinese acceptance of its occupation of Shandong. But Tokyo now also pushed for greater influence in China as a whole. Economic concessions in other regions were sought. Beijing was asked to agree that it would not allow other powers to obtain naval bases on its coast. In a final set of demands, China was asked to accept Japanese advisors throughout its military and governmental administrations, to make Tokyo its main arms supplier, and to agree to joint Sino-Japanese policing of certain areas of the country.[3]

Unsettled, American officials disagreed as to the best means of preserving the kind of political-economic framework they wanted. From Beijing, Ambassador Paul Reinsch pushed for an active and assertive response to Japan's challenge, while policy makers back in Washington worried about antagonizing Tokyo and thereby perhaps precipitating even bolder moves. Without the military power necessary to confront Japan, they were more inclined to temporize. House, for example, urged "great caution" on the president. The United States, he admonished, was "not at present in a position to war with Japan over the 'open door' in China."[4]

The approach ultimately taken conformed closely to ideas set out by Lansing. He was fairly confident that the United States would gain much more influence in East Asia after the war. America's leverage would come especially from its financial and economic power, which would then be enormous. In the meantime, the United States should try to prevent Japan from becoming entrenched throughout China, but avoid a confrontation. Such a holding action he felt could be advanced by voicing acceptance of a special position for Japan in Manchuria and Shandong. This the United States did.[5]

Japan might also be contained with the help of other powers. In 1913, Wilson had broken with other interested Western nations in recognizing the new Chinese republic and in pulling out of the international consortium (afterward, the administration had based its policy on the cultivation of a special relationship with the strongman Yuan Shikai). In the spring of 1915, however, Washington appealed to London, Paris, and Saint Petersburg to intercede with their Japanese ally. Not surprisingly (given there was a war on), this had but limited results, but it presaged further planning the Wilson administration would soon engage in. That looked toward American participation in a reconstituted international consortium after the war and the rebuilding of what former Secretary of State Knox termed a league of nations for China.

Principally because it had upset Great Britain, the Ōkuma government eventually did set aside its final set of demands. But it then insisted, successfully, on the rest. Washington's reaction at this time (May 11, 1915) was to announce that it could not "recognize any agreement or undertaking" impairing its treaty rights, the "territorial integrity" of China, or "the international policy relative to China commonly known as the open door policy."[6]

Japan did not however cease trying to expand its influence throughout China. It pursued closer ties with political factions there, pressured Beijing for economic concessions, and discouraged the Chinese government from offering contracts to others. In response, and at the strong urging of Reinsch, the Wilson administration exhorted American bankers and businessmen to step up their activity in the country. A surge of interest did materialize, especially on the part of the American International Corporation, a huge new investment trust that had been put together by Frank Vanderlip of the National City Bank. But this enthusiasm soon flagged, not only in the face of Japan's opposition, but also because of complications with Russia and France. They objected that some proposed American projects threatened their interests. Further discouragement ensued after Yuan, in 1916, moved to reestablish the old political structures of China with himself as emperor. This precipitated a rebellion against his rule and plunged the entire country into confusion (lasting even beyond Yuan's death by illness in midyear).[7]

A turning point of sorts came in late 1916 when Terauchi Masatake became prime minister. His advent reflected misgivings on the part of many Japanese political figures about the course of his predecessor, Ōkuma, especially about the tensions that had developed with the United States. Looking to the future, there was concern about Japan's dependence on American trade. Tokyo was also impressed with the enormous expansion of American economic power since the beginning of the war (no doubt as well with the recent passage by Congress of legislation providing for a dramatic buildup of the U.S. fleet). There seemed strong reasons to improve relations between the two states. Indeed, it was hoped that Japan might thereby, after the war, be able to benefit from access to American capital.[8]

By 1917, a path was thus finally opening toward the kind of modus vivendi for which Lansing had been angling. In exchange for assurances about Manchuria and Shandong, and acceptance of a greater strategic role for Japan in the region, Tokyo was willing to reaffirm support for the open door. Eager to ease tensions between the two powers as it prepared for war in Europe, the Wilson administration indicated its readiness, in May, to receive the Japanese diplomat, Ishii Kikujirō. Talks undertaken with him resulted, later in the year, in the so-called Lansing-Ishii agreement. Washington acknowledged that Japan had "special interests" in East Asia. Simultaneously, both powers pledged support for the open door and for China's independence and territorial integrity. Each government could read the statement as it wished, but from the standpoint of the Wilson administration what had been achieved was protection for the open door and the possibility even of challenging Tokyo's policy in Manchuria, under more favorable conditions, at a later date.[9]

*   *   *

Historian Donald Yerxa, among others, correctly observes that the Wilson administration's approach toward the Caribbean constituted not a new departure, but more a "culmination" of the policies pursued by its predecessors.[10] As already noted, Wilson came to the presidency in 1913 announcing his impatience with any further revolutions there. He believed it imperative that the countries of the region have governments that were close to Washington and that behaved as it wanted. What the outbreak of the Great War seems principally to have done is intensify this quest for stability and control.

The region had come to be seen as having unparalleled importance for the U.S. role in the coming twentieth-century world, for both economic and strategic reasons. Above all, it surrounded the approaches to the canal. Wilson saw the waterway as of world historical importance. He spoke in such terms repeatedly during the campaign of 1912 and in the months leading up to the Panama Canal's completion and opening in August 1914, just as the first maneuvers of the war in Europe were unfolding. To him, the closest parallel was to be found in developments following the Ottoman conquest of Constantinople more than four centuries earlier. That event, in the former historian-political scientist's view, had blocked East-West trade through the Mediterranean, forcing European merchant fleets out onto the Atlantic Ocean. "[A]t that moment," he maintained, "England, which had been at the back of the nations trading with the East, suddenly swung around and found herself occupying a place at the front of the nations. . . . Something not so great as that, but nevertheless as revolutionary in our trade is going to happen as soon as the canal is opened."[11] In addition to its commercial importance, the canal was seen to have immense military value, this by virtue of the fact that it would allow American naval vessels to much more easily be shifted between the Atlantic and Pacific oceans. It would be of great utility should any of Washington's overseas objectives lead it into confrontations with major sea-power rivals. And, like Suez for the British, the Panama Canal would allow the United States to contend more easily for influence and for the political and economic arrangements it wanted in areas far from home.

So that the canal could serve these purposes, it had become accepted that the United States should exercise—to draw on the title of historian David Healy's classic study of the relationship—hegemony throughout the surrounding region (if America became involved in a great-power conflict, such hegemony would also eliminate the possibility of the United States being vulnerable to an assault from that southerly direction).[12] To secure that, Washington had sought sites for bases in the Caribbean, simultaneously warning rivals against pursuit of the same. And it had sought to influence the political conduct and composition of the governments of the region's small states.

The United States had pursued financial oversight of those governments. And successive administrations had endeavored to build up

America's economic presence (creating in turn more stakes to protect). The navy patrolled this Caribbean "maritime empire"—spread out across roughly a million square miles—and set troops down on the ground on numerous occasions (at least seven times in the period between the Spanish-American War and the outbreak of World War I).[13] Cuba had been occupied twice, and American forces had been left behind in Managua after an intervention in Nicaragua in late 1912.

A pro-American regime had first been helped to come to power in Nicaragua by the Taft administration, and it was subsequently kept in power, in the face of local opposition, by a landing of twenty-three hundred marines. President Adolfo Díaz subsequently ran unopposed to succeed himself in office, and his victory, appropriately enough, was then celebrated with a reception on board the U.S.S. *California*.[14]

When it came to office, the Wilson administration kept a contingent of marines in the capital, Managua (ostensibly as a legation guard), precisely because this was a weak government, without widespread popular support. The new American president's commitment to constitutional process in the Caribbean was a reflection of his desire to put an end to disorder there. It did not stem from a commitment to democracy, which a deeply racist Wilson in fact doubted the majority of the people in the region had the capacity for. Nor, self-evidently, did the stationing of American leathernecks in Managua reflect a commitment to the principle of self-determination.

At least in this part of the world, little separated the views of the president and Bryan. The Great Commoner openly referred to the peoples of Latin America as "our political children."[15] Upon becoming secretary of state, his immediate goal with regard to Nicaragua was to try to strengthen Díaz. His government had mounting financial difficulties, and the worry was that if these were not addressed unrest would develop again. Picking up on a project his predecessor Knox had been working on, Bryan promoted a treaty whereby the United States would purchase the option on a potential canal route across Nicaragua and also obtain naval base rights on both that country's Pacific and Caribbean coasts. The proposed three-million-dollar deal would tie up strategic loose ends for the United States while simultaneously improving Díaz's financial standing.

Senate Democrats forced the administration to remove another provision that essentially would have given Washington the legal right to intervene at will in Nicaraguan affairs. But even then the treaty was ratified only in 1916, after the General Board of the Navy claimed that the base rights might be of importance if the United States wound up in a war with Germany.

In February 1914, Bryan wrote the president that Nicaragua under Díaz had "gone farther than any other Central American state in asking us to take part in her affairs."[16] But this did not prevent conflict between Washington and Díaz once it came time, in 1916, for Nicaragua to hold elections to choose Díaz's successor. Instead of his choice, the State Department was determined to see installed the strongman Emiliano Chamorro, a more prominent figure in the Nicaraguan president's Conservative Party. Chamorro had become a Washington favorite since becoming Managua's minister to the United States in 1912. Díaz tried to resist, but the issue was laid to rest when Admiral William B. Caperton, at the head of three cruisers and a regiment of marines, showed up to make it clear that that was futile. The majority party (and more nationalistic) Liberals (who had been ousted in 1910) were informed that their candidate was unacceptable. As a result, Chamorro won unopposed that October.

Further triumphs for democracy and self-determination were registered elsewhere. By early 1914, the administration was moving to set up a financial receivership in Haiti, similar to what its predecessors had created earlier in the Dominican Republic.[17] This was seen as a way of ending political instability that that country had been going through since 1910 and of making sure that its long-term political and financial ties were in the direction of the United States. As different figures gained control of the presidency, each in turn was offered protection in office in exchange for agreement to such a protectorate.

By 1915, that had become a condition of U.S. recognition. An irritated Wilson finally decided to "take charge" of "the dusky little republic."[18] The marines were ordered to occupy it (they would remain for nineteen years), press censorship was imposed, the customs houses were taken over, and a compliant Haitian politician was installed in the presidency. He subsequently signed a treaty providing for American oversight of the country's finances.

The Wilson administration's simultaneous efforts to expand U.S. financial control over the Dominican Republic actually had the effect of destabilizing the presidency of Juan Isidro Jiménez. They generated a popular revolt in early 1916. American forces were landed to keep him in power. But, to Washington's amazement, Jiménez finally decided to step down rather than collaborate further. Nor could any other politician be found to play the desired role (we "positively have not a friend in the land," commented Admiral Caperton upon his arrival), with the consequence that the country was now put under direct American military rule.[19]

Taking over from Bryan, Lansing, at Wilson's direction, initiated talks that would lead, in 1917, to American annexation of the Danish West Indies (today known as the U.S. Virgin Islands). Strong pressure was brought to bear to get Copenhagen to sell Saint Thomas, Saint John, and Saint Croix (Lansing refused to rule out the possibility that Washington might otherwise just seize them). The thinking was that if Germany did become a stronger European power as a result of the current conflict, it might eventually come to control these possessions of its northern neighbor. The administration was determined to foreclose any avenue by which Berlin might ever challenge America's Caribbean position.[20]

To secure order, and thus control, in the region, Wilson came to office believing that the United States had to adopt the position that it would never recognize any government there brought to power by means of a revolution. The president was persuaded by the advice of Professor Jacob H. Hollander, of Johns Hopkins, who argued that to do otherwise would be to "reward political violence and upheaval."[21]

This policy led directly to a confrontation between the administration and a new government that came to power in Costa Rica in early 1917. Federico Tinoco, who had been serving as the minister of war, became president as the result of a revolt he led against Alfredo González Flores. Wilson refused to grant Tinoco recognition. His intent was to isolate the new government and, since U.S. recognition was of critical importance to the international standing and financial and political survival of the small states of the Caribbean, to make it impossible for it to carry on.

Tinoco sought to demonstrate that he had majority support. To win Washington's favor, his government would also decide, later in the year, to follow America's lead and declare war against Germany. But the issue was never one of popular will or of Costa Rica's diplomatic orientation. It was rather, so far as Wilson was concerned, that Tinoco had to be made an example of for defying his prohibition. Surprisingly, the government stayed in power for two years before finally collapsing in 1919.[22]

In Cuba, meanwhile, the sitting president, Mario G. Menocal, who was a favorite in Washington, ensured his reelection in 1916 by what was widely, and correctly, identified as fraud. When a revolt then sprang up against him, American marines and bluejackets were deployed so as to assist his government in putting it down. Ten thousand rifles and two million cartridges were sold to Menocal. Again, the consistent theme was order and control.[23]

Just the previous month, in his "peace without victory" speech, Wilson had proclaimed to the world that a settlement of the Great War would have to be founded on "the equality of nations" and the principle that "governments derive all their just powers from the consent of the governed."[24] However the president chose to see it, the contrast with his administration's behavior in the Caribbean could not be more plain.

*   *   *

After the outbreak of war in Europe, the Wilson administration redoubled its efforts to improve U.S. ties with the states of South America. One objective was to preempt the possibility of Germany successfully contending for influence there should it win the war. More broadly, administration figures wanted to solidify and secure Washington's leadership of the hemisphere (as well as to align it behind the United States in the wider world). They hoped especially that the Great War would lead to a historic reorientation toward the United States of South America's finance and trade. In pursuit of such ends, American leaders tried to rally the governments of the southern continent behind an expanded notion of Pan-Americanism. They also sought, ultimately with much greater effect, to capitalize on the opportunities created by the war's disruption of South America's traditional economic ties with Europe.

Once it became clear that the war would last longer than a few months, House urged Wilson to rearrange his priorities. The president should give more precedence to foreign than domestic affairs. For starters, he should pay "greater attention to the welding together of the two Western Continents." Prior U.S. policy in this regard had been counterproductive. "In wielding the 'big stick' and dominating the two Continents," the president's adviser argued, the United States had "lost the friendship and commerce" of Latin America and "the European countries had profited by it." That could now be reversed.

He suggested that the United States offer to sign a pact with the Latin American countries. It would feature a guarantee by all of the "Republics of the two Continents" of each other's territorial integrity. Such a guarantee, House thought, would relieve the concerns those countries had about Washington's intentions. The way might then be opened for them to cooperate with the United States in meeting both extrahemispheric and hemispheric challenges to the kind of order in the Americas Washington desired. House also told the president that the plan he had in mind for Latin America might serve as a model for the stabilization of Europe once the war had ended.[25]

With Wilson's strong encouragement House subsequently described "this proposed League" to Bryan and then laid his plan before the ambassadors of the "ABC" countries, Argentina, Brazil, and Chile.[26] If the biggest states of South America went along, it was thought, the others were sure to follow. Hopeful that the United States might indeed be prepared to redefine the Monroe Doctrine and forge a more equal relationship, Argentina and Brazil initially responded quite favorably.

Chile was more reluctant. This was because the suggested pact provided for the expeditious settlement by arbitration of unresolved disputes over territory. Santiago worried that Chile's continued hold over provinces it had taken in the 1880s from Peru (following the War of the Pacific) might be called into question.

In addition to providing for a collective guarantee of (finally established and settled) international boundaries, the plan also called upon signatory countries to (1) agree not to have resort to force between and among themselves before a dispute had been referred to an outside commission, and (2) to place under government regulation the production and sale of arms. These provisions were also seen as advancing the goal of Latin American stabilization.

Despite Chile's hesitation, administration officials were convinced that the pact would ultimately be accepted. Wilson expressed enthusiasm about the direction of hemispheric affairs when he presented his annual message at the end of 1915. The countries of the Americas, he avowed, were becoming "cooperating friends." There was a "growing sense of community of interest" that was likely to give them "a new significance as factors in international affairs." Indeed, he optimistically suggested that they would form "a unit in world affairs."[27]

When he finally made the plan public the following January, the president also voiced the hope that it would facilitate the maintenance of conditions the United States wanted to see prevail *within* the Latin American countries. He told delegates to the Pan American Scientific Conference that it was "just as much to our interest to assist each other to the orderly processes within our own borders as it is to orderly processes in our controversies with one another."[28]

Not only did Chile continue to have misgivings. In early 1916, Brazil also began to balk at the proposal. Wilson's reaction is instructive. He suggested to Lansing that the ABC countries' "cooperating friend," the United States, was "in a position to make their isolation very pronounced and unenviable" if such resistance continued.[29]

The project finally collapsed altogether in midyear as a consequence of Washington's Mexican policy. The dispatch by the president of an American army into northern Mexico in March (see below) brought the United States and the government of Carranza, to the threshold of war. Numerous South American states suggested mediation and proffered their good offices, but—fearful that the outcome would not be in line with his objectives—Wilson refused. In the eyes of Latin America, that response raised serious questions about Washington's promises of a new era of equality and collaboration. As a result, all further consideration of the president's pact came to an end, and Wilson himself became much less popular in Latin America.[30]

Regardless of the failure of the pact, the outbreak of the Great War did lead to a dramatic reorientation of South American finance and trade (and that eventually would carry with it important political implications). As historian Mark Gilderhus points out, by mid-1917 U.S. trade with Latin America had increased, over mid-1914, by more than 100 percent.[31]

After an initial disruption, exports across the Atlantic—especially to the Allies—picked up in 1915. But South America had also long been dependent on Europe for finance, shipping, and a large proportion of its manufactured products. These were lost for the duration of the conflict. Even those who hoped that the war might help Latin America to pursue diversified economic development recognized that they would have to look to the United States, at least temporarily, as Europe's replacement.[32]

Officials in the Wilson administration were among the first North Americans to become aware of the opportunities presented. The Departments of State and Commerce created a new Inter-Departmental Committee on Pan-American Trade only three days after Britain entered the war. The next month, Bryan and Redfield presided over a Latin American Trade Conference. Participants included experts from the two departments and representatives of important American export organizations. Credit and exchange facilities were among the key deficiencies they mentioned that impeded a dramatic expansion of trade. Redfield and Treasury Secretary William Gibbs McAdoo subsequently turned their attention to those needs.

McAdoo invited Latin American finance ministers to Washington for a Pan-American Financial Conference in May 1915. The meeting created an International High Commission to address hemispheric trade problems. The secretary of the treasury then personally led a U.S. delegation to the commission's first meeting, held in Buenos Aires in 1916.

U.S. exports to South America grew rapidly during 1915 and after. And this expansion was paralleled by a similarly dramatic growth of American branch banking. Simultaneous efforts were made to expand north-south shipping. The eagerness with which a broad array of American government and business figures pursued the opening that the Great War provided suggests that Wilson was not alone in his appraisal of the situation. In his annual message for 1915, the president referred to this as "an opportunity which may never return again if we miss it now."[33]

*   *   *

The Wilson administration's policy toward Mexico showcased a number of the same themes and contradictions evident in its actions elsewhere in this period. Not only was international cooperation treated as an approach, to be used or not depending on whether it advanced Washington's objectives. By persistently trying to shape from the outside Mexico's politics, the president again violated his proclaimed commitments to democracy, self-determination, and the equality of nations. An administration avowedly committed to peace once more resorted to military pressure as a way of trying to achieve its goals. Likewise, when an explanation seemed required, such actions were justified by the president on the grounds that the United States was a disinterested party merely seeking to help another country "save herself and serve her people."[34]

Like its predecessors, the Wilson administration was committed to a policy of U.S. "paramountcy" and strategic control in North America. Ideally, it wanted to see Mexico align itself with Washington in international affairs. It also wished a regime in Mexico City that would respect its "international obligations."

Its policy in 1913–14 had simultaneously been influenced by the conviction that the acceptance of a change of government via revolution in Mexico would send the wrong signal to the adjoining nations of Central America and the Caribbean. Wilson's test of wills with Huerta had begun with the latter's refusal to accept that point of view.

As Europe edged toward war, during the summer of 1914, Huerta was chased from power. But Washington continued to withhold recognition from the interim government subsequently established in Mexico City. This was not merely because the administration wanted first to be able to say that Mexico had turned away from revolutionary methods of succession. Wilson was also looking for a way of pushing aside Carranza, the "First Chief" who had led the Constitutionalist forces in opposition to Huerta. Wanting an orderly Mexico, that looked to Washington for guidance, Wilson bridled at Carranza's nationalism. He also harbored doubts that Carranza was strong enough to bring an end to instability in that country.

By fall, events appeared to be moving in the direction desired by the American president. Fissures had been developing for months in the anti-Huerta coalition and it finally broke in half, into pro-Carranza and "Conventionist" pieces, after a Constitutionalist convention held at Aguascalientes in October. As the two sides moved toward a test of arms, Washington officials came to believe, and hope, that Carranza would soon be removed by Francisco ("Pancho") Villa. Quite mistakenly, they viewed Villa, the most prominent of the Conventionists and the most charismatic and effective of the military leaders who had fought against Huerta, as someone who would not only establish the stability they wanted in Mexico, but also cooperate with the United States. While they held quite different hopes for that country's future, Carranza and Villa were in fact both ardent nationalists.

Contrary to expectations, Villa's forces were torn to pieces during the first two major battles of this conflict, early in 1915. Alvaro Obregón, Carranza's leading general, successfully employed machine guns and tactics borrowed from the fighting then raging in Europe. U.S. officials explored alternatives. They looked for other generals with whom they might work. They tried to muster the ABC countries behind their objectives. Simultaneously, they continued to give support to Villa, even if only as a way of putting pressure on Carranza and delaying his victory. Still holding out hope that Washington could shape his course, the administration finally decided it had no choice but to deal with the First Chief. In the fall, it recognized him as the de facto head of the Mexican government.

Villa's aid was cut off. Not only did he feel betrayed, he also suspected that Carranza had acceded to demands that would compromise Mexico's sovereignty. His forces dwindling, Villa finally responded, on March 9, 1916, with a raid on the New Mexican town of Columbus. He expected Washington to react by dispatching troops into northern Mexico. The First Chief would then either find himself embroiled again with the United States or, if he acceded to the troops, be revealed as someone who would not stand up for the Mexican nation.

Mexican officials told Washington that they would accept "hot pursuits" across the border, but not large, open-ended missions. A U.S. expedition of five thousand troops nevertheless crossed into that country fully six days after the raid took place. General John J. Pershing, the American commander, was unable to find Villa amid Mexico's vast northern expanses. But his troops were not withdrawn, and as the weeks passed, friction with the local population developed and relations with Carranza grew increasingly tense.

On June 20, a clash occurred between Mexican and American forces. The president considered asking Congress for the authority to occupy northern Mexico. But he held back when Carranza accepted a suggestion by Lansing that a joint commission address relations between the two states.

Wilson saw this as yet another chance to shape the whole direction of Mexico's new regime. American delegates asked that Mexico pledge to carry out its obligations to foreigners (as Washington defined them) and grant the United States formal and sweeping rights to military intervention. But Carranza resisted, insisting that the focus of the talks be on future procedures for border security and the withdrawal of U.S. troops. Wilson was forced to stand down only after tensions began to mount between Germany and the United States at the beginning of 1917. As war with Germany loomed on the horizon, the president saw no alternative but to get Pershing's forces out of Mexico.[35]

PART III

Military Intervention (1917–18)

Take your actions all together from the Conscription Act to the Embargo—what a record that is! Of course it has saved the Allied cause, which would otherwise have been lost—in great measure if not wholly. And the British know that and freely say so. This in itself is a conquest over British "arrogance" which makes us henceforth the masters of the English-speaking world.

    —Ambassador Walter Hines Page to Woodrow Wilson, September 3, 1917

[I]t is not an army we must shape and train for war it is a nation.

    —Woodrow Wilson, 1917

[T]here ought not to be a man in the United States who isn't now willing to take orders and not ask any questions.

    —Woodrow Wilson, December 8, 1917

[T]he world is at his feet, eating out of his hand! No Caesar ever had such a triumph!

    —Secretary of the Interior Franklin Lane (speaking of President Wilson),
       following a cabinet meeting on November 5, 1918

CHAPTER 5

"The Whole Force of the Nation"

In March 1917, Lansing urged President Wilson not only to become militarily involved in the conflict raging in Europe, but also to recast the war as one of "democracy" versus "autocracy." The suggestion reflected the secretary of state's long-held view that future stability required a change in the very structure of Berlin's government, particularly the powers reserved to the kaiser in the realm of foreign affairs. Convinced that Germany bore primary responsibility for the conflagration, Lansing believed the ability to commit that country to war had to be taken out of the hands of a few individuals. Otherwise, other nations would have to stand in a constant state of military readiness to defend their interests.

Lansing was hardly a champion of the common man. What he envisioned was a liberalization of the German system principally in such ways as would give greater power to that country's upper-middle and professional classes. Decision making would be less centralized, and it would be procedurally more complicated for Germany to go to war again. He also assumed that such elements, by contrast with the kaiser's retinue, would be less disposed to take the risks that military conflict with other great powers entailed.

To Lansing (and other members of the administration who would come to share his view), such a crusade—in tandem with the collapse of tsarist power under way at this time in Russia—would complete the process whereby "democracy" had been replacing "autocracy" in Europe and North America since the eighteenth century. Lansing argued that framing the war in such terms would embolden dissent in Germany, galvanize public support for the war in those countries ranged against the Central Powers (all of whom would be deemed to "represent the principle of Democracy"), and enhance "our future influence in world affairs."[1]

As late as March 20, when he met with his cabinet members to solicit their views, Wilson protested "that he did not see how he could speak of a war for Democracy or of Russia's revolution in addressing Congress."[2] But the president was quickly converted. It helped that he too had now concluded—on the basis of his reading both of the diplomacy of the previous winter and of the Zimmermann telegram—that the existing government in Berlin could not be trusted and had to be altered. But what probably most appealed to Wilson at this time was the potential Lansing's formulation offered for mobilizing Americans behind the war. The president was worried that much of the U.S. public continued to lack enthusiasm for military involvement and would not rally to the idea that Germany's "submarine blockade" merited that response.[3] The idea of a final, titanic struggle between "democracy" and "autocracy," meanwhile, might both heighten the public's sense that America was itself in jeopardy and counter the criticisms he was likely to face.

Since the 1890s, the most damaging critiques of U.S. military interventions had been those that had alleged that they were in the interest not of most citizens or of the people of the involved countries but rather of a few selfish (or egoistic) Americans. Critics had warned that such activity risked entangling the United States in expensive overseas troubles which could weaken and undermine the republic. Wilson (principally in connection with Latin America) had previously sought to counter or anticipate such criticism by arguing that, whatever his predecessors' motives, his administration was driven by a sense of responsibility and a wish to be of service to the world. In 1917, the "democracy" versus "autocracy" theme offered the president a way of trying to define entrance into the European maelstrom in similar terms.

A war for "democracy" might also advance Wilson's longer-term goals more effectively. The president had lately come to view belligerency as his ticket to participation in the peace conference (so that he would not have to observe the proceedings through a "crack in the door"). The country therefore needed to be prepared for a mission that went beyond the question of how Germany from this time forward would, or would not, use its U-boats.[4]

On April 2, Wilson went before a joint session of Congress to request a declaration of war. In his address, he rehearsed his differences with Germany over the submarine and announced that he had now concluded that "armed neutrality" would be "ineffectual." Wilson wanted Congress to "accept the status of belligerent," which he maintained had been "thrust upon" the United States. After surveying the measures of mobilization and cooperation with the Allies that this course would entail, he moved on to define the conflict more broadly in terms of the "democracy" versus "autocracy" theme. The president said he wanted to make "clear . . . what our motives and our objects are." These were to "vindicate the principles of peace and justice in the life of the world as against selfish and autocratic power and to set up amongst the really free and self-governed peoples of the world such a concert of purpose and of action as will henceforth ensure the observance of those principles." "We are now about to accept," he boldly proclaimed, "gauge of battle with this natural foe to liberty and shall, if necessary, spend the whole force of the nation . . . [to fight] for the ultimate peace of the world and for the liberation of its peoples, the German peoples included. . . . The world must be made safe for democracy."[5] Despite Wilson's eloquence, and the air of crisis created by the sinking of American vessels, the president's stance did not go unchallenged. Senator Stone, the Foreign Relations Committee chair, saw the United States embarking on a great "national blunder." And two insurgent Republican senators took the floor to dissent at length. On April 4, George Norris of Nebraska and La Follette of Wisconsin challenged the contention that the administration had pursued a course that was neutral. "The only reason why we have not suffered the sacrifice of just as many ships and just as many lives from the violation of our rights by the war zone and the submarine mines of Great Britain as we have through the unlawful acts of Germany in making her war zone in violation of our neutral rights," the latter alleged, "is simply because we have submitted to Great Britain's dictation." La Follette was skeptical of Wilson's claim that this was a war "for democracy, for the right of those who submit to authority to have a voice in their own government." "The President has not suggested," he said, "that we make our support of Great Britain conditional to her granting home rule to Ireland, or Egypt, or India [three of London's numerous overseas holdings]. We rejoice in the establishment of a democracy in Russia, but it will hardly be contended that if Russia was still an autocratic government, we would not be asked to enter this alliance with her all the same." If Wilson really wished to demonstrate his commitment to democracy he could put the war resolution before the American people in the form of a referendum, one the Wisconsin senator believed the president would lose.[6]

In the end, six senators—three midwestern Republican insurgents and three Democrats from the West and South—refused to endorse the war, as did fifty members of the House. (Many others in both houses, according to historian Justus Doenecke, went along while nursing strong reservations.)[7]

*   *   *

The administration now proceeded to mobilize America so as, it hoped, to decide the European struggle. Little did policy makers realize how precarious the Allied position was becoming (though it became a distinction with little practical difference, the president insisted that the United States had become the Allies' "associate," that it had still not joined their—or any— alliance). This became evident only after the declaration.

But from the outset it was decided to put on a major display of American might, this so as to establish for the United States an international reputation for power and effectiveness and, more particularly, to enhance Washington's leverage on the shaping of the peace. House told Wilson on March 27 that it was important for him to meet the crisis "in a creditable way so that his influence would not be lessened when he came to do the great work which would necessarily follow the war."[8] At least so far as Wilson, House, and Lansing were concerned, this consideration underlay all of their war-making activities.

As had already become evident in Europe, a confrontation with other strong industrial nations required not just the assembling and dispatch of military forces. In the twentieth century, armed might depended upon complex systems of continuous economic support, upon the constant funneling of food, clothing, and materiel to the front. And those systems, in turn, had to be grounded on the enthusiastic sacrifice and commitment of a state's civilian population. The citizenry had to work hard, to commit to the cause, and to bear sacrifices. The people, as such, were the critical bedrock of strength for the rival major powers. Urged by House to look to the European precedents, it did not take long for Wilson to understand these principles. As he put it, "[i]t is not an army we must shape and train for war it is a nation."[9]

*   *   *

Critical to that process was the molding of public opinion. This was perhaps especially true for a nation with strong antistatist and antimilitarist traditions.[10] As the administration saw it, Americans' lack of fervor had to be converted into its opposite. Public enthusiasm had to be created, then harnessed and deployed.[11] And, as part of that effort, competing voices of continued skepticism had to be squelched. Slow to take effect, this campaign would ultimately contribute to a condition of frenzied hysteria on the part of many Americans. Simultaneously, it would contribute to an abridgement of what others considered bedrock American rights.

The key vehicle for the creation of such enthusiasm was to be the Committee on Public Information, created by executive order just a week after war was declared. An energetic young Wilson supporter, George Creel, was chosen to lead the agency. Fittingly, he was an accomplished practitioner, as one historian has put it, of that era's "advocacy journalism."[12] Creel absolutely idolized the president and believed without reservation in his message. He would go on, some have argued, to occupy a position of closeness to Wilson unrivalled by any but House (both were viewed as unconditionally devoted and unthreatening; the president rarely felt secure around those he felt might challenge him either politically or intellectually).[13] Wilson took great interest in the activities of the CPI, and he made sure that Creel carried considerable influence within his administration.

After the war, Creel would describe his CPI as "a vast enterprise in salesmanship, the world's greatest adventure in advertising."[14] That vastness was captured in the broad range of activities it pursued. By way of the many specialized divisions that were created within it, the CPI issued press releases, mounted ad and poster campaigns, produced movies (like *The Kaiser, the Beast of Berlin*), and organized speaking tours. It sponsored parades, pageants, mock battles, and patriotic sing-alongs, prepared foreign language materials, distributed curricula for schools, and circulated enemy atrocity stories. Tens of thousands of "four-minute men" were organized to deliver brief, essentially prepackaged, talks to crowds at theaters, schools, and churches.

Tapping into the evolutionary-racialist outlooks that were a major currency of that time, CPI materials employed what were intended to be terms and imagery that were lurid. The "democracy" versus "autocracy" theme was dialed up a notch. Germany—before the war celebrated by many educated Americans as a model of advanced social experimentation—was depicted as barbaric and bestial, as a threat not only to American freedom, but to civilization, indeed to basic morality and decency. Its challenge could not go unanswered. America had to save the world by undertaking what was often characterized as a divine mission.

That latter idea was promoted by none other than the president himself. "[W]e are to be an instrument in the hands of God," Wilson maintained, "to see that liberty is made secure for mankind." It was a holy crusade, indeed one that intentionally referenced the Christian expeditions to the Levant of the Middle Ages. As the opening subtitle of the CPI film *Pershing's Crusaders* put it, "The young men of America are going out to rescue Civilization. They are going to fight . . . to save Democracy from death. They are marching on to give America's freedom to the oppressed multitudes of the earth. The mighty exodus of America's manhood to the plains of Europe may well be called 'The Eighth Crusade.'"[15]

Many of the CPI activities focused on the presence in America of peoples of recent immigrant background. "Old stocks," like most of those in the agency, had long been anxious to see new immigrants become more "Americanized" (by which was meant that they should adopt the norms and follow the leadership of "real Americans" like themselves). That anxiety was intensified by the war, just as the war was also seen as a fresh opportunity to promote such an essentially submissive definition of patriotism. What Creel hoped to do, as he put it, was to weld all Americans into "one white-hot mass" behind his president.[16]

*   *   *

Historian David Kennedy has persuasively argued that the "overarching purpose of the CPI . . . was to create . . . a popular mood . . . that would minimize any necessity for the formal statutory enforcement of such policies as conscription, food conservation, industrial coordination, or war financing."[17]

It might be added that Creel also hoped to minimize the need for the suppression of dissent.[18] But this does not mean that the administration did not move aggressively to intimidate dissident voices, and to suppress them if, despite its best efforts, they continued to be heard.[19] Continued debate and criticism, it was implied, signified disloyalty to the country and would be so treated. Such—along with its efforts to manipulate opinion via fear and emotion—were the ironies of the administration's claim to be leading a crusade on behalf of "democracy." "I think that there ought not to be a man in the United States who isn't now willing to take orders and not ask any questions," said the president.[20]

The principal legal grounds for such a campaign were acquired by way of the Espionage Act, drawn up in the attorney general's office and enacted by Congress at the beginning of June 1917 (eleven months later, this was expanded by way of an amendment that produced what commonly came to be referred to as the Sedition Act).[21] Though initially framed as a law to deal with spying and foreign subversion, the Espionage Act included provisions that both the postmaster general, Albert S. Burleson, and Attorney General Thomas W. Gregory immediately began to employ to crack down on dissent. Under its Title XII, the postmaster general was given the power to deny use of the mails to any materials advocating "treason, insurrection, or forcible resistance to any law of the United States." Burleson interpreted this as giving him the authority to ban any publications that contained articles critical of the war, questioning the administration's motives or the way the war was being financed, or critical of any of the Allies. Still more broadly, he appears also to have set out to cripple the foreign-language press and the left-wing press, including especially periodicals associated with that wing of the Socialist Party that refused to endorse belligerency.[22]

More than two thousand people were meanwhile prosecuted by the justice department for speeches, letters to a newspaper, or simple offhand comments that were critical or questioning. Federal authorities repeatedly construed such acts as violations of Section 3, Title I of the Espionage Act that prohibited interference with the recruitment or performance of the U.S. armed forces. A favorable judiciary, combined with an increasingly inflamed public mood, created the conditions under which about half of these cases led to convictions, the most famous of which was of Debs, the popular labor leader and frequent Socialist presidential candidate. For a speech in mid-1918 that was critical both of the war and, more particularly, of the repressive atmosphere that had by then engulfed the country, Debs was sentenced to ten years in prison.[23]

The Department of Justice also sanctioned the creation of an organization called the American Protective League. It eventually came to include a quarter of a million volunteers. Claiming to be federal officers, and brandishing badges that said "American Protective League—Secret Service," its members illegally took people into custody, for example citizens whose draft status they questioned, and took it upon themselves to investigate tens of thousands of Americans whose loyalty they held in doubt. APL reconnaissance characteristically included acts of burglary, phone-tapping, the opening of private mail, and the interception of telegrams.[24]

Still other organizations grew up, stimulated by these efforts. With the blessing of state and local governments, tens of thousands of "councils of defense" were set up around the United States. Originally the idea was for them to help with the economic mobilization of the country. As that job came instead to be taken over by national agencies focused on different sectors of the economy, these local bodies of volunteers increasingly turned to other tasks, among which were promoting public enthusiasm for the war and suppressing dissent. People were investigated by them for "disloyalty," hauled before "slacker courts," encouraged to keep an eye on their neighbors, and warned that they were "under surveillance." Other, similar organizations had titles like the Minute Men, the Knights of Liberty, the Sedition Slammers, and so on.

Pacifists, pacifist religious sects (like the Mennonites), radicals, and, above all, Americans of German ancestry were particular targets of such activity. In some cases, the federal government simply lost control of tendencies it had set in motion, but it was frequently also slow to condemn or rein in vigilantism.[25]

*   *   *

Washington hoped and expected to bedazzle the world with American power. The objective was not only to win the war but to ensure a decisive U.S. impact on the peace. Critical to this process was the harnessing of what by the time of the Great War had become the greatest manufacturing economy on earth.

It took the administration until the winter of 1917–18, however, before it began adequately to appreciate what this would entail. In previous wars, procurement had largely been conducted by the various military bureaus, each of which bought from civilian producers what they required. For all practical purposes, and despite the early creation of a businessman-dominated federal Council of National Defense (and associated National Defense Advisory Commission that in theory provided for the scientific coordination of government and industry), this model continued to prevail at the beginning of World War I.

It eventually became clear that the unprecedented scale of the war, and of what the United States was undertaking, required much more innovation. By late 1917, essentially uncoordinated military purchases were running at cross purposes with one another, threatening not only mobilization but also the civilian economy. And gigantic bottlenecks were being created along all of the rail routes in the eastern half of the country. As well, the administration was beginning to face growing criticism and charges of incompetence from some in Congress, especially on the Republican side of the aisle.[26]

As a consequence, the military was forced to yield some of its authority. Overall coordination of procurement was assigned to a War Industries Board. And the railroads were temporarily nationalized. By spring 1918, Wilson had assembled what has been called his "war cabinet."[27] This included relevant department heads, Secretary of the Treasury McAdoo (in charge of the new Railroad Administration as well as of the financing of the war), Secretary of War Newton D. Baker, and Secretary of the Navy Josephus Daniels. It also included a handful of energetic individuals who were given responsibility for organizing key sectors of the economy through temporary agencies.

For example, Herbert Hoover became chief of the Food Administration. A successful prewar executive of a mining engineering firm, Hoover coordinated food relief for war-torn Belgium before U.S. entry. Operating under the authority of the Lever Act of 1917, he was charged with ensuring sufficient food for American forces and their allies. In pursuit of this objective, as one historian has noted, Hoover "rejected rationing or price controls." He relied instead on "high prices and patriotism." "To stimulate production, Hoover forced the American and Allied governments to pay high prices for agricultural goods." To curb demand, he employed propaganda to get American civilians to do without.[28]

The Lever Act also gave the president the power to control the price of fuel (principally coal). Harry Garfield, an old friend of Wilson's, son of a former president, and the president of Williams College, became fuel administrator. Yet another, much more forceful, member of the war cabinet was former Chicago manufacturer Edward N. Hurley, head of the U.S. Shipping Board and the Emergency Fleet Corporation. During the late nineteenth and early twentieth centuries, the expanding U.S. foreign trade had relied heavily on the merchant fleets of other nations. Advocates of government support for the development of an American merchant marine had repeatedly been thwarted. But the outbreak of the Great War generated more widespread concern about dependence on foreign carriers, while it at the same time struck many as an opportunity for the United States to win trade from European rivals. U.S. belligerency, it was believed, would require still more shipping under American control. In late 1916, Wilson was finally able to get Congress to create the Shipping Board and to allot it fifty million dollars. The legislation empowered the government itself, once war was declared, to undertake the creation and operation of a merchant marine. Eventually, under Hurley's direction, the Emergency Fleet Corporation built, purchased, seized (from Germany and Austria), and leased (often through pressure on neutrals) what by late 1918 would be the world's largest such fleet.[29]

The most important of such war cabinet officials was Bernard M. Baruch, who became the leader of the War Industries Board in early 1918. He sought to ensure an ample stream of industrial goods for the war effort while simultaneously minimizing dislocation of the economy and helping to position American business for postwar international competition.

Baruch wanted to forestall the degree of government control over business that was characteristic of some of the European belligerents (what he did instead was to provide new ideas about how government might help businessmen, especially to manage competition). He operated largely on the basis of positive incentives and a search for common ground.

Of a business background himself (he had made a fortune as a speculator on Wall Street), Baruch guided an agency that was staffed heavily with "dollar-a-year men" on leave from major corporations. He and his staff relied, like Hoover, largely on good prices to achieve their goals (Baruch ultimately expressed disappointment in patriotism as a motivator). Where businessmen were not cooperative, as for example was the case with the automobile industry (which did not wish to curtail its production of pleasure cars for the civilian market), the WIB threatened to limit supplies of raw materials.[30]

*   *   *

The administration harbored a great fear that labor stoppages might interfere with efforts to marshal and display power overseas. Though industrial workers in America had since the late nineteenth century sought repeatedly to organize and obtain improved wages and conditions, they had before the Great War achieved but limited results. After 1914, however, their bargaining position changed dramatically. Employers were more eager to ensure a stable and contented work force so as to take advantage of incoming Allied orders. What had been a high volume of immigration from Europe was cut off. And once the United States became itself a formal participant in the conflict, once it began economically to mobilize and to form a large army, the labor market tightened further. Workers were confronted with a historic opportunity to exert leverage on management, and their determination to achieve wage gains intensified as they saw the high profits corporations were beginning to make and they confronted a wartime inflation of prices. Militancy grew.

Anxious to keep production humming, the administration created such bodies as the National War Labor Board and the War Labor Policies Board. Through such agencies, it moved to ensure that vital industries had enough workers, to mediate disputes, and to establish standard nationwide policies. To a considerable degree, the government intervened so as to promote levels of compensation, hours, and conditions that would head off strikes (where unsuccessful, it on several occasions intervened forcibly to put work actions down).

The administration also cultivated the support of conservative labor leader Samuel Gompers, president of the American Federation of Labor. He sought to woo workers away from more radical figures and programs and toward support of the war (at the behest of the government, he even went on a mission to Europe to promote the Allied cause). Gompers beseeched workers in war industries not to strike.

In undertaking such roles, the AFL president believed he was advancing the kind of trade unionism he supported. Among the tangible gains he achieved was government support for union organizing and collective bargaining in war-related industries (crucially though, in exchange for pledges not to strike). But, most of labor's gains would be washed away after the armistice.[31]

*   *   *

The war, of course, had to be paid for. And to win it, Washington also had to make it financially possible for its increasingly exhausted allies to remain in the field. These tasks were the responsibility, chiefly, of McAdoo, the forceful and ambitious treasury secretary (who was also married to the president's daughter).

At the outset of belligerency, he pledged to pay for one-half of the war by way of taxation, suggesting among other things that this would be better for the nation's credit. Taxes grew, and the income tax in particular now became an important source of revenue. But borrowing eventually assumed a role that was much more important (taxes ultimately covering one-fourth to one-third of a total war expenditure of thirty-eight billion dollars). McAdoo concluded that his original goal would be too burdensome for the economy and he worried that it might undermine the government's success in raising money by other means. He came instead to rely heavily on the sale of bonds.

Eager to minimize the government's costs, McAdoo hoped to market these to the country by taking advantage of the kinds of passions being stoked by the CPI. As he put it in his memoirs, he "did not intend to sell the bonds on a commercial basis." Rather, he wanted their purchase "to be the expression of a fundamental patriotism." His objective was to "capitalize the emotion of the people." "Any great war," wrote McAdoo "must necessarily be a popular movement. It is a kind of crusade; and like all crusades, it sweeps along on a powerful stream of romanticism." So as to cultivate and benefit from such "romanticism," the Treasury Department mounted Liberty Loan bond sales campaigns that many even at the time—like future president Warren G. Harding—characterized as "hysterical and unseemly." In addition to rallies headlined by popular film stars, these featured in particular a wide variety of sensational posters. One of the most famous, but representative, by artist Frederick Strothmann, depicted a gargantuan German soldier, with a blood soaked bayonet, looming over the Atlantic horizon. The caption enjoined Americans to "Beat back the Hun with Liberty Bonds."

Far more money had to be raised than initially expected. As one sales campaign followed another, the treasury secretary found that higher interest rates had to be offered. All told, by mid-1919, five—roughly monthlong—drives were mounted, four Liberty Loan campaigns and then one Victory Loan campaign (under McAdoo's successor Carter Glass). McAdoo wanted as many Americans as possible to invest in the war. This was not only because he wanted to raise money, but also to solidify the public's sense of ownership in and commitment to the endeavor. Toward this end, the Treasury also marketed war savings stamps and certificates to lower income Americans less able to purchase bonds.[32]

More than ten billion dollars were loaned to the Allies. Though in the postwar period many American leaders would describe this lending as a favor, McAdoo well understood the degree of self-interest that was involved. He recognized that the dollars the U.S. government sent "through these loans to Europe were, in effect, substitutes for American soldiers."

The treasury secretary imposed strict controls over how the money was to be used as well. All of the proceeds had to be spent in the United States. As for President Wilson, it was his hope that the loans would provide invaluable financial leverage in achieving his aims at the peace conference. When the war was over, he told House in July 1917, he thought Washington would be able to force France and Britain "to our way of thinking, because by that time they will, among other things, be financially in our hands."[33]

＊　＊　＊

The first of the American armed forces involved in the conflict was the navy. For Washington to exert leverage over the war's outcome, it went without saying, the crucial sea lanes across the North Atlantic had to be kept relatively free of German interference. More broadly, victory depended on the Allies not being cut off from the supplies they depended on from other parts of the world.

Up until the spring of 1917, British leaders had discounted the idea that the U-boat blockade constituted a serious threat. But Berlin now had many more submarines to deploy. The Admiralty noted with growing alarm in March and April how much cargo they destroyed.

American officials were apprised of the mounting toll only when a U.S. Navy liaison officer arrived in London during the second week in April. This was Rear Admiral William S. Sims, a longtime advocate of modernization and efficiency who had been serving as president of the Naval War College. Sims was among those who endorsed the use of convoys as a way of dealing with the submarine challenge. Groups of merchant and transport ships would be escorted together to British and French ports by destroyers and other vessels useful against submarines. Such a system began to be used in late May, and eventually it did significantly reduce Allied losses.[34]

U.S. destroyers began to be dispatched to European waters in the spring of 1917, but these were in limited supply. A great debate then erupted when Sims and the British Admiralty proposed that the U.S. Navy alter its existing building program so as to concentrate on destroyers and other antisubmarine craft in preference to capital ships. Responding to Wilson's proposal that America build "incomparably the greatest navy in the world," Congress had provided the funds for a vast expansion of the U.S. Navy, over a three-year period, in late 1916. But reflecting the legacy of Mahan, the funds provided were for large capital ships, dreadnoughts, and battle cruisers.

Initially, officials in Washington were reluctant to change course. Admirals, like Chief of Naval Operations Benson, worried that that would work to the advantage of whichever naval rival, or rivals, emerged triumphant from this conflict. But they relented in June, once convinced that victory might hang in the balance. The next month Secretary Daniels directed that, for the duration, all new building focus on the smaller craft. Over four hundred antisubmarine vessels were commissioned in 1917–18.[35]

Eventually, several hundred American vessels operated in European waters. In addition to pursuing U-boats and performing convoy duty, they helped to lay new, more advanced mines across the North Sea. It also became U.S. policy to reinforce Britain's long-standing blockade on Germany. As part of this, Washington pursued various methods of helping to ratchet up the pressure on Europe's neutrals.[36]

*   *   *

Wilson was anxious from the outset to put on a display of American power so as to enhance his leverage at the conference table. He wanted and expected the U.S. role in the defeat of Germany to be seen as important. But exactly what role the United States would play as a belligerent was in fact not firmly settled when he made his decision for war. Contingency planning and Wilson's earlier musings had not featured the idea of an American army being sent across the Atlantic. Thinking instead had pivoted around the hope that Berlin might give way simply under the weight of the material, financial, and naval power the United States could bring to bear.[37]

This had been the view of the British as well. Despite the new U-boat campaign, leaders in London were quite optimistic early in 1917. They thought that American assistance along such lines, combined with the success they expected from the western Allies' upcoming spring offensive, would soon guarantee them the upper hand over the Central Powers (and their own allies as well). As late as March 20, Lloyd George asserted that the Allies were on the verge of a "victory in which the British Empire will lead. It will easily then be the first Power in the world."[38]

But in the weeks following the U.S. declaration, it became clear to the president that nothing less than a pledge to send ground troops across the ocean would do. The April "Nivelle offensive" on the Western Front cost the armies of the British and French empires (they included a significant number of troops from Canada and French West Africa) many casualties without achieving the looked-for great breakthrough (indeed, it quickly gave rise to mutiny within some French units). Victory might very well require the dispatch of an American expeditionary force. Allied military representatives (including the famous French general Joseph Joffre) who began to show up in Washington beseeched the administration to make such a commitment. And it became apparent that the United States would not have as great a voice at the peace table if it did not agree to also put soldiers on the ground in Europe.[39]

The administration set about the creation of a much larger army. And it decided that most of this expansion should be sought via a draft (by contrast with the war with Spain when expansion had been accomplished simply with volunteers). This was seen as essential to the task of mobilizing efficiently and effectively the whole nation for war. Not only did it promise the numbers needed. Officials were also trying to learn from Britain's mistakes. There, at the beginning of the conflict, important war industries had been disrupted because vital skilled workers had signed up for military service. Conscription would afford Washington more control and oversight so as to assign individuals to the activities where they might best be put to use.

A number of southern and western politicians, especially Bryan Democrats and insurgent Republicans, viewed a draft as highly distasteful. Speaker of the House Champ Clark (D-Mo.) commented that for his constituents there was "precious little difference between a conscript and a convict." In fact, unable to get the assistance of key Democratic leaders, the

White House had to rely on Julius Kahn, a regular Republican, to maneuver the draft legislation through the House.[40]

Acutely concerned about public support, the administration designed its subsequent conscription efforts and recruiting drives with great care. Throughout 1917–18, it was clearly hoped that the two approaches would reinforce each other.

Paralleling the CPI and Liberty Bond campaigns, recruitment materials demonized the enemy while summoning young American men both to pursue glory and do their duty. They should enlist so as to protect their country, their families, and their womenfolk. One of the most famous posters, drawn by H. R. Hopps, depicted Germany in the form of a giant crazed gorilla. The Atlantic Ocean was rendered as a mere pond that he had just crossed. On the far coast, the skyline of Europe was in ruins. The beast was now clambering onto a shore labeled AMERICA. Dressed only in a Prussian helmet, labeled MILITARISM, the animal bore in his right hand a huge club emblazoned with the word KULTUR, set in quotes to mock Germany's pretensions. In his left, he carried a beautiful fair-complexioned young woman, her hand to her face, whom he had just violently seized. "Destroy This Mad Brute," read the poster's caption, "Enlist." Approximately 1.3 million Americans did.[41]

As the vital draft machinery was set up, meanwhile, administration officials sought to downplay its coerciveness and even to keep the uniformed military largely in the background. Virtually everything—in particular, the registration and deferment process—was handled by local, civilian volunteers.

They wanted to avoid the animosities and resistance that conscription had engendered in the era of the Civil War. Terms like "selective" and "service" were employed in preference to conscription or draft. President Wilson even proffered that this was "in no sense a conscription of the unwilling; it is, rather, selection from a nation which has volunteered in mass."[42]

To start things off, men who were between the ages of twenty-one and thirty-one were summoned to register in their hometowns on June 5, 1917. Secretary of War Baker urged local officials to treat the day as a festive and patriotic occasion. Authorities simultaneously announced that Selective Service would make public the names of those who complied.

Administration figures breathed a sigh of relief when this first round was completed relatively smoothly. Nine and a half million young men came forward. Over the following months the rolls were expanded by another fourteen million. This proved sufficient for the War Department's purposes. Draftees came to constitute 72 percent of U.S. forces during the Great War (those forces grew to an overall size of about four million). At the same time, more than three hundred thousand registrants evaded induction when called, and an estimated three million eligible men simply failed to register for the draft at all.

At the behest principally of the French, who were eager for a boost to their country's morale, General Pershing, late of the Mexican intervention, was dispatched immediately to the continent at the head of an American division. But the bulk of the American Expeditionary Force had yet to be formed. At the end of the summer of 1917, new recruits were brought together for training at hastily assembled camps throughout the country. The working assumption was that a large American ground force would not be ready to go to Europe until well into 1918. Once built up there, the U.S. military and the Wilson administration hoped and expected that it would play a central role in the defeat of Germany during 1919. In the meantime, the French and British would largely shift over to the defensive.[43]

Training and shaping these troops was seen to require more than an emphasis on specific military skills. The Wilson administration cherished the idea that the United States would field an army that would stand out from others and be a beacon to the world, as well as win the hearts of all Americans. Military service would promote greater national order and efficiency. And the belief was that to achieve such objectives, American soldier-crusaders had to be focused and pure.

Among other things, this required that the American army be insulated from both alcohol and illicit sex. Such temptations and distractions could sap the health and performance of the AEF. Both were also morally objectionable to many Protestant old-stock Americans. The administration's attitudes in this regard mirrored powerful moral and hygienic reform impulses in America in this era (indeed, national prohibition would be one outcome of the war). (Ironically, and tragically, it now appears that American training camps may actually have been key points of origin for the first wave of the great global influenza pandemic of 1918–19.)[44]

Bodies like the Committee on Training Camp Activities, headed up by reformer Raymond Fosdick, tried to monitor soldiers' off-camp fraternization with prostitutes as well as other young women. They arrested thousands, and closed down nearby red light districts and burlesque houses.

Alcohol meanwhile was banned not only at all training camps but in surrounding areas, and it was made illegal to serve such beverages to soldiers,
even at one's home. Soldiers were encouraged to engage in what were considered more wholesome activities arranged for them on bases by such
organizations as the YMCA.[45]

No previous American soldiers had ever been subjected to such a formal
program of indoctrination and motivation. Beginning in the fall of 1917,
all recruits were issued a copy of the *Home Reading Course for Citizen-
Soldiers* prepared by the War Department. It extolled American military
traditions and sought to justify, on selfless grounds, involvement in this
conflict. The pamphlet sought to lay fears to rest and to prepare the young
men for the upcoming "great game of war." Lectures and speeches, as well
as drills, were devised to enflame emotions against Germans. At the same
time, special coaches were dispatched to the bases to promote camaraderie
and commitment through patriotic singing.[46]

"One-hundred percent Americanism" and "Americanization" were
major rallying cries of old-stock elites in this period. Wilson himself repeatedly expressed his suspicion of what were called hyphenated Americans.
But in its efforts to utilize recruits of recent European-immigrant background, the War Department felt compelled to take official note of them
as such. While "Americanization" remained the ultimate goal (and was
promoted via language, civics, and citizenship classes), foreign-born soldiers were placed in ethnic platoons, under the leadership of officers of
their same ancestry who had spent more time in the United States. These
platoons were then eventually attached to regular divisions. According to
historian Nancy Gentile Ford, the department's Foreign-Speaking Soldier
Sub-Section associated these "platoons with an immigrant 'colony' and the
larger companies with the American 'melting pot.'"[47]

Deeply racist in its assumptions, the War Department meanwhile
resisted training any African Americans for combat roles on the theory that
they, as a race, simply did not have what it took to make frontline troops.
They were segregated and largely, though not exclusively, relegated to labor
battalions.[48]

The emphasis on efficiency also led the War Department to experiment
with the idea that it could employ intelligence tests that would allow each
soldier optimally to be matched with the right job. Ultimately, 1.7 million
recruits were tested by university psychologists. But many officers doubted
the test's worth, and the results generally came back too late to be of

relevance. The exam was in fact of little value in the measurement of mental aptitude—not to speak of other traits pertinent to military duty—as it "tested to a soldier's education level and economic background and included culturally biased questions." What it actually did was to ensure results that reconfirmed the reigning class and evolutionary-racialist ideas of the era. The scores supposedly provided scientific evidence that peoples of "Anglo-Saxon" stock were superior to other Europeans, and that they in turn were superior to peoples from places other than Europe.[49]

In part because of the broader confusion and delays in mobilizing the economy, the troops were not actually prepared very well for combat. At least stateside, inefficiency and disorganization were more the rule. There were huge delays in completing the camps, and many soldiers did not see the kind of weapon they were expected to use until they were on the other side of the Atlantic. According to historian Edward Coffman, during late 1917 a substantial proportion received "relatively little training beyond physical conditioning and drill."[50]

Large numbers of soldiers nevertheless began to be transported to Europe by early 1918 (though not as rapidly as London and Paris wanted). This took place ahead of the schedule originally intended, not because the AEF was ready sooner, but because the Allied position on the Western Front had begun to appear desperate. In the fall of 1917, Italy had suffered a major defeat at Caporetto. Its ability to preoccupy the Central Powers on that front now seemed in doubt. British forces had taken large losses, and suffered great demoralization, after their failure to achieve a breakthrough in Flanders at the Third Battle of Ypres. Still more important, in the wake of continuing political upheaval, Russia was moving toward complete withdrawal from the war. Starting in late 1917, Germany was able to transfer many of its forces from the Eastern Front to northern France. Berlin hoped, and the Allies feared, that it might succeed in breaking through British-French lines there before any impact by American ground forces could be felt.

Even amid this crisis, major differences remained over how these U.S. forces would ultimately be deployed. From spring 1917, London and Paris had pushed for American soldiers to be integrated into their armies, the argument being that this would be the quickest way for them effectively to be used, while the United States had staunchly resisted. Under the impact of events, a somewhat greater flexibility was shown in the spring of 1918, but only on the understanding that this limited amalgamation was temporary. Pershing stood firm for the creation eventually of an independent

American army in France, determined that it not be robbed of the glory that it (and he) would be due. And Washington backed his decision. It knew that any other position would rile American opinion. Still more important, Wilson was determined that the United States be seen as playing a major role in the conclusion of the war.[51]

CHAPTER 6

To the Fourteen Points Address

At bottom, the Wilson administration's war efforts were shaped by one overriding, and long-standing, goal. That was to restore and put on more secure foundations the essentials of an international order with which Washington had long identified, an international order within which the United States, it was believed, could and would increasingly assume a pre-eminent role. Determined to defeat Germany, to end the threat that it was seen to pose to that order, the administration sought to mobilize U.S. society. It strove to focus against Berlin America's financial, manufacturing, and military might.

Yet, more seemed required. In his efforts to end the conflict along lines he found desirable, the president had, in the period of American "neutrality," taken note of—and tried to exploit—growing popular war-weariness in Europe. During the winter of 1916–17, for example, he had endeavored to speak over the heads of the warring governments and to capitalize on such feelings via his "peace without victory" address.

That weariness did not abate in 1917–18. Rather, the strains of the conflict weighed more and more heavily, discontent mounted, and growing numbers on both sides began to raise questions about their government's intentions. Put most simply, people asked: When will this war ever end?[1] Such sentiments on the part of citizens in the Allied countries constituted a challenge to Washington in that they threatened to undermine its coalition's military resolve. Exhaustion and dissent on the part of the peoples of the Central Powers, meanwhile, increasingly came to appear to the president and his advisers as tantalizing vulnerabilities.

In response, Wilson felt called upon to engage in much more public diplomacy. Most notably, he gave speeches, delivered for occasions selected for the notice they would draw, that were then further publicized and distributed—by the State Department and the CPI—overseas.[2] The president sought to separate the peoples of the Central Powers from their governments by assuring them that they themselves would actually benefit if their countries gave up the fight. He sought to rally the peoples of the Allied countries, as well as of the United States, by arguing that they should not settle for anything short of victory. Wilson now insisted that there could be no real triumph for peace and freedom in the world without that.

In the winter of 1916–17, the president had been prepared to make peace on the basis of Germany agreeing both to evacuate Belgium and northern France and to collaborate on measures aimed at disarmament and the avoidance of future war. But after the spring of 1917, he no longer saw that as sufficient. As Berlin consolidated it leadership over its coalition, and its armies gained control over more and more of Eastern Europe, the prospect was raised that Germany could emerge from the war as a much more formidable rival—capable of challenging the kind of international order that Washington wanted—even if it agreed to retreat from Belgium and France. That was a result that Wilson would not countenance. He also maintained that the leaders of Germany could not be trusted. The president still preferred that Germany not be crushed as a country, but, as noted, he now believed that a pro-American stabilization of Europe would have to include regime change there (even if retention of the kaiser as a figurehead was an idea that continued to be entertained). Wilson had a particular outcome and settlement of the war in mind and he wanted to ensure that the anti-German coalition would fight on so that those results could be achieved.

From mid-1917, Russia represented a growing and especially serious challenge to the administration's plans. Although initially there had been hope that the overthrow of the tsar would usher in a more effective Russian military effort against the Central Powers, figures in Washington were by late spring beginning to worry that Russia might in fact leave the war. And, indeed, while the Provisional Government of Russia continued to prosecute the struggle, its perseverance in the face of repeated setbacks and mounting popular antiwar sentiment actually wound up being the most important factor contributing to that government's overthrow in the fall. Following their seizure of power, the Bolsheviks sought not only to disentangle Russia from the fighting, but also to encourage antiwar and social revolutionary uprisings throughout the rest of Europe. They embarrassed Russia's military partners by publishing the contents of secret treaties revealing that early on the Allies had agreed, in the event of victory, to divide up choice territories belonging to the Central Powers in Europe and elsewhere. These documents seemed to contradict Allied claims that they fought only to thwart German conquests and end "Prussian covetousness."

It was against this backdrop that Wilson delivered his Fourteen Points Address in January 1918. With it, the president hoped he might still keep Russia from leaving the war and rally the Allied publics. The president insisted that, far from participating in a war of greed and self-interest, he was crusading on behalf of "the principle of justice to all peoples and nationalities, and their right to live on equal terms of liberty and safety with one another, whether they be strong or weak." Wilson called this "the culminating and final war for human liberty."[3] In a world thirsting for such liberation, the president's address—despite its stark contrast with his own recent record in such places as Mexico, Central America, and the Caribbean—was to make him, during the balance of 1918 and for a while into 1919, the repository of many peoples' hopes.[4]

*　　*　　*

The possibility that there might continue to be widespread sentiment for negotiations and peace, while he was now urging unremitting war against Germany, materialized as a real challenge for Wilson as early as spring 1917. It did so, initially, in connection with events in Russia. As noted, the overthrow of the tsar made it easier for the president to describe American belligerency in his war address as a crusade against autocracy. House hoped that it would put an end to any future prospect of a German-Russian-Japanese alignment forming in opposition to the kind of international order desired by the United States. Other figures were flattered by the thought that Russia might now adopt political arrangements more like those of the United States. Concern grew during April and May however over mounting evidence that popular support for the war in Russia was less than wholehearted and also highly conditional. Particularly notable, deep suspicions were being voiced on the part of members of the powerful Petrograd Soviet, composed of representatives of insurgent soldiers and workers, as to what Russia's goals, and those of the Allies, were.

House told the president on May 6 that, in addition to minimizing the impact of Germany's U-boats, the key to victory was keeping Russia in the war. Two weeks later, Tumulty, a key political adviser as well as the president's secretary, broached the possibility that a "separate peace" movement might break out. It could, he told the president, "promote currents of peace throughout the world." These would be "much to our injury and embarrassment." He endorsed a suggestion raised in the *New Republic* to the effect that Wilson make a declaration designed to "strengthen Russian" commitment to the war. This might be done by reassuring Russia that self-aggrandizement was not the goal of the United States. In language that already anticipated his speech of the following January, Wilson addressed such a statement to the Provisional Government the very next day. America, said the president, was "fighting for no advantage or selfish object of her own but for the liberation of peoples everywhere . . . for the undictated development of all peoples." All should "unite" in this "great cause of human liberty."[5]

The campaign to keep Russia fighting proceeded along other lines too. On April 10, both House and Lansing advised the president to dispatch a delegation to the new Russia. Its objective, the secretary of state later urged, should be to extend American greetings to "the new and powerful member which has joined the family of democratic nations" and to make the case that it was the duty of those who loved democracy to "render harmless" autocratic Germany. Following up, a mission was dispatched to Russia in May, led by former Secretary of State Root. Upon its return in August, it recommended, most prominently, that financial aid be extended to the Provisional Government (on the condition that it stayed in the war) and that an American-funded propaganda campaign target Russian public opinion. The United States had already advanced a large loan to Russia in May. To this were now added hundreds of millions of dollars of aid. Propaganda was developed. And American railway, medical (Red Cross), and other experts were sent to that country as well (these included, on the model of U.S. army training camps, YMCA officials to promote Russian military morale).[6]

Other challenges to continuation of the war existed early in 1917 as well. Both Mexico and Argentina expressed interest in neutral countries

coming together to promote and facilitate an end to the fighting. Among
the bigger states in Latin America, these were two that had contested U.S.
domination previously. American officials, in response, quite energetically
made clear their displeasure.[7]

In Europe, meanwhile, Dutch and Swedish socialists called for representatives of socialist parties and trade unions from neutral as well as warring
countries to meet during the coming summer in Stockholm. Their hope
was that such a conference would lead both to a reconstitution of the Second (Socialist) International, which had fractured along national lines in
1914, and to a push for peace. Though much discussion and planning took
place, in the end the meeting was never held. It foundered in part as a
result of the competing nationalist perspectives of many of those who were
invited, but also because both the Allies and the Wilson administration
simply refused to provide passports to those of their citizens who wished
to attend.[8]

From 1914 to 1917, the two belligerent sides—as well as the "neutral"
aspirant to world power status, the United States—had either favored or
discouraged moves for peace depending on how a settlement at any given
time would advance or set back their perceived interests. It was such considerations that made Wilson impatient with any talk of an end to hostilities
now (while they would lead Germany to flirt with peace during the coming
months). Although he had advocated "peace without victory" in January,
the president insisted that those who advocated an end to the war at this
time were either fools or agents of Berlin. A worthwhile peace, he maintained, could come only as the result of the enemy's defeat. (In addition to
military means, Wilson thought this should be promoted, as House had
been urging, by efforts to heighten dissatisfaction with continuance of the
war on the Central Powers' side.[9])

In an address delivered on Flag Day, June 14, 1917, meant for both an
American and an international audience, Wilson sought to rally support
for his views. "The military masters of Germany," he maintained, "denied
us the right to be neutral." But the German people were themselves in the
"grip of the same sinister power." The whole world was struggling to prevent that power from achieving "mastery." Any calls for peace from Berlin
were meant to "deceive all those . . . who stand for the rights of peoples
and the self-government of nations." In response, there was but "one
choice," and "[w]e have made it," said the president: "Woe be to the man
or group of men that seeks to stand in our way."[10]

*   *   *

Nevertheless, proposals for ending the fighting short of a victory by either side did not cease. In August, a major initiative was undertaken by the pope. Pronouncing itself appalled at Europe's apparent march toward self-destruction, the Vatican offered to mediate a settlement on the basis of terms in many ways redolent of those put forward by Wilson just seven months before. Pope Benedict XV essentially called for there to be a settlement without annexations. Northern France and Belgium would be evacuated. Germany's colonies would be returned. Disputes over border territories between Germany and France, as well as Austria-Hungary and Italy, would be settled peacefully, taking into consideration popular will. Indemnities, for all practical purposes, would also be eschewed. The powers would all commit to a system of enforced arbitration of disputes, to a program of disarmament, and to the freedom of the seas.[11]

House pressed Wilson not simply to ignore or reject the proposal, communicated to the belligerents at the beginning of the month and then published two weeks later. Having at this point become apprehensive as to whether victory could in fact be achieved, he expressed fear that such a reaction might guarantee Russia's alienation and also frighten those people in the Central Powers who might otherwise criticize their governments' continued prosecution of the war.

He urged that the president instead try to hijack the initiative. Up to this point, the administration had been content to mute the differences between its war aims and those of the other members of its coalition. Any other course was viewed as futile and counterproductive. (Once the war was won, Wilson had told his adviser in July, "we can force them to our way of thinking.") But House now believed that adopting a clear stance in opposition to annexationist war aims was called for. Washington should in essence turn to its advantage its disinterest in more territory. This might rally popular opinion in the Allied countries, including Russia, while putting pressure on Berlin to either do the same or face domestic upheaval.

House actually implied that it might make sense to try to end the war as soon as possible, even if that meant relenting on immediate regime change, this to a considerable extent because of the situation in Russia. He worried about the collapse of the Provisional Government. That would bring with it the loss of that ally and the strong likelihood that in the future it would come to be dominated by Berlin. The Provisional Government's survival meanwhile might ultimately lead to the kind of political change the United States desired in Germany. "On a basis of the status quo ante, the Entente could aid Austria in emancipating herself from Prussia," he told the president. The threat to future stability inherent in the Allies intended carve-up of the Ottoman Empire might be avoided. On the other hand, if the war went on too long, American power would be depleted, and the U.S. ability to shape the peace settlement might diminish.[12]

House knew that he was "running counter to the advice of Lansing, [Second Assistant Secretary William] Phillips and others in the State Department," as well probably to the feelings of the president.[13] And he was right, though not without influence. In the end, Wilson's response to the Vatican's initiative was essentially dismissive. It rejected peace as a possibility so long as Germany's leaders remained in place. At the same time, the president did accept House's advice to again try to promote opposition to the war on the part of the German people. He pointedly distanced himself in his note from "dismemberment" or a punitive peace.[14]

In September, Berlin broached the prospect of peace, hinting to London that it might forsake bases on, and influence over, coastal Belgium in exchange for a settlement that restored to Germany its colonies (this presumed a British ability to control the attitude of France as well as a readiness to write off Russia). But the idea ran into staunch resistance. It came less from Lloyd George than from other members of his war cabinet, like Balfour, Milner, and Curzon. The prime minister was told that it was in Britain's interest to do all it could to prevent Germany from emerging from the war as a more powerful state. That would follow if it were not prevented from acquiring new territory and influence to its east. Not only might it become dominant as never before in Europe, it also—via Russia—might gain a way of threatening Britain's Asian holdings.[15]

A similar attitude led Wilson in the fall of 1917 repeatedly to discourage talk of peace anytime soon, though he cast the need to prevent German success in terms of freedom and democracy. In early October, Wilson received delegates from a new group, the League for National Unity, at the White House. According to a newspaper account, they described "[a]gitation for a premature peace . . . as seditious, and those [U.S. citizens] who attacked the allies of America . . . [as] enemies of their country." The president endorsed the purposes of the group and opined that Americans "needed guidance to remember that the war should end only when Germany was beaten and Germany's rule of autocracy and might be superceded by the ideals of democracy." The president declared, the article continued, that the United States was "fighting now for the same ideals of democracy and freedom that have always actuated the nation." He "gave warning that it should not be forgotten that German success would mean not only prevention of the spread of democracy, but possibly the suppression of that already existing."[16]

These themes were then the centerpiece of a major speech that Wilson gave to the American Federation of Labor in early November. "Look at the map of Europe now!" he told his listeners.

> Germany is thrusting upon us again and again the discussion of peace talks—about what? Talks about Belgium; talks about northern France; talks about Alsace-Lorraine. Well, those are deeply interesting subjects . . . but they are not the heart of the matter. Take up the map and look at it. Germany has absolute control of Austria-Hungary, practical control of the Balkan States, control of Turkey, control of Asia Minor. I saw a map in which the whole thing was printed in appropriate black . . . and the black stretched all the way from Hamburg to Bagdad. . . . If she can keep that, she has kept all that her dreams contemplated when the war began. If she can keep that, her power can disturb the world as long as she keeps it, always provided . . . the present influences that control the German government continue to control it. . . . Power cannot be used with concentrated force against free peoples if it is used by free people.

"Germany," the president continued, "is determined that the political power of the world shall belong to her. There have been such ambitions before. They have been in part realized, but never before have those ambitions been based upon so exact and precise and scientific a plan of domination."[17]

For all practical purposes, Wilson was now inviting the German people to overthrow their government. This fit into a broader pattern that had become characteristic of both sides in the war. As the conflict became more desperate, the contending great powers became more and more inclined to welcome and foment political upheaval behind their enemies' lines. Germany had sought to promote revolt in Ireland and had facilitated the

Bolshevik leader Vladimir Lenin's return to Russia. The British were encouraging Arab revolts against the Ottoman Empire in the Middle East. Principally through the use of rhetoric and propaganda, Wilson was now seeking to bring about the victory, with regime change, that he was hoping for over Berlin.

*   *   *

But Wilson also hoped to use these methods to influence his allies. By the time he gave his speech to the AFL, the anti-German coalition was confronted with yet another crisis. In late October, the Italian army had suffered a calamitous defeat at the hands of German and Austrian forces on the Isonzo River, near Caporetto. It took heavy casualties and suffered a breakdown in discipline and morale. Hundreds of thousands of troops surrendered or were taken prisoner, refugees streamed southward from the border region, and Central Power military units penetrated deep into the area to the north of Venice. As with Russia, this ally seemed in danger of collapse.[18]

The British and French raced troops to the Veneto to try to stabilize the situation. Although Wilson succeeded in getting Congress to declare war against Austria-Hungary, as a way of boosting Italian spirits, the president accepted his army's counsel not to plan for the same. Dispatching military forces to Italy would extend and make more complicated American chains of supply. It would also fragment American power and diminish its impact on what was seen as the all-important front in France.

The administration did however mount an immense propaganda and aid offensive in that country. This was meant to rally Italian popular support for the war (to this point lukewarm) for however long it took to achieve victory. As historian Daniela Rossini notes, in the long run it was also meant to boost U.S. influence among the population in such a way as would achieve for Wilson influence with Rome over the terms of the peace.

The Red Cross and YMCA were the first to arrive. Beginning in November 1917, Red Cross workers, uniformed adjuncts of the U.S. Army, began to distribute aid to refugees and to set up canteens and rest houses for Italian soldiers. Generous cash payments were distributed to families of poor soldiers. And propaganda was distributed, arguing that Italy could not lose the war, connected as its fortunes were now to the invincible United States.

YMCA workers arrived in January. Focused more on the troops at the front, they too trumpeted American material wealth and superiority, as well as idealism. To improve morale, they organized recreation, sponsored movies and other forms of entertainment, and liberally distributed cigarettes, snacks, stationery, postcards, and magazines.

A major operation was then inaugurated in the spring by the CPI. It distributed favorable news stories, pamphlets, and photos about the United States and extolled American contributions to the war. Speakers circulated throughout the country. Commercial films from the United States were distributed (on the condition that CPI-produced propaganda films be shown along with them). Wilson's speeches were freely dispersed, as were posters, a large number bearing the image of the president himself. One official wrote Creel that the "President's poster picture inscribed with the Italian words 'for the rights of the peoples' is framed and hangs in countless simple homes throughout Italy." Many other observers testified that, during 1918, the campaign had the effect, almost literally, of turning Wilson into a figure of adoration for many rural peasants.

The president was absolutely convinced of the importance of public opinion in world affairs and he followed closely, may even closely have participated in planning, the CPI's activities. His hope was not only to keep his coalition partners fighting, but to build up a public sentiment that could be used to pressure those governments to follow his lead when it came time to conclude the peace.[19]

*   *   *

Come November, House was in Western Europe again. He had crossed the Atlantic to attend an inter-Allied conference in Paris meant to lay the groundwork for more coordination in the anti-German cause. The war against the Central Powers was not going well. The convoy system and other measures were increasingly effective, but the U-boat remained a problem. And British forces were being "swallowed up by the mud" at Passchendaele (near Ypres).[20] Meanwhile, it looked as though the Allies might soon face much more pressure on the Western Front. This was partly because Italy's ability to fight was in doubt. Even more important was the situation in Russia. To the president's chief foreign policy adviser, these circumstances made the need for a bold new public relations initiative essential.

The Bolsheviks had seized power at the start of the month, and on November 8 Lenin, in his capacity as chairman of the Council of People's Commissars, launched a peace offensive. His Decree on Peace was aimed not only at all of the governments that were at war, but also at their peoples. Quite at variance with the stance of the western Allied governments, he called for a generalized cease-fire followed by talks—conducted "absolutely openly"—leading to a settlement of the entire conflict. Lenin hoped that the governments on both sides would be pressured by their exhausted populations to respond to his call and that the conclusion of the war would mark a first step in the continent-wide triumph of socialist reconstruction.

According to the decree, the settlement should ideally entail no annexations or indemnities for either side. The right of people to self-determination should be acknowledged, and the colonial system should come to an end. It condemned the idea that the war might continue "simply to decide how to divide the weak nationalities among the powerful and rich nations." Two weeks later, the Bolsheviks published, and for Russia disavowed, the secret treaties dividing up territories that had been concluded by the Allies.[21] By the time of the inter-Allied conference, a cease-fire had been arranged with Germany, though negotiations were being held in abeyance by Leon Trotsky, the People's Commissar for Foreign Affairs, in the hope that the western Allies would feel the need to attend.

Neither the United States nor any of the western Allies had any interest in entering into these negotiations. And they were upset with the Bolsheviks. But they were put in an awkward position before the world and their publics. They also confronted a situation with regard to Russia that might greatly complicate their hopes of victory. If that power left their coalition, Germany could transfer a large number of troops from Eastern Europe to the Western Front. Moreover, the blockade might be negated. Berlin would be able to get supplies from the east.

The powers at the Paris conference decided to temporize and equivocate. They expressed a willingness to reconsider their objectives in consultation with Russia when the political situation there stabilized. They hoped that it would meanwhile become clear that Berlin would not in fact settle on the basis of no annexations. And, as a hedge against Russia's withdrawal from the war, they authorized London to pursue again with Austria-Hungary the possibility of a separate peace.

But House wanted them to go further. He had long desired a more vigorous ideological offensive, one that would rally the Allied publics while undermining popular support in Germany. And, he was increasingly of the belief that discussion of war aims differences between the United States and its partners should no longer be deferred. Hoping that he would be "aiding the military situation," House encouraged the conference to declare that the Allies and the United States were not waging war for the purpose of territory or indemnity; the sacrifices they were making were to destroy militarism and the threat it posed to freedom. As he put it in his diary, the United States was "not embarrassed" by any such desires. It ought, therefore, to make a virtue of that. His resolution was designed to ensure support for the war from the American and Allied publics, to undermine German and Bolshevik propaganda, to influence Russia against settling separately with Berlin, and to make it more difficult for the other states to maintain war aims (particularly in regard to territory and indemnifications) at variance with the American program.[22]

But the Allies, most notably Italy and France, resisted. House returned to the United States arguing not only that the effort to transport troops to Europe had to be speeded up, but that the president had soon on his own to make a broad public statement.

*   *   *

The result was what would come to be called the Fourteen Points Address. Home from Europe, House met with Wilson in mid-December. "An important decision, the President and I made," he later wrote in his diary, "was to formulate the war aims of the United States."[23]

Back in September, Wilson had asked House to assemble a body of experts who could pull together the detailed information the administration would need to promote the kind of settlement it wanted at the end of the war (the president once again demonstrating a predilection for working outside of the Department of State). Out of this soon emerged what came to be called the Inquiry, a group of historians, political scientists, economists, geographers, lawyers, and others housed at the headquarters of the American Geographical Society in New York. The operation was headed up by Sidney E. Mezes, who had been serving as the president of City College. He regularly provided updates on the organization both to Wilson and to Colonel House (who, conveniently, was also his brother-in-law).[24]

At their meeting in mid-December, the president urged House to ask Mezes for information that might be useful in their current task. From this time forward, House and several members of the Inquiry collaborated on assembling key building blocks of what would become Wilson's speech.

The immediate objective of the address was to meet the public relations situation created by Allied exhaustion, the publication of the embarrassing secret treaties, and the possibility of an end to fighting between Germany and Russia. Wilson and his advisers wanted to make the argument that the United States was after disinterested ends that all people should support and fight on for. These were liberty and everlasting peace.

But the ultimate purpose of such a public relations offensive was, of course, to promote an outcome of the conflict in line with the administration's long-prized objectives (which were related to concepts like peace and freedom in only contingent ways). These were to restore and more effectively secure the international order to which American policy makers had become attached. More specifically and immediately, they involved settling the interrelated questions of European disorder and German might.

The Inquiry team focused heavily on these topics in the draft materials they furnished at House's behest, which makes discussion of them crucial to any understanding of the Fourteen Points and American war aims. They placed particular emphasis on preventing Germany from ever becoming a more formidable power. They also reflected a belief that granting greater degrees of autonomy to aspiring nationalities in Central Europe might provide both leverage on Berlin and more stability on that continent in the future (an idea House had embraced by 1915).

Beyond leaving Belgium and France, the draft materials stipulated that Germany had to be denied control over Middle Europe and the region extending southeastward through the Ottoman Empire to Baghdad (in other words, Berlin needed to be prevented from achieving a position where—as Wilson had put it—it could "disturb the world"). This could be addressed in a number of ways. The recommendations maintained that Germany and Austria-Hungary should be pushed apart. Austria-Hungary's fear of a nationalist breakup should be capitalized on. The Dual Monarchy ought to understand that safety from that was dependent on it keeping its distance from Berlin. Meanwhile, the surging nationalist outlooks that had been developing within the empire should be directed toward a federal solution (rather than independence, not favored at this time) which would reduce within Austria-Hungary the "German-Magyar ascendancy." Poland should be made into an independent state. Italy should be given boundary rectifications, but not all the territories stipulated in the heretofore secret Treaty of London. Such would simply lay the groundwork for another war.

A German-dominated Middle Europe and Berlin-to-Baghdad Axis ought also to be checked by the neutralization-internationalization of the Straits. The Ottoman Empire should be broken up. Like Poland, Armenia should be cultivated as a friendly country. The Arab portions of the empire should not be divided up into formal colonies handed out to the different Allied powers (as called for in the secret treaties), a step House and Wilson had long seen as paving the way for future conflict and instability. Rather they should be put under the, presumably collective, protection of the "civilized nations."

As for Germany itself, the existing degree of concentrated, especially Prussian, power in its political system needed to be broken up. Germany needed to know that if it underwent such political restructuring it could be a candidate for partnership in the world with the other big powers. At the same time, an uncooperative Germany needed to keep in mind that it might be excluded from commercial activity in the "outer world" and prevented from participation in the planned-for league of nations.[25]

With the draft materials and maps provided them by the Inquiry team, House and Wilson worked up the speech and "finished remaking the map of the world" (as the former put it) at the White House on the weekend of January 4–5, 1918. The president almost certainly played the central role in reconciling the various rhetorical-political purposes of the address with the administration's more specific long-term aims.

Understanding the temporal context is important. By this point, the Bolsheviks had given great prominence to ideas that a number of European antiwar groups had been promoting since 1914. In November and December, they had roundly denounced secret diplomacy, condemned annexations and indemnities as improper war aims, and championed the right of all peoples to self-determination. They alleged that the two big-power led blocks had been struggling for similar and unworthy ends. Recently, even quite establishment figures within Wilson's coalition had gained attention by questioning the logic of continuing the war. Late in 1917, Britain's former foreign secretary, Lord Lansdowne, wrote a widely discussed letter to the *Daily Telegraph* asserting that the fighting "has already lasted too long." "We are not going to lose this war," Lansdowne told his countrymen, "but its prolongation will spell ruin for the civilized world and an addition to the human suffering, which already weighs upon it." Wilson was eager to counter these voices and to rally American and Allied peoples behind a continuance of the fight (similar motivations led Lloyd George to rephrase and partially reformulate British aims in a speech on January 5).[26]

Such public relations concerns account for much of the language contained within the Fourteen Points Address. But most of the points, or aims, cannot be understood without reference as well to long-standing U.S. great-power goals. Via both rhetoric and substance, what Wilson was seeking to do was promote the kind of peace he wanted in Europe and, by extension, the world.

The structure of the address, as finally delivered before Congress on January 8, progressed from general terms to particulars (with one exception to be noted below).[27] In his first point, the president championed the concept of open diplomacy that would "proceed always frankly and in the public view," a commitment that, as time would tell, was susceptible of quite a wide range of interpretations. Point 2 advocated freedom of the seas, "except as the seas may be closed in whole or in part by international action for the enforcement of international covenants" (this a very important qualification that, it was hoped, would mollify Britain and make it possible for the powers that would dominate a postwar league to again cut off commerce to any state that threatened to alter the international order they wanted). The third point called for the "removal, so far as possible, of all economic barriers and the establishment of an equality of trade conditions among all the nations consenting to the peace." Wilson and his advisers knew that the United States would thrive commercially under such conditions. As they saw it, greater movement away from protectionism and closed doors would also depoliticize trade and reduce a major source of conflict among the powers. Point 4, calling for a reduction of nations' armaments "to the lowest points consistent with domestic safety," was likewise aimed at the stabilization of the postwar order, while Point 5 may be read as expressing the hope that the international system might be spared upheaval from colonial rivalries or resentments.

Trotsky's biting comments of just the week before are likely to have been relevant to Wilson's discussion of this topic.[28] He had ridiculed the Allies, calling them hypocritical for claiming to be fighting to free weak nations (like Belgium and Serbia) from the Central Powers' grip while remaining silent about their own subject peoples. "[T]o demand self determination for the peoples that are comprised within the borders of enemy states," he argued, "and to refuse self determination to the peoples of their own state or of their own colonies would mean the defense of the most naked, the most cynical imperialism." Trotsky directly referred to "Ireland, Egypt, India, Indochina, et cetera."[29] (The once-secret treaties had in fact revealed an Allied willingness to dispense with the self-determination of still other peoples.)

Wilson's comments, though weak, tentative, and vague in the extreme, would nevertheless be grasped onto by many peoples, particularly subject populations in the British and French empires, with a great deal of hope. What he did was to pronounce himself in favor of a "free, open-minded, and absolutely impartial adjustment of all colonial claims, based upon a strict observance of the principle that in determining all such questions of sovereignty the interests of the populations concerned must have equal weight with the equitable claims of the government whose title is to be determined." (A month later he was bolder, pronouncing himself a champion of, and actually using the term, self-determination.)[30]

Much of the speech was directed at Russian sentiment and the situation in that country.[31] Keeping Russia in the war, or at least at odds with Germany, was one reason for proclaiming, and putting in the most favorable light, American war aims. Wilson's address opened with a direct and extended reference to the Russo-German talks that had gotten under way in late December at Brest-Litovsk. The president complimented the Russian representatives. They had been "sincere and in earnest," just, and wise. Though Russia's power "apparently is shattered," it was not adopting a subservient attitude toward the Central Powers who were intent upon retaining the lands they had occupied. The Russians continued to support a "humane and honorable" peace in a way that "must challenge the admiration of every friend of mankind." "Whether their present leaders [the Bolsheviks] believe it or not," he insisted, "it is our heartfelt desire and hope that some way may be opened whereby we may be privileged to assist the people of Russia to attain their utmost hope of liberty and ordered peace."

It was against this backdrop that Wilson enunciated Point 6, wherein he demanded the evacuation of Russian territory and supported the idea that that country be given an "unhampered and unembarrassed opportunity" to work out its own affairs. In words whose spirit would contrast sharply with the tenor of the policy pursued by the United States and its allies in the coming months, the president declared that "[t]he treatment accorded Russia by her sister nations in the months to come will be the acid test of their good will, of their comprehension of her needs as distinguished from their own interests, and of their intelligent and unselfish sympathy."

Point 7 insisted that Belgium had to be "evacuated and restored." This step was of crucial importance to the long-term stability of the postwar order, for without it, the president stated, "the whole structure and validity of international law is forever impaired." In Point 8, Wilson declared that all French territory "should" also be "freed and the invaded portions restored." Much discussion among the Americans had attended the specific case of Alsace-Lorraine, the provinces that Germany had taken in 1871 after the Franco-Prussian War. Ought the possibility that France might compromise on their recovery be provided for? Should the possibility that Germany might retain equal economic opportunity there be advanced? In the end, the president asserted that "the wrong done to France . . . which has unsettled the peace of the world for nearly fifty years, should be righted, in order that peace may once more be made secure in the interest of all."[32]

Point 9 again reflected the concern with long-term stabilization. It did not overtly challenge the Treaty of London. But, rather than endorse that, it recommended that a "readjustment" of Italy's frontiers "should be effected along clearly recognizable lines of nationality."

"[A]utonomous development" was meanwhile suggested for the "peoples of Austria-Hungary" in Point 10. This reflected the administration's desire to maintain some leverage on Vienna. The same suggestion, in Point 12, in regard to the fate of the non-Turkish nationalities of the Ottoman Empire, reflected its desire to block a Berlin to Baghdad Axis and postwar great-power rivalry over that empire's remains.

Eleven addressed the Balkans. Rumania, Serbia, and Montenegro "should be evacuated" and "occupied territories restored." Serbia should also have "free and secure access to the sea." Wilson presumably believed that beyond this the route to stability lay in allowing borders to be drawn in line with peoples' national identities. These boundaries could then be prevented from being challenged via "international guarantees." How hard arriving at such borders would in practice be was likely not understood.

Point 13 stated that an "independent Polish state should be erected," containing "territories inhabited by indisputably Polish populations," and with access to the sea. Its "independence and territorial integrity" should then also be "guaranteed by international covenant."

The president decided to "round out" his list with a final broad provision, the fourteenth point, which consisted of a reiteration of Wilson's support for a "general association of nations" that, after the war, he hoped would hold his settlement in place.

* * *

In addition to mobilizing U.S. financial, manufacturing, and military might, the Wilson administration vigorously employed public diplomacy in its efforts to achieve what it considered a favorable conclusion of the war. From the spring of 1917 onward "Peace without Victory" was no longer seen as satisfactory. The administration wanted to see changes made in the structure of the German government. It also wanted to see Berlin thwarted from becoming a more formidable world power via formal or informal expansion in Europe and to the southeast. In the face of mounting exhaustion and international sentiment eager to see the conflict end, Wilson ironically became the most important voice pushing to keep it going.

In the interest of unity, the president's initial inclination was to downplay the differences that existed between himself and his European partners over war aims. He knew that his plans for a settlement (especially in regard to territorial changes and indemnities) that might solve the problems posed for the United States by European instability were not shared by the Allies. But he assumed that Washington would be able to prevail on these questions once the fighting was over. The war aims discussion, which Wilson had himself (in late 1916 and early 1917) intensified, nevertheless only continued to become more central amid the exhaustion that was felt on both sides.

Once the Bolsheviks, and to a lesser extent Germany, put the Allies on the defensive, the stage was set for the president to change course. It now seemed imperative that aims be set forth, and that that be done in such a way as would rally the peoples in his coalition (and ideally lessen the will to fight in Germany). Wilson was uniquely placed to do this precisely because, while most certainly driven by self-interest, the administration's goals had little to do with either territorial acquisitions or indemnifications. Indeed, U.S. interests were viewed as best served by a settlement that did not entail such terms, seen as only likely to breed further discord in the future.

If the president and House believed that a statement of aims now had to be made, the occasion also presented an opportunity. For, to the extent that those goals could be phrased in such a way as would command popular enthusiasm, the administration might finally be able to take control over the settlement from its partners, even before the conflict ended.

As things turned out, the speech did serve Wilson's purposes in a number of ways. It helped rally support for a continuance of the war. (Sixty million copies of the address were distributed abroad by the CPI.[33]) It enhanced the president's stature and leverage within his own coalition (though none of the Allies at this point revised their aims in light of it). And, eventually, it even facilitated Germany's willingness to discuss peace on American terms. In the end, however, it was too vague to provide a blueprint for a "Wilsonian" peace. It also failed in what arguably was its most ambitious and important short-term objective, namely keeping Russia as an ally in the war.[34]

CHAPTER 7

Casting Every Selfish Dominion Down in the Dust (1918)

During early 1918, Britain, France and the United States braced themselves for the possibility of a powerful new German offensive on the Western Front, made possible by Russia's military collapse. All of them continued to hope that the Central Powers might be deprived of a complete victory in the east. If serious military pressure from that direction could not be revived, at least Germany might be prevented from gaining control over Russian food and other resources, a development that would largely negate the blockade. London, for its part, worried that, in the absence of resistance, Germany might eventually be able to move across Russia and contest Britain's control of the Indian subcontinent.[1]

But the three allies disagreed both as to how they should try to influence events in Russia and as to the amount of resources (especially military) that should be devoted to that task. Wilson worried that heavy-handed interference would be counterproductive, both in terms of influencing Russia's direction and in terms of world opinion. It would risk, in other words, undermining the ideological offensive that the president had mounted with his Fourteen Points Address. In addition, military strategists in the United States maintained that the war would ultimately be won on the Western Front. So far as American forces were concerned, therefore, that was where they should fight. It would also be difficult logistically for any great number of American troops to be diverted elsewhere, a step—the president knew—also likely to be difficult to explain to the American people.[2]

These concerns initially led Wilson to resist the British and French when they pressed the idea of Allied military operations in Russia. But, by mid-year, he finally relented, even agreeing to the dispatch of some American troops. Though Wilson was no friend of Bolshevism (a force he would increasingly come to see as a threat to the kind of international order he wanted), in mid-1918 he was motivated less by the desire to extinguish that (even if the intervention he envisioned would work in that direction) than by a desire to advance two other objectives. With an eye on the eventual peace settlement, Wilson was anxious to maintain good relations, and influence, with his major European allies (it helped that he thought he had come upon a plan that would minimize the backlash he feared). Simultaneously, he worried that, without some U.S. participation, the intervention in Russia of another ally, Japan, might jeopardize American visions for the arrangement of postwar Asia.

Germany's new offensive in France finally began in late March. It put enormous pressure on the Allies throughout the spring. But the breakthrough Berlin hoped for never came. And with Paris still out of reach, its army finally began to lose steam. From July, the momentum shifted ever more rapidly to the Allies, who were now joined by a large and growing army from the United States. Eventually, it became apparent that the tide had turned.

Allied and American leaders began to entertain the idea that the war might be won before the end of the calendar year. But even the most optimistic were then surprised at the speed of the Central Powers' disintegration in late summer and early fall. Domestic turmoil and economic collapse threatened each exhausted member of that German-led coalition, and its constituent governments soon began to pursue separate deals with the Allies.

German leaders explored an armistice in October. Their decision to approach Wilson and, through him, to try to get the Allies to concede the conditions suggested in the Fourteen Points convinced the president that success, as he had been defining it, was near. Now he had both an opening and more leverage with which to commit England, France, and Italy to his ideas for the peace, to his plans for a postwar international order along the lines of what Washington had long been seeking. House ultimately handled the details of pre-armistice negotiations with the Allies. But, both he and Wilson came away with an exaggerated sense of what they had achieved.

*   *   *

By early 1918, all administration figures were doubtful that a serious Eastern Front could be revived. But they did hope that Germany might at least be prevented from acquiring Russian territory, trade, or resources.

What influence the United States could have on that was unclear. One thought, promoted by Lansing as early as December, was that aid could covertly be supplied to generals who were contesting Bolshevik power and who might be willing to continue fighting against Germany. Wilson subsequently signed off on a program whereby limited support would be funneled, in conjunction with Britain and France, to the Don Cossack General A. M. Kaledin in southern Russia. Kaledin's movement, however, collapsed early in the new year.[3]

Another idea, promoted especially by American representatives in Russia, was for the United States to try positive engagement with the Bolsheviks. The view in Washington was that the Bolsheviks were weak and would not long remain in power. The American ambassador (to the Provisional Government), David R. Francis, insisted that at least for the moment they were the strongest force in Russia. It was important to keep the Bolsheviks and Germans apart. He was successful in getting the administration to allow informal discussions with the new regime, a course simultaneously followed by Britain and France. For the United States, the key figures in these talks were William V. Judson, the head of the American military mission to Russia, and then, after he departed, Raymond Robins, of the American Red Cross. The latter, in particular, hoped to woo the new Russian government with the prospect both of aid and of mutually advantageous trade. In late January, Robins recommended that the United States consider extending recognition, something eagerly desired in Petrograd. The president briefly considered this—or at least de facto recognition—as a way of heading off a German-Russian peace treaty, but he held back, apparently because of British opposition. Such a step was also strongly opposed by Lansing on the grounds that it would bolster the Bolsheviks in power.[4]

Negotiations had been taking place, on and off, between the Bolsheviks and Central Powers at Brest-Litovsk (today the city of Brest in Belarus). In February, they reached a climax when it became clear to Trotsky how high the cost of ending the war would be. Berlin wanted Russia to relinquish control over many of what had been the empire's most valuable territories in Eastern Europe. Its objectives were to reduce Russia as a major power, to contain Bolshevism, and to secure Germany an economic and strategic sphere of influence in that region. In the short term, such influence would give the Central Powers much needed access to the agricultural produce of the Ukraine. In the longer run, it would enhance Berlin's competitive position among the great powers and provide security for the projection of its power into the Middle East. Germany partly sought to engineer this via the encouragement and manipulation of anti-Russian nationalist forces in the region (like its Allied counterparts, putting itself forward as the protector of small nations).

Assuming a stance of "no war, no peace," the Bolsheviks withdrew from the talks on February 9, only quickly to be confronted with a renewed German military advance. Soon Petrograd itself seemed threatened. After negotiations were resumed, the surrender of even more territory was demanded. "Left Communists" and left-wing members of the Socialist-Revolutionary Party—at this point aligned with the Bolsheviks—advocated rejection of the Treaty of Brest-Litovsk, signed on March 3, but Lenin prevailed, arguing that the survival of any base at all for world revolution was now at stake. As it had done with the Fourteen Points Address, the administration in Washington continued rhetorically to appeal for close relations between the United States and the Russian people, but it rejected aid to or recognition of the Bolshevik regime.[5]

Still another, overtly interventionist, idea for blocking German access to Russian resources had meanwhile been submitted for Washington's consideration at the very end of January. This was contained in a secret memorandum from the British government. Though little had as yet been achieved, London still looked forward hopefully to the development of military forces in southern and southeastern Russia that would work side by side with the Allies. Given sufficient aid, the memo argued, such forces might be able to prevent Germany from gaining control over the grain, iron ore, and coal of that region. The aid could be delivered by means of the Russian port of Vladivostok and the Trans-Siberian Railway, running west across Asia. But for that to work, the route had to be under Allied control. The British suggested that Japan be asked to take up that task.

London anticipated American objections. To meet them, at least in part, it proposed that Japan be invited to act as a mandatory for all the Allies. The memo also acknowledged that some would argue that these steps might "do more harm than good to the Allied cause in Russia" in that they "would involve the temporary control by foreigners of many thousands of miles of Russian railway, and those foreigners would be drawn from the very nation by which Russia was defeated within recent memory [Japan, in the Russo-Japanese War of 1904–5]." It claimed, however, that British intelligence was picking up contrary indications. Such steps might actually be welcomed. Moreover, their importance, particularly in preventing Germany from alleviating the pressure of the blockade, warranted any risks.[6]

That was not the general reaction in Washington. The military value of the gambit seemed questionable and the threat of alienating Russian sentiment, even to the point of throwing that country "into the arms of Germany," seemed great. Despite the continued prompting of England, House could not help feeling "that they have lost their perspective." "We are treading upon exceedingly delicate and dangerous ground," he wrote Wilson, "and are likely to lose that fine moral position you have given the Entente cause. The whole structure which you have built up so carefully may be destroyed . . . and our position will be no better than that of the Germans." Intervention might not only be counterproductive in these terms. U.S. officials worried that, if invited to intervene (in a mandatory capacity or not), Japan might seize upon the opportunity to expand the scope of its influence in Northeast Asia.[7]

Washington's first formal reaction was to reject Britain's proposal. It asserted furthermore, that if, in the future, occupation of the Trans-Siberian was considered, it should be with an eye to that being undertaken by a multinational force, not by Japan alone. But the British (joined by the French) continued to press their case. Wilson wavered. At the end of February, he drafted a statement saying that while the United States still did not think the plan wise, it would not object if the other powers requested Japanese action. Tokyo would of course, the draft read, not act in such a way as would affect the long-term fate of Siberia. Days later though, the president reverted to his original stand and incorporated that in a formal note. Convinced it could not move forward without U.S. assent, Japan announced that it would for the time being hold back.[8]

But Allied appeals continued and the administration appears to have increasingly worried about seeming unsupportive. After the ratification of the Treaty of Brest-Litovsk and the onset of Germany's massive offensive in France, House—still dubious of the merits of the envisioned intervention—opined that it might be worth launching if only for the sake of Allied morale.[9]

Still uneasy about Siberia, Wilson responded in positive terms when London and Paris broached the possibility of an intervention in northern Russia that would include American troops. The Allies wanted control over military stores that had been stockpiled at the ports of Murmansk and Archangel before Russia left the war. The administration took the position that it was not being inconsistent. It held that the military value of this mission was clear. Given that Japanese forces would not be involved, the risk of a Russian backlash was also smaller, though the western powers would still have to be careful not to appear as if they meant to interfere in the country's politics. An undertaking was made that would see roughly five thousand Americans landed in that area in late summer.[10]

Washington's willingness to endorse, and indeed participate, in an expedition to northern Russia did not however reduce the Allies' desire to win American backing for a larger intervention in Siberia. With the emergence of the so-called Czech Legion, Wilson finally began to be more receptive to that. The Czech Legion consisted of tens of thousands of troops who had deserted, or been captured, from the Austro-Hungarian army earlier in the war. Hoping to promote Czech independence, some had then fought alongside the Russians against the Central Powers. But with the end of formal hostilities on the Eastern Front, those troops were now seeking to leave Russia, via Vladivostok, in order to fight in France. Traveling eastward on the Trans-Siberian Railway in May, a number clashed with local Bolsheviks. The Legion henceforth took sides in the unfolding Russian Civil War and gained control over large stretches of that line.

Wilson envisioned the Czech Legion as a force that might advance U.S. and Allied goals without the complications that he and his advisers had feared. The Legion's power might embolden the formation of more Russian forces who would work with the western powers. Fears of a Russian backlash against Allied interference would, he hoped, be unlikely. As the president saw it, the Bohemians and Slovaks were Russian's Slavic "cousins." And Japan's role could, it was thought, be limited in geographic scope and size compared to what the British had envisioned. That, in turn, would allow Washington to contain Japanese ambitions by matching Tokyo's small force with one of its own. Wilson expected that the American public would endorse the idea if it was framed as Americans going to the Czech Legion's rescue.[11]

Little of this would turn out as Wilson hoped, but in mid-1918 the president thought he had found a way forward that would at least partially satisfy England and France (he still ruled out any effort to reconstitute an Eastern Front). Overriding the continued objections of his generals and secretary of war, Wilson told the latter: "Baker, I wholly agree with all you say from a military point of view, but we are fighting this war with Allies and I have felt obliged to fall in with their wishes here."[12] By August, an American force that would reach about ten thousand was beginning to arrive in Northeast Asia from California and the Philippines.

*   *   *

By that time, ironically, the situation in northern France was already changing. The more than three-year-old stalemate was coming to an end. Berlin's powerful offensive had fallen short and the tide of the war had turned.

During the winter of 1917–18, largely as the result of developments in Russia and Italy, Germany had been able to move forty-four divisions to the Western Front, this in preparation for what its generals hoped would be an offensive that would end the conflict. By spring, it had achieved an edge over the Allies of 191 to 178 divisions (in some other areas, most notably transport, tanks, and food, the Allies retained an advantage). General Erich Ludendorff, the architect of Berlin's plans, saw this offensive as Germany's last chance of victory. He wanted to capitalize on its numerical superiority before a large American force could reinforce the armies of Britain and France. Via a succession of well-placed blows, his goal was to break through the Allied line, separate the British and French, and render Paris vulnerable.

The first of these blows, coming on March 21, was aimed at the southern sector of the British line in the area of the Somme. The scale of the assault, if not the location, came as a surprise to the defenders, with the result that over the next several days German forces made dramatic gains. The Allies were shaken. Having established a superficially greater coordination in the fall (after Caporetto) with the creation of a Supreme War Council (to which Wilson had attached a permanent military—though not political—representative, General Tasker Bliss), they now appointed a commander-in-chief for the entire region, the French general Ferdinand Foch.

A second attack, against British Empire forces to the north in Flanders on the River Lys, took place in early April. Again the Allies were forced back. Then, after a pause of a month, a massive assault was launched on the French sector in the vicinity of Champagne. Huge gains were made, and the Germans found themselves by the beginning of June within forty miles of Paris. Panic ensued there, many began to flee, and in London consideration was given to the withdrawal of the British Expeditionary Force from the continent.

That wound up, however, being the highpoint of the German campaign. Succeeding drives during the second week in June and again in mid-July stalled out quickly. Berlin's forces were overextended, exhausted, hit hard by the flu, and increasingly difficult to resupply. While their ranks were diminishing, moreover, those of their enemy were now rapidly increasing.[13]

Hundreds of thousands of American troops were beginning to arrive per month in France by late spring 1918 (so as to accelerate this process, it had been agreed that their weaponry would largely be provided by the French). By late July, they would number over a million. Many continued to lack training, and until May tensions persisted over their command. The Allies still wanted to incorporate the new troops into their own, now increasingly pressed and depleted, armies. At the beginning of the year, Pershing had again told Baker that "when the war ends, our position will be stronger if our army acting as such shall have played a distinct and definite part."[14] Under the impact of the crisis, the American general finally agreed to temporary brigading, but only on the condition that an explicit commitment be made by the British and French to the creation soon of an independent U.S. army. That was eventually formed at the end of July.

On the anniversary of the U.S. entrance into the war, the president told his countrymen that there was only one response they could make to Germany: "Force, Force to the utmost, Force without stint or limit, the righteous and triumphant Force which shall make Right the law of the world, and cast every selfish dominion down in the dust."[15] On that very day in April, American troops attached to the British army participated in the defense of Amiens. Others fought, with the French, in late May and early June at Chateau-Thierry and Belleau Wood. Still larger numbers would be involved in both sectors when the Allies began their counteroffensive during late July and August. But it would not be until September that American forces began to undertake major assignments on their own, ones they were still not well prepared for. These were to the east in the region of the Meuse-Argonne.

Wilson would later maintain that American troops won the war on the Western Front. That was a considerable exaggeration.[16] The principal U.S. contributions to the defeat of the Central Powers came in the realms of finance and supply (specifically supplies of steel, petroleum, and ships). Nevertheless, the appearance of very large numbers of U.S. troops had a by no means negligible effect on both Allied and German morale (their military role would likely have been far more important had the war lasted on into 1919).

On August 2, the German army went on the defensive. By September it would be seeking merely to return to the fortified position, the so-called Hindenburg Line, it had occupied in 1917. But as the Allies gained momentum, even that proved impossible to hold. Germany's position deteriorated further.[17]

Crises also beset the rest of the Central coalition. Fearful both of collapse and dismemberment (nationalist uprisings were now being actively encouraged by the Allies), Vienna felt the need to call for peace talks on September 14 (they were rebuffed). Soon after, the Ottoman Empire's southern defenses gave way before an assault led by Britain's General Edmund Allenby, his forces subsequently driving on in the direction of Damascus and Beirut.

Most serious of all—outside the Western Front—was the sudden collapse of the Bulgarian army, coming after a military standoff of over two and a half years. Rejecting the obvious comparison with what the Germans had done in Belgium, the Allies had maintained an army in the north of neutral Greece from the end of 1915 (the year Bulgaria had joined the war on the Central Powers' side) to mid-1917. They had then demanded the abdication of King Constantine, so as to bring to power a pro-Allied government in Athens led by Eleutherios Venizelos. Over time, Berlin's ability to support the Bulgarians declined, and that made it possible for the deadlock on this "Salonica Front" finally to be broken. A bold Allied offensive in mid-September compelled Sofia to sue for peace. The German command was stunned. Not only had the Allies cut them off from Constantinople, but Austria-Hungary was now in greater jeopardy. Moreover, the Balkans might be expanded into a major front.[18]

Above all because of the pressure it faced in France, Ludendorff was convinced that his army needed to regroup. It would otherwise be able neither to resist the Allies nor to put down the social unrest within Germany that he increasingly feared. He and other military leaders urged that Berlin should explore what kind of peace might be achieved on the basis of Wilson's Fourteen Points. If it was unacceptable, the thinking was that the war could be resumed. Along with members of the foreign ministry,

Ludendorff argued that there should also be a rearrangement of the German government so as to give the appearance of the regime change for which Wilson had been calling. On the night of October 4/5, a new chancellor, Max von Baden, dispatched a message to the U.S. president requesting a cease-fire and talks.[19]

*   *   *

This approach from Berlin seemed to provide Wilson with a golden opportunity—if, that is, Germany was truly beaten. The president believed he might use it as a way of committing the Allies to peace talks predicated on his ideas. As yet, neither Britain, nor France, nor Italy had committed to them. On the contrary, as victory came in sight, there seemed to the president more and more evidence that his partners were resuming methods of competition that would lead to conditions he did not want.

The British and French were vying over which of them would control the endgame in the Ottoman Empire, a prelude it seemed to a competitive, potentially explosive, carve-up of the Middle East. Italy, which had been promised Austro-Hungarian territory when it entered the war (in the Treaty of London of 1915) appeared determined to expand into the still roiling Balkans. Washington policy makers thought that the Allies might yet be planning to discriminate against other powers economically after the war. France, in particular, still seemed inclined toward the imposition on Germany of a too-punitive peace. And, on the other side of the world, Japan was sending many more troops than Wilson liked into Northeast Asia.

Never mind the solidification by the United States of a sphere of influence for itself in the western hemisphere, its own burgeoning merchant marine and navy, the fact that Wilson had actually held back on shipping for the Atlantic so as to build up American trade across the Pacific and in Latin America during the war, or the fact that the reconstruction and stabilization of the kind of international order it wanted in the eastern hemisphere proceeded very much from Washington's own pursuit of—what it saw as—America's self-interest. The president now saw himself as poised for a final struggle with backward "selfishness."[20]

In September, House had asked the president, "Do you not think the time has come for you to consider whether it would not be wise to try to commit the Allies to some of the things for which we are fighting?" "As the Allies succeed, your influence will diminish," he warned him.[21] Wilson's first effort to do this came with a speech at the Metropolitan Opera House in New York on September 27, 1918. Since 1914 the administration had been determined to play a central role in determining the terms under which the Great War would end. On one level, this address was meant to signal again to the other powers that that was its intention. On another, it was designed broadly to review what U.S. objectives were.

Washington wanted to reconstruct the kind of international order it desired and then provide greater safeguards against its destabilization, against future rearrangements of power, and against the exclusion of the United States from world markets. Wilson's goals would entail, he suggested in his speech, the elimination and exclusion of special alliances and politicized economic rivalries that he believed had in the past been the root cause of eastern hemisphere conflict. The powers of what he saw as the troublous Old World should instead commit to a "common concert to oblige the observance of common rights." The "indispensable instrumentality" for this was a League of Nations, and, the president maintained, the establishment of that had to be a part—it was "in a sense the most essential part"—of the peace settlement itself.[22]

Berlin's early October request for talks on the basis of the Fourteen Points, predicated on its hope that these might protect Germany against the loss of territory and heavy indemnities, might allow Wilson to carry this process further. The president's inclination was therefore to try to determine if his own goals with regard to Germany had been achieved and then, if so, to present the accomplishment of an armistice on such terms to the Allies as a fait accompli. Unsurprisingly, his partners resented what they saw as his effort to control the dialogue with Berlin. No more surprising, Wilson expressed resentment at any such insinuation.[23]

Wilson and House had always believed that too complete a victory over Germany would lead to an unstable settlement. The Allies would push for too much at the peace table. Germany would nurse a desire for revenge. The opportunity would be lost to transform Berlin into a buttress of eastern hemisphere order. The administration even continued to cherish a long-term vision whereby Germany (through membership in a pact or a league) would ultimately collaborate with other powers like Great Britain and the

United States to, as House had put it before the war, "ensure peace and the proper development of the waste places, besides maintaining an open door and equal opportunity to everyone everywhere."

But the president and his key adviser were also determined that Germany had to be taught a lesson and accept changes that would prevent it from becoming a threat again to the kind of international order that the United States wanted. These would include limits on its arms, the evacuation of all of the territory it had gained control over—to the east as well as west—and a political system sufficiently liberalized to prevent a small coterie from easily taking their country to war. Such concerns shaped Wilson's subsequent negotiations with Berlin (as in the end did ideas from the Allies and the need to be sensitive to domestic American opinion, much of which was worked up to a frenzy by this time against Germany).

In his initial response to Berlin, drawn up after consultation with Lansing and House and dated October 8, the president sought clarification. He wanted reassurance that Germany was ready to actually accept the Fourteen Points, that it was prepared immediately to begin the withdrawal of its forces from *all* occupied territories, and that the new chancellor was not speaking only as the agent of those who had been running the war. Although the note took the form, as Lansing put it, of a "[q]uery not a reply," it made America's European partners nervous. They told Wilson that Berlin needed to know that the Allies would never accede to an armistice except under such terms as Germany could not regroup and then restart the fighting. The prime ministers of Britain, France, and Italy wanted any armistice agreement to be drawn up in close consultation with Allied military authorities so as to ensure against that. They also noted that the Allies had never adhered to the Fourteen Points and insisted that negotiations to discuss them should be held.[24]

In its answer to Wilson's questions, on October 12, Berlin assured the president that it accepted the Fourteen Points and asserted that it was "ready to comply with the propositions of the President in regard to evacuation." It insisted that the new German government had been formed "in agreement with the great majority of the Reichstag" and spoke in the name "of the German government and . . . people."[25]

Two days later, Wilson replied that it had to be "clearly understood that the process of evacuation and the conditions of an armistice are matters which must be left to the judgment and advice of the military advisers" of the United States and its partners. "No arrangement" would be accepted that did not safeguard their "present military supremacy." Nor would an armistice be considered unless Berlin reined in its U-boats and took steps to ensure against depredations on the part of its retreating forces. The president, finally, was determined that Germany comply with what he had called for in his most recent Fourth of July address. Wilson had said that he wanted to see destroyed or reduced to impotency "arbitrary power" that could "separately, secretly, and of its single choice disturb the peace of the world."[26] At the same time that he sent this note, the president dispatched House to Europe to confer with Allied leaders.

Even though the cease-fire now under consideration was much less favorable than what had initially been envisioned, Berlin's answer of October 20 confirmed that it was willing to proceed. The driving factor remained conditions on the battlefield, especially the evident exhaustion of Germany's troops on the Western Front. There was a growing fear of invasion. But anxiety about domestic upheaval—stemming from popular impatience with continuance of the war—was also increasing. Germany confined itself to stating that it trusted Wilson would not approve of armistice conditions that would be irreconcilable with the honor of the German people and a peace of justice. It rejected the charge that its forces had acted inhumanely, but ended its unrestricted U-boat warfare. Again it insisted that its governmental changes were fundamental.[27]

Responding on October 23, Wilson announced that he was now prepared to take up Germany's request with America's partners "with the suggestion that" if the Allies were "disposed to effect peace" on the basis of the Fourteen Points "their military advisers and the military advisers" of the United States be asked to devise cease-fire terms. He added that he remained of the opinion that sufficient steps to curtail the power of the emperor had not been taken. If they were not, the United States would have to demand from Berlin "not peace negotiations, but surrender." These words were not only meant to ensure one of the administration's long-held goals. They were also designed to appease the enormous hostility toward the kaiser that had been built up at home in the United States. Yet it is by no means clear that the president was unwilling to accept something short of an end to the monarchy or even Wilhelm's abdication. Increasingly apprehensive about social unrest in the aftermath of the war, Wilson had in a meeting with his cabinet just the previous day "said he was afraid of Bolshevism in Europe, and the Kaiser was needed to keep it down—to keep some order."[28]

After his own objectives with regard to Germany were met, Wilson's hope had been that the Allies would feel compelled by public pressure to move toward an armistice and peace talks predicated on the Fourteen Points. It quickly became clear, however, that their acceptance of neither a cease-fire nor the Fourteen Points would be automatic. Britain, France, and Italy were loath to abandon their key goals. They also resented what they saw as the effrontery of the president trying to commandeer an unfolding victory that they felt was principally their hard-won own.

The Allies were more than happy to draft armistice terms. They had in fact already begun to do so. But they pushed for the inclusion in them of far-reaching provisions that—once accepted—would not only make resumption of the war on Berlin's part impossible, but, in key ways, predetermine the peace.[29] The United States would face a daunting challenge should it try to contest what Allied leaders claimed were provisions necessary to stop the fighting safely.

In connection with a meeting by House with Allied leaders in Paris, American policy makers essentially decided that they would concentrate on gaining their partners' formal adherence to the Fourteen Points. Once hostilities had ended, provided those had been accepted, Wilson and House believed that they would possess sufficient leverage to insist on the settlement they wanted, both at the peace conference and then through the League of Nations.[30]

But even this, it quickly became clear, was not going to be easy. House essayed a threat. He told the prime ministers that Wilson would otherwise "have no alternative but to tell the enemy that his conditions were not accepted by his Allies." The result might be that the United States would pursue a separate peace. But his interlocutors called his bluff. Lloyd George said he would deeply regret that, but the Allies would "go on fighting." Georges Clemenceau agreed.[31]

House then struck a deal with the French. Meeting privately with Clemenceau, on October 30, he apparently traded France's acceptance of the Fourteen Points for U.S. acceptance of some or all of the cease-fire conditions that Paris wanted. Clemenceau particularly wanted House's support for the occupation of the left bank of the Rhine, a provision that London had been opposing.[32]

Britain's support for most of the Fourteen Points came more easily, but Lloyd George adamantly resisted agreement to Point 2, which ostensibly championed the "freedom of the seas." Like the others, this point was susceptible of different interpretations. But none were really acceptable to a power that historically had seen its preeminent position in the world as tied to its sea power. The prime minister wanted, at a minimum, explicit qualifications.[33] London's stance reignited resentments of Britain that had burned red-hot in the Wilson administration in 1916. It also touched directly on what the president saw as a major cause of wars in the eastern hemisphere. For these reasons, a heated struggle ensued.

Wilson wanted not so much to protect the "freedom of the seas" as to rein in London's ability to deploy "blockades" unilaterally and to harness the Royal Navy to what he saw as common Anglo-American interests. He wanted naval power to be deployed by the great powers collectively in the eastern hemisphere via the League of Nations. The president had said as much earlier in the fall when talking with Sir Eric Geddes, First Lord of the Admiralty, who at the time was visiting the United States. When asked by Geddes what he meant by "the freedom of the seas," Wilson later told House that he replied "that vaguely he had in mind that any nation having become an outlaw as Germany was today, would be compelled to feel the weight of the united naval power of the world. He [the president] was distinctly opposed to any one nation exercising this power."[34]

The issue occasioned sharp words. On October 28, House told Sir William Wiseman, who had been acting for months as his go-between with the Foreign Office, to inform British negotiators that the United States would no sooner "submit to Great Britain's complete domination of the seas . . . than to Germany's domination of the land." If need be, America would create a bigger military establishment than Britain's. Subsequently he added that unless Lloyd George relented, "all hope of Anglo-Saxon unity would be at an end."[35]

President Wilson still hoped that such considerations would be decisive. Speaking broadly, he told House on October 29, "It is the fourteen points that Germany has accepted. England cannot dispense with our friendship . . . and the other Allies cannot without our assistance get their rights as against England."[36] Lloyd George nevertheless held out, and in the end all he would do is pledge, in a letter to the president, that the British would discuss the matter. Looking forward to the power he expected Washington would wield after the fighting was over, House chose to consider this a victory.[37]

Wilson's adviser came away from these talks in Paris feeling that Washington had basically achieved its goals with regard to the Allies. "I doubt whether any other of the heads of governments with whom we have been dealing quite realize how far they are now committed to the American peace programme," he cabled the president.[38] House was optimistic. But whether Washington would actually have the leverage to transform what had been achieved, namely formal acceptance of much of that—still quite imprecise—program, into the peace settlement it desired, was a question that remained to be answered.

*   *   *

The more pressing issue for Washington and the Allied leaders had to do with Germany. Would it accept an armistice on the terms that were going to be offered? On November 5, Lansing informed Berlin that the Allies had indicated their willingness to negotiate peace on the basis of the Fourteen Points, subject to two qualifications. Agreement could not be reached on Point 2. Furthermore, the Allies would insist that "compensation will be made by Germany for all damage done to the civilian population of the Allies and their property."[39]

The "terms of an armistice" were then communicated to German representatives by Foch on November 8. These provided for evacuation of Alsace-Lorraine and all territory Germany had come to occupy in Western Europe since 1914. All positions occupied in Eastern Europe would likewise need to be relinquished (though the timetable for this was subsequently modified in the interest of Central Power forces being used to combat disorder and social revolution in that area). Treaties that Berlin had concluded in Eastern Europe, most notably with Russia at Brest-Litovsk, were to be renounced. Germany's army would surrender a large proportion of its aircraft, heavy artillery, and machine guns (though the demand for the latter was quickly modified by Foch so that the military might suppress domestic German unrest). The U-boat fleet would be surrendered and much of the surface fleet interned (the latter had not played a significant role in the war, but the British Admiralty was determined to use this occasion to ensure that Berlin was reduced to a "second-rate Naval Power"). The blockade would continue, Germany would allow the occupation of its territory on the left bank of the Rhine, as well as U.S. and Allied control of three bridgeheads across that river. A strip of territory to its east would be demilitarized.[40]

These were sweeping provisions, far exceeding what German leaders had had in mind when they initiated armistice discussions in early October. Many U.S. and Allied officials doubted that Berlin would go along. They would not negotiate. What was expected was that, for a time, the fighting would continue.[41]

But too much had changed. Germany was left with no alternative but agreement. Its military position had continued to deteriorate. It had lost all of its allies. And, to a degree only belatedly perceived by the enemy, Berlin was now confronted by domestic insurrection. Over the previous ten days, soldiers and sailors at bases within Germany had begun to revolt. Protests broke out throughout the country in opposition to any continuance of what now seemed futile suffering. Demand grew for the emperor's removal.

That in fact transpired on November 9, the day after the cease-fire terms were received. Max von Baden simultaneously yielded the chancellorship to the Social Democratic Party leader Friedrich Ebert, who was immediately given the honor of ratifying Germany's defeat. The armistice went into force on November 11.[42]

*   *   *

However heady Wilson must have been feeling as the fighting in Europe came to a decision, one development in the days leading up to the cease-fire could not but have been disconcerting. That was the Republican triumph in the congressional off-year elections on November 5. The GOP's seizure, if only by two seats, of the Senate, in particular (by a wider margin, it also gained control of the House), suggested that the president might have a more difficult time than he had hoped getting his way with the Allies over the peace treaty and then getting that treaty ratified by the Senate (two-thirds of the upper house would have to register its approval).

Republicans claimed that the election constituted a repudiation of Wilson's foreign policy leadership. The vote does not in fact seem to have turned on that issue. But the president himself had given credence to this idea. Because he was fearful that he would not have the seats he wanted, Wilson had—in what many saw as a contradiction of the "politics is adjourned" wartime pose that he had been affecting—essentially tried to turn the election into such a referendum himself. Ten days before the election, he had asked voters to help the Democrats retain control of both houses as proof that Americans "wish me to continue as their unembarrassed spokesman in affairs at home and abroad."[43]

Wilson still did not seem to doubt that he would be able to rally Americans behind his program and indeed that this would suffice ultimately to enable him to dominate the Senate. But, as the fighting came to an end, he almost certainly did feel more pressure to show his counterparts in Europe just how substantial a force they were dealing with.

PART IV

The Paris Settlement (1919–20)

"Self-determination" is not a mere phrase. It is an imperative principle of action.
—Woodrow Wilson, February 11, 1918

[President Wilson] speaks to the masses in terms of the new diplomacy, but he deals with the leaders by means of the old.
—Ray Stannard Baker, March 8, 1919

Disguise it from ourselves as we may, the basic idea of the League is to begin some form of government for the world in which the ideas of the best class of men in the great civilized powers shall dominate.
—General Tasker H. Bliss, U.S. delegate to the Paris Peace Conference, 1919

[O]ne can see why the question is so constantly asked whether his [President Wilson's] talk means anything at all. His oratory is so great, and he is so convincing that he has been able to sway the multitudes in nearly all lands. But if he is not careful, the feeling of distrust for him will become universal.
—Edward M. House, May 31, 1919

CHAPTER 8

The Future of Europe—and the World

Deciding he would represent the American government there in person, President Wilson looked at the Paris Peace Conference as an opportunity to reconstruct and put on a more solid basis the international order Washington wanted.[1] Viewing Europe as central to the problem, the president aspired to inject greater stability into affairs on that continent. He hoped thereby to provide against future upheavals in trade; still more important, to ensure against changes in power relationships that might jeopardize the kinds of political and commercial arrangements desired elsewhere (above all—though increasingly less exclusively—in the western hemisphere and East Asia).

The administration expected to exercise considerable leverage over the proceedings. That would derive, as policy makers saw it, from the economic and military might the United States had demonstrated since 1917, from the debts owed the United States by its allies (combined with their hope of financial help), and from the enormous international popularity that had been built up behind the president as a consequence of the formulas set out in his Fourteen Points Address and elsewhere.[2]

During the war, Wilson had made a number of pledges. He had called for a nonvindictive settlement, for peace proceedings that would include discussions with the enemy, for a new and open—as opposed to traditional and secret—diplomacy. He had championed the self-determination of peoples, the equality of nations, and general disarmament (the reduction of national armaments "to the lowest point consistent with domestic safety").

Once it got under way in Paris, the conference began to depart rather quickly from these. Given his objectives, Wilson often felt he had to compromise. In other cases it is evident that his promises meant much less than appeared. The "smaller" allies were offered participation in plenary sessions that did little, while decision making was monopolized by the United States and major Allied powers in meetings, shrouded in secrecy, held behind closed doors. The Central Powers were left to await their fate, which turned out to be harsher than they had expected. The Americans exhibited interest in heading off a new arms race, but they were also determined not to cede Britain, as a matter of right, continued supremacy at sea.

Many colonial peoples had taken seriously Wilson's call for a new world order. Irish, Egyptian, Indian, Vietnamese, Korean, and other nationalists looked expectantly toward Paris, only to find that self-determination for them was not on the agenda.[3] But nor was it pending for the extra-European possessions of the Central Powers, though their ties to Germany and Turkey were definitely to be sundered. In Central and Eastern Europe, a number of new states were recognized by the big powers as independent, but even here—as for a century had been true in Latin America—their sovereignty was meant to be conditional on the discharge of their (great-power-determined) "international obligations"; ideally also on their acceptance of the tutelage of those powers.

France, in particular, would come to see the new states as vehicles for the containment of Germany and, farther east, of Bolshevism. But for Wilson, their creation also stemmed from his desire to put an end to European nationalism's explosive potential. The president and House wanted to provide against a replay of the developments in the Balkans that had helped to bring on war in 1914. Little did they appreciate just how much volatile material would remain, how difficult it would be to establish clear-cut territorial boundaries along ethnic lines in this part of the world, or how sweeping might be the ambitions of some of these new products of the national idea.

Wilson expected that the inexperienced and weak new states were likely to become the target of other powers' territorial expansion. This was among the reasons he was eager to create the League of Nations.[4] Its establishment had become the president's most important priority by the time he reached Paris. Wilson expended political capital and was willing to devote precious time so that this issue might be addressed before any other. He was also determined to have the League's charter—or "covenant"—attached to all of the peace treaties.

Throughout history many people had dreamed and spoken of a "parliament of man," and the concept had generally come to have attached to it an unselfish, as well as utopian, flavor. But the devil was, so to speak, always going to be in the details. The only way to really comprehend what Wilson had in mind is to examine the structure of the particular league he endorsed and how those plans were related to earlier projects he—and his predecessors—had promoted.

This league was viewed as a mechanism, indeed—given the reluctance of average Americans to become "entangled" in the Old World—perhaps the only mechanism by which the United States might on a regular basis constitute a factor in eastern hemisphere affairs (while in theory it would have a scope that was universal, it was never looked at by Wilson as an institution that would compromise, as he had put it in 1913, Washington's "paramount influence" in the Americas).[5] While freeing up American might so that it might be used in the eastern hemisphere, the new body was also intended to impose restrictions on particular behaviors by great powers there that might unsettle the international order to be reconstructed following the Great War. And finally, principally by way of great-power dominance of its powerful Executive Council, this league was envisioned as a mechanism that would ensure "the proper development of the waste places"—of the underdeveloped countries—while "maintaining an open door and equal opportunity to every one everywhere," as House had put it in 1913.

Only after planning for the league was under way did the triumphant allies, principally the leaders of France, Great Britain, and the United States, really come to focus on a settlement with Germany, the most formidable of the Central Powers. Discussions on that would drag on through the spring (while peace treaties with Austria, Bulgaria, Hungary, and Turkey were drafted over a period of many more months, after Wilson and his counterparts had left for home and turned over the details to their subordinates).

* * *

Reconstructing and stabilizing the kind of international order desired inevitably necessitated the containment of any further challenges or disruptions. At the beginning of November, Lansing and Wilson read a report by State Department official William C. Bullitt warning of widespread discontent with the old order of things and of a possible "bath of Bolshevism" throughout Europe after the war.[6] Herbert Hoover voiced fear of "Bolshevism and rank anarchy," connecting these—particularly throughout Central and Eastern Europe—to the likelihood of "raging famine."[7] House opined that the president should mark the signing of the armistice with a "message to the world" that included a "steadying note." "The world is in ferment," he wrote, "civilization itself is trembling in the balance."[8] Before a joint session of Congress on November 11, Wilson took that tone. "The present and all that it holds," he said, "belongs to the nations and the peoples who preserve their self-control."[9]

The best way to head off revolution, administration leaders were convinced, was with food. Rapidly, House, Wilson, and Hoover moved to set up a relief program under the latter's direction. The distribution of foodstuffs would address conditions that promoted unrest, while the provision or denial of the same would be used as a means of influencing politics in recipient countries.[10] Of great importance, American agriculture would simultaneously be relieved of the burden of towering end-of-the-war surpluses. The U.S. government would provide credits in those cases where the targeted countries could not immediately pay.

The administration insisted that since food of American provenance would predominate, the United States should have control. This was in line with a general inclination, now that the fighting was over, to eschew the pooling of resources and end the role of inter-Allied bodies. Officials wanted Washington's influence to prevail over that of Britain or France. Branding the relief as American, Wilson hoped, would win appreciation and support from those people and governments who received it. There ensued a massive—largely American-controlled—program, coordinated from Hoover's headquarters in Paris. It extended throughout the continent, though the inclusion of Germany had to await the modification of the blockade over the next several months.[11]

Wilson had already been assured by the American ambassador to Italy, Thomas Nelson Page, that he was "adored" by the "common people" of Europe.[12] To him this was confirmed by the rapturous public welcomes he received—in France, England, and Italy—following his arrival on the continent in mid-December. It was an idea paired in the president's mind with the thought that—as he told members of the Inquiry aboard the U.S.S. *George Washington* on the way over—his Allied counterparts "did not really represent their peoples."[13]

But Wilson quickly discovered that Lloyd George and Clemenceau were not willing to accept the implication that they should simply fall in with his views. Clearly more skeptical of the meaning of Wilson's popular reception, and judging rightly that he would not take up lightly the alternative of breaking with them, they also knew that they controlled stronger legislative majorities within their governments than did he. Would Wilson, whose party had actually lost control of both the Senate and the House in November, in fact be able to deliver on the agreements he made in Paris?[14]

The first big challenge Wilson confronted came at the end of December from France. French leaders, in this case quite like their counterparts in Britain, resented Wilson's failure, as they saw it, to acknowledge sufficiently the role their country had played in the defeat of Germany, what the war had cost them, or their right to play a role second to none in shaping the peace. In a speech before the Chamber of Deputies, Clemenceau was defiant, and he made clear how limited were the commitments he felt he had made under the Fourteen Points. It would be foolish, he suggested, for France to rest its security on a league. He would not oppose it, but he looked upon the idea as a supplement to other guarantees it would need. The League was best discussed after more important issues had been settled.[15]

House pronounced the speech a great diplomatic blunder that might "cost France many millions that she might otherwise have had from us."[16] He had worked with Clemenceau against Lloyd George to get the Fourteen Points accepted two months before. Now he told the president "that in my opinion we would have to work with England rather than with France if we hoped to get the things for which we were striving through." Wilson, he wrote, "needed some persuasion before he agreed with me, but finally did so."[17]

At the end of the war, British-American relations became frayed and tense again, as they had been in 1916. On both sides there were expectations of heightened trade rivalry and competition for oil.[18] Financially and economically in disarray, London worried about a United States that was stronger than ever and now possessed of a large merchant marine. Washington suspected that London might deviate from its historic commitment to the open door, also that the empire might seek to acquire more territory. It was uneasy about London's control of transoceanic cable routes. Differences over the treatment of Germany, especially about reparations, loomed. London feared an American challenge to its naval primacy, and the two powers had already squared off over the question of freedom of the seas. In his State of the Union address, just before he set sail, a determined Wilson had called upon Congress to recommit to the ambitious, "naval programme which was undertaken before we entered the war."[19] Three days later, aboard ship, he vented in private that if Britain did not agree to limits on its naval power "we would build the biggest Navy in the world . . . and then if they would not limit it, there would come another and more terrible and bloody war and England would be wiped off the face of the map" (the thought that such a conflict was possible was in fact widespread among planners in the U.S. Navy).[20] For his part, Lloyd George had recently remarked that Washington's unilateral approach to relief appeared a bad precedent for a cooperative League of Nations.[21]

Yet the two governments continued to share much in common in terms of the kind of international order they wanted. And there were ways each saw working with the other as of potential value. In particular, as the conference approached, Wilson needed support for his goal of having the League receive priority, and British leaders decided to give him that.

The Lloyd George government did so for a variety of reasons. Some prominent figures had concluded that a league would be a valuable mechanism for stabilizing international affairs after the war. The idea was also popular at home. Others emphasized that it might be a starting point for a close working relationship with the United States. As Grey had hoped, it might be a means of harnessing U.S. power to the maintenance of the peace, even to the development of a "pax Anglo-Americana." In this regard, Jan Smuts, the influential South African member of the Imperial War Cabinet, thought he saw a path by which the British Empire could pursue a course more independent of France. For still others, the principal attraction was that such support might win Britain greater leverage over other, more heatedly contested policies. And, indeed, following London's decision, Wilson showed a marked inclination to defer controversy over navy building and argued that creation of the League would make irrelevant the question of "freedom of the seas."[22]

*   *   *

The Paris Peace Conference—actually what was supposed to be a preliminary inter-Allied conference before the negotiations with Germany (that

never really came)—formally got under way on January 18 when all delegates assembled together in a large hall at the Quai D'Orsay, the home of
the French foreign ministry. But it quickly became apparent that the real
business would be done not only by groups that were smaller, and therefore
more wieldy, but by bodies composed principally of representatives of the
major powers. This was even true of the commission set up to establish the
League of Nations. Ostensibly a "parliament of man," an institution that
might reflect the recently vaunted equality of nations, the League would be
established mainly as the result of British and American collaboration. The
British ambassador to France, Lord Derby, expressed the idea on January
6. Reporting on a conversation with House, he wrote Balfour that the latter
had told him Wilson was determined to work with London. "The amusing
thing is he apparently contemplates that the League of Nations shall begin
by a joint agreement between England and America and that other Nations
will then be told you must come into this or take the consequences."[23]

The tone had in fact already been set during the previous week. On
January 12, what would come to be called the Council of Ten began to
meet. This body, composed of the premiers and foreign ministers of Britain, the United States, France, Italy, and Japan, decided how the conference
would be run. Key was the idea that the great powers would dominate
decision making about the peace (Japan's role to be confined principally to
issues related to the Far East). (In late March, the Council of Ten would be
superseded by an even smaller, more manageable inner Council of Four,
composed of Wilson, Lloyd George, Clemenceau, and the Italian premier,
Vittorio Orlando.) Smaller powers (in terms of might, by no means necessarily population or geography) would be offered an opportunity to make
presentations to the Council on issues of importance to them. They would
participate in occasional, mostly perfunctory, plenary sessions and might
be enlisted in the work of what were envisioned to be several, great-power-
dominated, committees or commissions. The hope was to keep them busy
and mollified, though in its operation this system was to generate considerable resentment.[24]

In early December, it had been agreed among the major powers that
they would each send five delegates to the conference. Which other countries would be included, and how many delegates they would have,
remained open. Over thirty nations, who had either declared war on or
broken relations with Germany, sought representation. On the theory
(voiced by Lansing) that those Latin American governments that had

followed Washington's lead in the war would also vote with it at the peace conference, the United States supported the inclusion of eleven other western hemisphere nations. These included countries, like Cuba and Panama, where there were American military bases, and others, like Nicaragua and Haiti, which were under U.S. occupation.[25] (The Inquiry meanwhile had proceeded on the assumption that the United States would also have a "dominating influence" at the conference in regard to any discussions relating to the Americas.)[26]

Brazil, which had long sought to enhance its position in South America by distinguishing itself as a supporter of the United States, succeeded in winning Wilson's help to get more than the two seats it initially was assigned. Eventually, despite Lloyd George's misgivings, it received three, the same as war-torn Belgium and Serbia. The president also put himself forward as China's sponsor at the conference, asking for it to receive more than one seat (it got two).[27]

The British prime minister meanwhile asked for separate representation for India and each of the self-governing dominions, this largely in response to their pressure for acknowledgment of their huge wartime contributions. (House took this as a portent of the British Empire's eventual disintegration.)[28]

Along with Wilson and Lansing, the American commissioners consisted of House, General Bliss (Washington's representative on the Supreme War Council), and the retired career diplomat Henry White, chosen because the president—surely unfortunately, given his objectives—could not bring himself to include a more prominent Republican, like Taft. Wilson rarely, in any event, took any of them except House into his confidence. Otherwise, over the course of the conference, he sought advice from men who had been part of his war cabinet, such as Baruch, Hoover, and Vance McCormick. Experts from the Inquiry and the Treasury and State Departments had been brought over to provide the president and House information as needed. All told, there were more than thirteen hundred American personnel in Paris, headquartered at the Hôtel Crillon.[29]

Another revealing, and heated, procedural discussion among the big powers revolved around the question of the official language of the conference. At European diplomatic gatherings, French had reigned unchallenged since the eighteenth century. However, at the meeting of the Council of Ten on January 15, Lloyd George and Wilson contended for English *and* French. The president claimed that English had become the diplomatic language of the Pacific. It was also spoken by more people. Perhaps more to the point, Wilson said that while French had undoubtedly been "the language of European diplomacy in the past," "we were now dealing with a new case," the "rest of the world had come into the arena." "A new Great Power was now concerned in the business of world diplomacy. He referred to the United States, whose language was English. The precedent in favour of the French language in diplomacy was only a European precedent. The language of diplomacy on the other side of the globe was English." The French were wounded but eventually gave in, Foreign Minister Stéphen Pichon nevertheless remarking that even Bismarck, "who was no friend of France," had raised no objection to French being the language of the Treaty of Berlin."[30]

In the run-up to the formal opening of the conference, the members of the Council also considered what the policy on press access should be. A hundred reporters were in Paris from the United States alone. They and others may or may not have expected a literal implementation of open diplomacy ("open covenants . . . openly arrived at"), but there is little question that they expected, and wanted, more than they received. Wilson now contended that what he had meant was simply that there would be no more secret treaties. He and the other great-power leaders were largely of a mind, determined to keep as tight a lid as possible on their proceedings. Feeling the need to make a gesture, it was agreed that most plenary sessions might be opened to the press. The president enlisted the American journalist, and Wilson devotee, Ray Stannard Baker as his press liaison. But as things turned out, Baker was starved of information and his boss wound up giving very few interviews. House was not alone in fearing that such arrangements would complicate Wilson's ability to hold onto and marshal public opinion.[31]

*   *   *

Pursuant to a resolution passed by the Council of Ten on January 22, the second plenary session, on the twenty-fifth, created a commission to work out the details of the League of Nations. Wilson became chair. At the behest of Lloyd George and Clemenceau, who were seeking to mollify the "smaller" states, the lesser Allies were allowed token representation, something the president had resisted.[32] But Wilson would, in any event, largely dominate the ensuing process, working along with Britain's Lord Robert Cecil (as well as House, Smuts, David Hunter Miller, an American specialist on international law, and C. J. B. Hurst, of the Foreign Office).

The British and American delegates succeeded in having a draft that they had already reached considerable agreement on made the basis for discussion when the commission began to meet on February 3. Two noteworthy challenges were subsequently mounted, but the essentials of this "Hurst-Miller draft" went on to become the League's "covenant."[33]

One challenge came from representatives of "smaller" nations. Noting that the draft relegated real control over the League to an inner Executive Council, they expressed resentment that membership on that body was to be composed only of major powers. Epitácio Pessoa, of Brazil (soon to become that nation's president), opined that the Council would not be an "organ" of the League but rather of "Five Nations [the United States, Britain, France, Italy, and Japan], a kind of tribunal to which everyone would be subject." Paul Hymans, of Belgium, ventured that the "smaller" countries should have an equal number of seats.

Wilson in January had taken the view that the world's many "smaller" states might be allotted places up to such number as they were still outnumbered by the great powers. At first, he defended the draft, which reflected Cecil's preference. But in the face of "small"-state complaints, the commissioners fell back to the president's earlier position. "Small" nations, selected by the League membership, would occupy four seats (on a rotating basis), while five others would belong (on a permanent basis) to the major powers.[34]

Another challenge was mounted by France. A week after Clemenceau's explosive speech before the Chamber of Deputies, House had talked with the prime minister and come away feeling that he had convinced him that the League was "for the best interests" of his nation. House had argued, he recorded in his diary, that developments since 1914 had left but "one great military power on the Continent," namely France. England "would not look with favor" on this situation and would seek, as it historically had, to promote a counterbalance. Paris and London also had points of potential disagreement and conflict throughout the world. Neither Britain nor the United States had been compelled "to come to the aid of France" in the present war, House told Clemenceau. Would the French "not feel safer if

England and America were in a position" where in the future they would be obligated to do so? Given the isolationist outlook of the American people, the president's adviser implied, if France "lost this chance which the United States offered through the League of Nations, it would never come again."[35]

House may have increased Clemenceau's interest in a league, but the kind of organization the prime minister inclined toward was quite different than that embodied in the Hurst-Miller draft. The French felt that the Anglo-American model would not provide much protection for their interests, particularly if Germany rearmed in secret and suddenly launched another war. They wanted a league that for an extended period would bar Germany. And they wanted one that would act as a vehicle to hold their defeated foe to stringent terms. Such a league would have to have an army that it could readily employ, drawing on international forces. To the exasperation of delegates like House, Wilson, and Cecil, Paris's delegates vigorously pressed for these ideas before the commission, starting on February 11.[36]

The British and American delegates saw the French conception of the League as a threat to the kind of stabilization they wanted after the war and as an effort to tie their nations' interests to those of France. Acting together, they accepted inessential changes but rallied the commission against the thrust of Paris's proposals. Wilson argued that Germany's economy had collapsed. It would also not be able to hide its preparations (he assumed as well that it would be deterred by the U.S. commitment to the League). He explained that political reasons would make impossible American acceptance of the French model. And he disparaged Paris's idea as verging on "international militarism." Cecil, still more bluntly and openly, admonished the French much in the way that House had privately warned Clemenceau a month before. The League was an Anglo-American "present" to France. If spurned because it did not amount to more, the alternative would likely be that London and Washington would stand apart from the continent and forge an alliance just between themselves.[37]

One additional controversy emerged immediately before the draft Covenant was scheduled to be presented to the conference as a whole. Since the turn of the century, Japanese (like other Asians) had faced discriminatory treatment when seeking to emigrate (or even travel) to many places around the Pacific that had come to be dominated by peoples of European background. Such places included Australia, New Zealand, British Columbia, and the west coast of the United States. The Japanese government, and public, had been deeply offended. Having become a major power and having fought beside the British Empire and the United States in the Great War, Tokyo now wanted these prejudicial policies and practices expunged, even if at first only on a rhetorical level. It also felt that the British and American response would signal whether the League was meant simply as a vehicle to ensure Anglo-American dominance internationally.

On February 13, Makino Nobuaki, one of Japan's delegates on the commission, moved an amendment to a clause already in the draft that was meant to protect people against discrimination on the basis of religious belief. It took as its starting point a major theme that Wilson had been emphasizing over the previous year. "The equality of nations being a basic principle of the League of Nations," the amendment read, "the High Contracting Parties agree to accord, as soon as possible, to all alien nationals of States members of the League equal and just treatment in every respect, making no distinction, either in law or in fact, on account of their race or nationality."

This has come to be referred to as the "racial equality clause." Neither Woodrow Wilson nor any of the people close to him believed in such equality. Indeed, the president believed in quite the opposite, a world composed of many distinct "races," of different capabilities, in which all of those who were not of English, Scottish (like himself), or Dutch background were somewhere back down a figurative trail behind—and needing the guidance of—people like himself. He was also well aware of the hostility that would be aroused toward both him (and the League) in the western United States if language along the lines of what Makino desired was adopted. Yet Wilson also wanted Japan in the League, principally so as to restrain and redirect that power and prevent it from challenging, particularly in the Pacific–East Asia region, the kind of international order Washington sought.

House had earlier tried but failed to finesse the issue by suggesting more anodyne language to the Japanese. On February 13, instead of meeting Japan's wishes, the commission decided to avoid all reference to religious tolerance, as well as racial equality, from the draft. In response, Tokyo's delegates made it clear that they would raise the matter again at a later stage.

The best outcome for the United States, House came to believe, would be for the British to be seen by Japan as the principal obstacle. Prime Ministers William Hughes, of Australia, and William Massey, of New Zealand, were vociferous and blunt in their opposition. At a commission meeting many weeks later in April, the Japanese asked merely for language endorsing "the principle of equality of nations and just treatment of their nationals" to be included in the Covenant's preamble. This won the backing of most of the delegates. But the British voted in opposition, while Wilson and House abstained. In his capacity as chair, the president then ruled, on dubious grounds, that without unanimity an amendment of this kind could not be entertained.[38]

*   *   *

On February 14, just prior to his departure that evening for a short trip back to the United States, Wilson read the text of the commission's handiwork aloud to the conference's third plenary session. The most important features can be summarized briefly. The Covenant provided (1) for a Body of Delegates that would meet at regular intervals and within which all member states would have one vote; (2) for an Executive Council composed of the five major-power allies in the war plus four other members selected by the Body of Delegates; and (3) for a permanent administrative Secretariat, led by a Secretary-General chosen by the Executive Council. New members might in the future be added to the League by the positive affirmation of two-thirds of the Body of Delegates. Such would have to be "self-governing countries," able to give "guarantees" of their intention to observe their "international obligations," and they would have to accept the League's "principles" as to the size of their naval and military establishments. For all members, this size was to reflect what was considered necessary for "national safety and the enforcement by common action of international obligations."

Article 10 constituted an undertaking on the part of members "to respect and preserve as against external aggression the territorial integrity and existing political independence" of all states who belonged to the League. If any such challenge materialized, "the Executive Council" would "advise upon the means by which this obligation shall be fulfilled." *Any* threat of war was a matter of League concern (Article 11), "whether immediately affecting" any of the members or not, and the organization reserved "the right to take any action . . . deemed wise . . . to safeguard the peace of nations." In accordance with Articles 12 to 17, members were to agree to refer disagreements between them, not resolvable via diplomacy, "either to arbitration or to inquiry by the Executive Council." To deal with judiciable disputes, the Executive Council would create a Permanent Court of International Justice. Any member (or nonmember) that disregarded these procedures for settling conflicts would be subjected to isolation and to such military action as decided upon by the Executive Council.[39]

Article 19 outlined provisions by which many of the territories that had been controlled by the Central Powers would be turned into "mandates" under the supervision-tutelage of the League. Article 21 aimed "to secure and maintain freedom of transit and equitable treatment for the commerce" of all members. All existing international bureaus, including a new one addressed to the particular problems of industrial labor, were henceforth to be housed by the League in accordance with Articles 20 and 22.[40]

The Covenant represented the most recent and comprehensive of U.S. efforts to stabilize the international order it wanted since Washington had begun to move out onto the global stage at the end of the nineteenth century. Its antecedents included not only the arbitration treaties, world court projects, periodic Hague conferences, and league ideas that a number of American leaders had supported, but also mechanisms by which the United States had sought to inject order into particular geographic regions.[41] Among these were the various initiatives by which Washington had endeavored to exercise supervision and bring stability unilaterally to lands in the Caribbean and, collectively, with other powers, to China. Likewise, they included Washington's efforts to substitute a "harmonious approach" for a politically competitive and potentially conflict-inducing state of affairs among big powers interested in the latter country (this was an approach that Wilson had earlier deviated from but come back to in 1917). In the western hemisphere, the United States had striven to prevent any other great power from playing a political-military role. In China (as in Siberia since mid-1918), where such was not feasible, the strategy had been to prevent unwanted activity on the part of others by absorbing them into an approach that was collective.

In the western hemisphere, as well as China, U.S. policy since the end of the nineteenth century had been to shore up and stabilize political boundaries and frameworks for trade that had been established earlier in the 1800s. Wilson indeed described the thrust of his league as an effort to have the "doctrine of President Monroe" adopted "as the doctrine of the world."[42] The idea was to depoliticize boundaries and trade frameworks, to take them "out of politics" (as the Taft people had put it, or "neutralize" them, in parlance employed by both Knox and House), so as to secure the international arena as American leaders believed it should be, realizing in the process, they had no doubt, a worldwide "community of interest."

Not unlike a number of other prominent American political figures, especially after August 1914, House and Wilson had become convinced that global order required measures that went beyond those that had been at the forefront of discussions at The Hague (in 1918, Wilson was not even in favor of a court being provided for in the Covenant). From 1913, House had actively supported a political "pact" or "league" under the lead of Great Britain and the United States. And the administration's favored prototype for this was the regional Pan-American Pact, promoted from late 1914. Under this, the nations of the Americas would collaboratively address both internal and external challenges to the kind of hemispheric order desired by Washington. International boundaries, which had been a particular source of conflict in South America in the past, would be settled, after which the territorial inviolability of every state would be ensured by a collective guarantee. No country would have recourse to force over any issue before a dispute was referred to conflict settlement mechanisms. And there would be greater regulation of the region's arms. Wilson and House hoped that these ideas, to their annoyance still not implemented in the Americas, would provide a model for the postwar stabilization of Europe and, by extension, the rest of the world.[43]

The most fundamental threats to the maintenance and stability of the kind of international arrangements desired by American leaders had for years been seen to lie in activity and attitudes by others—including the U.S. public—defined as "irresponsible" or "selfish." In response, policy makers had sought ways of inducing or, if necessary and the stakes were high enough, forcing other countries to "behave." The idea was to get countries and peoples to accept the international order Washington desired and, in their domestic affairs, uphold what were asserted to be their obligations to outsiders. The right of countries to sovereignty, so far as American leaders saw it, was actually conditional on such conduct, on countries being both able and willing to "behave."

The league championed by House and Wilson in 1919 would promote such "proper" conduct by a variety of means and on several levels. The major powers of the eastern hemisphere were, in essence, offered a deal.

They would consent to limits on their freedom of action. They would help sustain the international order that was going to be reconstructed at Paris. In exchange, they would be guaranteed a permanent seat at the high table of global (or at least eastern hemisphere) affairs. As House and Wilson saw it, their security would be enhanced. They would live in a world where there would be greater scope for their economic expansion, less chance of friction and conflict among them, and improved supervision of, and therefore possibilities in, the underdeveloped world (this by virtue of the leverage the powers would—if united—be able to exert; viewed another way, by virtue of the fact that countries like China would no longer be able to play the powers off against one another and evade "reform").

The other powers would see more to gain than lose by this deal, it was hoped. In the face of British and American agreement, they also would believe they had little option. But, should any formidable states not come into this pact, the idea was that they would be intimidated from challenging the international order reconstructed at Paris by the overwhelmingly preponderant power possessed by the states that did (the president's "concert of power").[44] Wilson put great stock in the deterrent value of the League, and that was one reason he thought it unlikely the United States would have forcefully to intervene across the Atlantic to uphold the kind of order it wanted again. While Wilson and House described the balance of power as an inadequate, undependable method of stabilization (partly because Washington—because of domestic American sentiment—did not seem easily able, either in East Asia or Europe, to play the role of ultimate balancer), they were, as previously noted, by no means disinterested in questions of the distribution of world power.

In his first concrete efforts to flesh out a plan for a league, House had in mid-1918 actually ventured that the "League might be confined to the Great Powers." "If the smaller nations are taken in," he wrote Wilson, "the question of equal voting power is an almost insurmountable obstacle." He pointed out that several of the "smaller nations have indicated a willingness to come into a League of Nations only upon condition that the voting power of each country shall be the same." (This was comparable to a controversy that had dogged American efforts to set up a new, more juridical, world court during the Roosevelt and Taft administrations.) The problem with this was that they could outvote the big powers while the latter would shoulder all of the burdens for upholding an international system that, House was sure, was in everyone's best interest. At most, he suggested, the "smaller nations" might have "representation without voting power, just as our Territories have had representation in Congress without votes" (not an analogy that would have been appreciated by the "smaller" states). In response, Wilson insisted that the "small" nations could not be excluded from the League because that would be "contrary to all our protestations concerning them." Yet he granted the force of House's argument.[45]

The issue was ultimately resolved at the conference by a plan that offered all "small" states membership, though equality only in a Body of Delegates of limited importance. Since the "small" states could not dominate, a deal was now possible that carried clear advantages. The "small" states were still likely to prefer participation to nonparticipation, as that seemed to offer enhanced recognition, acceptance, and protection against aggression. In exchange, membership would entail on their part acceptance and execution of what the major powers defined as their "international obligations."

Many peoples, of course, especially in Africa and Asia (and the Western Pacific), still lived in territories that were not legally independent but under outside rule. In general, Wilson and his advisers were not eager to see that situation changed. They were not confident that the peoples who lived in those areas were ready to "behave," as they were not seen biologically as "self-governed" peoples. Instead, they should continue under the tutelage of outsiders until they could and would "behave" in a manner that was consistent with "civilization."

However much an independence where Africans and Asians conducted themselves as the "civilized" world's leaders wanted constituted an ideal, therefore, Wilson was not anticolonial in the context of 1919. The Central Powers should lose their territories in Africa and Asia. They had mistreated their colonial peoples, he was now sure (though that was not the main reason the president supported the view that they should lose those lands).[46] But he was not in favor of independence for those who had been "liberated."

At the same time, from Washington's standpoint, formal colonialism also carried with it great dangers, these flowing principally from the fact that the policies pursued in colonies were a function of decisions taken unilaterally by individual "home" nations. Colonialism represented the ultimate politicization of the competition by "advanced" states for markets and influence in the underdeveloped world. As such, it constituted a potential—in many places an already existing—obstacle to participation in those regions on the part of the new leader of "civilization" (namely, the United States). Simultaneously, it entailed the prospect of future "advanced"-state conflicts over territory, which in turn carried the risk of instability and undesirable reconfigurations of power.

The mandate system would, as Wilson and House saw it, work against these problems arising in the lands being detached from Germany and the Ottomans. On the one hand, it would promote the stabilization of the international order being reconstructed by providing supervision for those peoples "incapable" as yet of "responsible" independence. On the other, it would also work toward such stabilization by taking those lands "out of politics." It would restrain the "greed" that might otherwise lead to friction over trade or territorial positions, "greed" that might lead to a new war, to the exclusion of American economic access, or to new aggregations of power. (What Wilson may have hoped to do with the forfeited territories of the Central Powers was to push a new system of "civilized" oversight that might not only check the unilateral activity—"selfishness"—of rivals in those lands but even point the way more broadly to an internationaliza-tion of the other empires the European powers had constructed, especially since the mid-nineteenth century.)[47] Instead of simply being annexed by the various conquerors (a naked division of spoils that would also "dis-credit the conference"), Wilson wanted Central Power territories unready for independence to legally be turned over to the League to be supervised, through individual trustees or mandatories, under imposed conditions (such as maintenance of the open door).[48]

If there was one distinctively Wilsonian element of the Covenant, it was Article 10. Providing for a positive and collective guarantee of the "territo-rial integrity" and "political independence" of all members, this found its way into the Covenant largely at the insistence of the president. Lloyd George, like Lansing, had preferred a "negative guarantee," wherein each member would forswear hostile activity against another until League mech-anisms had been given ample opportunity to settle a dispute. Violation of that pledge would turn a country into an "outlaw" and occasion an Execu-tive Council meeting to determine the appropriate response.

But the "positive guarantee" had been a part of the Pan-American Pact idea and was championed by the president on the grounds that it would show that the League was serious (during the commission's discussions the French had supported him on this). To Wilson, it was "the key to the whole Covenant," the embodiment of what he meant by making the Monroe

Doctrine the "doctrine of the world." The prewar Hague approach had been too "wishy-washy." Responding the previous August to an early British blueprint for a league (drawn up by the government-appointed Phillimore committee), the president had complained to Wiseman that it had "no teeth." Wilson was determined to have a league that would be "virile." He saw Article 10 as the centerpiece of his plan for postwar stabilization. It would also become, in the United States, one of the most debated of the Covenant's provisions.[49]

At the plenary session on January 25 that set up the League of Nations commission, President Wilson had spoken before the assembled delegates. Following House's advice, he told them that the United States was, "[i]n a sense," "less interested in this subject than the other nations here assembled." This was because "[w]ith her great territory and her extensive sea borders," it was "less likely that the United States should suffer from the attack of enemies than that many of the other nations here should suffer." U.S. ardor for a league derived not from "fear and apprehension," but rather from "ideals." The tone of the speech was consonant with the central theme that had been and would continue to be featured throughout Wilson's term in office, including the time he spent in Paris: the United States was the one disinterested, unselfish power, acting on behalf of "the cause of justice and liberty for men of every kind and place." That the president said this, likely even convinced himself that it was the case, does not however relieve historians from taking cognizance of his project's quite clearly Washington-centered purpose.[50]

CHAPTER 9

The Treaty of Versailles

Discussion of the settlement with Germany proceeded more slowly. It was also attended by much greater disagreement on the part of the most interested major powers. By March it was clear to House and Wilson that they had achieved a lot less than hoped in the armistice negotiations of late fall. British and, especially, French leaders, however eager to have good relations with the United States, were demonstrating their determination to pursue objectives seemingly at odds with the Fourteen Points and a reintegrative peace. These were in line with what they took to be their own vital foreign policy and domestic political interests.

It was also increasingly clear that they had the backing not only of their political establishments, but—again especially in the case of France—of their own publics.[1] Economic leverage was less than expected as well. The Allies owed huge sums to the United States. But the Treasury Department concluded that this indebtedness should not be discussed at Paris. Decisions might be taken before it was clear what their impact would be on American "financial safety," on Allied trade policies, or on the U.S. international competitive position. Administration figures also became convinced that any negotiations that would reduce the debts were likely to enflame U.S. public opinion.[2] Wilson's hope of financial leverage was consequently reduced to the hope that the European powers would want to please Washington so as to be eligible for credits and to attract private American investment.[3] Meanwhile, the United States was to some extent dependent on the Allies, particularly in regard to the maintenance and repatriation of the American army.[4]

However much the president and his family circle would eventually place the blame on his longtime adviser, both Wilson and House were coming to see compromise as critical to continued global influence.[5] Wilson and House were likewise beginning to worry that any extended delay in achieving a settlement—given the languishing European economy and the spread of Bolshevism—might jeopardize fundamentally the international order they wanted to reconstruct.

Continued amity with Britain and France, at some level, seemed crucial at a time when the reintegration of neither Japan, nor Germany, nor Russia could be taken for granted. It seemed essential to the establishment of the League of Nations. That body was envisioned as a mechanism that would secure and stabilize the desired international order. It was designed ideally to hold in place what American leaders considered a well-made peace, one where major sources of potential dispute had already been removed. Over time, however, House and Wilson placed more and more emphasis on the idea that the League might be able, after the fact, to rectify a settlement substantially different from what they had originally intended.

The Big Three (Italy and Japan played no significant role in these discussions) all had different views, reflecting what they took to be their country's interests, their nation's geographic proximity to Germany, and their historical ties and experiences with that power. Facing massive reconstruction costs, and convinced that Germany before long could again become the most powerful state in Western Europe, Clemenceau pressed for a decidedly onerous settlement. He and other French leaders wanted a partial dismemberment of the large, populous state created in 1871. They also wanted to impose heavy reparations. For France, like Britain, the desire for the latter was influenced, though not created, by the position on Allied debts taken by the American delegation. The Allies wanted these to be written down dramatically. They argued that, in light of the far greater number of casualties they had suffered, the loans should be thought of as America's particular contribution to victory. If the debts were in fact not going to be written down, then it was all the more important to Allied prospects that Germany be made to pay. (To their argument that "their fight was our fight," House rejoined, in the privacy of his diary, that we never "feared that they [Germany] could defeat us or dominate us.")[6]

The British occupied an intermediate position. Lloyd George was determined to put an end to Germany's ability to act as a player on the extra-European world stage, much of which objective had already effectively been achieved by the terms of the armistice. Like Clemenceau, he was also determined to collect sizable reparations and had in fact locked himself into such a posture by the tenor of the campaign he had run in the recent, late 1918, British elections. Otherwise, as evidenced particularly by his disinclination significantly to reduce Germany's boundaries in Europe or to see too many Germans governed over by the new Poland, the British prime minister was hopeful that the settlement might be sufficiently measured as to guard against the creation of a spirit of revenge. London wanted stability on the continent and worried that a too harsh peace would not achieve that. It hoped to see Germany restored as a major trading partner. And British leaders, finally, wanted to guard against the possibility that the European balance of power might in the future be upset in favor of France.[7]

For his part, Wilson had since 1914 taken the position that Germany needed to be taught a "lesson." And his punitive inclinations had been hardened by the war and by concern as to how deep Germany's recent political changes went. In the lead-up to the conference, however, the president continued to call for a peace that might be received as just and moderate enough to pave the way for Germany to be brought, in a supporting role, into the international order desired by the United States. This included a desire for a reparations bill that would be within Germany's ability to pay. Wilson wanted a Germany that would quickly begin to attract investment, rebuild, and contribute to a Europe that would be stable and, once again, a consumer of American trade (and, in the case of the Allies, able to pay its debts). After a brief period of "probation," he hoped to see Germany become a member of the League of Nations. During the war, the president had tried to make a virtue of America's lack of interest in indemnities or annexations. His credibility, and therefore that of the peace, appeared to hang in the balance.[8]

Wilson did not succeed. The resultant Treaty of Versailles instead represented a compromise of these three viewpoints. Such an outcome derived from the pressure each of the leaders felt not to risk a rupture in their alliance and the consequent destruction of the triumphant position in the world it had allowed them collectively to achieve.[9]

*   *   *

Among the most contentious issues at Paris were those dealing with European frontiers, in particular the postwar borders of Germany and of the new states to its south and east. U.S. policy toward all these boundaries was dominated by its concern to reconstruct and stabilize the kind of international order it wanted. In most of Central Europe it thought this could be done principally via the formula of "the consent of the governed." With regard to the new states, Washington sought endorsement by the powers of borders reflective of the ethnic distribution of the peoples of the region (though it also proved willing to mix in considerations of strategic and economic viability). Such presumably would constitute realization of the nationalist yearnings that, since the nineteenth century, had grown up in this part of the world. Becoming (hopefully) legitimate and stable, these boundaries could then be guaranteed by the League of Nations. "We are trying to make a peaceful settlement," the president told a plenary session in late spring, "that is to say, to eliminate those elements of disturbance, so far as possible, which may interfere with the peace of the world, and we are trying to make an equitable distribution of territories according to the race, the ethnographical character of the people inhabiting them. And back of that lies this fundamentally important fact that, when the decisions are made, the Allied and Associated Powers guarantee to maintain them."[10]

With regard to Germany (and ethnic Germans), more complex considerations entered in. Like its allies, the Wilson administration was eager to contain that country's power in the future.[11] In keeping with its pre-armistice planning it wanted especially to ensure against the reemergence of a German-dominated Mitteleuropa. Consequently, the "Germanness" of an area might not be decisive if it was considered important to the economic or strategic viability of a neighboring new state. Such was the case with some of the territories assigned to Poland and Czechoslovakia (or simply detached from Germany, like Danzig). Along with its allies, Washington was also adamantly opposed to the expressed wish of Austrians (in the principal ethnically German portion of what had been the empire of Austria-Hungary) to self-determine themselves into an amalgamation with their northern neighbor.[12]

Self-determination was ultimately more a strategy than a principled commitment. It nevertheless remained the case that the Wilson administration wanted to prevent the creation of vengeful and irredentist sentiment in Germany that could lay the seeds for future conflict. House and the president repeatedly voiced their desire to avoid creating anything analogous to the French obsession after 1871 with the recovery of Alsace-Lorraine.[13] Moreover, there was American and world public opinion to contend with. "Consent of the governed," "self-determination," "no annexations or indemnities," these were among the formulas that Wilson had endorsed to rally support for the war and to advance America's agenda in the world. Success for the administration's efforts seemed to require that it at least be able to make the argument that its course did not seriously contradict such announced positions. Continued American public support for a major role in the world depended on this (just as, more broadly, the viability of the League of Nations seemed to depend on global opinion). That was what would give the League the deterrent weight Wilson was counting on.[14]

Such considerations were particularly central to the administration's reactions to French proposals for the treatment of Germany's border areas, especially in the west. (In the case of Poland, in the east, they acted as a limit on just how many Germans should be incorporated in the newly reconstituted state.) At the armistice negotiations, House had justified acceptance of French demands for the occupation of the Rhineland on the grounds that it would be temporary. He and Wilson hoped that the creation of the League, combined with the disarmament of Germany, would eliminate the need and desire for other security steps.[15]

But the French government had other ideas.[16] France had lost a higher share of its male population in the war than any other belligerent. It no longer possessed a Russian ally. France was deeply in debt to both England and the United States, and its economy lay in shambles. French leaders remained in awe of their larger and, they were convinced, more dynamic, eastern neighbor, and they feared that in the future it might overawe them. As they saw it, this called for decisive strategic realignment of the territory along Germany's western border. Together with other measures, it was hoped such realignment could ensure French security if not predominance. France might restore its status as a power, not only in Europe but abroad.

Clemenceau wanted to expand French influence in Belgium and Luxembourg. He wanted the return of Alsace and Lorraine. Much more controversially, at least from the standpoint of Lloyd George and Wilson, he was determined to rearrange the politics of the lands to the immediate north and east of those two provinces, along the Rhine. Although only formally laid out on February 25, in a memorandum drawn up by his close adviser André Tardieu, the general drift of Clemenceau's thinking had become known in Paris weeks before. The plan called for the termination of Germany's sovereignty over the territory west of the river, for the Allied occupation of the left bank and key bridgeheads to continue indefinitely, and for the forfeited territory to be turned into a buffer state.[17]

Looking ideally to arrange things on the continent so as to avoid expensive, on-the-ground commitments, both the British and the American conference participants recoiled from the occupation idea. And they worried that the creation of a Rhenish republic would sow the seeds of another war. Wilson and House expressed other concerns as well. The plan was in contradiction with the idea of self-determination. It would alienate, rather than reintegrate, Germany. And it might precipitate a thoroughgoing redistribution of world power. House told Balfour that

[t]he French have but one idea and that is military protection. They do not seem to know that to establish a Rhenish Republic against the will of the people would be contrary to the principle of self-determination. . . . If we did such a thing, we would be treating Germany in one way and the balance of the world in another. We would run the danger of having everything from the Rhine to the Pacific, perhaps including Japan, against the Western Powers.[18]

Before Wilson's departure in mid-February, House told him that he would try to move the conference along more quickly. Ideally, the broad outlines of a German settlement would be ready for the president's consideration upon his return. But, House cautioned, progress was clearly going to require compromise—not he hoped of principle, but of detail.[19]

Two weeks later, his pessimism had deepened. "It is now evident," House confided to his diary on March 3, "that the peace will not be such . . . as I had hoped. . . . I dislike to sit and have forced upon us such a peace as we are facing. We will get something out of it in the way of a League of Nations, but even that is an imperfect instrument."[20] With regard to the Rhineland, he cabled the president four days later that Clemenceau was taking a "very unreasonable attitude." House had apparently been open to a compromise premised on the idea that a separation that was not necessarily permanent might be allowed. But the French premier wanted "the Rhenish republics to be perpetually restrained from joining the German Federation."[21] Wilson asked that House "not even provisionally consent" to separation, "under any arrangement," and instead "reserve the whole matter until my arrival."[22]

Once back, the president immediately fell in with a plan that had been devised by Lloyd George to address French security. This was for the United States and Britain to promise to come to France's military aid in the event of unprovoked German aggression. While House was dubious that such an obviously "entangling" treaty would be ratified by the Senate (even if he still valued it as a strategy to move the conference along), the president was inclined to frame the idea as a mere stopgap—once the League was up and running, it would quickly be superseded. Both Lloyd George and Wilson hoped that the proposal would put an end to talk of anything but a short-term Rhineland occupation.

Clemenceau was receptive to the guarantee and agreed in return to abandon the idea of the region's wholesale separation from Germany. But he continued to push for an extended occupation. He also asked for the demilitarization of the river's east bank and for a French right to reoccupy the Rhineland in the future if Germany violated any provisions of the peace. Simultaneously, the premier insisted on French control of the coal-rich Saarland area, abutting Lorraine and Luxembourg, as recompense for the destruction by the German army of coal mines in northern France.

On March 25, Lloyd George circulated to his associates the Fontainebleau Memorandum, a paper drafted by his private secretary, Philip Kerr.[23] Taking stock in general of the settlement that was shaping up, the document warned against a too-onerous peace. It held up as the greatest danger the possibility of the Bolshevik Red Army and the Germans being driven together. Before what had now become the Council of Four, Wilson two days later seconded the British leader. He asserted that "our greatest error would be to give her [Germany] powerful reasons for one day wishing to take revenge."[24] Clemenceau rejoined that "America is far away, protected by the ocean. Not even Napoleon himself could touch England. You are both sheltered: we are not."[25]

With regard to the Rhineland, Wilson and Lloyd George supported demilitarization. But, Clemenceau wanted more, holding out for a fifteen-year occupation, with phased withdrawals, all reversible if Germany failed to abide by any of the peace settlement's provisions. Wilson, and then Lloyd George, finally accepted this in mid-April. The issue of the Saar was settled on the basis of substantial concessions to France as well. The French were to be given economic control and ownership of the mines, with the territory formally to be detached from Germany and administered by the

League. The inhabitants would be consulted about the area's ultimate political disposition, but only after these arrangements had been in place for fifteen years.[26]

*   *   *

In keeping with its desire to teach Germany a "lesson" but also to integrate that power, as an important prop, into the kind of world order it sought, the American delegation supported meaningful, but relatively moderate, reparations for its wartime partners. The Americans hoped that a definite figure could be agreed upon at Paris and that it would be set with a view to what Germany had the capacity to pay "within a reasonable time" (they suggested no more than thirty years).

With the exception of Belgium, for the violation of whose neutrality Germany had to be punished, the American delegation took the position that the enemy should be assessed for the civilian damage it caused but not for Allied war costs. Those, it insisted, had also been ruled out by the terms of the undertaking made with Germany in the fall. And they would violate Wilson's public promises not to pursue indemnities.[27]

The British and French, who had spent heavily on the war and whose economies were in disarray, not surprisingly disagreed. Their leaders were acutely aware of loud voices at home insisting that Germany should pay heavily. Lloyd George and Clemenceau were at the same time inclined themselves toward the belief that more than moderate reparations made sense (all the more in light of the attitude the United States was taking on Allied debts).

Clemenceau saw heavy reparations not only as a way of helping to rebuild France, but also as a means of maintaining leverage over his nation's eastern neighbor. From Lloyd George's standpoint, if Britain was confronting major economic hurdles, as it set out to again compete in trade with the other powers, it made good sense for Germany to be encumbered (and, he noted, "somebody had to pay" for the war!).[28] Though he often spoke in tones of reintegrative moderation, Lloyd George actually acted, on repeated occasions, in ways likely to push reparations higher. The prime minister was not deaf to the arguments of his Treasury experts, who argued that demanding too much could be counterproductive economically. He simply seems to have been eager to push for as high a level as might possibly be sustained.[29]

Aware of the domestic political expectations its partners had to deal with, increasingly mindful of the fact that the United States was in the minority on this issue, and eager not to destroy the alliance or unduly prolong the conference, the Americans—House and Wilson especially—made a series of concessions. Though they staunchly resisted British and French arguments in February that war costs ought to be admissible (as well as intimations that the reparations issue was bound up with that of the debts), U.S. financial experts were, for example, sympathetic to their counterparts' need for home-front cover. Two of them, John Foster Dulles (who was also Lansing's nephew) and Treasury Department official Norman Davis, thus made suggestions that would become Articles 231 and 232 of the treaty. The victorious powers would affirm (in Article 231) that they were in fact morally entitled to collect compensation for "all the loss and damage to which the Allied and Associated Governments and their nationals have been subjected." But, as a practical matter, they would only seek compensation for all the damage done to the "civilian population . . . and to their property," because more would exceed Germany's capacity to pay (Article 232).[30]

Lloyd George continued to insist that he remained politically vulnerable. Under a formula that focused on civilian damage, England would collect glaringly little compared to France. The prime minister wanted soldiers' pensions to at least be included. And, ultimately, the president agreed. To the objections of his experts that this decision could not logically be defended, Wilson rejoined, "Logic! Logic! I don't give a damn for logic. I am going to include pensions."[31]

The Americans had wanted the discussion to move on to what Germany's capacity was and, from there, to a specific amount that it would be asked for. They floated figures that went as high as thirty-five billion dollars.[32] But, the Big Three could not agree on an amount to be included in the treaty, Clemenceau and Lloyd George taking the position that, under the prevailing political conditions in their countries, any total would be rejected as too small. Fearing that they were right, Wilson finally told his delegates to try to meet their counterparts' "suggestions, as otherwise . . . their ministries might fall and we would have no governments to make peace with for some time to come."

In the end, the plan was "to postpone the fixing of the amount Germany is to pay" and leave the "determination of claims" to a commission to explore and report on over the course of the next two years. For identical reasons, Wilson subsequently conceded two other points insisted upon by the French premier, both of which were likely to increase the reparations burden. While Clemenceau pledged that there would still be room for liberality, after the fact, he wanted the bill to be arrived at on the basis of a toting up of claims, rather than capacity, and for there to be no limit set as to the time frame within which Germany would be expected to make payments.[33]

In the treaty, Germany would essentially be asked to sign a blank check.

*   *   *

Arrangements were finally made for representatives of Germany to be presented with a draft of the treaty on May 7. This would occur after an outline summary (no more) of the document was run past the full conference for its approval on the sixth.[34] The Germans would then be given limited time to, in writing, respond.[35]

Beyond its provisions for the Rhineland, Saarland, Alsace-Lorraine, and reparations, related above, the treaty called for Germany to lose small amounts of territory along its (prewar) borders with Belgium and Denmark and much larger amounts of territory, in the east, to Poland.[36] The country would largely be disarmed, and Germany would be stripped of all of its territories outside of Europe as well as most of its merchant marine.

The president expressed satisfaction with the work of the Council of Four. He asserted that it had "completed in the least time possible the greatest work that four men have ever done."[37] Once they too had had a chance to absorb the whole treaty, however, that was not the typical reaction of his compatriots in the American delegation. They worried that the treaty would negatively affect postwar prospects for stabilization. Although Wilson averred that the conference had "been able to keep tolerably close to the lines laid down at the outset," most of his advisers were upset at how far the treaty seemed to depart from the reintegrative emphasis of the Fourteen Points.[38] They also feared that its financial features were unworkable and would lead to future upheaval. Hoover later wrote that upon seeing the whole document, the morning before it was to be presented to the Germans, he was struck that it "contained the seeds of another war."

The provisions on reparations alone would "pull down the whole Continent and, in the end, injure the United States."[39] Baruch, Davis, and other financial advisers expressed similar forebodings. Lansing characterized the treaty as almost "hopelessly bad." The terms were "immeasurably harsh and humiliating." He told Ray Stannard Baker that the League would be assigned the task of guaranteeing an "unjust settlement."[40] Bliss had similar misgivings, while James Brown Scott, an expert in international law attached to the delegation, proclaimed the settlement "the worst ever drawn," one guaranteed to render another conflict "inevitable."[41]

House too was negative in his appraisal.[42] But, and this was almost certainly the private perspective of the president as well, he had long since become reconciled to the fact that it would not be what he wanted and had concluded that—from the standpoint of his most important priorities— any of the alternatives to closing on the settlement were worse. These, most prominently, were the continuance of disorder (along with the spread of Bolshevism) in Europe and the breakup of the alignment between the United States, Britain, and France. In terms of the reconstruction and stabilization of the kind of international order House and Wilson wanted, the fragmentation of the alliance might invite challenges (including by France) that would set American objectives back even further. Better to get the League established and hope that it (and maybe the Reparations Commission) could address what U.S. leaders disliked about the settlement.

The document did not perhaps add up to the "Carthaginian peace" that some claimed (or even match the severity of the Treaty of Brest-Litovsk). Germany was far from totally dismembered. Strategically, with the appearance of numerous small states in place of large empires to the east, it was in many ways in a stronger position than before the war. Several historians have maintained that the reparations bill, finally set in 1921, could have been paid.[43]

Nevertheless, the treaty was hardly an instrument likely to encourage the reintegration that American policy makers had desired (Clemenceau, of course, insisted that such was impossible; unless firmly dealt with, it was certain that Germany would challenge the Allies again).[44] In the face of criticism, Wilson took refuge in the thought that the issue was not whether the treaty was harsh—he said Germany had earned that—but whether it was just and fair, which he insisted it was.[45] But this begged the question as to how reintegration would be served if Germans saw the treaty, rightly or wrongly, as the opposite of that.

As indeed they did. In fact, the Social Democrats and their partners, who had inherited control of the German state in late 1918, many of whom had been calling since 1917 for a "peace of understanding" with the Allies, received the unveiling of terms as a major disappointment and betrayal. During late 1918 and early 1919, they had put great faith in the fact that the settlement was supposed to be based, in the main, on the Fourteen Points. They had read the most positive possible interpretations into Wilson's formulations and entered, as one philosopher of the time put it, into a kind of "dreamland" state. The United States would want a good relationship with a Germany that had now been politically restructured and become the republic that Wilson had called for. The United States would desire an economically strong and stable Germany that could become a bastion against the spread of Bolshevism. The Americans would appreciate how the new government acted early in 1919 to put down revolution on the left as well as reaction on the part of unreconciled nationalist elements. In exchange, the new government hoped to see self-determination for all ethnic Germans respected. It dreamed of this reformed Germany being accorded a leading role in the League, and of Berlin—under the League's supervision—retaining a role in the underdeveloped world.[46]

Against this backdrop, and in the absence of the negotiations through which they had wanted to make their case, Germany's leaders reacted with shock and anger to the terms they were handed. They viewed as ominous the failure of the Allies to stipulate a figure for reparations. At a minimum, the uncertainty would cloud prospects for economic revival. Worse, it seemed to promise a figure that, when finally presented, would be far higher than hoped. They bemoaned the losses of territory and population, lamented that Germany was left out of the League, and complained that the disarmament envisioned appeared one-sided. In ways totally unanticipated by the Allies, German leaders took great exception to Article 231 (which came to be called "the war guilt clause") and its imputation, as they saw it, that Berlin bore sole responsibility for the conflict.[47]

In its response to the terms, delivered on May 30, Germany emphasized what it saw as the treaty's unfair and dramatic divergence from the Fourteen Points. The financial levies apparently envisioned, it protested, were likely to destroy the nation's economy and subject its people to perpetual slavery.

Berlin made a counteroffer on reparations. It accepted disarmament, but called for plebiscites in Alsace-Lorraine, Austria, and the Sudetenland.

Germany also wanted to retain much of the territory the treaty ceded to Poland (or, in the case of Danzig, turned into a free city under the supervision of the League) as well as its overseas colonies. It wanted only a brief occupation of the Rhineland and immediate German membership in the League.[48]

Lloyd George worried that Germany would not sign the treaty. He received the backing of his cabinet and of other members of the British delegation to propose modifications on a number of questions. These included Germany's borders with Poland, the length and scope of the Rhineland occupation, reparations, and how long Berlin would have to wait for membership in the League. The French noted, as they had before, that whenever Britain tabled concessions they generally were at France's, not England's, expense. Clemenceau maintained that Germany would sign. He also insisted that any significant changes would bring about his government's fall.[49]

To his personal physician, Cary T. Grayson, Wilson complained of Lloyd George's conduct. He claimed that the British were now "doing their best to get the very things that they had prevented" him from incorporating in the treaty in March. Nearly a month was wasted, during which the president had fought to secure a settlement where "while Germany was punished for her past crimes, she was still allowed to retain her place in the concert of nations." Mistrustful of the prime minister, Wilson was determined not to be led into a "trap." Any changes would have to start with agreements between Britain and France.[50] The president subsequently told Grayson that "various persons" had pointed out that "a change at the present time would be a very serious problem, as it could be depended upon to change the German attitude of humility to one of aggression."[51]

On June 3, the president attended what, somewhat amazingly, was the first general meeting of the American delegation with him at the conference. Wilson, on balance, argued for a cautious approach toward modifications, and he did so largely on the ground of keeping the British, French, and Americans together. "The great problem of the moment," he said, was "the problem of agreement, because the most fatal thing that could happen, I should say, in the world, would be that sharp lines of division should be drawn among the Allied and Associated Powers." That was a likely prospect if major areas of difference, like the Rhineland occupation, were immediately revisited. The key thing now was to get the League started, let some time elapse, and let excited emotions and political feelings cool. "What is necessary is to get out of this atmosphere of war, get out of the present exaggerated feelings and exaggerated appearances, and I believe that if we can once get out of them into the calmer airs it would be easier to come to satisfactory solutions."[52]

One argument for modification did impel him to action though. Seconded by Morgan partner Thomas Lamont, who was also in Paris as a Treasury Department adviser to the U.S. delegation, Davis pushed the president to try again to get a fixed amount, one that Germany could pay, set for reparations. This would allay worry among the Germans, especially because they thought that the Reparations Commission would interfere in their internal affairs. It would allow them to restart their economic life. And, given "Europe's financial situation," it would also help "France and Italy and the other countries" get "on their feet."[53] Wilson subsequently raised the question in the Council of Four, but Clemenceau and Lloyd George remained opposed. In the end the one significant concession offered by the victors was for a plebiscite to be employed to determine the fate (Polish or German) of coal-rich Upper Silesia.[54]

On the sixteenth, the Germans were told that they had five days (later extended to a week) to accept the revised document. Many in Paris believed that they would refuse, and, with that in mind, the Allies prepared for a resumption of military operations. Tensions increased further after the twenty-first, when word arrived that most of the German surface fleet, interned off of northern Scotland at Scapa Flow, had been scuttled by its officers and sailors. To the Big Three, this defiant act was a blatant and ominous "breach of faith."[55]

Fevered debate took place in Germany. The treaty was widely unpopular, but while some argued for outright rejection and resistance, others urged the acceptance of what seemed inevitable. Things could be worse. More of the country was likely to be occupied or, alternatively, thrown into chaos. The four-month-old government of Philipp Scheidemann resigned on June 20, to be replaced two days later by another led by Gustav Bauer. It offered to sign with reservations, but was answered with an ultimatum to accept (which it did) or refuse by the end of the deadline the next evening.[56]

Five days later, in a ceremony fraught with meaning—the first kaiser had been crowned there following Prussia's victory over France a half century before—the treaty was signed in the Hall of Mirrors at Versailles.[57]

Americans in Paris: The Russian Revolution, the Royal Navy, Power in the Western Hemisphere

Trying to reassemble, and put on firmer foundations, the kind of international order they desired, Wilson and "his peacemakers" felt compelled to engage with other issues as well while in the French capital during the first six months of 1919. Some of these problems were not only inherently difficult of solution. They tested the harmony of the victorious coalition of great powers that the president was counting on collectively to superintend the world (or at least the eastern hemisphere) in the postwar era.

They were numerous. Throughout this period, the continuance of turmoil, especially revolutionary turmoil, in Russia stood as a challenge to the establishment of the European peace and order that Wilson and his advisors wanted. Meanwhile, in early spring, American policy makers confronted efforts by Britain to contain America's rise as a naval power. Not unrelated, the president felt the need to ask the other powers for changes he wanted in the League of Nations Covenant, these deemed important (in the wake of his visit back to America) to the League's chances of being accepted by the U.S. Senate.

The assignment to specific powers of territories in the "colonial world" slated to be mandates created concerns. So too did Italy's insistence that, "no annexations" be damned, it be given territory well down the previously Austro-Hungarian coast of the eastern Adriatic.

Wilson's stand in opposition to this Italian bid, which helped dramatically to undermine his popular standing in that allied country, contrasted sharply with compromises he was making elsewhere, perhaps above all with his decision to go along with the desire of Japan—a more feared ally—to take control of the Chinese coastal province of Shandong. That move, taken above all because of his hope to contain Japan's activities more generally in East Asia by attaching Tokyo to the League, in turn seriously complicated the president's efforts to promote U.S. influence in China. After the conference, it would also contribute to political problems for him before the American public. These issues will be addressed in this chapter and the following two.

*   *   *

French leaders were furious at the Bolshevik's early 1918 repudiation of Russia's state debt, much of which was held in France. Paris was likewise upset at the loss of a long-standing partner against Germany and terrified of the inspiration Bolshevism seemed to be providing to uprisings elsewhere in Europe. It wanted no dealings whatsoever with the new Soviet government. Instead, many French leaders pushed for Marshal Foch to be unleashed. They pressed for a much larger military intervention to be mounted, one that would overthrow the Bolsheviks and set up a new regime.[1]

But such a move seemed foolhardy, if not impossible, to Wilson (as well as Lloyd George). The Allied and Associated publics were tired of war. Americans, in particular, had never been in favor of U.S. troops entering Russia. And there were already voices, led by progressive Republican senator Hiram Johnson, asking why—in the wake of the armistice with Germany—doughboys were still in Siberia and Archangel.

The United States and Britain, not France, would have to bear the costs of such a campaign. An expanded intervention would further embarrass the claim that Wilson believed Russians should be allowed to work out their own future. And the president's military advisers were dead set against it. While Foch was ready to go, even some French generals, like Franchet D'Esperey, were arguing that it was too late for an intervention in European Russia to make any difference.

At the least, most military men accepted that a new intervention would have to be massive to have any chance of success. Drawing on his experience with another large state in the throes of social revolution, Mexico,

Wilson felt that there was a greater likelihood that an increased foreign military presence would be counterproductive, that it would unify the Russian populace behind the Soviets. Indeed, he felt that the troops that were in Russia should for this, among other reasons, get out.[2]

Wilson, despite his animosity toward the Bolsheviks, therefore objected to the French plan for the dispatch of a large army to Russia. He felt that the Allies (by which label, at Paris, he meant to include the United States) would have to look for other ways of influencing events in that vast country and of pursuing their interests, these most immediately being to prevent events in Russia from making more difficult the reestablishment of order elsewhere on the continent. Engagement might be explored (though he was not eager to help a government he disliked solidify its position). So too might less overt means of shaping that country's political order. The political containment and isolation of the Bolsheviks meanwhile was Wilson's fallback policy, the president being confident that that would ensure, in the not too distant future, the overthrow or at least dramatic transformation of the regime.

Since mid-1918, the Bolsheviks had, as historian David McFadden puts it, "faced civil war [specifically "White" military forces that often benefited from Western material support], foreign invasion, and virtual isolation from the rest of the world."[3] The Allies had pressed neutral nations to break relations, and the blockade on Germany had been extended to include Russia. Yet, having fought back, often with extreme measures, the regime still appeared ascendant at the beginning of 1919, perhaps in popular as well as military terms. This was the reality that both Wilson and Lloyd George felt they had to deal with in the run-up to Paris.

Soviet foreign minister Georgi Chicherin had been pushing, especially since the armistice, for negotiations with the Allies. To enhance the prospects for that, Maxim Litvinov was appointed a special emissary and, in December, sent to Stockholm. Both made clear that the Bolsheviks were prepared to make major concessions. When he met with Lloyd George and Balfour in London on December 30, the president suggested that the Allies should ask Litvinov "formally and definitely what his proposals were."[4]

This sentiment lay behind the dispatch by Wilson of William Buckler, a foreign service officer who had since 1917 been a confidant and collector of information for House, to Stockholm in mid-January. Buckler met with Litvinov over the course of three days, on the last along with Arthur Ransome, a British newspaper correspondent. On the eighteenth, Buckler reported that the Soviets "conciliatory attitude . . . is unquestionable." They were anxious for peace and trade, to get which they would compromise on all outstanding points, including foreign debts and "protection to existing foreign enterprises and the granting of new concessions." "[P]ropaganda in foreign countries would cease at once," and the regime would recognize the independence from Russia of Finland, Poland, and the Ukraine. He cited approvingly Ransome's view that the continuance of intervention only strengthened the hand of Bolshevik extremists, "whereas a policy of agreement with the Soviet Government will counteract their influence, will strengthen the Moderates and by reviving trade and industry will procure prosperity, the best of all antidotes to Bolshevism."[5]

Wilson was intrigued, perhaps above all by the seeming desperation of the Bolsheviks for peace. The latter were looking for direct negotiations. But, the president and his colleagues came together instead around an idea that originated with Lloyd George, Cecil, and the Canadian prime minister, Robert Borden. This was to propose to both the Soviets and the various White forces that they conclude a cease-fire and send envoys to the Island of Prinkipo (in the Sea of Marmara) to confer in the presence of representatives of the Allies. The objective would be to find common ground and end the fighting in Russia, the reward for doing which would be representation at the conference in Paris.[6]

Implicit in this was the notion that the Soviets would be offered peace in exchange for significant concessions. But the French could not reconcile themselves to any dealings with the Bolsheviks at all. In the Council of Ten, Clemenceau went along with the proposal, on the grounds that the Allies needed to stay united. But, from behind the scenes, France encouraged White leaders not to go along.

Unwilling to halt their current military offensives, the Soviets ignored the call for a cease-fire. Yet they made things awkward for the Allies by agreeing to attend the Prinkipo meeting. The Allied leaders eventually decided that there was no point going ahead if none of the other factions were going to participate.[7]

In mid-February, just before Wilson took temporary leave to go home, the new British war minister, Winston Churchill, came to Paris. He urged the Allies greatly to increase the scale of their military intervention in Russia, even if they had to do so by calling for volunteers. But Lloyd George, who was back in England, and Wilson both opposed such a course. The president was inclined instead to double back and pursue a more direct follow-up to Buckler's discussions. He said he now thought it would be worthwhile for American representatives to meet informally in Russia with the Bolshevik leadership.[8]

Such thinking was a prelude to the secret dispatch to Moscow several days later of the American delegation's man most familiar with events in Russia and Eastern Europe, Bullitt.[9] Top British officials were very involved in the arrangements for this mission, but the French were kept in the dark for a month. Despite what the French were later told, it was understood that Bullitt was, if possible, not only to get more information, but to "prepare the way for further discussions."[10] He met with Soviet officials, including Chicherin and Lenin in Petrograd and Moscow during the first two weeks of March, the meetings with the latter finally eventuating in the outlines of a proposed agreement. To Lenin, if not to Trotsky and some others, granting significant concessions was the price the Bolsheviks would have to pay for securing the Soviet regime (the analogy was made with the decisions made the year before in the run-up to Brest-Litovsk). Not all would necessarily be permanent, particularly if White military leaders, like General Anton Denikin, in the South, and Admiral Aleksandr Kolchak, in the East, did not have popular support.

Crucially, the proposal that he and the Central Committee approved called for the Allies to remove their troops from Russia, lift the blockade, and suspend aid to the Whites. In turn, the White's de facto control over an enormous amount of Russian territory (more than had been in play at Brest-Litovsk) was to be accepted and undergirded by a pledge of non-aggression on the part of all parties (including the Allies). Bullitt was also given assurances in regard to "the financial obligations" of the Russian Empire.

Bullitt viewed this as a favorable opportunity to promote peace and stability in Russia, to steer the revolution in a more moderate direction (he personally believed that a move toward "social democracy" was inevitable and should not be opposed), and to stabilize Russia's relations with the rest of the world. The Bolsheviks were conciliatory, and peace with them, he wrote Wilson on the sixteenth, could be had.[11] But, whatever advantages they might see in it, his agreement immediately began to strike his superiors as problematic.

House initially wanted to follow up. He told the Italian prime minister that the best course would be for the Allies to "draw up a treaty . . . practically upon our own terms . . . and send this treaty to Moscow for their signatures." His reasons were largely geopolitical and strategic. He told Orlando that Russia "wanted to resume relations with the outside world. If we met her in a reasonable way she would agree to leave the boundary lines as they stand today; to stop all fighting on all fronts, and to agree not to use any propaganda in any of the Allied countries. . . . If we did not make terms with them, it was certain that as soon as we made peace with Germany, Russia and Germany would link up together, thereby realizing my prophecy that, sooner or later, everything east of the Rhine would be arrayed against the Western Powers." If they did come to terms, "the general Russian dislike for Germany" would give the Entente a dominating influence in Russia. House said it was "footless to say we preferred some other plan." There was none. The Allies had either to "reckon with the de facto Government, or remain in a state of war, or semi-war" with them. "We cannot intervene, everyone admits that," he told the prime minister.[12]

Nevertheless, Wilson and Lloyd George decided not to take the risk. Even if formal recognition were avoided, they would have to confront the opposition of the French at a sensitive time in the negotiations over the treaty with Germany. Perhaps more important, House noted that what Bullitt had negotiated would undoubtedly help to stabilize the Soviet regime. That was something that all the Allied leaders had a hard time with, and new developments, in Eastern Europe and in their own countries, were reinforcing their hesitancy. The triumph of a radical revolution in Hungary, under Béla Kun, was reigniting fears among the "forces of order" in Allied countries that Russian Bolshevism was aggressively on the move. Simultaneously, postwar social and labor strife in the United States was beginning to give rise to an anti-Bolshevik hysteria, later known as the Red Scare. Questioned by journalists, after news of the mission to Russia had begun to leak out, Lloyd George took the position that he did not know what the Americans had been up to. The president, for his part, decided not seriously to consider Bullitt's proposals. (While disappointment with the Treaty of Versailles was also important, the failure of Wilson to explore the possibilities of peace with the Soviets was a major factor leading to Bullitt's resignation from the State Department in mid-May.)[13]

By the end of March, as a consequence, House was moving on to another plan. This would be to address, and capitalize on, the material prostration of Russia (something that had figured very prominently in Bullitt's reports) that had been brought about by the civil war and the blockade. He thought that the Soviets might be so desperate as to agree to a cease-fire without the Allies having to discuss with them a political settle-ment. A large-scale international relief effort, coordinated by a prominent neutral, would be proposed, with a cease-fire being stipulated as a precondi-tion, this on the grounds that it was necessary for a successful operation.

House worked closely with Hoover in developing this idea (the latter touting its merit to Wilson by noting that it would avoid any question of recognition). And together they enlisted the Norwegian explorer and humanitarian Fridtjof Nansen to head up the enterprise. But while the Bolsheviks were interested in discussing the shipment of food, they insisted that a cease-fire could be had only via negotiations looking to an overall settlement. In response, the Allies instructed Nansen not to proceed.[14]

A better option had, in any event, seemingly just arisen. One of the White military leaders, Kolchak, seemed to be gaining momentum in his fight against the Soviets. This former commander of the Black Sea Fleet had in November seized control of the city of Omsk, in southwestern Siberia, and declared himself the Supreme Ruler of All Russia. At the beginning of the year, British observers had sized up Kolchak's military situation as "distinctly bad." But he gained considerable ground in April and May, to the point where Lloyd George began to propose in the Council of Four that the admiral be given further support, on the condition that he give assur-ances that he had no intention of trying to reestablish an unpopular autoc-racy. This led to a note being sent to Kolchak by the Allies on May 27, in which, in return for such guarantees (and acceptance of a central role for the League in the determination of Russia's western boundaries), ammuni-tion and supplies—assistance in helping them become the government of all Russia—were offered to his forces.

However, Kolchak no sooner provided the kind of reply desired than he began to suffer dramatic reverses. Apparently getting wind of the Allies' possible recognition of the admiral, Trotsky made the Eastern Front the top priority for the Soviet Red Army. It quickly regained lost ground, casting in doubt—though not yet altogether destroying—the hopes that had been raised by the Big Four back in Paris just as the Allied leaders were preparing to leave the conference.[15]

*   *   *

British-American relations became more fractious as the proceedings at Paris went on. Reparations (and the related issue of Britain's indebtedness to the United States), discussed above, was one major area of disagreement. Another, not entirely unrelated, was that of the two powers' relative strength at sea. Financially drained, London, as it assessed its situation, became increasingly anxious to hold down expenditures for the future. But it was also eager to maintain Britain's status as the world's supreme naval power.[16]

Ultimately more important than Washington's attitude on the freedom of the seas, from London's perspective, was the question of the plans the United States had for the continued build up of its fleet. During the war, America had interrupted the long-range program decided upon in 1916 (with its heavy emphasis on capital ships) to focus on the construction of destroyers and other small craft (see Chapter 5). But in December Wilson had called for a resumption of the original plan. And the U.S. Navy had proposed a follow-up program that was even bigger. The president's call, in 1916, for the United States to have "incomparably the greatest navy in the world" seemed back on course.[17]

For Britain's leaders, what to do was a major dilemma. They saw little prospect of England being able to out-build the United States. Chief of Naval Operations Benson warned Wilson that London might try, as an alternative, to have the German navy divided up in such a way as would give England the lion's share.[18] Eventually, the Lloyd George government settled on a strategy of trying to get the United States to abandon its naval expansion as the price of Britain's continued collaboration on the League.[19]

In late March, First Sea Lord Wester Wemyss offered that the United States should publicly acknowledge London's "right" to supremacy. And First Lord of the Admiralty Walter Long suggested that the United States reconsider completion of the 1916 program as well as shelve the more recent proposal of the General Board. To which American leaders responded that there could be no serious discussion of such matters until the League was established. For their part, the British rejoined that they might not cooperate over the League unless the United States addressed their concerns. With friction mounting, Lloyd George and Wilson delegated House and Cecil to try to reach an agreement.[20]

The president wanted to limit naval expansion, this because of its expense and because he recognized that resistance would grow on the part of Congress and the public. American authorities were also acutely aware of "the apparent inconsistency of the United States in advocating a general reduction of armaments, while itself undertaking an intensified Naval Building program."[21] But the administration had long been committed to a policy quite at odds to what the British were demanding. Wilson was determined not to concede to the Royal Navy the right to supremacy that it was demanding. His long-range goal was rather to achieve for the United States the right to occupy a position of naval power equal to that of England. The administration had been strongly suggesting for months that Washington would otherwise demonstrate that it could out-build Britain. Cecil confided to his diary that while it was "unreasonable for Wilson to build a large Navy and insist on everybody else joining the League of Nations," he was "sure that any attempt to combine the two will only irritate the Americans without securing any advantage."[22] He therefore asked House if the United States might not reassure Britain that "when the Treaty of Peace containing the League of Nations has been signed you would abandon or modify your new naval programme."[23] House replied that "[i]f the kind of peace is made for which we are working . . . I am sure you will find the United States ready to 'abandon or modify'" the new program. He pointedly added, "by which I understand you to mean our programme not yet provided for by law."[24]

House was referring here to the plans that, in 1918, had been forward by the General Board. He was anxious that the naval issue not interfere with creation of the League, but the 1916 program was not on the table. "It is to be noted," House wrote in his diary, "that I promise nothing whatsoever. It is merely the spirit of his suggestion that I am accepting. I particularly reserve and insist upon the completion of our past naval program."[25]

He predicted, correctly, that Lloyd George would "catch the point" and not approve. As he no doubt guessed, however, the British were in the end likely to acquiesce because they had no acceptable alternative. Good relations with Washington seemed important to the prime minister, while a worsening of those was only likely to bring about the kind of naval race that Britain could ill afford.

Lloyd George held that House's letter was unsatisfactory because "it left him [the United States] still able, by building his accepted programme, to build a fleet nearly equal in numbers and superior in armament to the British Fleet." He wanted Washington to also abandon construction of the ships provided for but not yet begun under the 1916 program. And he implied that this would be the price of Britain's support for an amendment to the League Covenant explicitly recognizing the Monroe Doctrine (see below). When Cecil raised this prospect with House, the latter refused to bargain, saying that if London wished to turn the amendment down, "they were privileged to do so." Here "the naval battle of Paris," as it has been called, stood until well after the conference was over, the British having to content themselves with U.S. assent to a memorandum stating that Washington was not embarking on a quest for outright supremacy.[26]

*   *   *

During Wilson's trip home in late winter, misgivings had been expressed by a number of Republicans about features of the League Covenant (a few voiced hostility to the entire idea).[27] On March 3, Henry Cabot Lodge, the incoming chair of the Foreign Relations Committee, made public a statement—which would come to be known as the "Round Robin resolution"—endorsed by more than a third of those who would be serving in the Senate during its next session. It asserted that "the constitution of the league of nations in the form now proposed to the peace conference should not be accepted by the United States."[28] And it urged that American negotiators in Paris make their top priority the conclusion of the peace with Germany. The League idea could be taken up later.

Wilson would need two-thirds of the votes in the Senate for ratification. Yet his initial reaction to this Republican gambit was dismissive and defiant. Before leaving to return to the peace conference, the president declared that he intended to work for a treaty with Germany from which the Covenant could not be separated.[29] Initially, he also insisted that the Covenant would not be modified.[30]

Wilson maintained this attitude for about two weeks. Finally, he bowed to advice and embraced the idea that some changes in the Covenant had to be sought if he were not to court defeat. Senator Gilbert Hitchcock (D-Neb.), the outgoing chair of the Foreign Relations Committee, and ex-President Taft, a leader of the League to Enforce Peace and supporter of the Covenant, urged what they saw as minor revisions. They expressed confidence that these would satisfy enough senators to ensure ratification. Hitchcock and Taft suggested, for example, that the document should include language that would guarantee that American domestic affairs were outside the purview of the League. There should be clear steps by which the United States could withdraw from that body if it so desired. Both also urged the inclusion of language stipulating that nothing in the Covenant could interfere with the Monroe Doctrine.[31]

As the president saw it, the United States was going to be in the driver's seat and thrive as a consequence of the League of Nations. Far from being threatened, American interests would be served. The League was going to ensure American leadership. The power the United States was destined to have within the institution would be more than adequate to fend off any of the threats meant to be protected against by the proposed changes. In fact, the ability of the United States to shape events elsewhere in the world might be diminished to the extent that language laying out limits on the League's powers (or broaching the idea that countries might ever want to leave the organization) was included. Wilson worried that French support might be jeopardized if the League was weakened or if American support seemed less than wholehearted. As he and House saw it, more explicit mention of the Monroe Doctrine was not only unnecessary, it might serve to encourage Japan to carve out a sphere of influence for itself in the Far East. They worried, finally, that the effort to seek revisions to the Covenant would put leverage in the hands of the other powers. Wilson would have to face the possibility (later borne out in the dispute with London over the American navy) that other powers would want things in return.[32]

Nevertheless, by late March, the president was convinced that the effort would have to be made. On the twenty-second, the League of Nations Commission began meeting again, now to consider amendments and revisions. Efforts were made by France, and for the most part turned away by Wilson and Cecil, to nudge the Covenant back in the direction of the kind of league Paris had pushed for earlier in the conference.[33] France (and Belgium) also was disappointed in its preference to have Brussels designated as the home of the League (and to have French established as the organization's official language). Instead, the British and American preference for Geneva prevailed.[34]

The most important changes in the Covenant conformed to those the Americans had been looking for. Wilson succeeded in amending Article 15 so as to exempt from League action any dispute "solely within" the "domestic jurisdiction" of one of the parties.[35] Then the preamble to the Covenant was rewritten to provide that "after two years' notice" a member of the League, provided that "all of its international obligations" had been fulfilled, might withdraw. In pushing for this provision, the president was at pains to assure the French that "he did not entertain the smallest fear that any State would take advantage" of it.[36]

At the end of the second week in April, the differences over naval building having for the time been composed, Cecil, as historian Alan Sharp nicely puts it, "backed Wilson in his attempt [explicitly] to prevent the League interfering in the American hemisphere without United States approval."[37] At the commission's meeting on the tenth, the president introduced an amendment, initially intended to be attached to Article 10, stating that "[n]othing in this Covenant shall be deemed to affect the validity of international engagements such as Treaties of arbitration or regional understandings like the Monroe Doctrine for securing the maintenance of peace."[38]

Again, the principal opposition came from the French. Some of this, no doubt, was a by-product of the heated discussions in the Council of Four at this time over the settlement with Germany. But it clearly also reflected French concerns about the nature of the American commitment to Europe. One delegate, Fernand Larnaude, requested a definition of the Monroe Doctrine and expressed concern as to whether mentioning it would affect the United States becoming involved outside the western hemisphere. Coming—by prearrangement—to Wilson's aid, Cecil rejected the idea that the doctrine needed to be clearly defined. The president's "amendment had been inserted in order to quiet doubts, and to calm misunderstandings." It "did not make the substance of the Doctrine more or less valid." Cecil "understood this amendment to say . . . that there was nothing in the Monroe Doctrine which conflicted with the Covenant, and therefore nothing in the Covenant which interfered with international understandings like the Monroe Doctrine."

Not satisfied, Larnaude pointed to the fact that Article 20 of the Covenant called upon all states to make their "international engagements conform to the spirit of the League." They could stand if not inconsistent. Therefore, why the need for the president's amendment? If "there was nothing in the Monroe Doctrine inconsistent with the Covenant it would not be affected." Wilson insisted that if the United States joined the League it would be "solemnly obliged" to become involved "when the territorial integrity of any European State was threatened by external aggression." To assuage French concerns about the possible impact his amendment might have on the commitment undertaken in Article 10, he and Cecil offered to attach it instead to Article 20. Larnaude supported that idea, but he subsequently also asked for language that would make explicit that nothing in the doctrine would prevent the United States from "executing their obligations under this Covenant." To which the president replied that he feared Larnaude's wording would lead to an "unwarranted suspicion" being "cast upon the Doctrine."[39]

In the end, the revision—in Wilson's wording—prevailed, this according to House by dint of "Anglo-Saxon tenacity."[40] House was of course referring not only to the president but also to the support Wilson received from Cecil. That, in turn, was a function of Cecil's commitment to working with the United States over the League as well as of Lloyd George's eventual decision not to follow through on his threat to tie London's support to U.S. policy on its navy. But there may in fact have been payoffs made to Britain for its support, including the president's agreement the prior week to accept pensions as a basis for German reparations and Wilson's heavy-handed ruling in Britain's favor at the last meeting of the League commission on the "racial equality" clause. Yet another reward may have come a few weeks later when Wilson acceded to the idea that the Dominions would be eligible to sit as temporary members on the League's Executive Council.[41]

Comparatively little discussion in the meetings of the League commission focused on the fact that the United States had been using its "doctrine" to ensure that, except by Washington's consent, no other power could play a political or military role in the western hemisphere. Jayme Reis, of Portugal, "asked whether the Monroe Doctrine would prevent League action in American affairs." Wilson "replied in the negative," but then elaborated in a way that sidestepped the thrust of the question, asserting, as he had before, "that the Covenant was nothing but a confirmation and extension of the Doctrine." Another delegate asked if in the case of a hypothetical dispute between Paraguay and Uruguay the League "would have the right to come to the aid of whichever . . . was supported by the decision of the Executive Council." It would, of course, but only with U.S. consent in the Executive Council. There had never been any intention by Wilson to allow any compromise of Washington's "paramount influence" in (and over) the Americas.

The inconsistency of the president's "internationalism"—a league for the world that would not affect the validity of a "regional understanding" in the western hemisphere—was certainly much noted elsewhere, as

Wiseman pointed out in a cable to the British ambassador to the United States a week later. "Wilson has lost much of his popularity in England and does not get much support now even from liberal and labour press," he told Reading. "American insistence on the Monroe Doctrine in the Covenant has created a very bad impression. It is thought that the American attitude is 'everybody else must abate their sovereignty except America!' "[42]

CHAPTER 11

Americans in Paris: The Colonial World

Wilson's approach to the "colonial world" in 1919 is best discussed in two parts: first, his policy toward the territories of the defeated Central Powers, and, second, his attitude toward the colonies of the Allies.

As noted, the centerpiece of the president's policy toward the extra-European territories to be taken away from the Central Powers—principally, the Arab portions of the Ottoman Empire (composing much of the Middle East) and Germany's possessions in Africa and the Far East–Pacific—was the League mandate idea. Much historical literature has attributed this idea to Smuts, in particular to suggestions he proffered about the new international organization in his sketch of a league, produced in mid-December 1918.[1] Wilson certainly looked favorably on the South African's proposal that the League act as a "successor" to the defeated empires. But Smuts was thinking of this as a policy principally in connection with territory in Europe and the Middle East.[2] Moreover, the idea of League mandates had in fact already been talked about among the Americans.[3]

The more important point to make is that the mandate concept had its roots in earlier great-power practice, including U.S. practice. Assigning "guardianship" or "trusteeship" status to a country signified that direct outside supervision was not intended to amount to ownership, that what was being asserted was a temporary arrangement, to be distinguished especially from annexation. The latter was something Wilson was in fact eager to stem as a tactic of great-power competition. And, driven by a desire to stabilize the postwar order, he wanted to encourage the idea that forcible changes of boundaries were passé.

Taking on trusteeships is essentially what Washington claimed it was doing—via financial receiverships and military occupations—in the Caribbean and Central America.[4] A key difference, of course, was that while Wilson had no intention of sharing this "unselfish" labor (and there is little doubt he had convinced himself of its altruism) in the Americas with any other power, he was determined that such work of "civilization" in the Central Powers' former territories not be undertaken by any of the other powers unilaterally. It should, rather, be internationalized.

Just before Christmas 1918, he told the British ambassador to France that he thought the German colonies "ought to be neutralised and worked in the common interests of humanity."[5] The best analogy here would be with the predominant thrust of American policy toward China since the turn of the century, where promoting collective oversight—principally via international financial consortia—had come to be seen as the way to contain the unilateralism of rivals, such as Russia and Japan, who were seen as threats to the open door.

Ideally, Wilson hoped to see the territories of the Central Powers put in the "mandatory" hands of small, "disinterested," "advanced" nations (like those of Scandinavia, he suggested). He told members of the Inquiry, aboard the *George Washington* on his way to Europe in December, that the German colonies should be declared the common property of the League of Nations and administered by small nations. The resources of each colony should be available to all members of the League. Small states were better than large ones for this duty, according to the president, because the possibility existed that, in the latter case, the mandatory might develop into the "owner."[6]

Here he had to compromise. For the most part, the conquerors, several of them great-power rivals of the United States, would be assigned the mandates (in some cases on terms not dramatically different from annexation).[7] But it nevertheless appeared at Paris that the president would be successful in compelling these "mandatories" to, in most places, exercise authority on the basis of American-endorsed ground rules—prominently including the open door and access for American missionaries—and be subject to review by the Executive Council of the League.[8]

Some of the Central Power territories were held to be of exceptional interest to the United States. For example, Japan had overrun the German-controlled Mariana, Caroline, and Marshall Islands in the Pacific during the fall of 1914. American policy makers, urged on by their naval advisers, were extremely anxious to prevent Japan from asserting sovereignty over these territories because they lay athwart U.S. lines of communication between Hawaii and the Philippines. The mandate idea was seen as very serviceable in this case, because by way of it Tokyo could be limited in its ability to develop the islands militarily.[9]

A greater range of concerns drove U.S. policy toward the Middle East. One important one was American commercial and missionary access. But, familiar with the dangers long associated with the so-called Eastern Question, the Wilson administration was also anxious that the region not become the flash point for another great-power war. Such, it was feared, might be the result of the big European powers each pursuing their interests there unilaterally.

In the Fourteen Points Address, Wilson had promised the "Turkish portions" of the Ottoman Empire a "secure sovereignty" (which—see below—did not necessarily translate into freedom from outside influence). But, coming away from the war, Washington ideally wanted the largely Arab lands to the south that had been part of that empire to be organized into one or more mandates under the immediate oversight of one or more small, neutral nations.[10] It also wanted the straits—the Bosporus and the Dardanelles—leading into and out of the Black Sea to be taken out of European great-power competition and turned into a barrier against any future effort by Germany to assemble a zone of influence extending from Berlin to Baghdad (this despite the worry that had been articulated by House that such an approach might work to undermine the position of Britain and the United States at, respectively, Suez and Panama).[11] The cause of stabilization, finally, was seen to require some attention to the feelings of the people, especially the Arabs, in the region.

There was never much chance that the big European victors would not figure in. In late April 1917, just after the U.S. declaration of war, Balfour had divulged to House some of the secret understandings that the Allies had made to one another. The Middle East figured prominently. The Allies, House recorded in his diary, "have agreed to give Russia a sphere of influence in Armenia and the northern part" of Anatolia. The British sought Mesopotamia (for its oil and because it lay athwart a major "overland" route to India). The French would have their sphere. There was agreement that Constantinople should be internationalized and that the Ottoman Empire should be dismantled, but as for the rest, House commented, "It is all bad and I told Balfour so. They are making it a breeding place for future war."[12]

Russia dropped out of this picture after the Bolshevik Revolution, but that only had the effect of intensifying tensions between France and Britain, particularly as the latter now saw less value in a French role. Setting the stage for charges of double-dealing, London had meanwhile already made promises implying independence for most of the region in a successful effort to enlist the Arabs in the defeat of the Ottomans. (It then muddied the waters further, in November 1917, when, via the Balfour Declaration, Britain announced its support for "the establishment in Palestine of a National home for the Jewish people.")[13]

Given these ambitions, and the strong military position the British in particular had come to occupy in the Middle East by the end of the war, American policy makers no doubt considered themselves fortunate that they were at least able to have the mandate approach to that region accepted at the beginning of 1919. Yet concerns remained, especially as to whether the open door would be respected and as to the attitude of the Arab people. These centered especially on France. Historically, it had never felt that it could compete on the basis of the open door. More pressingly, by late winter 1919, there were growing signs that its effort to occupy the areas it wanted, in Lebanon and Syria, would—at least in the latter case—be met by substantial, and embarrassing, local opposition.

At Paris, Faysal ibn Husayn conducted diplomacy on behalf of an envisioned independent and unitary kingdom of the Arabs in southwestern Asia. His father, Husayn bin Ali, was king of the Hejaz (the region along the east coast of the Red Sea that embraced Mecca and Medina), who with the encouragement of the British had risen up against the Ottomans. Leery in general of what the mandate system might portend for Arab independence, Faysal was particularly opposed to the French becoming the mandatory for Syria, fearing that this would lead, as in other areas around the Mediterranean, to substantial French settlement. He maintained that the local people should at least be able to weigh in on who their mandatory would be.

In the Council of Four on March 20, Wilson inquired of Edmund Allenby, the British general whose forces had taken Damascus the previous October, what the result would be if the French were invited "to occupy the region of Syria." Allenby (according to the notes taken by Maurice Hankey) "said there would be the strongest possible opposition by the whole of the Moslems, and especially by the Arabs." "If the French were given a mandate in Syria," he asserted, "there would be serious trouble and probably war. If Feisal undertook the direction of operations there might be a huge war covering the whole area. . . . [T]he consequences would be incalculable." Unnerved, Wilson subsequently suggested that an Inter-Allied Commission be sent to the region to ascertain the inhabitants' wishes (starting from the premise that there would be a mandatory). "If we were to send a Commission of men with no previous contact with Syria, it would, at any rate, convince the world that the Conference had tried to do all it could to find the most scientific basis possible for a settlement," he commented.[14]

This was agreed to, but when France delayed selecting its commission-ers, Wilson ultimately dispatched the men he had appointed, Henry Churchill King and Charles R. Crane, to the Middle East on their own.[15] From Beirut, they filed a preliminary report in July. It testified to a desire "for as early independence as possible" in the region and "[u]nexpectedly strong expressions of national feeling." If there were to be mandates, there was especial antipathy to any role for the French. They greatly praised Fay-sal. "Given the proper sympathy and surroundings," the commissioners thought there was "no danger of his getting adrift" or taking bold moves "without Anglo-Saxon approval."[16]

A final report was filed when they returned to Paris in August. In light of the opinions King and Crane had canvassed, it recommended that Syria, Palestine, and Lebanon "be kept a unity," Faysal be made king, the Zionist program be "seriously modified," and the mandate assigned either to the United States or Britain (the latter also to be allotted Mesopotamia).[17] In the end, however, the report had no practical significance. As historian Laurence Evans notes, the idea was for it to be presented to the conference when it took up negotiation of the Turkish treaty. But the United States wound up withdrawing from the conference before that took place.[18] The distribution of the Arabian mandates was eventually settled between the British and the French, with the latter getting Lebanon and Syria (and Pal-estine, Trans-Jordan, and Mesopotamia going to Britain). The regions far-ther south were accorded formal independence within what was envisioned as a general British sphere of influence. Arab nationalism, meanwhile, was emerging as an increasingly significant force.[19]

Lloyd George had early on expressed a desire to have the United States take one or more mandates. "[B]y making the offer to America," he told associates at the end of 1918, "we would remove any prejudice against us on the ground of 'land-grabbing.'"[20] He did not see the United States as a likely competitor either in Africa or the Middle East.

By May he had come to focus especially on Armenia and Constantino-ple.[21] The prime minister no doubt saw this as something that would reduce Britain's expenses, in particular as an American mandate in those areas would act as a buffer against potential expansion in the future on the part of Russia or Germany.

Wilson himself, for a time, warmed to the idea. Historian George Louis Beer, the American Colonial Delegate to the Peace Conference, had (partic-ularly in the context of Africa) been talking up the need for the United States to do its "share in caring for derelict territories and peoples."[22] In late June, Wilson told the Council of Four that he thought the Senate might accept a U.S. mandate for "the [Turkish] Straits, with a strip of territory surrounding the entire area." America would go there "to guard them, in the interest of all nations."[23] The next day, at a press conference, he men-tioned both Constantinople and Armenia.[24] But, back home, by August, as he began to appreciate the struggle he had before him over the treaty, Wil-son was adopting a pose of much greater caution.[25]

*   *   *

As noted, in his quest for victory over Germany during 1918, Wilson had proclaimed the Great War one for self-determination, the equality of nations, and the consent of the governed. The struggle, he had said, was one for all the people. America's mission was to act "not for a single people only, but for all mankind." The "plot" of the war the United States was engaged in, he declared in an Independence Day address, was "written plain upon every scene and every act." "On the one hand" stood "the peoples of the world," and "not only the peoples actually engaged, but many others also . . . of many races and in every part of the world." On the other stood a tiny group of German leaders who stood only for their "selfish ambitions."[26]

This language of universal rights, combined—as historians such as Erez Manela have noted—with the obvious power commanded by the United States, caught the attention not only of people in the subject territories of the Central Powers but also of advocates of independence in the—much larger—Allied "colonial world."[27] Genuinely hopeful and excited that something was going to come of such rhetoric, many of the latter chose representatives to travel to Paris and lobby on behalf of their people's freedom.

But the cause of independence in such lands had never been one that Wilson intended to take up. Particularly given his interest in the stabilization of a reconstructed international order, the president certainly looked with favor on various reforms. He endorsed improvements in the treatment and training of colonial peoples (just as, especially against the backdrop of the Bolshevik Revolution, he supported some measures for the amelioration of the conditions of industrial workers around the world). These ideas directly mirrored Wilson's response to social instability at home in America in these years.

Someday those peoples might ideally be brought to a condition where they would act as he would have them on their own (the end result the president envisioned, for example, for the Philippines). But precisely because of his interest in stabilizing the kind of international order he wanted, the president was not going to champion independence for people he deemed—drawing on his social evolutionary, racialist outlook—irresponsible and unready.

The case of Ireland, meanwhile, vividly demonstrated that even where he believed people might have more self-government, the president was not going to do anything on their behalf that might undercut relations with a major ally. Wilson's impact, as Manela suggests, was simultaneously to stimulate anticolonialism at the end of the war and, over time, to spread disillusionment about where he himself stood.

Many nationalist figures appealed directly to the president for support, but for the most part they were either ignored, told that the conference already had too much to do, or encouraged to view the League, once it was established, as the forum where they should pursue their appeals.[28] From within the French Empire, Wilson received a petition by cable from Tunisian nationalists. He was also asked for an audience by the man who was to become the most prominent Vietnamese figure of the twentieth century, Ho Chi Minh. After traveling throughout the world, including to the United States, Ho—still in his twenties—had arrived in Paris during the war and immediately become involved in émigré politics. The Vietnamese community included many who had been recruited to work in French factories during the conflict (while still others from "French Indochina" had made up labor battalions near the front). Under the name Nguyen Ai Quoc (Nguyen the patriot), Ho (born Nguyen Tat Thanh) drafted and circulated widely a petition calling for political autonomy. House acknowledged its receipt and promised to bring it to Wilson's attention, but that was as far as things got. A decade on, Ho told colleagues that many had been misled by the president's wartime "song of freedom."[29]

Missives were also dispatched, and representatives sent, on behalf of freedom for Japan's largest colony. With, in fact, the acquiescence of the United States, Tokyo had consolidated its influence over the Korean Peninsula in the period after the Russo-Japanese War of 1904–5. In 1910, Japan formally annexed that country.

But resistance was widespread, and at the end of the Great War, on March 1, 1919, some nationalists—intentionally employing the language that had been used by Wilson—signed and circulated a declaration of independence. This sparked major demonstrations and what historians have come to refer to as the March First Movement.

The official U.S. position was that Korea was part of Japan. The State Department did everything it could to distance Washington from the protests. It also refused assistance to Korean nationalists living in the United States who wanted to travel to Paris. Nationalist Kim Kyusik, who had been living in exile in Shanghai, did get there. But he failed to get a meeting with any of the American higher ups, "even in an unofficial way."[30]

Not surprisingly, appeals were also made on behalf of territories under the control of London. For decades a movement had been developing in India, the "jewel in the crown" of the vast British Empire, on behalf of a greater role for Indians in the governance of the subcontinent.[31] During the war, more than a million men from there participated as soldiers in the British war effort (in both Europe and the Middle East). The subcontinent's economy was affected by the conflict as well. Many locals hoped that India would be rewarded after the war with political reforms. And, as was also the case with the French and Indochina, the promise of such was ultimately held out, in 1917, in a declaration made by Secretary of State for India Edwin Montagu.

Initially received with favor, the vagueness of Montagu's pledge eventually invited doubt, just as the sacrifices of wartime continued to fan the desire for significant change. Wilson's rhetoric of 1918 was seized upon as new evidence that the latter might be in reach, and it also formed the basis for reformulated demands. At this time, groups like the Indian National Congress still focused on the achievement of dominion status as their goal. But they increasingly insisted that it should be people in India, not London, who controlled the process of reform and that Indians should be able to "self-determine" the timing and nature of change. The Muslim League, for example, asserted that in light of Allied statesmen endorsing self-determination, the subcontinent "should have the immediate opportunity of freely exercising that right."[32]

The Indian National Congress hoped to have reformers represent India in Paris. But this was denied. Still optimistic, one of its choices for that mission, Bal Gangadhar Tilak, tried to carry on the campaign from London. He wrote directly to Lloyd George, Clemenceau, and Wilson, but with little result. Tilak told the latter that the "world's hope for peace and justice is centered in you as the author of the great principle of self-determination." But the only acknowledgment he received from the president was a letter from his secretary, Gilbert Close, assuring him that "the matter of self-determination for India" would be taken up "in due time" by the "proper authorities." Back in India, meanwhile, a move by the government to extend emergency powers that had been enacted during the war led to widespread protests and then repression.[33]

Nationalism was also becoming an important force in Egypt. Although technically still a part of the Ottoman Empire, it had become increasingly autonomous during the nineteenth century. European influence and inter-est in the country grew from midcentury, especially after the opening of the Suez Canal in 1869. And that passageway, in turn, came more and more to be valued by Britain as a strategic and commercial link with all of the regions around the Indian Ocean and farther east.

Riots in protest of European dominance of the economy in 1882 led to the intervention of British troops, who subsequently remained in occupa-tion. Then, in 1914, after Egypt's putative suzerain entered the Great War on the side of the Central Powers, London formally declared the country to be a "protectorate." It became a major base of military operations against the Ottomans. Martial law was imposed and significant demands were made on Egyptian resources and labor power.

At the end of the war, demands for independence coalesced in the cre-ation of a new political party, the Wafd, whose leaders, rebuffed by London, were eager to take their case to the peace conference. Appeals for support were directed to the American consul general in Cairo and also to Wilson, on the grounds of the latter's rhetoric about "self-determination." But these received only perfunctory responses. Continued agitation by the party led to its leaders being sent into exile, in Malta, in March, which in turn set off demonstrations on the part of a broad cross section of the population.

Allenby was sent back to the region, now as the high commissioner. Also, in an effort to stem the turmoil, it was announced that the leaders would be allowed to travel as they liked. The focus shifted to Paris. Expecting that Sa'd Zaghlul and other Wafd leaders would soon arrive there, Balfour moved to preempt them. Through Wiseman and House, he implored the United States immediately to recognize the protectorate and thereby deprive the Wafd of the claim that they had, or would soon have, Wilson's support. Issuing a statement that expressed sympathy with the desire of Egyptians for "a further measure of self-government" but denouncing efforts to achieve such "by anarchy and violence," the Americans obliged. When Zaghlul reached Paris, Wilson refused to meet him.[34]

One of the thorniest challenges the president faced, as a result of his "self-determination" rhetoric, came in connection with Ireland. This was due to the electoral importance of Americans of Irish descent. They had for many years not only been a key Democratic voting bloc, but also a constituency sympathetic to a change in Ireland's relationship to Britain. Both in Ireland and among Irish Americans, there were high expectations that Wilson would champion formal discussion of that country's political status at Paris.

Long aware of Irish American feelings, and reminded of them often by his political operative-adviser-secretary Joseph Tumulty, the president had hoped for years that England would grant Ireland home rule, or dominion, status (and this view appears to have been conveyed to Balfour, at least by Lansing, after the United States became a belligerent). This, it was anticipated, would please Irish Americans. Still more important, it would remove a major impediment to Britain and the United States collaborating in international affairs. There would never be "real comradeship between America and England until this issue is definitely settled and out of the way," Wilson told Tumulty.[35]

The relationship with London, in fact, remained the most important consideration. On the eve of the president's departure for Europe, in December 1918, Senator Thomas J. Walsh (D-Mont.) wrote Wilson that "[w]e shall not escape the harsh judgment of posterity if we do not insist on the same measure of justice for the people of Ireland" that the United States had declared it its "purpose to exact" for those "held unwilling subjects of the Central Powers." The president said he could promise nothing, but he would "use my influence at every opportunity to bring about a just and satisfactory solution."[36] Wilson had, however, already assured

Wiseman, ten months before, that "as far as he was concerned he would not allow Ireland to be dragged into a Peace Conference."[37]

In the aftermath of the British suppression of the Easter Rebellion in the spring of 1916, home rule had given way to the creation of an independent republic as the favored objective of nationalists in Ireland. Sinn Fein, the political champion of that course, became the largest political party. Independence was declared in January 1919, following which the nationalists' hope was that this status might be recognized by the conference in Paris. However much support independence had in the United States though, Wilson was eager to keep the issue at arm's length. Sinn Fein representatives were denied access to any but low-level American officials.

During Wilson's brief trip home in late winter, Tumulty urged the president to grant an audience to American backers of independence lest he disaffect important political support. Wilson complied, but at the meeting he pronounced the issue a "domestic affair for Great Britain and Ireland to settle themselves." The "Irish race," the president complained on his way back to France, was "very hard to deal with."[38] Many Democrats, including Wilson, subsequently began to worry that the issue might complicate the task of treaty ratification.

In April, three prominent Irish American Democrats, including Frank P. Walsh (who along with Taft had headed up the National War Labor Board), followed the president to Paris. Their hope was to gain safe conduct for Sinn Fein leaders to travel there; failing that, to lobby themselves on behalf of independence. Feeling pressed, House and Wilson each met with Walsh. Help was promised on safe conduct. Wilson also said he would address the Irish question himself *after* there was a peace settlement. At the urging of the Americans, Lloyd George allowed the three to visit Ireland. But when, once there, they spoke publicly on behalf of independence, the prime minister exploded in fury and placed restrictions on their visit. Wilson subsequently characterized Walsh and his associates as selfish "mischief makers," and curtailed his contacts with them.[39]

From the end of 1918, considerable support had built up in Congress behind the cause of Irish independence. On June 6, a proindependence resolution passed the Senate, sixty-one votes to one. This was sponsored by William E. Borah (R-Idaho), an opponent of the League and a supporter of the idea of self-determination for Britain's colonies. It called for the Irish case to be brought before the conference. After confirming what Lloyd George's reaction would be, Wilson decided that he would try to side-step responsibility back home by asking if Clemenceau would not raise the issue. The latter, predictably, ignored it, and that is where things remained.[40]

More familiar with Wilson than people from other parts of the world, figures from the Dominican Republic showed up in the French capital too. They pushed for an end to the U.S. military occupation of their country—now in its third year—on the grounds that it violated self-determination. But they only found sympathy from among some of the Latin Americans in attendance at the conference. Appeals to the conference also came from the Philippines, a U.S. colony, and Haiti, which, like the Dominican Republic, was under U.S. occupation.[41]

*   *   *

Wilson also sought to keep W. E. B. Du Bois, the prominent American scholar and civil rights activist, at arm's length in Paris. After the United States became a belligerent, Du Bois, in his capacity as editor of the NAACP journal *Crisis*, had (in July 1918) called upon African Americans to "close ranks" behind the president's course and rally behind the war effort, this on the grounds that a thankful nation, ideologically championing democracy and equality abroad, would subsequently have to address racial oppression in the United States. Several hundred thousand African American men joined the armed forces and two hundred thousand were sent to Europe (as part of segregated units). But a great number were restricted to duty as laborers, while those who went to the front often did so without adequate supplies, equipment, or training. Their contributions and abilities were disparaged and derided by many in the American high command, which also took official umbrage at a French public and military that treated African American servicemen, in its view, with excessive regard. Such treatment, it maintained, constituted a threat to the U.S. postwar social order (Wilson himself fretting that African American soldiers were the most likely means by which Bolshevism would cross the Atlantic and reach the United States).[42]

In December 1918, Du Bois set off to France with a mandate from the NAACP to compile a history of the experiences and activities of African American soldiers in the war. He also harbored another ambition, and that was to lobby the conference on behalf of the future of Africa. As Du Bois saw it, the "destiny of mankind for a hundred years to come" was going to be decided in Paris. And he wanted to seize the opportunity to put the colonies of that continent on a path to political independence, a course that he was sure would redound to the improvement of peoples of African descent in the western hemisphere as well. Seeking to garner consideration for Africans, just as other "little groups who want to be nations" were trying to do for themselves at Paris, Du Bois worked to assemble a Pan-African Congress in the city alongside the peace conference. Initially, this met a wall of resistance on the part of the major powers. But Clemenceau finally relented and provided assistance, perhaps as gesture of thanks to Blaise Diagne, a member of the French National Assembly from Senegal, who had signed up many tens of thousands of men from French West Africa to fight for France.[43]

Du Bois had developed a plan whereby a vast area of Central and Southern Africa would gradually be helped and prepared by the League, and by sympathetic whites and members of the African diaspora, to become an autonomous state. Its territory would start with colonies there that Germany was being forced to forfeit (Kamerun, German South-West Africa, German East Africa, and Togo). But, ideally, it would also come to include the large adjacent and connecting colonies of the Allied countries of Portugal (Angola and Mozambique) and Belgium (the Congo), all of which German expansionists had hoped to meld into their empire (and had referred to as Mittelafrika).[44]

Not unlike many proponents of change at the time, Du Bois was hoping for a League of Nations quite different than what the great powers had in mind. Indeed, his would have the power to challenge the major states, in particular over discrimination against the "Negro race" in the colonies, in South Africa, and in the United States. He hoped it would have the ability to "oppose the doctrines of 'race' antagonism and inferiority." "Peace for us," Du Bois wrote in the spring of 1919, "is not simply Peace from Wars like the past, but relief from the spectre of the Great War of Races which will be absolutely inevitable unless the selfish nations of white civilization are curbed by a Great World Congress in which black and white and yellow sit and speak and act."[45]

The Pan-African Congress was held, from February 19 to 21, at the Grand Hotel. There were fifty-eight delegates in attendance. Not surprisingly, most were not from the African colonies. Sixteen African Americans, who were already in Europe, participated (State Department policy was to deny passports to Americans who wanted to travel there). And a number of resolutions were passed, in the hope that they could be presented to the peace conference.[46]

But nothing came of Du Bois's efforts. However much they disagreed over mandates and how they might be arranged, none of the big powers had any interest in the "withdrawal of Europeans from Africa" that the American scholar-activist desperately sought.[47] Indeed, Britain and France, the two powers that between them controlled most of the continent, had a direct interest in just the opposite. And the U.S. officials at Paris were meanwhile certain that it would be a very long time before the Africans were "ready." Steeped in the view, just the opposite of Du Bois's, that nothing positive had happened in Africa until the Europeans arrived, they could only conceive of Africans as "savages," as Lansing put it, in need of outside control.[48] The withdrawal of that would be anything but conducive to the stabilization the United States sought.

However much he spoke, and probably saw himself, as the champion of "all mankind," Wilson was in fact the most antiblack president the United States had had since at least the time of Andrew Johnson right after the Civil War. He showed D. W. Griffith's film *The Birth of a Nation* (originally *The Clansman*) in the White House and endorsed its racist view of Reconstruction. He allowed members of his cabinet to segregate their departments. He hesitated even to condemn lynching and mob violence directed against African Americans, lest he upset his political party's southern white electoral base. And, he sought to impress acquaintances with insulting, but what he took to be entertaining (supposedly in dialect), "Negro stories."[49]

A great upsurge of violence directed against African Americans both in the U.S. South and North, where many had migrated in search of employment during the war, broke out over the course of the spring and summer of 1919, seeming—along with Wilson's positions at Paris—to mock the hopes that Du Bois had entertained just a year before.[50]

CHAPTER 12

Americans in Paris: The Adriatic and Shandong Controversies

Two issues, brewing since the beginning of the conference, assumed pressing importance for Wilson once the basic outlines of the Versailles Treaty had finally been decided. Each pitted him against a prominent ally deemed important both to the overall settlement and to the League. One controversy revolved around Italy's demand that it be allowed to acquire territory formerly belonging to Austria-Hungary that extended well down the eastern shores of the Adriatic Sea. The other pertained to Japan's desire to be granted the rights that Germany had exercised, up until late 1914, on the Shandong Peninsula in China.

The president opposed the wishes of both powers. Yet, albeit with some conditions, he ultimately yielded to Tokyo, while he resisted giving in to Rome. Much discussion of his decision on Shandong has been framed to explain why Wilson felt it necessary on that occasion to (again, it should be noted) violate his "principles" (specifically on self-determination, the consent of the governed, and the equality of states). Explanations of his course in the Adriatic, meanwhile, have focused on why here he felt he could—or had to—stand by them.

In fact, neither episode involved a principled stand. And what has generally been obscured is that there was a unity to the president's diplomacy in both cases. That becomes evident when each is viewed against the backdrop of what really drove Wilson's approach—to almost every question—at the peace conference, namely a quest to reconstruct and put on a more solid basis the kind of pro-American international order that he desired.

*   *   *

At a crucial point during the conference, Wilson did publicly criticize Italy's leaders on grounds of principle. This was part of an effort to refurbish a reputation that by that point had been seriously compromised by the president's deviations from what most understood to be the meaning of the Fourteen Points. Indeed, historian Sterling Kernek suggests that the president's decision to air his differences with Orlando and his foreign minister, Sidney Sonnino, on April 23 was aimed more at audiences outside Italy (particularly in the United States) than in.[1] The published statement is, however, an inadequate guide to what drove Wilson's Adriatic policy.

The president did have real problems with Italy's claims, but they need to be traced back to his interest in a stabilized postwar Europe. In regard to the South Slavs, Wilson was never a principled champion of self-determination, consent of the governed, or national equality. The Fourteen Points had not called for those regions that, with Serbia, would later be joined together into the state of Jugo-Slavia (the Kingdom of the Croats, Slovenes, and Serbs) to become independent of Austria-Hungary. Point 10 had merely said that the "peoples" of that empire "should be accorded the freest opportunity of autonomous development."[2] Support for independence came only in mid-1918 after Washington concluded that Vienna would never sign a separate peace.[3] More important, although he objected to the *extent* of Rome's demands on the east coast of the Adriatic, the president was willing in 1919 to accept a boundary that would concede to it considerable territory there that was predominantly peopled by Slovenes and Croatians.[4] His stance was a far cry from the apparent meaning of what Wilson had said the previous year in Point 9, namely that "[a] readjustment of the frontiers of Italy should be effected along clearly recognizable lines of nationality."[5]

The president went to Europe eager to keep Italy in the triumphant-great-power fold. Indeed, it was probably for that reason that the United States, almost immediately, conceded to Rome the whole of South Tyrol, up to the strategically valuable Brenner Pass. That was an area that, toward the north, contained a quarter million German speakers (who otherwise would have been incorporated into the rump state of Austria).[6] But Wilson wanted to limit the degree to which the settlement in the Adriatic was likely to offend the sensibilities of the new South Slav nation. Particularly in the

Balkans, but not unlike elsewhere in Eastern and Central Europe, he was eager to avoid a result where a mood of disappointed nationalism might fester and contribute, as in 1914, to the outbreak of another war. The retention of Austria-Hungary would have been worth trying in order to win the Great War. But, for stabilization, Wilson was now hoping for a situation where the new Jugo-Slavia—composed of what he called a "turbulent people"—would accept its boundaries.[7]

Ten days before the armistice, Wilson wrote House that this was "the time to win the confidence" of the peoples living in the "pieces" of the former Austria-Hungary. "[T]he peace of Europe," he said, obviously thinking of 1914, "pivots there."[8] Well aware (though he would later claim that he was not) of the Treaty of London of 1915 (wherein the Allies, as part of their effort to bring Italy into the war, had signed off on its aspirations in the Adriatic), Wilson went to Europe expecting disagreement on this issue. His hope was that he could resolve it by being, by his lights, "very generous."[9] By this he seems to have meant conceding Italy South Tyrol plus much of Istria.

This was a major preoccupation for the president during and immediately after his trip to Italy at the New Year. Sonnino was interested in the Balkans as a field for Italian expansion, but Orlando was concerned above all about the coastal territories' potential impact on Italian politics. Acquisitions across the Adriatic (and elsewhere) would, he hoped, make what had been an enormously costly war seem worthwhile to his countrymen, among many of whom high expectations had been raised.

In his discussions with Wilson and others, however, the prime minister cast his case for the eastern Adriatic coast principally in terms of defensive, strategic requirements. Especially given the lack of suitable sites for bases on the Adriatic's western shores, the valuable harbors and islands across the sea, he insisted, had to be in Italy's hands. Wilson suggested other ways of addressing these concerns. And he subsequently confided to Grayson that he was "debating . . . how far he could disappoint" Italian "popular ambitions and still get through an amicable settlement."[10]

Several days later, the president sent Orlando a letter with a map. The letter had drawn on it the boundary line along the Adriatic coast as proposed in the Treaty of London, which he said he could not support, and another line that he said he could. This second line offered Italy much less (but still areas inhabited principally by South Slavs). In his letter, Wilson begged Orlando to see Italy's security situation in a new light now that

Austria-Hungary had collapsed and the League of Nations seemed likely to be realized. The boundaries proposed in the Treaty of London, he said, "were laid down as a frontier against" an empire "that no longer exists." He maintained that none of the successor states "will be strong enough seriously to menace Italy." And they would have to "accept from the League of Nations a limitation of their armaments." Beyond this, Wilson would back several other conditions: that the new "Jugo-Slavic State be erected on the understanding that it maintain no navy," that fortifications and arms on the east coast of the Adriatic be forbidden, that Jugo-Slavia, along with all of the other new states, agree that they would not discriminate against (Italian or other) "minorities within their jurisdiction," and that Fiume and Zara be turned into free cities and ports. He hoped that "Italy will accept this just settlement as her contribution to the longed-for peace of the World."[11]

But the prime minister clearly felt it was too late to reverse his course. In early February, he reaffirmed Rome's interest in the boundaries promised in the Treaty of London. He also expanded on those claims by asking for Fiume. This was a city that—because of an Italian population that lived in its central districts—had recently captured the imagination of the nationalists that Orlando felt his government had to attend to.[12]

The issue failed to get sorted out at lower levels in February and March, and thus remained to be dealt with by the Big Four as they began to wrap up the German treaty in April. In the middle of the month, the president handed Orlando a memorandum that largely recapitulated his arguments of three months before. With Austria-Hungary gone, Wilson insisted, the territories across the Adriatic from Italy were to be "organized for the purpose of satisfying legitimate national aspirations." He did not want them to be "hostile to the new European order but . . . interested in its maintenance." The president agreed that "the greater part of the Istrian Peninsula [containing a large number of Croats and Slovenes] should be ceded" to Rome. But he opposed "including Fiume or . . . the coast lying to the South of Fiume [principally Dalmatia]" (though he was willing to accept Rome's possession of the island of Lissa and the port of Valona [in Albania]). There was a need to avoid the "fatal error of making Italy's nearest neighbors on the East her enemies and nursing just such a sense of injustice as has disturbed the peace of Europe for generations . . . and played no small part in bringing on the terrible conflict through which we have just passed."[13]

Five days later, at a meeting of the Council of Four, the president reiterated that Fiume was a port that would be economically vital to the new states created by the collapse of the empire. He also averred that an outcome in the Adriatic such as Italy wanted would run the risk that the "people of the United States would repudiate" engagement in the postwar European order. Wilson said that there had once had been a time when he had not cared what happened in Europe. "Now, however, it was his privilege to assist Europe to create a new order. If he should succeed, he could bring all the resources of his people to assist in the task."[14] (In the meantime, as evidenced by a note he wrote to Norman Davis the same day, the president was determined to have the U.S. Treasury delay any further credits to Italy.[15])

The issue began to dominate the conference. Neither Lloyd George nor Clemenceau felt that Italy's contribution to the war justified the claims it was making. But they also saw no alternative to according Rome what it had been promised, if it insisted on the 1915 treaty. And if it did, that seemed likely to jeopardize continued U.S. involvement in Europe in the ways they were hoping for. On the following Monday, April 21, Lloyd George, Clemenceau, and Balfour put it to Sonnino and Orlando that they would all lose, that Europe could not "put itself back in working order" if the United States was not politically and economically a factor. But, facing a "nationalistic revolution" at home, the Italian leaders refused to budge and were angry. Having already compromised their principles "right and left" at the conference, Sonnino charged, the Americans were now trying to recover their "virginity" at Rome's expense.[16]

Wilson was apparently willing to grant more islands (so long as the offer was made through Clemenceau or Lloyd George), while the British prime minister began to ponder compensation for Italy in Asia Minor.[17] But the Italian leaders intimated that they might leave the conference and skip Versailles if their claims were not conceded. The president rejoined that the Western powers risked alienating the Slavs such that they might be driven into the hands of Russia and the Bolsheviks.[18] In the statement he published on the twenty-third, Wilson recapitulated all of the arguments he had made previously. He concluded by asserting that the United States had gone to war on behalf of a new order and new principles. "[T]he compulsion is upon her to square every decision she takes a part in with those principles," Wilson said.[19] Orlando took offense. The president, he alleged, was trying to interfere in Italian politics. He left the conference the next day, and, upon returning home, received a strong vote of confidence from the Italian parliament.

But Orlando had not achieved his objectives, and Britain, France, and the United States seemed prepared to continue without him. Financial assistance from the United States was being held up. Clemenceau and Lloyd George were suggesting that Italy's withdrawal eliminated their need to honor the Treaty of London. Austria's delegates would soon be meeting with the Allies to discuss its frontiers, including in the Tyrol. It became obvious that it would be dangerous not to return to Paris, which the Italian prime minister finally did on May 7.[20]

The powers remained as far apart as ever on the Adriatic, and their search for a solution, and maneuvering, continued. Just before Orlando's return, the Big Three learned that Italy had sent naval vessels to both Fiume and Smyrna (on the western coast of Asia Minor). The Treaty of London had included the promise that Italy would be rewarded in Asia Minor if the Ottoman Empire ceased to exist. To Lloyd George, Clemenceau, and Wilson, it appeared as if Rome was preparing to act on its own if the conference did not grant what it thought it was entitled to.

The three dispatched warships to those waters to keep a watchful eye.[21] But, among themselves, the Big Three now also began to explore new ways by which Italy might be brought around. Wilson was willing for there to be a plebiscite in Fiume, on the condition that if Italy should win there it would drop its other claims. With Lloyd George in the lead, the three also began to ponder, in essence, whether Rome's acquiescence in the Adriatic might be purchased at the expense of the self-determination, consent, and equality of someplace other than Jugo-Slavia.

On the thirteenth, the British prime minister asked the others to look at things from what he took to be Italy's standpoint. They were not being treated as equal to the other great powers. "They realized that there were a certain number of backward people to be taken in hand by more efficient nations. . . . No one, however, was asking Italy to undertake this burden. Consequently, their pride of race was hurt. . . . It would be much better to settle the question of Fiume in this sort of atmosphere," he said. "The principal Allied and Associated Powers were the real trustees of the League of Nations looking after the backward races, and for a long time, they would remain the trustees of the League of Nations. (President Wilson agreed.)" "Why should we not say frankly to the Italians," Lloyd George continued, " 'we have not quite worked you into the picture yet.' " They should be invited to "develop a part of Anatolia" and Italian emigration should be encouraged in that direction. The president agreed that Lloyd George "had stated the case on right principles." He, however, very enamored—at this point—of the Greek prime minister, Eleutherios Venezelos, wanted (the heavily ethnic Greek) Smyrna (along with the Dodecanese Islands) to be joined "in complete sovereignty" to Greece and for that country also to act as a mandatory over a surrounding area of Anatolia. Italy's point of entry, and sphere of activity, Wilson suggested, should be around the port of Makri. (As to the likely Turkish reaction to this, apparently neither Clemenceau nor Lloyd George voiced disagreement with Wilson's misguided assertion that they were a "docile people.") As part of this "comprehensive proposal" they were formulating, the president also urged that Italy be given more territory in East Africa, specifically in Somaliland.[22]

Then, over the next two weeks, the Big Three had a complete change of heart. This was brought on by two developments. Italy began to land and position troops in southern Anatolia in a way that, they worried, was a prelude to it acting unilaterally. Simultaneously, a Muslim delegation from India appeared before the Council to champion an undivided Turkey as well as the traditional role of the Ottoman Sultan as the caliph (temporal steward) for much of the Islamic world.[23] The British prime minister, in particular, no doubt with British interests throughout Southwest and South Asia in mind, became anxious that the Council not do anything that would shock "Mohammedan opinion."

On the nineteenth of May, Lloyd George told the Council that he would like to reconsider. "To put the Turks under the Italians when they thought themselves better men . . . would put the whole Mohammedan world in revolt." "[H]is present attitude," the prime minister continued, "was that it would be best to get the Italians out of Asia Minor altogether." Wilson said that until the "Mohammedan deputation" he had forgotten his statement about Turkish sovereignty in the Fourteen Points. Now he had a new idea. This was "in effect to give a mandate"—over the Sultan, and Anatolia—"to France without calling it a mandate." "That is to say," the nimble architect of the new international organization went on, "France would not be responsible to the League of Nations, she would be in a similar position as an independent friendly country advising the Turkish Government under treaty stipulations."[24] From this remarkable juncture, the discussion shifted back to efforts to find a U.S.-Italian compromise in the

Adriatic, Wilson now taking the position that he would allow Rome to have any territory there where the population voted for Italian sovereignty.

But agreement was never reached, even though the Italian government, under Orlando's successor Francesco Nitti, did by late summer shift a good bit. In August, it announced that it would yield the Dalmatian coast to Jugo-Slavia and accept Fiume becoming a neutral city under the League. Italian ultra-nationalists, however, now began to act on their own. Under the leadership of the nationalist poet Gabriele D'Annunzio, several hundred armed men, with the acquiescence of the Italian military, simply seized control of Fiume in September.[25]

When he left the conference at the end of June, Wilson's attitude toward Italy was that they "must be with us or outside us."[26] As for Turkey, which had for a time seemed to constitute a solution to his Balkan concerns, although he now opposed Rome having any role in its affairs, he still "thought some Power ought to have a firm hand" and that the Turks "ought to be cleared out" of Europe.[27] Yet Lloyd George and Wilson were disinclined to suggest that England or the United States exercise such a role in Asia Minor, and the British cabinet prevailed upon the prime minister to oppose it being assumed by France. Some offered that Anatolia might instead be influenced more informally, via outside financial pressure and Allied control of mandates around its periphery.

Events were in any event soon moving in an entirely different direction. Greek military operations in and beyond Smyrna were, already by summer, helping greatly to encourage the development of a Turkish nationalist movement that would challenge the big powers' plans for that region.[28]

*   *   *

The Shandong matter, revolving about Japan's desire to inherit the rights in a Chinese province that, via intimidation, Germany had acquired at the turn of the century, provides one of the most prominent examples of Wilson's willingness to depart from his "principles" at the conference. The decision he eventually made—to go along with Tokyo—was dominated, once again, by his desire to restore and stabilize the kind of international order he wanted.

The turning point in this episode came in late April, when Tokyo made it clear that it would walk away from the conference, the treaty, and the League if—all the more in light of the failure of the racial equality clause—Japan did not get what it saw as this just reward for its role in the war. As has been noted, the League was the key mechanism Wilson was looking to for postwar stabilization. Its big-power members would adopt a more harmonious approach to their competition in and supervision of the underdeveloped world (e.g., with regard to places like China). If Japan walked away from the conference (and it could plausibly do so more easily and successfully than Italy), the president worried that his plans not only for the Far East but for the eastern hemisphere more generally would be thrown into question.

Japan was perhaps the foremost example of a power whose freedom of action Wilson wished to see contained. Indeed, Washington's approach to world order had, to a considerable extent, developed since early in the century side by side with its experience trying to ensure against Japan dramatically challenging the open door and China's territorial integrity. A key lesson Wilson felt he had learned as a result of his administration's failed approach to East Asia during his first term was precisely that the U.S. effort henceforth should be to try to absorb Tokyo into a collective great-power approach. This should be pursued at least until the dreamed-for time when, it was imagined, a strong Chinese government, pro-American in orientation, and willing to arrange its policies in line with what Washington considered "responsible," came into being. In acting as he did in the spring of 1919, Wilson had in mind this "big picture."

Note has been taken of the reservations voiced by Wilson on the eve of American belligerency, namely his worry that it might be important for some part of the "white race" to remain strong so as to block challenges in East Asia by Japan. Later, concern that Tokyo intended to contest the framework the United States desired in the Far East was a central element in the administration's thinking about Allied intervention in Siberia. And that worry intensified when, contrary to the president's hopes, Tokyo began to flood Northeast Asia with troops at the end of the summer of 1918.[29]

Such is the backdrop against which to understand Wilson's course on Shandong. Needless to say, and to a degree he understood this, his decision would be costly. It would create confusion in the United States, where more and more Americans were striving to comprehend how what Washington was engaged in was an anti-imperial war. And it would lead in China, as in other parts of the underdeveloped world, to profound disillusionment with the settlement.

Wilson's decision confounded the hopes and expectations of virtually all politically active Chinese. China had itself become a belligerent on the side of the Allies in August 1917. As historian Xu Guoqi has noted, for many Chinese, involvement seemed to offer great opportunities. The recovery of Shandong was considered just one goal that might be achieved. It was hoped that China might win a role at the peace conference and that that would give it a chance to push for the return of all foreign concessions and leaseholds, to regain control over its tariff system, and generally to overturn the system of unequal arrangements and treaties that the country had been forced to accept by outside powers over the previous century. Unable either to finance or transport an army to Europe, China did provide 150,000 to 200,000 laborers for the Allied cause, which, in turn, alleviated military recruitment problems for Britain and France. Most of China's hopes, however, were destined to be disappointed.[30]

As was true in many other areas of the underdeveloped world, Wilson's wartime proclamations and addresses created great excitement and expectations in China. The impact there was especially far-reaching because China had been the target of a major CPI propaganda effort during the war's last months. The president and his Fourteen Points, as well as American foreign policy, were promoted in China via the publication and printing of thousands of photographs, posters, engravings, and buttons bearing Wilson's image, as well as by way of newsreels and the distribution of reprints of Wilson's speeches.[31] By the time China's delegation set forth for Paris, there was throughout that country's politically active population a widespread hope that the peace conference might usher in a new international order, grounded on the ideas of the equality of nations and the consent of the governed. Wilson was widely looked to as the champion of that, and there was great interest in the concept of a league.[32]

Disillusionment first began to set in when it was learned that China would get only two conference seats and then when it became clear that the proceedings would in any event largely be controlled by the great powers. Shandong subsequently became the main focus of China's delegation.

China scored a triumph when, to Japan's chagrin, it was granted the opportunity to have its views heard by the Council of Ten, this when, in late January, the future of Shandong first came up in connection with the German settlement. Wellington Koo, who was also the Chinese minister to the United States, made what by all accounts was an eloquent and forceful presentation. He emphasized that the people of the peninsula were Chinese and that the region had great historical and cultural importance for China by virtue of it being the birthplace of Confucius. The rights that had been obtained by Germany were nontransferable, and they had ended when China became a belligerent. Tokyo, he conceded, could point to treaties that Beijing had signed acknowledging the transfer, but these had been negotiated under duress.[33]

The Japanese were surprised and stung by this challenge. Shandong had become an objective of enormous importance to them, and their hope and expectation had been that the Chinese would follow the lead of Japan's delegates at the conference.

Blood had been spilled to defeat the German forces in northeast China, and the triumph had been sold to the Japanese public as a great victory. Moreover, powerful political elements were insisting that this issue was of vital importance to Japan. They thought Tokyo ought rightfully to play a leadership role in the whole region. China should accept Japan's guidance and other powers should deal with East Asia through Tokyo. Japan's future and its security would be in jeopardy if it were not accorded here something akin to a Monroe Doctrine of its own. If Japan was not granted Shandong, that would embolden the other powers. It would guarantee that China became the scene of intensified postwar great-power competition.

For the new, more cautious, Takashi Hara ministry that had recently come to power, there was an irreducible bottom line. Its delegates suggested from the beginning of the conference that Tokyo was willing ultimately to return the German leasehold in the province to China (with Japan nevertheless retaining key railroad rights and other concessions). But this could come about only following the other powers' acceptance of the full transfer to Tokyo of Germany's rights and as the consequence of subsequent, and satisfactory, bilateral negotiations between China and Japan.[34]

Over the following weeks, the United States came to be seen as the major threat. Both Britain and France had secretly assured Japan of their support over Shandong early in 1917. Meanwhile, Wilson's rhetoric was seen as a factor in the nationalist activity in Korea, and while the United States kept its distance from the March First Movement, Japanese diplomats were uncertain as to whether that would hold in the case of China.

Key specialists in the American delegation did indeed warn Wilson that failure to support China over Shandong would lead to a dramatic reduction of American influence in that country. And, in line with that perspective, the president initially spoke as China's champion, this when the topic came before the Council on April 15.[35]

Three days later, on Friday, April 18, Lloyd George commented that "[f]or the moment, we only have to see what is appropriate to put in our treaty with Germany." He did not see why Germany's leasehold "should not be treated in the same way as all other German territories overseas, which, we have decided, are to be handed over" to the Council to "dispose of as they see fit." Wilson endorsed this as the "best solution," and it was adopted. He then opined that both Japan and China would be impressed if this was followed up by all powers renouncing any spheres of influence they had in China (a longtime U.S. objective). Lloyd George was open to studying this "on the sole condition that the principle of the open door continues." "Certainly," rejoined Wilson.[36] That was, in fact, a central objective.

The following Monday morning, the two most prominent members of the Japanese delegation, Baron Makino Nobuaki and Viscount Chinda Sutemi, appeared at the president's residence to tell him that Tokyo would oppose Shandong being turned over to the Council. Indeed, Japan would not sign the Versailles Treaty if its wishes were not met. After Wilson related this meeting to the other members of the Council later in the day, it was Lloyd George (evidently fearful that acceding to Japan's wishes would open him to criticism from the Australians) who most staunchly resisted yielding. At his insistence again that Shandong "should be placed on exactly the same footing as all other German territory," the president responded that "to be perfectly fair to the Japanese he thought they would interpret this as a challenge of their good faith."[37] Wilson was already hinting at the position he would take up in the Council the next day.

His change of direction may have been reinforced by information he received from Clemenceau at the beginning of the morning session on April 22. After rereading the understandings entered into with Japan in 1917, the latter told Wilson, he was convinced that both London and Paris were treaty-bound to support the transfer of Shandong to Japan. Lloyd George agreed. Later in the day, the sanctity of treaties (including those signed between China and Japan) became the basis upon which the president spoke up for that outcome before the disappointed Chinese. But, in private, with his British and French counterparts, Wilson was more expansive. "Concerning Japan," he told them, "it is necessary to do everything to assure that she joins the League of Nations. If she stands aside, she would do all that she could want to do in the Far East."[38]

It was the very next day that the president, in the context of his dispute with Italy over the Adriatic, issued his statement that having gone to war on behalf of new principles the United States was compelled to square every decision it made "with those principles." With the exception of House, virtually all of his advisers wanted Wilson to make a stand against the transfer of Shandong to Japan. China experts, like Stanley K. Hornbeck and E. T. Williams, as well as other members of the legation, worried about the impact any other course would have on the U.S. position in China. The idea of Japan getting Shandong also clashed with the view they had come to cherish of the United States as the protector of China from "selfishness." That was also the outlook of Reinsch in Beijing (who would subsequently resign his post over the issue).[39]

But Wilson had decided to act on the basis of what he felt he had learned from his administration's activities in East Asia during his first term. Given its military strength in that region at this time, the best if not only way for Japan to be blocked from dramatically overturning the kind of framework Washington wanted was for it to be integrated into the collective great-power approach that would be provided by the League. If Japan did not get Shandong, he told Ray Stannard Baker on April 30, the day the Council made its final determination, the impact might not even be restricted to the Far East. His efforts to reconstruct and stabilize world affairs in general might be in jeopardy. The conference and the League could be at stake. "If Japan went home there was a danger of a Japanese-Russian-German alliance—and a return to the old 'balance of power' system." According to Baker's diary, the president told him "he *must* work for world order and organization against anarchy and a return to the old unilateralism."[40]

From Washington, meanwhile, Tumulty had provided comment from the standpoint of American and world opinion. Applauding the president's statement on the Adriatic, he had urged Wilson to continue to define the United States as in opposition to "any imperialistic peace." "[F]rom this distance," he told Wilson, "the selfish designs of Japan" were no more defensible than "those of Italy."[41] When the president informed his secretary and political adviser of the Council's final decision, he referenced again China's treaty obligations. He also encouraged Tumulty, "at such time as the matter may come under public discussion," to lay emphasis on Tokyo's assurances that it was going to restore China's sovereignty in the province, albeit while retaining economic privileges. Presciently, the latter cabled Dr. Grayson, indicating that he remained "afraid of the impression" that the "Japanese settlement" would make.[42]

In China, and within that country's Paris delegation, there was intense disappointment that the conference had seen fit to acquiesce in the transfer of Shandong from Germany to Japan. There was profound disillusionment, not surprisingly, with Wilson as well. "Little has been heard here of the famous fourteen points," commented Koo bitterly.[43] Hopes that had soared over the previous two years had now, one by one, all been dashed to the ground.

Within days, large demonstrations broke out, first in Beijing and then in other cities. Modern Chinese nationalism is today widely held to have begun with this May Fourth Movement, whose outlook was characterized by a broad disenchantment with the powers generally and the peace they were concluding.

In Paris, this mood was reflected almost immediately in talk among the Chinese that they might not sign the Treaty of Versailles. Hoping to head that off, a distressed Wilson unsuccessfully beseeched the Japanese to provide China with more specifics about Tokyo's plans to restore the province to Chinese control. China's delegates eventually suggested that they might sign but include a reservation excepting the treaty's provisions on Shandong. Wilson wanted to explore that, but Clemenceau and Lloyd George countered that it would open the door to other dissatisfied states doing the same. In the end, the decision was taken out of the delegates' hands. On the day of the signing, Chinese students resident in Paris surrounded the hotel where their delegation was housed and prevented any of its members from leaving.[44]

CHAPTER 13

The Campaigns for Treaty Ratification (Summer 1919–20)

The most important item on Wilson's agenda upon his return to Washington in early July was ratification of the Treaty of Versailles. This proved a more daunting challenge than he had expected.

As soon as the essence of the settlement with Germany had become public knowledge, in the spring, the president had begun to lose the backing of many prowar "progressives," particularly those who had placed a high value on the conflict ending in a "peace without victory." To them, the treaty's terms seemed likely, instead, to breed further strife. Their disillusionment was reflected in the pages of such journals of opinion as the *New Republic* and the *Nation*. Many of these were people who had begun to have qualms about Wilson even earlier, this because of his wartime record on civil liberties and because, even after the fighting was over, his administration did not seem inclined to move quickly on a domestic program of amnesty and reconciliation.[1]

But a far greater slice of the public had by war's end been whipped into frenzy about Germany, so much so that in late 1918 and early 1919 the president appeared more likely to be hurt by criticism that he was not on course to punish that country enough. This created a situation whereby, once they were released, the harsher than anticipated treaty terms had the effect largely of removing the German aspects of the Treaty of Versailles from significant debate. With the exception of the Shandong transfer, this proved especially true in the U.S. Senate.[2]

But what Wilson did face was significant controversy over the charter for the League of Nations, which he had made sure was attached to the settlement. In the end, the assent of two-thirds of the Senate, the proportion necessary for ratification, could not be mustered, and the president's unwillingness to countenance changes—beyond those that had been secured earlier in Paris—led to the entire treaty's failure.

* * *

This opposition must be attributed to a number of factors. They no doubt include the disaffection, in some cases intense alienation, of elements of the public, particularly many German Americans (upset that Berlin's membership in the League had been deferred) and some Irish Americans (worried about the institution's potential impact on Irish self-determination).[3] Yet there is general agreement that the League of Nations was broadly popular in mid-1919, when Wilson returned from Paris. Horrified by the recent carnage, hopeful that the Great War might never be replicated, most Americans had, at least for the moment, been won over to the idea. What Wilson failed to grasp was that this popularity still might not translate into the kind of pressure needed to get an unmodified Covenant ratified by the Senate, particularly if alterations could successfully be presented to the public as safeguards or improvements.

Opposition in that all-important Senate, meanwhile, stemmed from several causes not easily disentangled one from the other. These included partisanship, the desire to ensure for the Senate a major role in the formulation of American foreign policy, and personal animosity toward Wilson on the part of key senators. That every one of these motives would come into play in connection with the treaty, especially after it was formally submitted to the Senate on July 10, was eminently predictable. It is all the more remarkable, therefore, particularly given his party's loss of control over that body as a result of the November 1918 elections, that Wilson often bore himself in such a way as was likely to antagonize many of its Republican members.

The Republicans, like the Democrats, were aware of the League's popularity. Many were clearly worried about what success for the treaty, at least without some input, some alterations that they could take credit for, would do to their prospects (especially of recovering the presidency) in the upcoming elections of 1920. They wanted to play a role, even while they were also eager that any Republican impact be registered in such a way as would allow the party to avoid criticism should the treaty ultimately fail of ratification. (Simultaneously, they wanted to avoid reopening, over the treaty, the kinds of fissures in their own ranks that had been so disastrous to the party in 1912.)[4]

Though party loyalty seems to have suppressed any such worries on the part of the Democrats (through 1919 they voted largely as a block behind their president), it appears that concern for the power of the Senate as an institution was another factor that motivated some Republicans. Henry Cabot Lodge (R-Mass.), who as the new chair of the Senate Foreign Relations Committee would play a central role in creating and holding together the opposition to Wilson's Covenant, seems to have been driven, at least in part, by such a consideration. Throughout his long career, he had stood up for what he saw as the prerogatives of the legislative chamber he identified with, at times even in opposition to the wishes of Republican presidents (including his friend Theodore Roosevelt).[5]

The Senate had lorded it over both the House and the executive branch in the late nineteenth century. Then, after more assertive presidents came along at the turn of the century, many senators had continued vigorously to defend what they saw as their body's rightful powers. With regard to the conclusion of treaties, they were inclined to define broadly what "advice and consent," in Article II, Section 2 of the Constitution, required. And, in ways that prefigured specific developments in 1919, senators again and again insisted that their role had to be protected even in what were supposed to be general arbitration agreements. In the hope of winning easy ratification of the treaty to end the war with Spain, McKinley had shrewdly put three senators (including one from the opposition Democratic Party) on the five-man commission he appointed to negotiate that pact. Twenty years later, in late 1918, Wilson had unwisely passed up an opportunity to do something similar.[6] That decision more or less guaranteed that some senators would look at the president's handiwork with an eye to ensuring their institution's interests.

Personal animosity is also a part of the story. This is often discussed in connection with the attitude toward Wilson that had been harbored by Lodge, at least since 1912. The latter, by virtue of his multiple academic degrees and writings, had cherished the idea that he was America's preeminent "scholar in politics." That standing was challenged by the arrival in the White House of a former Princeton University president (who was a

Democrat no less). Lodge was also unnerved by Wilson's reinvention of himself, from a Cleveland Democrat into a "progressive," just at the time when he decided to enter New Jersey, and then national, politics. To the Massachusetts senator, this was a sure sign of someone who lacked "loyalty of conviction," had no core, was a weak opportunist, and therefore could not be trusted with matters of importance.[7] These early takes helped set the stage for Lodge subsequently to oppose, and to try to outmaneuver and show up, the president.

But Lodge's antipathy toward Wilson seems in fact to have been shared by many Republicans, both within and outside the Senate. Wilson was, by most accounts, a self-righteous and extremely self-important figure. He had also been extraordinarily successful. That profile made him someone guaranteed to rile many of the, often similarly self-important, figures in the opposition party. In an era when the Republicans held majority party status nationally, Wilson had twice won the presidency. He had exercised extraordinary powers during the war. And, by championing a league that he was essentially depicting as the world's long-awaited "parliament of man," he was bidding not only for shining glory, but perhaps also for a third term. Not unlike those who had once been drawn to, but were now disillusioned with, the president, there appears to have been an eagerness on the part of many Republicans to see Wilson embarrassed and taken down a peg.[8] (The antipathy, it cannot be doubted, was mutual.)

*   *   *

There were genuine foreign policy differences actuating much of the criticism as well. But, contrary to popular lore, the most important opposition on policy grounds did not come from senators holding an "isolationist" stance. The nearest approximation to that was the general position held by some former insurgent Republicans who objected to the League on the grounds that it was another step in the development of the United States as an imperial power. (Wilson's dominance of his party had by 1919 largely eliminated Bryanite elements with similar views.) For them, the League was reminiscent of the Holy Alliance of the early nineteenth century, by which the big powers of Europe had tried to collaborate to keep the world the

way they wanted it. Membership in the League, in the view of these senators, would put U.S. foreign policy on the side of the British Empire and
the big New York and London banks. But they constituted a very small
group, numbering only about half a dozen legislators (albeit such formidable figures as William E. Borah of Idaho, Hiram Johnson of California, and
Wisconsin's La Follette).[9]

Other Republicans certainly played to the widespread and long-held
American concern about entanglement abroad, unintentionally helping to
bolster a public attitude that would be problematic for globally oriented
policy makers in the postwar era. But, taking their cues from such Republican policy "experts" as the Pennsylvania senator and former secretary of
state Philander C. Knox and, still more important, the former secretary of
war and secretary of state (as well as former senator from New York) Elihu
Root, what most GOP senators actually objected to in Wilson's Covenant
was entanglement of a different sort, namely that relating to U.S. freedom
of action in its capacity as a major actor on the world stage.

Supporters, overall, of the foreign policy pursued by Republican presidents from McKinley onward, most senate Republicans, at least tacitly,
endorsed the idea that Washington should continue to promote "America's
interests" in the world and, in connection with that, reconstruct and stabilize the essentials of the international order that had existed before 1914.
Where they differed most with Wilson was in their weaker attachment to,
often downright dislike of, Article 10, wherein League members undertook
"to preserve as against external aggression the territorial integrity and existing political independence" of *all* members and accepted that, if the danger
of such aggression occurred, the Executive Council of the League would
"advise upon the means" by which that "obligation shall be fulfilled."[10]

Wilson cherished Article 10. To him, it was the very heart of the League
in that he saw it as pivotal to his plans for the stabilization of the postwar
order. Without Article 10, he felt that the League would not have the
"teeth" necessary to ensure that the world as reconstructed at Paris would
be maintained. Of key importance, it would lack the deterrent power which
the president hoped would obviate, or at least diminish, the actual need for
force to be used toward that end. This vital ingredient, as Wilson saw it,
had been missing from other conceptions of a league, just as it had been
absent from prewar Republican-led efforts at stabilization centering on
arbitration, mediation, and international law. Absent Article 10, he told a
press conference on the morning of July 10, the League would only be a

"debating society." If the Senate would not accept it, he had informed Lansing months before, "it will have to reject the whole treaty."[11]

Focusing on the latter part of the article, some senators feared that Article 10 constituted a threat to their chamber's foreign policy role. But just as important to Republican foreign policy influentials was anxiety about the nature of the pledge, or undertaking, that the United States would in the article be making. The president's assurance that no steps could be taken by the Executive Council of the League without America's assent was to key figures insufficient.[12] It did not put to rest their concern that the pledge being made in the first part of the article was too broad.

Worried that the article's deterrent value was not going to be strong enough, these critics did not want to see the United States embroiled in any and all conflicts around the world. Nor did they believe that public opinion would support that. Yet they feared that America's credibility as a power on the world stage, which they highly valued, could be at stake. "Nothing can be worse in international affairs," Root had written House the previous summer, having been consulted by the latter about his views on a league, "than to make agreements and break them."[13]

To avoid that situation, Knox had, beginning before the Paris conference convened, come forward with another idea. Taking the position that the postwar stabilization of Europe was the highest priority, he proposed that planning for a league be deferred. The United States should, for the time being, essentially just extend something like the Monroe Doctrine to Europe. Washington should make it clear that it would become involved if any effort were made to unsettle existing arrangements on that continent.[14]

But this proposal not only collided with the fact that the league concept was (at least for the moment) very popular. Other leading party figures felt that there was too much of value in the Covenant that Knox's course would risk losing. One of these leaders was Taft, who had been campaigning for a league longer than Wilson. He did not place the same value on Article 10 as did the president, but he also did not see it as a major problem. Standing on the same podium as his successor in New York in early March, he had explicitly rejected the idea that it would be unduly burdensome, arguing that different nations would be delegated to act by the Executive Council depending upon which were closest to any given challenge.[15]

Root articulated a third position. Though he wished the Covenant had given more encouragement to international law as a means of stabilization, he thought that it contained useful new measures promotive of that goal.

At the same time, for the reasons he had indicated to House, he was nervous about Article 10. Root was initially prepared to accept the article with a proviso that the United States was only committing itself, at this time, for five years. Later he took the position that Washington was better off rejecting any obligations under it altogether.[16]

*   *   *

Wilson insisted that anything less than a wholehearted embrace of Article 10 would compromise its deterrent value and lead to challenges of the postwar order that were otherwise far less likely to take place. It would weaken relations with France and jeopardize American international leadership.[17] Like Taft, he did not think that Article 10 would lead to the United States being called upon to act in remote areas of the eastern hemisphere.[18] At the same time, he also clearly did not think that the American public would accept a role guaranteeing the postwar order in Europe unless that role continued to be presented in universal, internationalist, as well as altruistic, terms.[19]

It had become clear by late June that Knox's idea of separating the Covenant from the treaty, still less his notion that the United States should declare a new doctrine relative to Europe, did not command sufficient support. Henceforth, Lodge put more emphasis on Root's suggestion that the Covenant be endorsed on the condition that there be more revisions. These would come in the form of "reservations"—including to Article 10—that would be part of the resolution of ratification.

Such an approach might unify the party and humble the president. But, as a strategy, it was not problem free. For, while the majority of Republicans wanted alterations in the Covenant, they differed a good deal among themselves as to what those ought to be. And some were open to this tack only because they were afraid that the Covenant could not be defeated altogether. Thus there were "mild reservationists" at one end of the Republican spectrum and "irreconcilables" at the other.[20]

The Republicans' thematic emphasis was on the need for steps to be taken to protect traditional U.S. policies, as well as American national sovereignty and freedom of action. Though he still played down the challenge it posed, Tumulty reported to Wilson in mid-July that the opposition was spreading the notion that the treaty required clarification in certain areas.

These included what the United States was pledging itself to in Article 10, the role of Congress in declaring war, whether the Monroe Doctrine had unquestionably been protected from League interference, and whether the United States would still control what it historically had considered its domestic affairs (he was alluding particularly to such matters as immigration and tariffs). Tumulty recommended the president take steps to head off anything that would interfere with the treaty's momentum.[21]

Wilson expressed a willingness to accept interpretive reservations, but he continued adamantly to oppose any that would be attached to the resolution of ratification. He insisted that clarifications were not needed and that, given the unsettled political and economic state of the world, conditions did not admit of the delay consideration of them might cause.[22] Almost certainly more to the point, Wilson, according to the *New York Times*, told Senator George McLean (R-Conn.) "that any action by the Senate in making changes in the treaty might be interpreted by nations abroad as meaning that the United States was only half-hearted in its engagement."[23]

During July and August, the president met with many, mostly Republican, senators, alone and in small groups. And, on August 19, he hosted the entire Senate Foreign Relations Committee at the White House (formal hearings on the treaty had begun at the end of July). His key argument on all of these occasions was that the revisions of the spring, in Paris, had already met senators' concerns. Reservations were uncalled for.[24]

But lack of success eventually led Wilson to try to sway senators by going over their heads to the country. In late 1898, McKinley had traveled to the South to garner support for the Treaty of Paris (ending the war with Spain, but simultaneously and controversially providing for the annexation of the Philippines).[25] And, in 1911, Taft had toured cross-country on behalf of "unlimited" arbitration pacts that had been negotiated by Knox. These latter treaties had, in fact, not escaped drastic alteration in the Senate (after which Taft refused to proceed with them further).[26] But, in terms of public speaking, the president no doubt reassured himself, Taft was no Wilson. Having considered the move for months, the president hoped that by deploying his formidable oratorical skills around the nation he ultimately could turn back the serious challenge in Washington that he was now beginning to realize he was facing.[27]

*   *   *

Already, numerous observers in Washington and elsewhere were discounting the possibility that the treaty could be ratified without reservations of some sort. Indeed, many in favor of ratification were urging the president to face that fact and strike a deal with the "mild reservationists."[28] Looking at the fight from this perspective, the speaking tour no doubt struck much of the country as a bid by Wilson to maximize his bargaining leverage before such negotiations took place. The result would be ratification (and membership in the League), with some reservations. Certainly few, at this point, took seriously the prospect that the treaty might not be ratified at all.

But getting the best deal he could was not the president's objective as he set out west across the country in early September.[29] On the contrary, his goal was to rescue the treaty that he had brought back with him from Paris two months before. And he refused to accept, would continue to refuse to accept, that that could not be done (indeed, he would ultimately imply that anything less would not be worthwhile, would not be viable, and would be rejected by America's partners). Article 10 remained Wilson's preeminent concern, but any of the reservations being discussed (or any reservations at all, for that matter) threatened, in his mind, to undo what he had accomplished at the peace conference. So far as Wilson was concerned, arguments such that the Monroe Doctrine had not been adequately provided for, that not enough had been done to prevent League interference in American domestic affairs, that the United States had to protect a right of withdrawal, that the role of Congress in the U.S. system had to be stipulated, were all spurious. They were a cover, beneath contempt, for partisan politics, or based on ignorance. They were also mischievous, insofar as these suggestions that the United States adhere to the Covenant under different terms than others, or with "privileges" that went beyond the revisions secured in April, might signal less-than-wholehearted commitment to the League (the League that the United States itself had proposed). That, in turn, might encourage less-than-wholehearted adhesion by others to an organization the precise purpose of which was to set bounds on the behavior of other states in ways that would benefit the United States (and, as Wilson would have it, the whole world). The prospect of American action under the Covenant would be taken less seriously. That would embolden potential challengers of the reconstructed international order. At the same time, it would diminish U.S. influence with other governments who were counting on American power.[30]

Many steps were taken to maximize the speaking tour's impact. Visits via a presidential train to practically a different city each day were meticulously planned out and promoted. Numerous reporters were taken along, to spread Wilson's words—and the positive reception they would hopefully elicit—throughout the entire country. Variants of several set arguments were repeated again and again, as the trip progressed, containing, it should be noted, useful insights into the administration's foreign policy thinking. But, as a recent student of rhetoric and of the western tour has made clear, the president also went well beyond his announced goal of "setting the record straight," of engaging in rational argument and dispensing information. Particularly as the challenges he faced seemed to mount, Wilson indulged in extreme forms of demagoguery, far removed from his avowed professorial oratorical ideal.[31]

The president's preparation for the tour consisted principally of his constructing a list of talking points.[32] From these he chose different issues to emphasize and arguments to employ at each stop, sometimes pitching his talk to a specific audience. Again and again he told his auditors that the purposes of the settlement with Germany and of the League were one and the same, to deter "selfishness." This was the first resolution of a war in history designed, not for the aggrandizement of strong nations, he maintained, but for the protection and freedom of the weak. It was unseemly that for partisan purposes some American politicians would turn away. In the past, he noted, Republican leaders had been advocates of a league. In fact, the idea had originated with them. There were some opponents of the League who he granted were conscientious. But these were people who would have America flout what he claimed were its obligations and destiny and remain stuck in the past.[33]

The reservations being talked about were unnecessary, Wilson maintained, the arguments for them specious. With respect to Article 10, nothing compelled the United States to accept the advice of the League council if it called for the use of force. A determination that there had been a violation of the article would have to be made unanimously by that body, of which the United States would be a member, anyway. There was, in any event, too much emphasis on the prospect of military action. Generally, nations would be deterred from violating the Covenant. And a discussion of the need for force would arise only "after it is evident that every other resource has failed." Other forms of coercion were envisioned (by which, among economic measures, the president made clear he included imposition of the kind of blockade that had been used by the Allies during the war against Germany). The Covenant also provided for numerous mechanisms and methods for the peaceful settlement of international disputes, and it would help mobilize public opinion against those who would threaten a disturbance.[34]

Peace, rather, was what was promised. Among the major advances provided for was establishment of the principle that any conflict that threatened to unsettle international relations would now be deemed the legitimate concern of League members not party to the dispute. Expanding on Article 11, which provided the authority for this, Wilson told an audience in Indianapolis on September 4 that "at present we have to mind our own business." But, under the Covenant, "we can mind other peoples'."[35]

Allegations that the Monroe Doctrine had been made less secure, the president claimed, had gotten things exactly wrong. Up until recently, he asserted in Tacoma, "there was not a nation in the world that could be induced to give" it official recognition. Now, "all the great nations" were united in doing so. The other proposed reservations likewise spoke to non-existent problems. And, Wilson maintained (even though he had been presented with legal counsel to the contrary), attachment of reservations to the resolution of ratification would only delay dangerously the restoration of order as that would require renegotiation of the peace treaty with all of the other powers.[36]

He sought not just to make the case that reservations were unnecessary. An equally important part of the president's strategy was to fan support for the League—to heighten public enthusiasm—by arguing that membership was something of vital importance to all Americans, and then to imply that any senator who was not prepared to vote for ratification without reservations was irresponsible and a League opponent.[37] In Wilson's speeches, joining the League implicitly meant doing so without reservations.

Not to join the League (on his terms) would, he insisted, be to betray a pledge that the United States (really he) had made to make sure that a conflict in Europe did not happen again. Such a betrayal would dishonor the sacrifices that American boys had recently and rightly made. And, he asserted, it would guarantee that other troops would need to be dispatched again. His was not the course of intervention, but of peace. "You would think to hear some men discuss this Covenant," he said, "that it is an arrangement for sending men abroad again just as soon as possible." To the contrary, claimed Wilson, "[i]t is the only conceivable arrangement which will prevent our sending our men abroad again very soon."[38]

And how might the need for a replay of the just completed struggle arise? To the extent that the president addressed this, he did so in terms of geopolitics. Students of the speaking tour have ignored this, perhaps because such evidence does not comport with the notion of Wilson the idealist. Nevertheless, on at least five occasions during the tour he spoke in these terms (referencing ideas that he had, in other contexts, been articulating since the middle of 1917). The president said that, in the future, Germany might most easily become a power capable of challenging the kind of Anglo-American led international order he wanted by expanding its influence to the east or in a southeasterly direction. Here were the countries whose territorial integrity and independence he had become most concerned about, many of them brand new entities in Eastern Europe and the Middle East. The route, Wilson said, had to be closed to "the material that Germany was going to make her dominating empire out of." If it was left open, there would be another war.[39] Generally, he spoke of the "Bremen to Baghdad" road, but at other times Wilson spoke of Russia. For example, at Coeur d'Alene, Idaho, the president said that "[a]t this moment the only people who are dealing with the Bolshevik government are the Germans. . . . They are making all their plans that . . . the development of Russia shall be as soon as possible in the hands of Germans. And just so soon as she can command that great power, that is also her road to the East. . . . If you do not guarantee the titles that you are setting up in these treaties, you leave the whole ground fallow in which again to sow the dragon's teeth with the harvest of armed men."[40]

Failure to join the League would create rivalry and tension with those powers who would remain to lead that body, argued the president. In such a world, the United States would have to be a "nation in arms."[41] It would also find it more difficult to ensure the foreign markets that it now needed more than ever (because of the industrial expansion that had taken place during the war). "If you put it on the lowest level," he said, "you cannot trade with a world disordered."[42] It was going to be necessary for the United States to advance billions of dollars for the reconstruction of Europe. "If we are to save our own markets and rehabilitate our own industries, we must save the financial situation of the world and rehabilitate the markets of the world." But, without being members of the League, and of bodies like the Reparations Commission, "we must put our money in the hands of those who want to get the markets that belong to us." It would be like "playing a hand that is frozen out!" Whereas, "[i]f we are partners," the president predicted (on the basis of the economic shift the war had brought about), "we will be the senior partner. The financial leadership will be ours. The industrial primacy will be ours. The commercial advantage will be ours. And the other countries of the world will look to us . . . for leadership and direction."[43] "The rest of the world is necessary to us," Wilson said in Helena, Montana, "if you want to put it on that basis." But "that is not the American basis," he immediately added. "America does not want to feed upon the rest of the world. She wants to feed it and serve it. America . . . is the only national idealistic force in the world."[44]

Failure to follow his vision, namely to seize the opportunity (and, as he had also convinced himself, the responsibility) the Covenant entailed, was ignoble as well. In Los Angeles, Wilson said that the only question critics "can ask us to answer is this—shall we exercise our influence in the world, which can henceforth be a profound and controlling influence, at a great advantage or at an intolerable disadvantage?" The choice for Americans was whether they were going to be "ostriches" or "eagles" (implying that these were the only ways by which his compatriots could relate to the world beyond America's borders).[45]

Americans, the Calvinist president confidently assured his flock in Saint Paul, were "the *predestined* mediators of mankind" (emphasis added). The "representatives of all the great governments of the world" had accepted what he described as "the American specifications" for the treaty. "Shall we have our treaty," he asked them, "or shall we have somebody else's? Shall we keep the primacy of the world, or shall we abandon it?"[46]

His opponents were not just wrong, not just ignorant. From the beginning of the tour, but especially as he began to suspect he was not having the effect he wanted on the Senate, the president became more wild and shrill. In his Kansas City address, he predicted that his Senate opponents were so base in their motives and outlook that they deserved to be "gibbeted" in the annals of history (and "they will regret," he added, "that the gibbet is so high").[47] Riding the Red Scare hysteria that was beginning to envelop the nation, Wilson suggested that that "poison" [of Bolshevism] would "steadily spread" until senators ended the uncertainty hanging over the peace by falling into line.[48] Reverting to rhetorical stratagems that had been central to wartime mobilization (and to the 1916 election campaign), the president sought to equate opposition to the treaty with disloyalty and foreign interests. Willingly or not, he implied, his critics were doing the enemy's work. Those who had been "the partisans of Germany are the ones who are principally pleased by some of the aspects of the debate that is now going on."[49] This theme—that his opponents were intentionally or unintentionally "un-American"—was front and center in what would turn out to be Wilson's last speech of the trip, in Pueblo, Colorado, on September 25. It "portended," according to one scholar, "some of the worst tendencies of the modern rhetorical presidency."[50]

*   *   *

Although other appearances were planned, Pueblo turned out to be the last stop on the president's tour. During the night following the speech, as the train rolled on toward Wichita, Wilson began to suffer from a severe headache, nausea, and a "highly nervous condition." His worried physician prevailed upon him to cancel the rest of the trip and return directly to Washington. Four days after returning there, on October 2, the president experienced an ischemic stroke. Dr. Grayson subsequently underplayed the seriousness of what had happened. He implied that Wilson was suffering from no more than severe exhaustion. But the stroke, combined with an infection he battled in mid-October, left the president, for many weeks, both weak and absent the ability fully to attend to his duties. In the interim, his wife and Grayson exercised control over Wilson's contacts and decided what would be brought to his attention.[51]

Meanwhile, though the president had spoken, for the most part, before large and enthusiastic crowds, there was little evidence that his tour had changed things in the Senate. Senators clearly did not feel politically threatened, as Wilson had hoped they would. Perhaps they did not view those who turned out to greet the president as representative of public opinion as a whole. Whatever conclusion Wilson drew, many Republicans likely doubted that those who applauded necessarily shared the president's stance that one could not be in favor of the League and also support some "clarifying" reservations. Senators were definitely aware that sizable crowds had in fact also turned out in September, often in cities the president had visited, to listen to outright opponents of the League. Senators Johnson and Borah, in particular, had challenged Wilson in this way. And those two senators had frequently received an enthusiastic response for their warnings that involvement in the League would allow the executive branch to side-step democratic control over American foreign policy and entangle the United States in wrongheaded interventions throughout the world (the very model of which, for these two senators, was the Allied intervention in Russia).[52]

Wilson had certainly not been helped by developments back in Washington. At the invitation of the Republican majority, former state department official and member of the peace commission, William C. Bullitt, had, on September 12, given testimony before the Foreign Relations Committee. During the hearing, he maintained that the secretary of state himself had expressed misgivings about the Covenant. Lansing had remarked to him on May 19, he asserted, that "at present" the League "was entirely useless." The disclosure made headlines throughout the country. And the damage was compounded when the secretary, reached at his home in Watertown, New York, initially reacted by saying that he had "no comment." (The problem was, he later told Polk, that he "could not flatly deny the testimony.") An incensed Wilson remarked to Tumulty that if he were back in the capital he would immediately demand Lansing's resignation.[53]

September had in fact witnessed a firming up of the reservationist position. Having been spurned in August by the president, who perhaps had thought his tour would force them to settle for no more than interpretative declarations (separate from the resolution of ratification), the "mild reservationists" had instead entered into negotiations with Lodge and, by extension, the rest of the "strong reservationists."[54] By the end of October, Republicans in the Senate had endorsed a total of fourteen reservations, the most important of which focused on Article 10. That reservation stipulated that the United States was assuming "no obligation" under that article "to preserve the territorial integrity or political independence of any other country or to interfere in controversies between other nations . . . or to employ" American forces "under any article of the treaty for any purpose unless in any particular case the Congress . . . shall . . . so declare."[55]

Still acting as the Democrats' floor leader on the treaty, Hitchcock met twice with Wilson in November and urged him to compromise, even going so far as to suggest that they accept the reservation on Article 10. But Wilson exhorted Democratic senators to vote against the treaty with the "Lodge reservations," making it clear that he would not accept the treaty with them. Reflecting his unshaken confidence as to where popular opinion stood, the president told Hitchcock that "[i]f the Republicans are bent on defeating this Treaty," he wanted "the vote of each, Republican and Demo-crat, recorded, because they will have to answer to the country . . . for their acts."[56] On November 19, the "irreconcilables" joined most Democrats in defeating the treaty with the "Lodge reservations" attached. Lodge then agreed to a vote on the treaty as originally presented. This time it was defeated with the "irreconcilables" adding their votes to the "strong re-servationists."[57]

*   *   *

Both Wilson and Lodge were unbending in the immediate aftermath of the votes of November 19. The latter's initial comments especially pleased the "irreconcilables," though the actions of one, Knox, revealed how divergent were the views of the senators who wound up in that group. In mid-December, the former secretary of state resurrected, again without success, his resolution calling for the Covenant to be separated from the treaty. He suggested that the Senate then approve the settlement with Germany. As to the League, to the discomfort of some other "irreconcilables" like Borah and Johnson, Knox proposed that Washington negotiate a loose affiliation with that organization until such time as conditions were worked out under which the United States could become a "full member."[58]

By January, however, Lodge was indicating a willingness to entertain compromise proposals looking toward the treaty's reconsideration. "Mild reservationists" were eager for such to be explored. There were indications that a significant number of Democratic senators might now be willing to break with the "no reservations" position. And Republican Party leaders, most notably Will Hays, the national chairman, were taking the view that it would be best for the treaty to be disposed of definitively before the upcoming presidential campaign.[59]

"Bipartisan conferences" looking toward compromise began in mid-January, 1920. From the outset, these were premised on the assumption that ratification would have to entail reservations. It was likewise accepted that there would be some modest concessions to the Democrats in regard to these, mostly in their wording. Apparently the discussants came close to agreement on a slight reformulation of the all-important reservation to Article 10.[60]

Lodge's pronouncement on January 22 that "the thing is going to work itself out," however, immediately caused a dustup, pitting against him some "strong reservationists," and, especially, the "irreconcilables." "Peace progressives," like Borah, among the latter group, threatened to bolt the party, while longtime maverick Lawrence Y. Sherman (R-Ill.) articulated the view that "Wall St. financial interests had obtained control of certain Republican leaders, preventing them from taking a stand against the League of Nations."[61] Lodge responded that he would entertain no change in the fundamental meaning of the reservations, nor would he allow them to be detached from the resolution of ratification. The course he was following, he argued, was in the best interest of the Republican Party. The president, he believed, would persist in the position he had taken. Responsibility for the failure of the treaty would then land entirely on the administration, and the Democrats would fall into disarray (precisely because he feared such discord, Hitchcock was soon trying to rein in the compromise-leaning Senate Democrats).[62]

The "irreconcilables" remained unconvinced. Their great worry was that Wilson might in the end ratify the treaty with reservations. In the aftermath of their uprising, the "bipartisan conferences" ceased. But Lodge continued to have contact with Republicans and Democrats who were eager to explore the prospects for ratification. And on February 9, he formally proposed the treaty's reconsideration.[63]

Success of course hinged not just on enough such-minded senators of each party reaching agreement, but on the president being willing to sign the treaty if it had attached to it the likely (slightly altered "Lodge") reservations. To the extent that he addressed the matter in the winter of 1920, Wilson was certainly not encouraging. What kept most figures who were seeking compromise going was the hope that the president would, in the end, have a hard time turning away. Senators of this view almost certainly misread their man. They definitely underestimated the continuing, albeit diminished, influence he had over his party.

In the wake of the November 19 votes, many of Wilson's Paris associates counseled settling now for the treaty on simply the best terms that could be gotten. The "vital" thing, House argued (in a communication that went unacknowledged), was "that the Treaty should pass in some form." "Objectionable reservations" could later be "rectified."[64] Hoover, Bliss, Lansing, and Norman Davis offered similar advice, as did the League to Enforce Peace. Signals eventually came from France and Britain as well to the effect that prominent figures there thought the most important thing was for the United States to be in the League of Nations organization.[65]

But, as early as mid-December, the president's thinking was moving in a different direction. Still holding out for treaty ratification without reservations, Wilson began to look for ways of capitalizing on what he remained convinced was the overwhelming support of the public for his position. His first idea was to explore the possibility of holding something akin to what in parliamentary systems would be called a snap election. The president pondered challenging those senators who had not agreed with him in November to resign their seats and immediately stand for reelection on this issue.[66] Shortly he settled on another plan, namely to try to turn the coming presidential election into a plebiscite on his stance with regard to the treaty (perhaps with Wilson as the Democratic candidate again as well). This the president unveiled in a message, composed with considerable assistance from Tumulty, sent to be read at the Democratic Party's Jackson Day dinner on January 8. "The maintenance of the peace of the world and the effective execution of the treaty depend upon the whole-hearted participation of the United States," it said. "[W]hen the treaty is acted upon," Wilson's missive continued, in a portentous allusion to the president's decisive role in the ratification process, "I must know whether it means that we have ratified or rejected it." Wilson rejected what had happened thus far, arguing that it did not represent "the decision of the Nation." But if his opponents disagreed, the "way out" was for "the next election" to be given the "form of a great and solemn referendum."[67]

The president's position, as outlined here, was entirely consistent with the one he had been taking all along, but given how out of touch it was with the political situation in the country at this point, it seems almost certain to have been influenced by the condition he was left in by his stroke. If the stroke intensified a rigidity and stubbornness in the president's personality that had always been there, it also cut him off from the world. Edith Wilson told Ray Stannard Baker two weeks later that "the President still has in mind the reception he got in the west [in late summer]," and believed the people remained in his, anti-reservation, corner (even during the western tour that had by no means been clear). On the other hand, the argument can be made that at least as early as the elections of 1918 the president had lost much of the skill with which in earlier years he had correctly read the public mood.[68]

Serious questions were raised about the value and feasibility of this idea. Except for his immediate White House circle and several cabinet members, few seem to have seen the president's attitude as constructive. Further missteps and blows to Wilson's stature followed. In February, after years of being dissatisfied with his secretary of state, the president finally fired Lansing. But he did so on the grounds that the secretary had been out of line to call together the cabinet when the president was indisposed. Much comment took the view that that criticism was undeserved and that Wilson was being unreasonable and petty. Further questions followed the president's subsequent appointment of the inexperienced, but sycophantic, Bainbridge Colby as Lansing's replacement.

Then there was the embarrassment of John Maynard Keynes's characterization of Wilson in his *The Economic Consequences of the Peace*, published in the United States the same month. Its principal argument had to do with what the author, who had been in Paris as part of the British delegation, saw as the unworkability of the treaty from an economic standpoint. But the book drew considerable notice as well for its depiction of the president as having been out of his depth at the conference. In addition, like many of those who had become disillusioned with Wilson, Keynes described the president as for all practical purposes a fake, who was endowed with all of "the intellectual apparatus of self-deception."[69]

Wilson nevertheless retained the loyalty of many Democrats in the Senate. Moreover, the course he was hinting at forced those inclined to disagree with him to think twice. Voting for the treaty with reservations might not only be futile, it might also put them on the opposite side of what could be the party's principal platform plank later in the year.

To suppress the numbers voting for the treaty with reservations, and avoid any chance of it being sent to him for his signature, the president eventually decided to make his position unmistakably clear. On February 24, Hitchcock reported to Wilson that the probability was that enough Democrats would vote for a resolution of ratification with reservations "to send the treaty to you unless something can be done to regain some of them." Many, he wrote, "will vote for the Lodge reservations on the theory that you will accept them ultimately. We might hold their votes if they could be made to understand that sending the treaty from the senate to the White House does not mean ratification."[70] The president's response came on March 8, in a letter addressed to the Nebraska senator and released to the press. Focusing especially on Article 10, it constituted a ringing defense of the treaty as written, and left no room for compromise. He urged that the country enter the League "fearlessly." "[P]ractically every so-called reservation," he wrote, "was in effect a rather sweeping nullification of the terms of the treaty itself. I hear of reservationists and mild reservationists, but I cannot understand the difference between a nullifier and a mild nullifier."[71]

Wilson's letter and stance appear to have had the effect of suppressing the number of Democrats who voted for the treaty with reservations when the vote finally took place on March 19, though many more did so this time. The treaty still fell seven short of the two-thirds vote it needed.[72]

*   *   *

The issue of League membership became more entangled than ever in politics during the 1920 presidential campaign. The Republican strategy of supporting ratification with reservations, as a way of achieving party unity and success, gave way. The "irreconcilables" could no longer be placated, as to a considerable degree they had been, with assurances that a treaty with reservations would never get past Wilson. "Mild reservationists" went to the convention in Chicago eager to have the party platform endorse that position. But it quickly became apparent that prominent and powerful League opponents like Borah and Johnson would, if it were adopted, either bolt or sit on their hands during the campaign.

Fairly confident of victory, Republican leaders were nevertheless anxious not to risk anything like a replay of 1912, just as they were also ambitious to secure solid control of Congress. As a result, a much more ambiguous plank, drafted by Root, was settled upon. In it, the party endorsed "an international association" that would "be based upon international justice," as reflected in the development of international law and "the decisions of impartial courts," and that would secure an "instant and general international conference whenever peace shall be threatened." This was "so that the nations pledged to . . . insist upon what is just and fair may exercise their influence and power for the prevention of war." Such language could be, and was, interpreted variously.[73]

After ten ballots, and stalemate between two early favorites, the convention selected a relative dark horse to be the Republican standard bearer.

The chief attributes of Senator Warren G. Harding of Ohio were that he was from an important swing state (whose governor, James M. Cox, many correctly predicted would become the Democratic nominee) and that he got along with all branches of his party. Harding's position on the treaty was not central to his obtaining the nomination. But it is no doubt important, from the standpoint of understanding the fate of the Covenant, that he had been a "strong reservationist" and critic. Probably more important, the senator was eager to take whatever course would avoid GOP disharmony and win him the most votes. By contrast with Cox, who broadly adhered to the president's ratification-without-reservations position, Harding exploited to the full his party platform's ambiguity on this issue during the campaign. The Republican candidate, on more than one occasion, excoriated the institution that had been provided for at the peace conference, only then to reassure pro-Leaguers that he did believe in an "international association." This allowed many of the latter to hope that a triumphant Harding, once in office, would find a way of having the United States become a member. Such, however, was asking for too much from a figure who, after his election, would see little reason why he should plunge his party, his new administration, and, given what he took to be the public mood, the country right back into turmoil over this foreign policy question. The majority party remained united and, in November, its candidate won a landslide that exceeded anyone's expectations. Shortly after his inauguration, Harding said explicitly that he would not push for American membership.[74]

The Republicans did not, after all, "answer to the country for their acts," as Wilson had predicted they would twelve months before (in fact Wilson himself had apparently become quite unpopular by 1920). There is in fact little reason to believe that the election even approximated the outgoing president's call for a "solemn referendum." By late 1920, many Democrats came to feel that it was a mistake "that the League was made a big issue."[75] What the Harding campaign had, by contrast, grasped was that there was a widespread and growing yearning on the part of many voters for what it dubbed "a return to normalcy." This, broadly, meant less talk about the League and much more emphasis on moving the country beyond the ferment, the dislocations, and the preoccupations of the war years.

PART V

The Republicans
Try Their Hands (1921–24)

I cordially favor a program of approximate disarmament, but when that day comes I want America to have the best [navy] that there is.
  —Warren G.Harding, February 20, 1921

[The Americans] had taken advantage of our complications in War to try and capture our International shipping position and were actually trading with South America while using our ships to convey their troops to France. They had done their best to wrest our Naval supremacy from us, and we had made the concession of equality to them in that respect. Today they were trying to wrest our financial and commercial supremacy.
  —Lloyd George, notes of his comments in Cabinet, July 25, 1922

The fellow who lends the money, is the fellow who makes the conditions and states the amount.
  —James Logan, U.S. observer, Reparations Commission, June 15, 1922

CHAPTER 14

Latin America and China

The overarching goals of the Republican foreign policy makers who came after Wilson remained those that had dominated his administration. These were to reconstruct and stabilize the basics of an international order that American policy makers had been committed to since the end of the nineteenth century. If there are, in some cases, more striking resemblances to the methods and approaches of the prewar administrations of McKinley, Roosevelt, and Taft (e.g., the greater emphasis on legal mechanisms of stabilization characteristic of the Republican administrations, embodied personally in the continued prominence of Root), the continuities in fundamental objectives, as well in many methodologies, across the entire era remain. Washington's most important priorities were (1) U.S. dominance in the western hemisphere, (2) retention of the open door framework in China, and (3) a Europe where the United States could trade and where unwelcome reconfigurations of power would not take place (in particular, those that might present a challenge to U.S. interests—as American leaders perceived them).

Unlike the Wilson years, American foreign policy making in the early 1920s was generally not centered in the White House. The presidents of this period were unexceptional figures. They were where they were principally because they were acceptable to most elements of a GOP that, while still the majority party nationally that it had been since the 1890s, was riven into numerous sparring factions: Insurgent versus Old Guard, East versus West, industry versus agriculture, large versus medium and small business, and protectionist, domestically oriented producers versus increasingly internationally oriented industrial and banking concerns.

This was an era of cabinet government, where, by and large, policies were developed by those appointed to lead the various departments of the executive branch. To head up the most important of such, Harding turned to party figures who were "stars" or heavyweights in the worlds of business or in the Republican Party, people who already stood well with the constituencies that would be most affected by and interested in their work.

Foreign policy was thus largely going to be developed in the State Department, not the White House. And to lead that organization, Harding decided to appoint one of the most prestigious figures of the GOP's "eastern establishment," former governor of New York, U.S. Supreme Court justice, and nominee for president (in 1916) Charles Evans Hughes. (Herbert Hoover—the former mining engineer, relief administrator, and, significantly, close adviser to Wilson in Paris—would carve out an important, but lesser, foreign policy role in the realms of trade promotion and commercial policy as head of the Department of Commerce.)[1]

Harding was not, though, the utter cipher often depicted by historians (nor was Calvin Coolidge, who replaced him after the former's death in July 1923), particularly when it came to the possible political implications of policies. Indeed, he quickly set limits on those who were going to devise his administration's foreign agenda.[2] It is highly significant, for instance, that the incoming president appointed in Hughes and Hoover, two figures who had been signatories of the Statement of the Thirty-One. This was a widely publicized declaration released to the press by a number of members of the GOP late in the 1920 campaign. Drafted by Root, the declaration, framed as an endorsement of Harding, was intended, as historian Richard Leopold notes, "to remind the nominee of his pro-League backers"—in other words of the fact that a sizable number of very prominent Republicans supported American involvement, albeit with reservations (especially with regard to Article 10), in the new international body that had been formed at the end of the war.[3] The subsequent appointments of Hughes and Hoover left no doubt that the administration's foreign policy orientation was not going to be one of disinterest in the wider world. But the president-elect made it plain early on that he opposed membership in the League of Nations, this above all for the reason that, as he put it in the winter of 1920–21, "the country does not want the Versailles League."[4]

The quote points to what *was* noticeably different about American foreign policy making in this period and to what has often led the Republican policy makers of the 1920s misleadingly to be labeled isolationist. Whatever their differences with Wilson, those who dominated policy formulation after 1920 had high regard for the overall record of his Republican predecessors. Yet, in their efforts to shape the kind of international order that American policy makers had long been committed to, they had to respect a domestic political mood now even more on guard against typical great-power international activity than what their prewar predecessors had confronted.

This was because the experience of the Great War had, within a relatively short period of time, generated a significant backlash in the United States (indeed, backlashes would be more appropriate). After 1919, the "white hot" commitment to an international mission, engineered by Wilson and the Committee on Public Information in 1917–18, largely evaporated. Promoted to overcome what had been tepid support for the war, that frame of mind came to be replaced by a range of different attitudes that presented serious challenges for policy makers to deal with.

These included an antipathy by many toward military spending, and, for some, the desire to see military methods marginalized as instruments of national policy. The horrors of the Great War gave rise, for example, to a large new peace movement, this one, more than its prewar counterpart, resting heavily on the country's mainstream Protestant churches (as well as many women veterans of the recently triumphant suffrage movement). It emphasized opposition to violence much more than the importance of order, which had been the characteristic tone of U.S. peace organizations before the war.[5]

A great disillusionment with the peace settlement spread, with disagreement arising as to whether the fault lay with Wilson or whether the world was simply irredeemable. Either way, legions of Americans were upset and disappointed with what they saw as the violation of wartime "principles," as in the case of Shandong. Over numerous matters in Europe, the Adriatic, and the Middle East, many registered their disgust with what they took to be the greediness of Washington's allies. They worried that the harshness of the Versailles Treaty would simply lead to another conflict. The results of the Great War, and of America's involvement in it, in other words, finally confirmed in many quarters the correctness of a policy of at least political and military nonentanglement (above all in regard to Europe), a sentiment impossible to ignore in Washington and among those responsible for policy.

Longtime insurgents and the most powerful of Wilson's radical critics, the (largely) Republican "peace progressives" (as historian Robert Johnson has dubbed them) continued to put forth foreign policy views at odds with those that, over recent decades, had become predominant in the executive branch. They remained a powerful force in Congress and continued in the postwar years to speak out against policies that they saw as taking the United States further down the road of militarism and imperial intervention (at the behest, they often alleged, of corporate or banking interests). A central theme was the corrosive effect such activity would have on America's republican political institutions.[6]

Meanwhile, the fevered propaganda of mobilization, combined with the Red Scare and the dislocations that the war created in America's agricultural economy, all created by the early 1920s a reactionary climate among many Old Stocks in small-town America. This entailed virulent strains of racism, nativism, and religious bigotry that were, in their essence, antipathetic to engagement with people, places, or things that could in any way be described as foreign.[7]

Confronted by this environment, postwar policy makers often felt themselves hemmed in, or if they ventured forth, directly challenged. Such a climate forced them to pursue an extremely circumspect course internationally.

As historian Warren Cohen notes, the United States was in the twenties actually "more profoundly engaged in international matters than in any [previous] peacetime era in its history."[8] But policy makers felt it imperative to steer clear of formal political commitments, above all in the eastern hemisphere, and they had to think more than twice before using or threatening military force even closer to home. In part to compensate, they began to place more and more emphasis on other instrumentalities or levers of power, particularly those bound up with America's newfound, and unrivaled, economic might.

*   *   *

By the early 1920s, the United States was well on its way to a position of all-round dominance throughout the western hemisphere. The underlying assumptions of policy makers since the late nineteenth century had been relatively straightforward. If Washington established itself as the only great-power player in this half of the globe, if it got the major European states to agree that, except with its permission, they would not exercise a political or military role, then—by virtue of geography and America's burgeoning economy—the United States would in the coming years assume a preeminent position.

Here, as in China, American policy makers had, generally, positioned themselves as defenders of an international status quo operating in their favor, seeking to shore up and institutionalize nineteenth-century political boundaries and frameworks for trade. This was the world as it should be, they were certain. And, not coincidentally, it seemed a world within which America's most "mature," "civilized" personages, its prominent political, business, and military figures, were destined to play a position of leadership. The overseas obstacles from the start were conceptualized as "others" who, unlike U.S. leaders, were "selfish" or "irresponsible," with the leaders of the European powers generally cast in the former role and the peoples of the other American states in the latter.

This project had seemed in possible jeopardy during the Great War, should Germany replace Britain as the dominant force on the other side of the Atlantic. But the Wilson administration had simultaneously seen the advent of that conflict as presenting a great opening, an opportunity, as that president himself had put it, "which may never return again."[9] This was particularly true in regard to trade and investment in South America. Although Americans had come to dominate in both categories in the Caribbean by 1914, the United States still lagged behind its European rivals, especially Britain, farther south. With South American ties to Europe disrupted by the conflict, Washington moved immediately to encourage and provide support for an American economic offensive throughout the hemisphere.[10]

This offensive was on occasion interrupted over the following decade. During the period of formal U.S. belligerency, American interest and resources were to some extent redirected. Inter-American trade was profoundly, if only briefly, slashed during the postwar recession of 1920–21 (which unquestionably also impacted the U.S. presidential election). It had to withstand the challenges presented by Britain's postwar effort to recover its position. And after the war, American bankers exhibited, until the early 1920s, nervousness about their ability to float new foreign loans in the U.S. market.

But, in the end, the offensive was stunningly successful, so much so that direct government assistance to American firms seemed less and less important with the passage of time. The Wilson administration had started things off by trying to address the needs that had already been flagged by its predecessors. These included shipping, the establishment of branch banks, and improvements in communication and the gathering of commercial information. Those that were unmet continued to be worked on during the era of Harding. Indeed, many of Hughes's trade advisers and Latin America experts had served under Wilson. Hoover (and his director of the Bureau of Foreign and Domestic Commerce, Julius Klein), meanwhile, built upon the work of predecessors like Redfield.[11]

The State Department in this period hoped to bring government financing everywhere in Latin America into American hands, this for political as well as economic reasons. As Wilson boasted on his western tour, at Paris all of the "great nations" had finally given official recognition to the Monroe Doctrine. A reorientation toward American sources for government financing would help close off indirect avenues whereby rivals might compete successfully for influence in the region.[12]

A similar overlap in objectives lay behind the Wilson-Harding-Coolidge administrations' policies in regard to undersea cables. From 1919 until success was achieved in the mid-twenties, the State Department wielded considerable diplomatic support and pressure on behalf of the creation of an entirely American network of such communications, one which would tie the two continents together. Until this point, particularly on the east coast of South America, Americans had largely been dependent on British and French firms, which, in an earlier era, had been conceded monopoly concessions. (First set up under All-America Cables, this new system was subsequently consolidated, in 1927, under the control of International Telephone and Telegraph, a U.S. multinational destined in the twentieth century to have an enormous impact in Latin America as well as elsewhere in the globe.) Again with Washington's assistance and encouragement, General Electric, American Telephone and Telegraph, Western Electric, and the United Fruit Company created the Radio Corporation of America, in part so that this entity could carry "the principal of the Monroe Doctrine into the [new] field of [radio] Communications" in Latin America.[13]

Oil was another area where the role of government was initially of great importance. The Great War had demonstrated the strategic and economic value petroleum was destined to have in the coming century. American companies had dominated production before 1914, largely on the basis of their control of fields located in the United States and Mexico. But afterward there were predictions—later proved hasty—that these sources would soon run dry (producers were unsettled as well by the economic nationalism manifested in the new Mexican constitution). From 1919, State Department resources began systematically to be used to search for possible new supplies abroad and to help American oilmen to obtain and hold onto concessions. New locations in upper South America were one focus. In the 1920s, U.S. firms, like Gulf and Jersey Standard, scoured the lands around the Caribbean in search of opportunities, coming to take especial interest in Colombia and, even more, in Venezuela around Lake Maracaibo. Initially, Washington sought aggressively to thwart the acquisition by Britain of any new sources in the region. But the government eventually pulled back for fear it would compromise its efforts in the British-dominated Middle East to insist on equal opportunity access to the oil of that region.[14]

Other resources in Latin America also attracted interest. Long before the war, prospects in agriculture (in tropical fruits and in older plantation crops like sugar, coffee, and tobacco) had drawn American investment into the Caribbean, though mining as well as oil opportunities had also been pursued in Mexico. From the Great War on, industrial raw materials gained in importance. It was in this period that the Guggenheim Brothers and Anaconda Mining moved heavily into Chilean copper. Throughout the Andean region, American capital chased opportunities in lead, tin, zinc, and nitrates as well. As economic historian Bill Albert notes, in Chile and Peru, the "mining sectors came to be almost completely controlled by large U.S. corporations."[15]

Between 1913 and the end of the 1920s, portfolio and direct investment in Latin America increased by more than 300 percent. This reflected the financial power that had come to be built up in the United States over the course of the war years, the diminishment of such power on the part of American rivals, and the prospects that investors believed might exist in that region. Over the period, as one economic historian notes, "British investment barely increased while U.S. investment soared." By the late twenties, it exceeded three billion dollars. As the United States had become the main source of new capital for the region, it was on pace soon to eclipse Britain.[16]

American exports to Latin America benefited from this investment, which was a major reason why it was encouraged by government officials.

It seemed especially important because the United States, unlike Britain, produced at home many of the primary products that the South American countries exported. (U.S. producers had also secured substantial tariff protection for some of these commodities.)

In the wake of the disruption of long-held British, French, not to speak of German, connections, and the development—with Washington's help—of essential commercial facilities, American industry also had a strong competitive edge after the war. This derived in part from the scale of enterprise that the huge U.S. domestic market had made possible over recent decades. It also stemmed from the more recent (but related) introduction of new approaches to mass production (such as the assembly line and "scientific management") which were to become the model for all other industrial countries in the next half century.

While their rivals had faced much more dislocation during the war, the largest American firms had become richer, stronger, and more up-to-date. No less important, U.S. industry (like that of prewar Germany) had come increasingly to be centered on the new generation of products that had sprung from the "second industrial revolution" of the very late nineteenth century and after. "The [trade] gains [in Latin America] made by the U.S. in wartime," concludes Rosemary Thorp, "were consolidated in the 1920s as her competitive advantage strengthened in the new dynamic products of the period." These prominently included automobiles, agricultural machinery, electrical and telephone equipment, and office machines. Britain, which had built its nineteenth-century trade preeminence around textiles, coal, and railway equipment, had, from this industrial standpoint, been unable to keep up.[17]

Exports from the United States to Latin America increased by 87 percent between 1913 and the end of the 1920s (which in fact understates the growth in sales by U.S. firms, since much American investment in the region involved the establishment of branch plants there). The United States accounted for 66 percent of Central America's imports in 1926, up from 56 percent before the war. In South America, the U.S. share, for the same years, grew from 20 to 35 percent. In every single Latin American country, meanwhile, there was during this period slippage, in many cases quite dramatic, in the market share held by Britain. By 1927, that was larger than that of the United States only in Argentina (one of England's principal food suppliers) and there only by the thinnest of margins.[18]

The U.S. government and American banks sought to capitalize on Latin American dependence on outside sources of investment to promote the political and economic policies and conditions they desired in the region. Particularly after Wall Street had begun to exhibit greater interest in foreign activity, most dramatically in the wake of the "Knickerbocker" panic of late 1907, Washington's Caribbean policy had come to emphasize financial oversight, planned and even directed by Americans, as a way of ensuring political and economic stability and order—as well as U.S. influence—in and among the small countries of that region.[19] After the war, it seemed possible that such "dollar diplomacy" might with advantage be utilized for more purposes and more widely.

Governments throughout Latin America were encouraged to enhance their chances of attracting financing for, and investment in, their countries by contracting for the services of a team of American financial consultants (on numerous occasions these were headed up by the Princeton economist Edwin Kemmerer).[20] These consultants prescribed generally the same program wherever they went. And it came with suggestions as to how it should be put into operation (not uncommonly including the idea that the host country hire a foreign adviser to oversee the plan's implementation). Ingredients included returning the nation to the gold standard, which everywhere had been suspended during the war (the United States returned to the gold standard in 1919), and getting the country to commit to a stable exchange rate. Clients were enjoined to create national banks with the exclusive right to issue notes and sufficient independence to maintain their nation's gold standard "peg." Governments were encouraged to maintain balanced budgets, restrain spending (especially on noninfrastructural projects), fight inflation, hold down wage levels, and maintain effective systems of revenue collection and debt-servicing. Historian Emily Rosenberg contends that, from the standpoint of "U.S. officials and business leaders, the purpose of [the] stabilization loans," which such plans paved the way for, "was to spread a globally integrated gold standard that would then provide a basis for rising levels of trade and investment." It appears that every independent state in South America, except Argentina and Brazil, brought in such American consultants.[21]

*   *   *

Stability would facilitate the development of trade and investment, which in turn would reinforce U.S. influence in Latin America and American leadership of the hemisphere in global affairs. It would also help to close off openings for influence to be acquired by outsiders to the hemisphere.

As ever, this issue was seen as most pressing and important in the Caribbean.[22] To achieve the kind of pro-American order that they wanted there, Harding-era officials employed, where they could, not only financial leverage and oversight, but a range of political and military pressures. There was no question but that Washington could—and would—ultimately set the boundaries on what were considered acceptable agendas and behaviors in the region, using force if needed. But, if they could not get the peoples of that area to operate on their own as the United States wanted, Hughes and figures in the Latin American division, like Sumner Welles and Francis White, preferred to employ the least unpopular and expensive methods of oversight.

In the period beginning around 1907, policy makers had hoped that they could substitute "dollars for bullets" in the Caribbean. But in 1912, Taft had stationed an oversized legation guard in Managua, Nicaragua, and in 1915 and 1916, Wilson had sent in forces to occupy Haiti and the Dominican Republic.[23] Such deployments of U.S. military power were viewed as especially problematic after the war. The extended presence of American troops in these countries quite blatantly clashed with American rhetoric about self-determination and undermined efforts to contain unilateralism on the part of U.S. rivals in other areas of the globe. It generated among the peoples in the affected countries anti-American enmity and opposition, antagonized people throughout the rest of Latin America, and was quite controversial at home in the United States. Even brief troop landings and the patrol of the region by American naval vessels elicited criticism.

In their quest to devise less costly and unpopular methods, policy makers sought to refine approaches formulated by their predecessors. Historian Dana G. Munro, who worked in the Latin American division in the 1920s, records that Root's earlier approaches continued to influence deliberations.[24] But there was clearly also thinking redolent of Woodrow Wilson. With the recent example of Costa Rica in mind, policy makers hoped that the mere threat of nonrecognition, and the financial and political isolation that that could bring, would discourage revolutions in the region. During the Roosevelt administration, Root had opined that the United States should seek to establish itself as the moral, ideally legal, guarantor of political order both within and among the countries of the Caribbean. The more that role was seen as a right, or even obligation, the more likely would it be that Americans would accept interventions; in turn, the more fearful of them would locals be. Actual use of force would less likely be needed.[25] Policy makers pressed again and again to have the United States become the author and superintendent of electoral laws that it authored or the sponsor of treaty agreements that it devised.

In keeping with their desire to employ less unpopular and expensive methods, policy makers, really from the last months of the Wilson administration on, sought to liquidate the military occupations of the previous decade. In the case of the Dominican Republic this was accomplished by 1924. Dominican leaders wanted the removal of troops to take place without conditions. But the State Department insisted that all acts of the occupation be embodied in a convention. The receivership, dating back to Roosevelt's time, also remained. A similar stepping back was weighed for Haiti. But there the department concluded that there were not yet elements and institutions within the country on which America could, as Munro puts it, "rely." Washington sought local elements that could and would make Haiti "behave" as the United States wanted. Unable to find them, it decided that more time was needed to reshape that society (the occupation continued until 1934). In Nicaragua, the oversized legation guard was withdrawn in August 1925, only to have American troops return to the country at the beginning of 1927.

Many historians have noted one tactic in particular that was coming to hold more and more interest for policy makers. "Removing the Marines and Installing the Puppets" is the apt title of historian Lars Schoultz's chapter on the Caribbean in the post–Great War period, included in his comprehensive study of U.S. policy toward Latin America. Like others, he sees the twenties as a transition period leading up to arrangements from the depression era onward, continuing for decades, whereby Washington would look to local military strongmen to maintain the conditions it wanted in many Caribbean countries. The notion that American-trained forces might be pivotal to the solution of Washington's problems in the region can be traced back to the (prewar) second occupation of Cuba. But, specifically in connection with the Dominican Republic, Nicaragua, and Haiti, this idea began to get much more attention during the Harding years.[26] As with financial receiverships, American-trained and -supplied constabularies were coming to be seen as a mechanism for neutralizing the "irresponsibility" of local peoples.

Policy makers had, meanwhile, for years been concerned that interstate conflict in Central America might also deter the development of American economic activity in that region or create an opening for the involvement of other powers. Fearful that a local war might soon break out and draw in three or four of those countries, Hughes sponsored a conference of Central American states in Washington during the early winter of 1922–23. As Munro puts it, the objective was to "revise and strengthen" treaties that Root had gotten these countries to sign at an earlier conference under U.S. auspices, held in 1907 in the same city.[27] Under Welles's supervision this time, the attending nations pledged that they would act to block help from their country being used to overthrow the government of any of their neighbors. New machinery for the settlement of regional disputes was also agreed to, some in fact consonant with mechanisms that a few years before had been included in the League Covenant. In this case, however, only one big power, the United States, would ever be a participant in the provided-for commissions of inquiry.

The League of Nations initially attracted a good deal of interest in Latin America. Brazil hoped that through participation in the League it might achieve a leadership status that had thus far eluded it in the Pan-American system. In particular, it hoped to secure a permanent seat on the all-important council. Disappointed in that quest, Rio withdrew from the League altogether in 1926.[28] Other Latin American states were hopeful that the League system might open up the hemisphere politically and give them a counterbalance to U.S. power. At the first meeting of the League assembly, for instance, Argentina moved to eliminate from the Covenant any notice of the Monroe Doctrine (this failed, and as a consequence Buenos Aires pulled out of the organization).[29]

For his part, the American secretary of state was determined that no such entity as the League—that the United States did not belong to and could not control—would play a role in order-keeping in the western hemisphere. Hughes even blocked League observers from being present at the first postwar Pan-American conference held in May 1923 in Santiago, Chile (where again, as in Washington earlier in the year, new conflict-settlement machinery just for the Americas—this time the Americas as a whole—was arrived at and embodied in the Gondra Treaty).[30]

Ironically, policy makers' greatest postwar anxieties about instability and "misbehavior" in the hemisphere centered on Mexico, right next door. As before the war, their concerns transcended Mexico itself (and the extensive American oil and mining holdings that had been acquired there). Now they embraced the possibility that "irresponsible" ideas about "international obligations" held by Mexico's leaders might constitute an objectionable model for Latin America as a whole.[31]

Carranza was still president when the fighting in Europe came to an end, and while (in his views on property rights and class distinctions) he was far from the Bolshevik he was often viewed as in Washington, he was an ardent nationalist who saw powerful American economic interests and the U.S. government as enemies of Mexico's development and independence. He supported the general international legal perspective that had been championed by Carlos Calvo, rejected what he saw as the pretensions of the Monroe Doctrine, and put strong emphasis both on the equality of nations and on the principle of nonintervention (of one country in another's affairs).

In this vein, he was also a supporter of economically nationalist provisions of Mexico's new constitution of 1917, among which was a stipulation, Article 27, that asserted that the land, rivers, streams, and subsoil resources of the country belonged to the Mexican people. Concessions might be granted to "aliens provided they agree . . . to be considered as Mexicans . . . [and not] to invoke the protection of their own Governments." This was not at all to the liking of those Americans who, mostly in the Díaz era, had been able to acquire a whopping 40 percent of Mexico's land and more than 60 percent of its oil properties.[32]

So long as the United States was preoccupied with the fighting in Europe, the State Department's motto had been "keep Mexico quiet." De jure recognition of the government had been accorded in September 1917. Washington did not approve of the country's new constitution, but it wanted to defer taking up serious differences with its neighbor until the war was over. When it was, some oilmen, members of Congress, and figures in the State Department immediately began to push for a harder line.[33] But Wilson felt that this could lead again to military intervention. That would potentially be costly and might result in the wholesale destruction of American property. It was likely to antagonize all Latin America, upset opinion at home, and jeopardize the treaty fight.

Carranza was overthrown in the spring of 1920 and eventually replaced as president by Obregón. Though the latter was more conciliatory toward Washington, Wilson decided to make recognition of his government dependent on Mexico formally committing itself to the U.S. position on the issues that had been in dispute. This was where things stood when Harding came into office, and that essentially became the policy of the new administration.

However, international creditors, represented by the House of Morgan's Lamont, were impatient to see Mexico resume payment on debts running back to the Díaz era. Seeing Obregón as someone they might be able to deal with, partly because he was anxious to restore Mexico's standing with foreign lenders, they took the position that excessive rigidity on Washington's part could be counterproductive. Rather than risk making him weaker in Mexico, they thought Obregón—whom they judged a potential force for the kind of stability they wanted in that country—should be bolstered.

Hughes and the State Department eventually came around to that point of view. The upshot was negotiations held in Mexico (the Bucareli Conference) in the spring of 1923, which produced two claims conventions and an implicit understanding, the essence of which was that Article 27 would not be applied retroactively. The Harding administration was pleased, though many American oilmen wanted more, and recognition followed.

Obregón, meanwhile, was accused by domestic opponents of selling out. He confronted an armed rebellion, whose suppression was aided by nonmilitary assistance from the United States. When that had been achieved, early in 1924, American policy makers were (prematurely) of the belief that, with the help of nonrecognition and dollar diplomacy, they had tamed the "misbehavior" south of the border they had been facing for so long.

*   *   *

In East Asia, the situation had always been more complex. American ambitions to become a trans-Pacific power and to shore up the nineteenth-century boundaries and open door trading framework in China, had for more than two decades faced challenges greater than those confronted in the western hemisphere. These included repeated manifestations of what Washington policy makers took to be Chinese weakness and "irresponsibility." They also consisted of the presence in East Asia of other strong powers who were suspected of goals at odds with America's "unselfish" objectives. Though problems of this sort seemed no less present in the postwar era, policy makers continued to pursue the basic goals that had been articulated by John Hay. And both the Wilson and Harding administrations were in fact hopeful that Washington had more leverage to bring to bear in the Far East now than the United States had had before the war.

Since late in the Roosevelt presidency, policy makers had flagged Japan as the major, new great-power threat to their aims across the Pacific (replacing Russia). The war made Tokyo a still more significant presence. Japan's economy had expanded (though the U.S. economy was still six times larger). The country was embarking on a program of naval expansion. Tokyo's troops were stationed in parts of Siberia. It had strengthened its sphere of influence in Manchuria. And Japan had also gained influence at Germany's expense, for example in the Shandong Peninsula. Moreover, Tokyo now appeared to be the power that carried the most weight in the Chinese capital city of Beijing. And, while some leaders of the British Empire were clearly concerned about this upstart's intentions, London and Tokyo were still allies. That relationship, American officials feared, could embolden Japan.[34]

China meanwhile emerged from the war in a state of political and, increasingly, financial disarray. Since the turn of the century, Washington had been looking to promote a central government there that would be both strong and compliant. But Beijing's authority had instead become weak (due in part, if few foreigners acknowledged it, to the pressures that had been brought on the country from the outside). Most recently, the rebellions sparked by Yuan Shikai's bid to become emperor in 1916 had resulted in a land where power had largely become dispersed among a handful of, often violently competing, regional warlords as well as the most popular nationalist figure, Sun Yat-sen, who had a base of operations in the far south at Canton (Guangzhou).

American leaders were cognizant, even if they underestimated its force, of the nationalist mood that had been developing, especially among many city dwellers. But from their perspective that mood was highly worrying. Sun had been in disfavor in Washington since 1913, while many of the issues that he and other nationalists were now embracing—including an end to the unequal treaties that the powers had imposed on China in the nineteenth century—were seen as evidence of the movement's "irre-sponsibility."[35]

Wilson had hoped that the United States would be able to use the League of Nations to make sure that Japan "behaved." But even after

America rejected membership in that body, policy makers believed they had meaningful influence that they might bring to bear (they were no doubt also pleased that Tokyo did become a League member). This derived from the fact that the United States had become by far the richest country in the world. Figures in Washington expected that America would be able to practice "dollar diplomacy" in the eastern hemisphere with far greater success than before the war. Its wealth would also allow the United States to build a navy immensely more powerful than Japan's. And such potential might not only make Tokyo uneasy. It could also help to break up the Anglo-Japanese alliance and align London and Washington more closely in China and in the western Pacific.

Wilson's objective during his second term had been to absorb Japan into a collective great-power approach toward China premised on the ground rules the United States desired. Not only the League, but a new consortium (the negotiations for which were concluded in May 1920) was to be used as a vehicle for that policy. Like the "neutralization" schemes and the consortium of the Taft era, this was seen as a means not only of restraining Japan from interfering with the open door—beyond Manchuria, where Washington had become amenable to concessions—but also of asserting a "guardianship" over China, this to last until such time as a strong, "responsible," U.S.-friendly government came into being. Ideally, no loans would be made to the country except by way of this second consortium. Along with other agencies, like the outsider-supervised customs service, it would control China's finances. The country would be maintained as one entity. It would supposedly be "rescued" from domestic and international politics. And its systems of economic and political administration would be remade.[36]

Another collective great-power policy pursued by the Wilson administration (and then continued under Harding) was an international embargo on the sale of weapons to any of the Chinese factions. The idea gained the adherence of both London and Paris. By the spring of 1919, Tokyo felt compelled to go along so as to avoid isolation. The embargo was meant to curtail wasteful spending, still more to be a spur to reconciliation and to the creation of a unified government for the whole country. The United States and Britain also came to see the embargo as a mechanism that might undermine the influence in Beijing of General Duan Qirui, who had become closely identified with Japan and seemed to stand in the way of unification. Although it was porous, the embargo did contribute to the

overthrow of Duan by rivals in the summer of 1920 (reunification nevertheless remaining elusive).[37]

*   *   *

Along with the consortium and the arms embargo, the Harding administration hoped that U.S. naval power might be able to hold Japan at bay until
the situation improved in China. Even before Harding was inaugurated,
however, domestic American threats to the continued upbuilding of that
leverage began to emerge. It was a major sign of the new administration's
agility that it was ultimately able to turn those challenges into a significant,
if overstated, foreign policy triumph.

As noted, a financially strapped British government came away from
the armistice in 1918 anxious to limit naval expenditures, while at the same
time eager to maintain London's longtime naval primacy. Well aware that
England could not win a naval building race with the United States, Lloyd
George, at Paris in 1919 and then again via Grey, who was dispatched to
Washington later that year, tried to get the United States to modify the
1916 program that it had resumed at the end of the fighting. These efforts
failed, as the Wilson administration held out for British acceptance of a
U.S. right to occupy a naval position equal to England.[38]

But, soon after Harding's election, the emergence of a strong sentiment
in the United States in favor of arms limitation began to raise the prospect
that American leaders might be deprived of the clout they wanted both
to force London's hand and to deter Tokyo. Of especial importance were
initiatives undertaken by Borah. In mid-December he introduced a resolution in the Senate calling upon the new administration to confer with
Britain and Japan with an eye toward an all-round reduction in naval
construction to "fifty percent of present estimates." In late January, he
introduced a second resolution calling for a six-month freeze in the American building program so that an inquiry could be made into what in fact
constituted a "modern fighting navy." This was in light of a growing
discussion—in the United States and elsewhere—of the military merits of
expensive battleships relative to new weapons such as the (airplane)
bomber and the submarine. Borah's call for a freeze got nowhere, but his
call for a disarmament conference became a rallying point for the peace

movement and for those who wanted to see a reduction in government spending and taxes. After initially trying to derail the initiative, the administration finally bowed before the growing support it was garnering in Congress. In late spring, the White House announced that it too was in favor of a disarmament conference.[39]

The Harding administration had never opposed economizing on expenses. Moreover, figures like Hoover were urging by spring 1921 that reductions in arms spending by the United States might encourage similar moves abroad, contributing to a restoration of the postwar world economy and, in particular, to the revival of European markets for American farm goods.[40] But the administration had not wanted to cut back on naval expansion if that meant sacrificing long-held objectives. Thus the president's statement in a letter early in 1921 to Lodge that he favored a program of arms limitation at some point, but that he first wanted to make sure that America had "the best [navy] that there is."[41] As late as April he was still maintaining that nothing in the way of arms limitation ought to be attempted until the 1916 program had been accomplished, expected to be in late 1924.[42] Yet the administration eventually began to doubt whether, in light of mounting public sentiment, the building program could be sustained.

There remained, of course, another path by which the relative sea power it sought might be achieved. Naval expansion was putting a much greater financial strain on both the British and the Japanese. It might be possible for Washington to get the naval ratios it wanted if it offered cutbacks in its building. The British government had indeed been signaling a possible willingness to reconsider its insistence on supremacy.

There were two goals above all that continuance of the 1916 program had been designed to achieve. One was to compel Britain to concede a U.S. right to share first place on the high seas, and the second was to deter Japan and, ideally, bind Tokyo more firmly to the kind of order Washington wanted in the Far East. With the Anglo-Japanese alliance soon up for renewal, the latter had recently become a major subject of British-American relations. The United States had repeatedly made it plain that it objected to that pact's continuation.

While secret British-American talks may already have been under way, both of these topics—arms limitation and London's Far Eastern policy—took center stage at the British Imperial Conference, convened in London in June 1921. Addressing the meeting (which included the leaders of the three British dominions bordering the Pacific), Lloyd George indicated his eagerness to enter into arms negotiations. He also asserted that there was no region where his government desired "more greatly to maintain peace and fair play for all nations and to avoid a competition of armament than in the Pacific and the Far East." Indeed, Britain, he said, wished "to work with" the United States "in all parts of the world."[43]

With the ball now clearly in its court, the Harding administration proceeded in early July to dispatch invitations to a conference in the American capital at the end of the year which would discuss disarmament as well as Far Eastern questions. Nine delegations would eventually attend. Powerful interests in Japan worried about what the British and Americans meant to discuss in regard to the Far East. But the government of Prime Minister Hara Kei was anxious not to antagonize either of those powers (or risk ties to American bankers), nor to appear as obstructive before international opinion.[44]

The most dramatic event of the Washington Conference, which lasted for nearly three months during late 1921 and early 1922, came at the outset, when Hughes boldly unveiled a proposal for the major naval powers immediately to stop building capital ships and agree that for a decade they would suspend further construction. No less sensational, especially from the standpoint of its impact on public opinion, the secretary said that the United States was prepared to scrap numerous (pre-dreadnought) battleships and that he wished Britain and Japan to do the same.

The key goals for the Harding administration at the conference were to get formal British acceptance of America's right to naval parity and Japan's agreement that the size of its navy would not rise to more than 60 percent that of the United States (achieving the latter, in combination with an end to the Anglo-Japanese alliance, would, it was hoped, firmly moor Tokyo to the arrangements in the Far East that Washington wanted). Toward those objectives, the secretary proposed that the United States, Britain, and Japan essentially build down to a capital ship ratio of 5:5:3. This course offered the possibility of success for American policy at great savings, but if Hughes was unsuccessful, if such gestures for "disarmament" were repulsed, administration leaders hoped that the consequence might be that the American public and Congress would then be much more willing to fall in line behind a continuation of the 1916 program.

Albeit after some compromises (Japan was allowed to salvage its new battleship, the *Mutsu*; the British and Americans agreed that they would not enhance bases in the western Pacific; and the fate of vessels other than battleships was for the time being left aside), Britain and Japan did accept the secretary of state's ratios for their largest capital ships (in addition, still lower ceilings were accepted by France and Italy). These arrangements were embodied in the Five Power Pact.

London also agreed that it would not renew the Anglo-Japanese alliance. In its place, Britain, the United States, Japan, and (at Washington's urging) France concluded the Four Power Pact. In that, the four pledged to respect each other's territorial holdings in the Pacific, to hold a "joint conference" if diplomacy could not settle a dispute arising between any of them, and to consult if the rights any of them claimed were "threatened by the aggressive action of any other Power." Though lacking the kind of commitments implied in Article 10 of the League Covenant, policy makers hoped that such provisions would help avoid conflict and disruptions of the existing Pacific order. Much the same purpose, in this case with respect to China, lay behind the Nine Power Pact, also concluded at the conference. In it, the signatories pledged to respect the open door as well as China's territorial and administrative integrity.[45]

The wording of the Nine Power Pact bound its signers to respect China's "sovereignty" and "independence" as well, but in practical terms those concepts fared poorly at the conference. The Nationalists had rejected participation when the United States refused their demand to be seated separately, rather than as part of a joint delegation led by Beijing. (Sun, as a consequence, announced that Canton would not regard what was concluded in Washington as binding.) But the delegation that came from China still articulated some nationalist demands. Indeed, Shi Zhaoji, its leader, urged that the conference address the proposition that "existing limitations upon China's political, jurisdictional and administrative freedom of action are to be removed."

Japan was prevailed upon to negotiate a reduction of its presence in Shandong (though it managed to hold onto privileges with regard to the railway that the Germans had built there). But the powers collectively resisted the idea that they should surrender their "rights" under what the Chinese termed the unequal treaties. They blocked an effort by the Chinese immediately to raise their country's import duties. And China's demand for an end to extraterritoriality was shunted off to a commission (which did not even convene until 1926).[46]

In meetings parallel to the formal conference, Japan agreed to remove its troops from Siberia. It also conceded to the United States control over cable lines to and from the strategically situated island of Yap, in the Carolines (which had become a Japanese mandate).[47]

Successfully framed as a meeting where peace and disarmament were the most important objectives, the Washington Conference treaties won both public approbation and relatively easy Senate ratification.[48] It goes without saying that the conference was also considered a policy, as well as political, triumph for the Harding administration.

Yet, while Japan appeared for the time being to have been reintegrated into the Far Eastern order the United States desired, it soon became apparent that that was not yet the case with China. Indeed, as historian Brian George puts it, "Following the Washington Conference, American observers were deeply concerned at the deterioration of authority in Peking."[49] And they simultaneously grew more concerned about the challenge presented by Sun Yat-sen. The United States would in fact participate in a great-power naval demonstration aimed at Sun in late 1923 when he moved to lay claim to the Canton customs. Sun for his part began looking more and more in this period for help from the new Soviet Union.[50]

Power repeatedly changed hands in Beijing, so much so that Coolidge would express nostalgia for Yuan Shikai. And by 1924, John V. A. MacMurray, the chief of the Far Eastern Division of the State Department, was asserting that Beijing could "scarcely to be considered a government at all." After Washington, the international bankers grew increasingly leery of lending money to China, while their Chinese counterparts became increasingly unwilling to entertain the consortium's conditions. Lamont, the most important American banker involved, was more and more inclined—to the chagrin of many in Washington—to do business in Asia by financing Japanese activity in Manchuria. American China policy found itself waiting for a China that could and would "behave."[51]

CHAPTER 15

Europe

Washington policy makers throughout the era under discussion in this study saw themselves as challenged by and pitted against what they saw as other people's "selfish" and "irresponsible" behavior. That behavior constituted the principal threat to the kind of world they wanted, which was based essentially on the global order that had taken shape under the aegis of Britain during the course of the nineteenth century. After the fighting of the Great War, the reestablishment of that order, ideally on firmer foundations, was seen as crucial to the realization of the leadership role policy makers desired and thought appropriate for the United States. European affairs were pertinent to this aspiration for two major reasons. First, the United States had historically found in that region a major market for its goods. Second, policy makers worried that further European conflict might yet bring about new aggregations of power that could pose a challenge to the kind of world they wanted.

Preferring not to be drawn into Old World problems, and aware that the American public had no interest in "entanglement," Washington figures had since the turn of the century sought to address Europe primarily in two ways. Without going so far as to formally become an ally, they had sought to bolster British power relative to Germany or any other European state whose policies might be more at odds with their aspirations. And they had promoted mechanisms of stabilization that would, they hoped, keep great-power competitions from eventuating in war, with all of its attendant risks. These mechanisms included mediation, arbitration, international law, international courts, a system of regular conferences at The Hague, and the idea—promoted from the end of the first decade of the twentieth century by some prominent Republicans and by the Wilson administration—of some sort of great-power pact or league.

After early 1921, policy makers essentially gave up on formal American membership in the League of Nations, indeed—at least for the time being—in a U.S. role in any similar association, though they did continue to hope that the Geneva-based organization might have a stabilizing role internationally (and Washington would by the mid-1920s come to have informal relations with that body).

But they continued to promote other, older approaches. For example, Harding, in 1923, called for American membership in the League-affiliated World Court (an effort that was ultimately unsuccessful).[1] And, more importantly, they looked to other means of (as they saw it) "depoliticization," which in the past they had felt comfortable trying only in the underdeveloped world. These included, most prominently, "dollar diplomacy" and what, starting with the Taft administration, had been described as the substitution of "dollars for bullets" in international affairs.

After 1919, a very strong public sentiment had reemerged domestically against U.S. political and military involvement in Europe. But the Great War also dramatically amplified and accelerated the development of new leverage that Washington policy makers hoped they could make use of. While America's European competitors saw their economies weakened and disrupted by the war, while Britain and France came to be saddled with debts in the billions (in the case of France, to both Britain and the United States), and while—after the Paris conference—all observers expected Germany to be dealing with large reparations, American economic might had grown enormously. Most importantly, the United States had become the home of vast capital surpluses.[2]

In line with Wilson's wartime thinking, that afterward the other powers would, for financial reasons, be "in our hands" (albeit like him underestimating how easy it would be to capitalize on that) postwar Republican policy makers expected "dollar diplomacy" eventually to be decisive. And, indeed, by mid-decade, in the wake of the Dawes Plan—which modified in important ways the results of Paris—they believed that it had been.

As had been the case with the Wilson administration, Republican policy makers hoped to see Europe's economy rebuilt, this in such a way as would align the region as a valuable trading partner and as a key participant in the kind of international political and economic order desired, also to promote European political stability. Via "dollar diplomacy" and other, often related, methods (such as nonrecognition), they hoped to address political as well as economic issues there that were perceived either as threats to stability or as deterrents to American investment.

As elsewhere, policy makers wanted to see European governments hold down public spending (in this connection, disarmament was seen as an economic measure as well as a step toward greater continental political stability), avoid inflation, stabilize their currencies, and return to the gold standard. Open door trade was perceived as a way of reducing the chances of conflict in Europe as well as of enhancing American sales on that continent.

Many of the more narrowly economic items on the American agenda for Europe in the 1920s were taken up by Benjamin Strong, governor of the Federal Reserve Bank of New York. Private American bankers, especially from the House of Morgan, played a variety of roles. And both Hoover and Secretary of the Treasury Andrew Mellon weighed in on numerous ques- · tions. But, by necessity, issues of both political and economic importance had at least to be overseen by Hughes and the State Department. Of such, two were especially prominent. These had to do with the future roles in Europe and the world of Russia and of Germany.[3]

*   *   *

Worries about Russia presenting a challenge to the kind of international order that Washington wanted were nothing new. Indeed, they dated back to the turn of the century. However, since 1917, their nature had changed. After the October Revolution, few American policy makers saw Russia as likely to be a great-power rival (for example, in East Asia) again anytime soon. Their concerns came instead to focus on whether Russia's resources might be organized by another power, alternately on whether the example provided by the Bolsheviks' ideas and policies, combined with their call for the working classes and colonial peoples of the rest of the globe to rise up, might continue to keep the world Washington wanted in turmoil.

The policy adopted toward the Soviets in 1921was essentially that which had been instituted by the Harding administration's predecessor. The political containment and isolation of the Bolsheviks had been Wilson's fallback position at Paris, and this was reverted to when it became clear over the course of 1919 that they were not likely militarily to be overthrown. Over the first half of 1920, Washington brought its troops home from Siberia and ended its trade embargo. But at the beginning of August, Secretary of State Colby announced that the American government was "averse to any dealings with the Soviet regime," this on the grounds that it was "based upon the negation of every principle of honor and good faith."[4] The United States could not work with it. Colby no doubt also feared that recognition would give the Soviet government an aura of legitimacy and a permanence that might encourage revolutionary activity elsewhere.

Hughes, after succeeding Colby the following year, reiterated this position.[5] Indeed, he made it clear that, so far as he was concerned, "any dealings" should include trade. Neither he nor Hoover thought at the beginning of 1921 that there was likely to be much of that anyway. At the end of seven years of war, revolution, civil war, foreign intervention, and sweeping requisitions (retroactively labeled "war communism"), the Soviet economy was in utter disarray. In any event, the secretary of state wanted the Bolsheviks to be made an example of rather than strengthened. And, at this point, his hope and expectation was that the regime was still headed, and soon, for collapse.

Two years later, with that regime still in place, Hughes said that the United States would consider recognition when the Soviets exhibited the "ability and disposition to discharge their international obligations," in other words when they demonstrated that they could and would "behave." The acid test by which the Soviets would show that they had committed to such a course would be when they acknowledged Russia's prerevolutionary debts and settled long-standing claims (to which Moscow replied that it too would have to be compensated, this for the destruction caused as the result of foreign intervention and the embargo-blockade).[6]

While refusing to deal with the Soviet government, and waiting for it either to be replaced or change, U.S. policy makers adopted a stance designed to court the Russian population and to distinguish between Washington's ideal and the existing regime. This included holding a place in their desired international order for the Russia that they wanted.

There was no commitment to use force, but—for geopolitical reasons— policy makers from the Wilson era onward repeatedly stated their support for the integrity of Russia's modern boundaries (making exceptions only for the independence of Poland, Finland, and Armenia).[7] Official policy (over Hoover's objection) was similarly to prohibit the acceptance for

American goods of Russia's gold, on the grounds that that did not belong to the Soviet regime and would be needed in the future.[8] Likewise, Washington continued to deal with the diplomatic representatives of the Provisional Government.[9]

When a major crop failure tipped large parts of the Russian countryside toward famine in mid-1921, Hoover successfully lined Hughes and Harding up behind a high-profile American role in providing food, clothing, and medicine. This would be via a revived, and technically private, American Relief Administration. Hoover had sought to use food to head off revolutions in Central and Eastern Europe after the armistice. His ARA had also funneled supplies to an anti-Bolshevik army marching on Petrograd in late 1919. Now the secretary of commerce (who would also resume direction of the ARA) hoped to deploy what had become a postwar glut of U.S. farm goods in such a way as might show up the Soviet government and greatly enhance among the Russian public American prestige. The subsequent program, funded by the U.S. government, private charitable contributions, and Russian gold (in an exception to the policy noted above), ultimately distributed a half million tons of food over the course of late 1921 and 1922. The relief program was widely hailed and appreciated, but, ironically, and contrary to Washington's intent, it had the effect of helping to stabilize the Soviet regime.[10]

However much Hughes opposed trade, pressure built on Washington to remove the significant obstacles that continued, even after the embargo, and to facilitate American business activity in Russia. With the passage of time, the regime's hold on power seemed increasingly secure, and more and more U.S. entrepreneurs were possessed of the thought that there was business to be done. The prospect also grew that others, particularly the British, but also the Germans, could preempt a lead role that otherwise might be had by the United States. Desperate to restore Britain's export position, Lloyd George's government signed a trade agreement with Moscow just as Harding was coming into office.[11]

Eager to revive production, the Soviets began in 1921 to pursue a New Economic Policy that promoted the revival of capitalist activity beneath the economy's "commanding heights." Simultaneously, Moscow stepped up its efforts to encourage investment from and trade with the major industrial states, as well as to secure recognition from the governments of those states. Lloyd George thought he saw in these developments a golden opportunity. More than ever, because of the loss of markets elsewhere in the world (like

Latin America), he saw trade with continental Europe as vital to Britain's recovery. Europe's revival was seen as dependent on Germany's, and that in turn was seen to require the reconnection of Germany profitably to hinterlands and markets toward its east. That could be done safely, as he saw it, if guided by an international consortium capitalized by British and other Allied sources. And Russia seemingly, because of its desperate condition, could be restored to a "normal" role.

The prime minister promoted a conference at Genoa in the spring of 1922 in the hope of realizing this "grand design." Even before it opened, things began to go wrong. The French were conspicuously uneasy, but so were the Germans and Russians. Resistant to British plans for their reintegration, Moscow and Berlin's representatives jolted the conference by meeting in the nearby resort town of Rapallo to sign a separate, bilateral treaty. The two states entered into full diplomatic relations, renounced claims against each other, established most-favored-nation trade relations, and even set the stage for a possible military agreement. Hughes meanwhile had refused to have the United States participate in the conference—though he did send an unofficial observer—in part because of the American policy of nonrecognition. The secretary also worked quietly to undermine the creation of an international consortium for Russia.[12]

Nonrecognition would remain a policy to which both Hughes and Hoover were committed. It would, in fact, not be abandoned by Washington until 1933. But, over time, Hoover in particular became interested in seeing American businessmen capitalize on commercial prospects with this regime that both men disliked. And he wanted that trade to be direct rather than through third parties, such as German and Baltic factors, who had to be paid commissions. Such was crucial, he had concluded by the end of 1921. Otherwise, he told the secretary of state, it might not be possible to preserve the "future Russian market for U.S. domination."[13] American trade with Russia began to take off from 1923. Echoing assurances that by then Hoover had already given businessmen, Coolidge, in his first annual message in December, stated that the U.S. government had "no objections to the carrying on of commerce" with Russia, even if it absolutely refused to recognize a "regime which refuses to recognize the sanctity of international obligations."[14] The Bureau of Foreign and Domestic Commerce, under Hoover's assistant Klein, was by then gathering and providing information to American firms interested in the Russian market. And five Soviet purchasing missions were being allowed to operate in the United States.

Despite Washington's unwillingness to enter into formal diplomatic relations (over the next year virtually all of the major European states did so), Moscow actually preferred buying goods from the United States, because after the war America was clearly the most technologically advanced nation. Historian Christine A. White notes that "[b]y the end of the 1923–24 Soviet fiscal year, American exports to Soviet Russia had surpassed those of Britain and Germany combined."[15] The products sold ranged from raw materials like cotton to Ford tractors.[16]

Hughes appears to have been more ambivalent about the development of this trade. But he did score one final victory over the Soviets during his term as secretary. This came as a consequence of the successful work he did behind the scenes related to the Dawes Plan, the implementation of which appeared to mean that, rather than looking to the east, Germany would be tied to the Washington-led, and American-financed, postwar international order.[17]

*   *   *

Germany had been at the very center of Washington's policy concerns going back to the eve of the war. In 1913–14, House had explored the prospect of it becoming more of a buttress, than a possible disrupter, of the international order that the United States wanted. From August 1914, Washington was anxious to see Berlin denied any major gains from the war and taught a "lesson." Notions of what that lesson should entail expanded over time. In addition, the Wilson administration decided that its foe's governmental system had significantly to be altered. But, during the fighting and afterward, policy makers continued to envision a largely restored Germany that would be reintegrated into the Europe, and world, that Washington desired, this in preference to a Germany on the outside, discontented and vengeful. Such an outcome not only was seen as crucial to the reconstruction of Europe as a trading partner, but was viewed as key to European stabilization.

These concerns were shared by the policy makers of the Harding administration no less than they had been by their predecessors. And they were what made those figures, again like their predecessors, regretful and uneasy about some of the compromises—particularly over damages and the occupation of German territory—that Wilson had felt compelled to make in Paris.

Foremost was how the conference had dealt with reparations. American diplomats had arrived in Paris in 1919 determined to see Germany pay restitution for civilian damages, but also anxious that such reparations be set before the conference concluded and be well within Germany's capacity to pay "within a reasonable time." As seen, no amount was fixed or time limit set. These matters were all turned over to a Reparations Commission to determine over the course of the next two years. It was also agreed that the commission would arrive at its total figure, at least in the first instance, by toting up claims.

In the aftermath, Wilson's hope was that a result more in line with his wishes might still be achieved. Lloyd George's views on reparations did moderate over time. British, as well as American, figures soon grew convinced that uncertainty over the issue and the prospect of Germany being assessed a high amount were blocking the recovery of the European economy.

But France's views hardened (while, after the Treaty of Versailles was rejected, the United States no longer had official representation on the Reparations Commission). The French government had always looked at reparations not just as a way of rebuilding its country, but as a means of keeping Germany down and under control. And that aspect of the question actually assumed more importance after 1919. The defeat of the treaty in the United States cast doubt on American involvement in the League and spelled an end to the Anglo-American security treaty. Having already agreed, at Paris, to a stronger Germany than it desired (by yielding on dismemberment), French authorities sought, as historian Patrick Cohrs has put it, "compensatory bases of security." These included military arrangements with London (that went beyond what that government was willing to accord), retention of a large army, and alliances with some of the new states of Eastern Europe. Paris also dug in its heels over any significant moderation of reparations. As a result, both the United States and Britain came to see France as a threat to European peace. From Paris's perspective, meanwhile, those powers were being insensitive to a wartime partner that had in the past half century twice been invaded by its eastern neighbor.[18]

For Britain and France, the issue of reparations was intertwined with that of inter-Allied debts. Both had said from the outset that greater moderation on the one might come if the United States was lenient on the other.

But as much as they wanted reparations to be limited, American leaders refused to acknowledge any relationship between the two questions.

This stance reflected their assessment of American public opinion, but also their own views. Having been rallied to fight the war on the grounds that its purpose was to help Europe and the world, Americans after 1919 seemed decidedly of the opinion that they had helped enough and that it had all really been for naught. Political leaders were also aware that cancellation, or dramatic write-downs, would have an impact on taxes, which they felt would not only be unpopular, but weigh down U.S. economic growth. They were not convinced that the debts were an impossible burden, if only the Allies would put their economic houses in order. And they were determined not to let these commercial rivals improve their competitiveness at American business's expense.[19]

There was receptivity, in the post-conference period, to the idea that interest payments could be postponed, but not to proposals that would deal with reparations and debts together. In August 1920, Lloyd George claimed in a letter to Wilson that the French prime minister had recently indicated some willingness to reevaluate his government's position on reparations. But Alexandre Millerand had, he said, insisted that his government could not accept less compensation for damages unless its debts were also scaled down. Britain could not act on what France owed it in isolation, but, Lloyd George suggested, it could and would as part of a general settlement. In his reply, sent in the fall, Wilson wrote that it was "desirable that our position be clearly understood in order to avoid any further delay in a constructive settlement of reparations which may arise from the hope that the debts to this Government can form a part of such a settlement." They could not. "This government has endeavored . . . to make it clear that it cannot consent to connect the reparation question with that of inter-governmental indebtedness." The delay, he warned, "which has occurred in the funding of the demand obligations is already embarrassing the Treasury, which will find itself compelled to begin to collect back and current interest if speedy progress is not made with the funding." This position, along with his view of reparations, remained that of Wilson's successors.[20]

The second compromise going back to the Paris conference that loomed over the new administration had to do with the Rhineland. Though they had successfully blocked the detachment of the region from Germany, Wilson and Lloyd George had nevertheless felt it necessary to accept Clemenceau's demand for its demilitarization. They had also acquiesced in a fifteen-year Allied and American occupation. The agreement provided for phased pullbacks from different zones over time, but also that the entire process might be delayed or reversed if Germany failed in any way to meet the provisions of the peace settlement. Given the prospect of a disagreement between France and Germany over reparations, this particular stipulation was potentially explosive. It appeared to carry with it the possibility of renewed conflict, or, at the very least, of tensions and turbulence that would set back the economic restoration and political stabilization of Europe. Even worse, by 1920 France had begun to expand on the occupation idea, insisting that language in the Versailles Treaty gave it the right—in the event of noncompliance—to place still more of western Germany under military control.

The occupation of any of its territory rankled in Germany, but both Germany and France valued the presence of American troops in the Rhineland (of whom there were still well in excess of ten thousand in 1921, centered in and around Coblenz). The former saw them as a check on French plots to promote separatism in the region, while they were prized by the latter as an ongoing symbol of U.S. support.

So long as there was going to be an occupation, American leaders hoped that U.S. troops could help to keep the lid on the situation. But the clear potential also existed for those troops to be drawn into any tensions that might develop, which in turn was unlikely to sit well with the American public (especially given that the United States had rejected the Treaty of Versailles).[21]

*   *   *

The presence of American troops on the Rhine no doubt also facilitated the conclusion of a favorable peace settlement with Germany. Congress took the view that the United States could simply declare the continuing state of war to be at an end. In the Knox-Porter Resolution—signed into law by Harding on July 2, 1921—that was stipulated alongside a statement reserving to the United States all the rights to which it would have been entitled under the Treaty of Versailles. But Hughes did not consider this sufficient for the accomplishment of his objectives. He wanted a firmer guarantee of American rights and also saw a return to normal diplomatic relations as critical to the promotion of trade, investment, and stability. Toward these ends, the secretary negotiated a separate peace treaty with Germany that was signed on August 25 and then ratified by the Senate in the fall.[22]

The Harding administration was eager to make progress on other important issues left over from the war as well. Among these was the question of Allied debts. It was not just impatience that motivated policy makers to push for quick agreement on how these would be paid. There was also the conviction that until the matter was resolved there could be no revival of the kind of international economic relations they wanted.[23]

On June 21, 1921, Mellon asked for legislation giving the Department of the Treasury the authority to negotiate, one-on-one, with the various Allied governments. But Congress was determined that it should have a say. By early 1922, it had created the World War Foreign Debt Commission, on which it would have representatives sitting alongside Secretaries Mellon, Hoover, and Hughes. It also set the broad parameters that it wanted the commission to adhere to. The most important were that the agreements should carry interest charges of no less than 4.25 percent and be paid off within twenty-five years. Once the commission was established, the State Department invited the debtor governments to send negotiating teams to Washington.

The most important debtors were France and Britain. That summer, Jean Parmentier, of the French Ministry of Finance, took part in discussions in the United States. But his principal objective was to argue the case why, for the time being, France was in no position to pay. Powerful voices in England, meanwhile, were still arguing for a dramatic reduction or cancellation of its debt. At the end of July, a bitter and angry Lloyd George told his cabinet that the Americans "had no adequate idea of the magnitude of the war effort of the Allies."[24] Other figures continued to protest that the money had all been expended in America on behalf of a common effort. In August, Balfour, now Lord President, floated an alternative, this essentially that all debts stemming from the war be written off. Britain and its associates had all, he stated, been "partners" in one common enterprise—which he described as the "cause of freedom." If it were in a position to do so, London would "remit all the debts" due it "by our allies in respect of loans, or by Germany in respect of reparations." Because of the American demand, this could not be done, but Britain would not ask those who owed it money to pay any more than would be required for it to pay off the United States.[25]

Officials in Washington were furious, all the more because the Balfour Note raised the possibility of England leading a common debtors' front. They now also began to face more criticism from internationally oriented American bankers and businessmen. But the administration held firm, continuing to insist that Europe's economic recovery would best be dealt with through financial austerity, currency stabilization, and a moderate reparations settlement.

In the end, British leaders felt they had no choice but to settle, lest they jeopardize Britain's credit position and London's standing as a major center of international finance. A settlement, a bit more lenient than what the Foreign Debt Commission had originally had on offer, was concluded in early 1923. This opened the way not only to debt agreements with the other allies later in the decade. It cleared the ground so that the British and Americans might ultimately turn to and collaborate on other issues, like reparations.

*   *   *

The Reparations Commission issued its long-awaited report shortly after the Harding administration came to power, and the Allies set a schedule by which the payments were to be made. They also asserted that failure to meet the prescribed terms would be met by the occupation of more German land, specifically the economically valuable Ruhr region to the northeast of the Rhine. Historians continue to debate how much of a burden meeting the London Schedule would have constituted. What is clear is that making the sacrifices necessary to do so had little political support. Faced with an ultimatum, German leaders promised fulfillment, but they did so from the beginning in the hope and expectation that it would soon be demonstrated that they could not comply.[26]

Upon coming to office, Hughes made it clear that he stood where his predecessors had. He told the Germans that the United States supported the idea that they should pay reparations. The secretary then told the British and French ambassadors that while that was the case, the administration wanted to see an economically robust Germany. From the standpoint of Washington's objectives, France had long come to be seen as the principal obstacle to moderate reparations and a reintegrative peace. But Hughes felt he had little leverage that could immediately be brought to bear. The situation would probably have to await that point where American financial might would prove decisive.[27]

Berlin initially complied. But at the end of 1921, it announced that it henceforth would be unable to meet the schedule. Temporary reductions in the amounts due were granted, while Germany, for its part, went in search of an international loan. In April, the Reparations Commission created a bankers' committee to look into the prospects for the latter. American officials hoped that this would eventuate in an overall reduction of reparations. One of the unofficial U.S. observers on the Reparations Commission, James Logan, was convinced that because France needed money from Germany to rebuild from the war, and Germany would seemingly not be able to come up with that money without a loan, Paris would eventually have no alternative but to heed American bankers. "The fellow who lends the money," he commented, "is the fellow who makes the conditions and states the amount." At this point, though, France held by its demand that there be no tampering with the total sums, and the effort to arrange a loan failed.[28]

By fall, French impatience with Germany was growing. So too were French efforts to reorient—at least economically—the occupied Rhineland. The other American observer, Roland W. Boyden, urged Hughes to convene an international economic conference. But the secretary rejected that suggestion for fear that the United States would be outnumbered and put on the defensive over its war debts position. Instead, he pressed the French premier, Raymond Poincaré, to reverse course, to revive the bankers' committee and to leave up to those "experts" the resolution of the problem of reparations. Meeting no success, on December 29, 1922, he then publicly urged this course. There could be "no economic recuperation in Europe," he told an audience in New Haven, "unless Germany recuperates. There will be no permanent peace unless economic satisfactions are enjoyed." "[D]istinguished Americans," Hughes promised, would be willing to serve on the new committee he was suggesting.[29]

Successful in getting the Reparations Commission to declare Germany in default, France and Belgium, with the support of Italy, began to move troops into the Ruhr during the second week of January. Britain tried to remain aloof, its forces staying put around Cologne, while American forces in the Rhineland were now completely withdrawn. The latter move drew divergent reactions. One French publication acidly commented, "To our friends and allies who came to fight on French soil, hail! To the occupiers of the Rhine who helped to frustrate the fruits of victory, good-by!" By contrast, the German press, at least initially, celebrated the American move.[30]

Paris's objectives were to get hold of much-needed coal and coke in this region, more generally to gain leverage over Berlin, or at least westernmost Germany. What had not been fully anticipated was the program of passive resistance that greeted the occupation. This was initially a spontaneous movement on the part of local businesses and workers, but it quickly won substantial financial support from the German government. The refusal of local workers to work and businesses to cooperate greatly frustrated the French. However, Berlin's subsidies exacerbated an already existing problem with inflation. And this soon spun out of control, creating economic distress and social and political tensions throughout the new republic.

By fall, Berlin felt compelled to abandon its measures. But the Poincaré government was no longer certain how to proceed. The operation had already been far more costly than expected. It was having an impact on France's economy and on the value of the franc. At the same time, the German state and economy appeared fragile. One option was to promote separatist forces in western Germany, in essence to revive some of the goals that France had pushed in 1919. But, after exploring that, Paris became fearful that it might isolate itself from Britain as a future ally and from American capital, without which, it worried, France might descend into financial crisis. In October, President Coolidge reiterated his secretary of state's proposal, of the previous December, to set up a committee of experts to put reparations on a new basis. Hoping (futilely, as it turned out) that France could set the terms upon which the committee's discussions would take place, Poincaré now accepted this idea as the potential solution to his problems.[31]

It appeared that the conditions had finally been reached under which American financial might could be brought to bear on behalf of U.S. leaders' plans for German—and European—economic reconstruction and stabilization. The idea was to have Germany's ability to pay appraised by "experts" and then for that to become the basis of a revised plan. The committee's deliberations took place in Paris at the beginning of 1924, a report being issued in April. An advantage of this approach, from the standpoint of the administration's management of American public opinion, was that the committee's activities were given the appearance of being nonpolitical and indeed of being merely technical in nature. Having American members serve in an unofficial capacity also allowed Hughes to sideline the Senate from the process by which committee members were selected. In reality, the secretary of state carefully managed, via Logan and the Reparations Commission, the appointment of the American members. He then met with them, and, in company with Hoover, saw to it that they were loaned staff members from the State and Commerce Departments. The most prominent American figures on the committee were the Chicago banker Charles G. Dawes, and—still more central to the formulation of the plan—the General Electric and Radio Corporation of America executive Owen D. Young. The "money doctor," Kemmerer, was a member of their staff.[32]

By spring, Hughes was already enthusing that the world was about to embark on a "new era." And Britain and France soon called for a diplomatic conference to take up the committee's recommendations (necessary because they envisioned alterations in the Treaty of Versailles) to be held that summer in London. Hughes initially entertained the hope that the U.S. government might avoid playing a formal role. But this was made impossible by the British Prime Minister Ramsay MacDonald's quick extension to Washington of an official invitation. (Historian Peter Buckingham notes that the Coolidge administration was still careful not to "acknowledge that acceptance meant formal American participation in a European diplomatic conference for the first time since Wilson left Paris.") In the end, the secretary crossed the Atlantic himself to lobby on behalf of the plan in Berlin, London, and Paris (the official American representatives were Logan and the American ambassador to Britain, Frank B. Kellogg).[33]

From the secretary of state's standpoint, the outcome of this entire process constituted another diplomatic success. Hughes's exercise in dollar diplomacy in Europe in 1924 did indeed work largely as he had hoped it would. France's need for currency stabilization assistance made it vulnerable to the threat—conveyed by both J. P. Morgan and American officials—that such would not be available if it did not change its policies. As a consequence, Paris agreed to a program that eased Germany's burden. It also surrendered its power to declare that country in default and to impose sanctions. Predicated on the idea of German economic unity and political integrity, the Dawes Plan also provided for the end of the occupation of the Ruhr within one year. The promise of a major loan, meanwhile, facilitated German political acceptance of a plan that, albeit on better terms, still required that country to pay reparations as well as accept a degree of foreign supervision (particularly by way of a Transfer Committee—that would replace the Reparations Commission—headed up by an American, S. Parker Gilbert, who had served as an under secretary in the Department of the Treasury).[34]

Conclusion

The Great War and American Foreign Policy considers a subject that, either in whole or in part, has been visited by historians many times over the course of the past century. But the contention here is that much perspective and understanding—both of that episode and of its place in the broader story of America's twentieth-century rise as a world power—have been missed, this because a specific topic in history has not itself been looked at against a broader historical background. A failure to do that was even characteristic of the famous "Revisionists of the 1930s," writers who in the post–World War I era subjected to intense scrutiny the Wilson administration's claims as to how and why America had become involved in that conflict.[1] A century after the war, such contextualizing is perhaps more easily achieved.

On balance, not only in the broader American public but also within the academy, the predominant view that prevails today is that the United States became involved in the Great War because it was compelled to do so by the way the conflict was fought by Germany. Once it became a belligerent, Washington was then governed by the desire to rescue the world and the United States from ever having to endure such an upheaval again. This is of course a formulation that echoes the assertions of the policy makers at that time. (It is also one that has since frequently been reused by American decision makers to explain U.S. foreign policy.) That a narrative emphasizing defense and rescue may be ideologically soothing goes without saying. It may not however adequately explain events.

The U.S. response to the Great War can fully be understood only when it becomes clear what, in Washington, that conflict was seen to challenge. To grasp that, a longer-range perspective is of enormous help. So too, it follows, is a willingness to consider that this topic cannot be looked at as simply a transatlantic story. For American leaders, the future of much of the non-European world, and their relationship to it, was also at stake.

Modern international relations have their origin in the extensive activities promoted by Britain's leaders during the decades following the fall of Napoleon in 1815. Freed from a challenge that had led them for many years to focus on the European continent, and (because of England's industrial development since the late eighteenth century) increasingly imbued with a sense of power and importance, they embarked on a course that would by the middle of the nineteenth century make London the seat of the world's first truly global power. Hallmarks of Britain's world role include the sea power by which it could make its influence felt far from home, dictate the terms by which all other countries used the world's oceans and seas, and guard the lanes of its commerce. It was also characterized by an emphasis on open markets—and a single gold standard—designed to ensure an international economy with Britain at its commercial and financial hub. Third, it was marked by a desire to see overseas areas that were deemed of especial strategic or economic utility secured against interference by other states and ruled internally in accordance with London's ideas of proper order and administration. To these characteristics must be added the strong desire to see British gentlemen validated on the global stage as both the bearers and proper leaders of a superior civilization.[2]

However successful it was for a number of years, this was an overseas project that generated both imitators and opponents, and by the late nineteenth century there was a proliferation of both. The leaders of other strong states came to see more expansive activity on the world stage as a way, as Mahan put it, of advancing their "wealth and greatness." And, depending on their location and the position they were starting from, that often meant pursuing courses of action with regard to naval power, foreign lands, and trade that caused friction with rivals.

Simultaneously, the pursuit by those big powers (and key elements in their societies) of greater influence and economic opportunities in places inhabited by "backward peoples" inevitably generated dislocations, resistance, resentment, and forms of push-back in the underdeveloped world destined to reverberate for generations (even if, until well into the twentieth century, this still was not seen by the most powerful states as an unduly expensive problem).

More than was the case with any other rising power, late nineteenth-century American leaders identified with the international order that had been promoted and presided over by London. Having come to view especially the rest of the western hemisphere and the vast empire of China as regions into which U.S. influence and trade should expand, they became anxious at the prospect that the kind of partitioning that had recently taken place in Africa might spread. And they responded by reasserting the Monroe Doctrine and stipulating Washington's interest in the Chinese open door. With these steps at the turn of the century, the United States began to announce itself as a power on the world stage.

Subsequently, more and more American leaders came to see the kind of world they wanted to preserve as requiring attention to relations among the other great powers. This manifested itself in two major ways: first, by means of a growing rapprochement with Britain, aimed in particular at propping up London's position outside the western hemisphere; and second, via interest in reforms that might promote stability.

From 1899, many U.S. figures began especially to worry that intensifying competition among the other powers—who were cheek by jowl in various parts of the eastern hemisphere—might erupt in wars that would bring rearrangements of power dangerous to the basic international order Washington wanted. Mechanisms and approaches were explored in the hope that they could not only help to contain great-power rivalries short of war, but simultaneously allow the powers to collaborate more effectively in the management of affairs in the less developed "waste" regions (outside the western hemisphere, which from the political and military standpoint had been declared off-limits to all powers but the United States).

When a general war between two coalitions of European powers (and Japan) broke out in 1914, what the Wilson administration actually was hoping to defend and rescue—ideally without military involvement—was a global order that American leaders had for some time felt would be conducive to the ascent during the coming century of the United States. They took particular note of the fact that the war pitted against each other Europe's two leading industrial powers, Germany and England (ranked second and third in the world in terms of manufacturing, albeit both well back behind number one, the United States, by 1914).[3] The conflict threatened not only to disrupt commercial and financial activity. It raised the possibility that London's power might be undermined and that Germany's might dramatically increase. For Washington, Britain was the more known quantity, and its policies in many areas were seen to overlap with those of the United States. Policy makers were much less sure what Germany's further rise might entail.

American leaders not only moved to shore up the basics of the existing international order. They also wanted to play a role in the settlement of the conflict, especially so as to provide, if possible, against something like it happening again. The Wilson administration hoped the Allies would fend off what was viewed as Germany's challenge to England. That was one of the reasons Wilson began, in practice, rapidly to depart from neutrality. The administration was also guardedly confident that London would prevail and it hoped that maintaining good relations with Britain would help the United States to achieve an important role in the settlement and in the postwar world. At virtually every stage of the Great War, the Wilson administration's policies continued to be governed by this overriding objective, namely to reconstruct and stabilize the essentials of an international order Washington had been concerned about for, by this time, at least two decades.

The administration did not want just any peace. (Indeed, on several occasions during the conflict Washington weighed in on the side of continued war.) It wanted Germany to be prevented from becoming stronger and taught a lesson. Yet it also did not want Berlin to experience a decisive defeat. That might lay the groundwork for another conflict by creating a German desire for revenge. It could strengthen other powers whose policies Washington worried about, like Russia. And it would remove any chance that German power might be harnessed to the "pact" project, that House had begun to explore in 1913–14, upon which basis it was thought desired postwar arrangements might dependably be ordered. This accounts for much of the subsequent friction between the United States and England, whose government was committed from the beginning to a more extensive reduction of German power.

Wilson wanted to avoid military involvement because of its expense, because he feared that it would jeopardize the United States playing a mediatory role, because so much of the American public and so many in Congress were opposed, and because he was afraid that Japan would take advantage of American belligerency to challenge the open door in China. But that desire was ultimately subordinate to the vision he cherished of the United States playing a role in the settlement of the war and becoming a—eventually the—central actor in the coming twentieth-century world. This priority is reflected again and again in the submarine crises.

Once he called upon Americans to fight, not only in defense of (his definition of) neutral rights but also to rescue the world and make it "safe for democracy," Wilson—with the keen endorsement of prominent leaders in the major opposition party—set about trying to mobilize the United

States so as to harness all its vast, if to this point largely latent, power for the realization of his goals. Ironically and tragically, this entailed some of the most dramatic assaults on democratic rights at home that the country had ever witnessed.

Wilson sought not only to demonstrate to all the power that Washington had at its disposal. From 1917, he was increasingly anxious to prevent any settlement of the war that would leave Germany strengthened to its south or east and also to see political change in Berlin. These were for the president among the most important reasons why "peace without victory" was no longer sufficient.

In pursuit of his objectives, the president increasingly engaged in public diplomacy. Before and during the war, the actual nature of Washington's commitment to concepts such as self-determination, the equality of nations, international cooperation, transparent diplomacy, and democratic governance had been made all too evident in the record of its behavior in Latin America and in the Far East. But in a world thirsting for change, Wilson was, for a short while at least, remarkably successful in putting himself forward as a principled champion of those ideas. The grand prize he sought was not only the military defeat of Germany, but also leverage over his allies in arranging the peace.

Wilson's central goal at Paris in 1919 was to reconstruct and, via reforms, put on more stable foundations a peace along very specific, and by no means particularly new, lines. His implicit model was in fact the *Pax Britannica* of the previous century, with the United States now playing a key role. Fans and critics alike have generally characterized Wilson's relationship to the war's settlement as he wished it to be seen: he was a disinterested quester after peace. But, even if the president came to see himself thus, there can be no more unhelpful way of trying to explain Wilson's (or any political figure's) actions than by simply accepting uncritically his own words.

In the president's view, the most important way of trying to achieve stabilization in the future was via a very carefully and deliberately designed "parliament of man," his League of Nations. The organization was a direct descendant of House's pact idea, but it also derived from all of those ordering mechanisms that Wilson's predecessors had been interested in from at least the time of McKinley. Confronted by domestic American concern about the pitfalls of overseas involvement, the League was the president's principal way of trying to make U.S. power a factor in eastern hemisphere affairs. Its objectives were to put constraints on the activity of rivals that might threaten the international order that Washington desired and simultaneously to bring as many of the other major powers as possible into a collective effort to oversee and "reform" the "backward regions" of that part of the globe. The hope was that challenges to the world set up at Paris, either from other powers or from within the to-be-supervised underdeveloped world, could be deterred by the combined might that the League's Executive Council would represent.

Ideally, the rest of the conference would achieve results that would help limit the tests that the League of Nations would face. This, for instance, was one of the reasons why Wilson and House were interested in offering a vent to nationalism in Central and Eastern Europe and why, simultaneously, the president was anxious to—by his lights—be "harsh" but "fair" to Germany.

Wilson's proclivity for reforms and relative moderation at Paris, it must be underscored, was aimed at stabilizing, not altering in any fundamental way, the world that had been created by the leading elements of the major industrializing powers in the late nineteenth and early twentieth centuries. And, as he showed at Paris, the president was prepared to deal harshly, not only with other powers, but also with revolutionaries and anticolonialists who seemed to represent a threat to the world he envisioned.

What the president faced upon his return home from Paris was not opposition on the part of most Republican leaders to the basic goals of his foreign policy, or even necessarily to a league. His fight with them was much more about U.S. freedom of action and about how Washington's credibility as a big power might be sustained on the world stage. The underlying commonality of purpose becomes all the more apparent when the activities of his successors in Latin America, China, and Europe are carefully explored.

Wilson insisted, of course, that what he was after was in the best interests of all Americans and of the entire world. After facilitating the first meeting between Balfour and the president, right after the United States became a belligerent, House registered in his diary the perceptive observation that "statesmen are apt to look upon the interests of their own countries from one viewpoint, and the interests of other countries from quite another."[4] This certainly held true for Wilson, who seems to have had an infinite capacity to define other countries' policies he did not like as "selfish" and "irresponsible" and his own policies as the reverse.

NOTES

Preface

1. Robert E. Hannigan, *The New World Power: American Foreign Policy, 1898–1917* (Philadelphia, 2002).

2. This notwithstanding the fact that much valuable information is also contained in the works of such chroniclers as Thomas J. Knock, John Milton Cooper, Jr., and A. Scott Berg. See especially Knock, *To End All Wars: Woodrow Wilson and the Quest for a New World Order* (Princeton, N.J., 1992); Cooper, Jr., *Breaking the Heart of the World: Woodrow Wilson and the Fight for the League of Nations* (Cambridge, 2001); Berg, *Wilson* (New York, 2013).

3. On which, for example, see William R. Keylor's comments in his review essay, "Postmortems for the American Century," *Diplomatic History* 25 (Spring 2001): 320–21.

Part I. Background (1890s–1914)

Epigraphs, in sequence: quotation from Bradford Perkins, *The Great Rapprochement: England and the United States, 1895–1914* (New York, 1968), 29; Roosevelt to Spring Rice, March 16, 1901, in Elting E. Morison, ed., *The Letters of Theodore Roosevelt*, 8 vols.(Cambridge, Mass., 1951–54) (hereafter *LTR*), 3:16; quotation from Tyler Dennett, *John Hay: From Poetry to Politics* (New York, 1934), 241; quotation from Charles S. Campbell, Jr., *Anglo-American Understanding, 1898–1903* (Baltimore, 1957), 180; "A News Report of an After-Dinner Speech in New York," January 30, 1904, in Arthur S. Link et al., eds., *The Papers of Woodrow Wilson*, 69 vols. (Princeton, 1966–94) (hereafter *PWW*), 15:149; address entitled "The Spirit and Purpose of American Diplomacy," delivered at the University of Pennsylvania, June 15, 1910, in Philander C. Knox Papers (Library of Congress, Washington, D.C.) (hereafter PCKP).

Chapter 1. The United States Steps Out

1. Lodge, "Our Blundering Foreign Policy," *Forum* 19 (March 1895): 16.

2. The broad story can be followed in Robert L. Beisner, *From the Old Diplomacy to the New, 1865–1900* (New York, 1975); Charles S. Campbell, *The Transformation of American Foreign Relations, 1865–1900* (New York, 1976); Hannigan, *New World Power*; David Healy, *U.S. Expansionism: The Imperialist Urge in the 1890s* (Madison, Wis., 1970); Walter LaFeber, *The New Empire: An Interpretation of American Expansion, 1860–1898* (Ithaca, N.Y., 1963); Walter LaFeber, *The American Search for Opportunity, 1865–1913* (Cambridge, 1993); and Milton Plesur, *America's Outward Thrust: Approaches to Foreign Affairs, 1865–1890* (DeKalb, Ill., 1971).

3. See Alfred Thayer Mahan, *The Influence of Sea Power upon History, 1660–1783* (Boston, 1890); *The Interest of America in Sea Power, Present and Future* (Boston, 1898); *The Problem of Asia and Its Effect upon International Policies* (Boston, 1900). On Mahan and his ideas and influence, see James L. Abrahamson, *America Arms for a New Century: The Making of a Great Military Power* (New York, 1981); Kenneth J. Hagan, *This People's Navy: The Making of American Sea Power* (New York, 1991), 161–258; Philip A. Crowl, "Alfred Thayer Mahan: The Naval Historian," in Peter Paret, ed., *Makers of Modern Strategy: From Machiavelli to the Nuclear Age* (Princeton, N.J., 1986), 444–77; Paul Kennedy, *Strategy and Diplomacy, 1870–1945* (London, 1984), 41–85; William E. Livesey, *Mahan on Seapower* (Norman, Okla., 1947); Clark Reynolds, *Command of the Sea: The History and Strategy of Maritime Empires* (New York, 1974), 402–18; Richard D. Challener, *Admirals, Generals and American Foreign Policy, 1898–1914* (Princeton, N.J., 1973), 12–23; and John Tetsuro Sumida, *Inventing Grand Strategy and Teaching Command: The Classic Works of Alfred Thayer Mahan Reconsidered* (Washington, D.C., 1997).

4. In Germany the idea was captured in a phrase employed by General Friedrich Bernhardi, later used by historian Fritz Fischer for the title of a volume he wrote on the controversy his studies of German foreign policy in the World War I era set off: *World Power or Decline* (New York, 1974).

5. Here I am referring to mass-produced, rifled weapons, improved armor, side arms, machine guns, etc., and to railroads, steamships, canals, the telegraph, submarine cables, and new developments in medicine and public health. Useful on these topics are Daniel R. Headrick, *The Tools of Empire: Technology and European Imperialism in the Nineteenth Century* (New York, 1981); Arnold Pacey, *Technology in World Civilization* (Cambridge, Mass., 1991), esp. chaps. 8–9; Philip D. Curtin, *Death by Migration: Europe's Encounter with the Tropical World in the Nineteenth Century* (Cambridge, 1989); and E. J. Hobsbawm, *The Age of Capital, 1848–1875* (New York, 1979), 48–71.

6. On American advantages, see Paul Kennedy, *The Rise and Fall of the Great Powers: Economic Change and Military Conflict from 1500 to 2000* (New York, 1987), 242–49.

7. Richard Olney, "International Isolation of the United States," *Atlantic Monthly* 81 (May 1898): 587–88; Bradford Perkins, *Great Rapprochement*, 29.

8. For a more extended discussion of this topic, see Hannigan, *New World Power*, chap. 1.

9. These themes are discussed in Christopher McKnight Nichols, *Promise and Peril: America at the Dawn of a Global Age* (Cambridge, Mass., 2011); Robert David Johnson, *The Peace Progressives and American Foreign Relations* (Cambridge, Mass., 1995); and Selig Adler, *The Isolationist Impulse* (New York, 1957), 15–173.

10. Rather, it was in a tradition that included McKinley's call for the United States to rescue the Cubans and Filipinos and the Taft administration's efforts to bring out the "altruism and unselfishness" of its "dollar diplomacy." See, for example, McKinley's speech of July 12, 1900, William McKinley Papers (Library of Congress, Washington, D.C.); Knox to Huntington-Wilson, May 20, 1910; and Knox's address of June 15, 1910, "The Spirit and Purpose of American Diplomacy," both in PCKP.

11. On the Caribbean, see Hannigan, *New World Power*, chap. 2.

12. Roosevelt to Hay, September 2, 1904, *LTR*, 4:917; Roosevelt to Root, May 20, 1904, *LTR*, 4:801.

13. James G. Blaine, *Political Discussions: Legislative, Diplomatic, and Popular, 1856–1886* (Norwich, Conn., 1887), 419. Blaine was the secretary of state under two Republican presidents, in 1881, under Garfield, and in 1889–92, under Harrison. For a discussion of his career, see Edward P. Crapol, *James G. Blaine: Architect of Empire* (Wilmington, Del., 2000).

14. See Olney to Bayard, July 20, 1895, U.S. Department of State, *Papers Relating to the Foreign Relations of the United States* (Washington, D.C.) (hereafter *FR*) *1895*, 545–62.

15. See Salisbury to Pauncefote, November 26, 1895, *FR 1895*, 563–76.

16. See, for example, Howard K. Beale, *Theodore Roosevelt and the Rise of America to World Power* (Baltimore, 1956, 1984), 394–95.

17. Roosevelt to Sternberg, October 11, 1901, *LTR*, 3:172.

18. Robert Bacon and James Brown Scott, eds., *Latin America and the United States: Addresses by Elihu Root* (Cambridge, Mass., 1917), 6–11.

19. See Donald R. Shea, *The Calvo Clause: A Problem of Inter-American and International Law and Diplomacy* (Minneapolis, 1955).

20. Root to Tillman, December 13, 1905, Elihu Root Papers (Library of Congress, Washington, D.C.).

21. Root, "The Monroe Doctrine," December 22, 1904, in Robert Bacon and James Brown Scott, eds., *Miscellaneous Addresses of Elihu Root* (Cambridge, Mass., 1917), 270.

22. See, for example, Joseph S. Nye, Jr., *Soft Power: The Means to Success in World Politics* (New York, 2004).

23. See *FR 1899*, 128–43.

24. *FR 1899, Appendix: Affairs in China*, 12.

25. Roosevelt to T. Roosevelt, Jr., February 19, 1904, *LTR*, 4:724.

26. Knox to Hoyt, October 8, 1909, and Knox address in Cincinnati, Ohio, October 1916, both in PCKP.

27. Hay is quoted using this expression in Norman Penlington, *The Alaska Boundary Dispute: A Critical Reappraisal* (Toronto, 1972), 47. For a more detailed discussion of this event and its aftermath, see Hannigan, *New World Power*, 141–57.

28. Robert E. Hannigan, "Reciprocity 1911: Continentalism and American Weltpolitik," *Diplomatic History* 4 (Winter 1980): 1–18; and Hannigan, "Continentalism and *Mitteleuropa* as Points of Departure for a Comparison of American and German Foreign Relations in the Early Twentieth Century," in Hans-Jürgen Schröder, ed., *Confrontation and Cooperation: Germany and the United States in the Era of World War I, 1900–1924* (Providence, R.I., 1993).

29. Roosevelt to James Creelman, March 7, 1908, *LTR*, 6:963–64.

30. Pepper and Davis, "Trade Relations with Canada, Newfoundland, and Mexico," May 23, 1910, PCKP.

31. This material draws on Hannigan, *New World Power*, chap. 6.

32. Quoted in Dennett, *Hay*, 241.

33. Quoted in Campbell, Jr., *Anglo-American Understanding*, 180.

34. Quoted in Philip C. Jessup, *Elihu Root*, 2 vols. (New York, 1938), 2:58.

35. Quoted in James Brown Scott, *The Hague Peace Conferences of 1899 and 1907*, 2 vols. (Baltimore, 1909), 1:427.

36. Here see Hannigan, *New World Power*, 192–200, 207–25.

37. Mark T. Gilderhus, *Pan American Visions: Woodrow Wilson in the Western Hemisphere, 1913–1921* (Tucson, Ariz., 1986), 8; David F. Healy, *Drive to Hegemony: The United*

States in the Caribbean, 1898–1917 (Madison, Wis., 1988), 164–65; E. David Cronon, *The Cabinet Diaries of Josephus Daniels, 1913–1921* (Lincoln, Neb., 1963), 6–7; "From the Diary of Oswald Garrison Villard," August 14, 1912, *PWW*, 25:24–25; "A Statement on Relations with Latin America," March 12, 1913, *PWW*, 27:172–73.

38. For a more detailed examination of Wilson's prewar Caribbean policy, see Hannigan, *New World Power*, 45–48.

39. "An Address on Latin American Policy in Mobile, Ala.," October 27, 1913, *PWW*, 28:449.

40. For a more detailed discussion of Wilson's prewar policy toward South America, see Hannigan, *New World Power*, 80–84.

41. "An Address to the General Assembly of Virginia and the City Council of Richmond," February 1, 1912, *PWW*, 24:111.

42. Gilderhus, *Pan American Visions*, 16–17.

43. "From the Diary of Colonel House," January 16, 1914, *PWW*, 29:135. There are two noteworthy biographical studies of House: Godfrey Hodgson, *Woodrow Wilson's Right Hand: The Life of Colonel Edward M. House* (New Haven, Conn., 2006); and Charles E. Neu, *Colonel House: A Biography of Woodrow Wilson's Silent Partner* (New York, 2015). Broadly speaking, the former is more analytical and interpretive, the latter more comprehensive with respect to House's activities and associations. "Colonel" was an honorary title bestowed on him by the Texas governor James Stephen Hogg in 1893.

44. For a more detailed examination of Wilson's prewar China policy, see Hannigan, *New World Power*, 127–31.

45. Ibid., 157.

46. This argument is laid out more fully in ibid., 165–75.

47. "An Address on Latin American Policy in Mobile, Ala.," October 27, 1913, *PWW*, 28:448–53.

48. "A Draft of a Circular Note to the Powers," October 24, 1913, *PWW*, 28:431–33; "An Outline of a Circular Note to the Powers," ca. October 24, 1913, *PWW*, 28:434.

49. "The British Embassy to Sir Edward Grey," November 14, 1913, *PWW*, 28:543–45.

50. Here see Hannigan, *New World Power*, 224–29 and below.

Part II. American "Neutrality" (1914–1917)

Epigraphs, in sequence: "From the Diary of Colonel House," August 30, 1914, *PWW*, 30:461–62; quotation from Phillips Payson O'Brien, *British and American Naval Power: Politics and Policy, 1900–1936* (Westport, Conn., 1998), 119; "From the Diary of Dr. Grayson," December 8, 1918, *PWW*, 53:338. Grayson, who held the rank of admiral in the USN, was the president's personal physician and a close confidante.

Chapter 2. Washington Reacts

1. Valuable overviews of the vast historiography include Jay Winter and Antoine Prost, *The Great War in History: Debates and Controversies, 1914 to the Present* (Cambridge, 2005); and John F. V. Keiger, "The War Explained: 1914 to the Present," in John Horne, ed., *A Companion to World War I* (Malden, Mass., 2012), 19–32. Noteworthy recent studies of the outbreak include Martin Gilbert, *The First World War: A Complete History* (New York, 1996), 1–34; Niall Ferguson, *The Pity of War: Explaining World War I* (New York, 1999); Hew Strachan, *The Outbreak of the First World War* (Oxford, 2004); David Stevenson, *Cataclysm: The*

First World War as Political Tragedy (New York, 2004), 3–35; Christopher Clark, *The Sleepwalkers: How Europe Went to War in 1914* (New York, 2013); Margaret MacMillan, *The War That Ended Peace* (New York, 2014); and Sean McMeekin, *July 1914* (New York, 2014). Many older works continue to be worth consulting. These include the studies of James Joll as well as of Fritz Fischer and his students. On the estrangement of Germany and England, see Paul Kennedy, *The Rise of the Anglo-German Antagonism, 1860–1914* (London, 1982). Also see V. R. Berghahn, *Germany and the Approach of War in 1914* (London, 1973); and Zara Steiner, *Britain and the Origins of the First World War* (New York, 1977). A concise collection of important documentary materials is Samuel R. Williamson, Jr. and Russel Van Wyk, *July 1914: Soldiers, Statesmen, and the Coming of the Great War* (Boston, 2003).

2. Justus D. Doenecke, *Nothing Less Than War: A New History of America's Entry into World War I* (Lexington, Ky., 2011), 20–21.

3. And impartial "in thought as well as in action." See "An Appeal to the American People," August 18, 1914, *PWW*, 30:393–94.

4. House to Wilson, August 22, 1914, *PWW*, 30:432–33; Wilson to House, August 25, 1914, *PWW*, 30:450; "From the Diary of Colonel House," August 30, 1914, *PWW*, 30:462.

5. "From the Diary of Colonel House," November 25, 1914, *PWW*, 31; 355.

6. "Memorandum for an Interview," ca. December 18, 1895, *PWW*, 9:365.

7. "From the Diary of Colonel House," August 30, 1914, *PWW*, 30:465.

8. I have drawn heavily in this section on John W. Coogan, *The End of Neutrality: The United States, Britain, and Maritime Rights, 1899–1915* (Ithaca, N.Y., 1981). Also see the classic study by Edwin Borchard and William Potter Lage, *Neutrality for the United States* (New Haven, Conn., 1937).

9. See Coogan, *End of Neutrality*, 214–15; Patrick Devlin, *Too Proud to Fight: Woodrow Wilson's Neutrality* (London, 1974); David French, *British Economic and Strategic Planning, 1905–1915* (London, 1982), 98.

10. Marion C. Siney, *The Allied Blockade of Germany, 1914–1916* (Ann Arbor, Mich., 1957), v; Coogan, *End of Neutrality*, 155–56.

11. Siney, *Allied Blockade*, 12–29; Coogan, *End of Neutrality*, 137, 167, Borchard and Lage, *Neutrality*, 65–69.

12. Hew Strachan, *The First World War* (New York, 2004), 42–44.

13. Ibid., 48.

14. See especially Avner Offer, *The First World War: An Agrarian Interpretation* (Oxford, 1991), 217–317; and French, *Planning*, 22–23.

15. Carlton Savage, ed., *Policy of the United States Toward Maritime Commerce in War*, 2 vols. (Washington, D.C., 1934–36), 2:200–201. A "paper blockade" refers to a declaration of blockade not accompanied by sufficient means of enforcement.

16. Quoted in Coogan, *End of Neutrality*, 173.

17. Ibid., 174–75.

18. Savage, *Policy*, 2:185, 195–206; Coogan, *End of Neutrality*, 172–74, 184–93; Siney, *Allied Blockade*, 21–27.

19. See Page to Bryan, October 19, 1914, in Savage, *Policy*, 2:219–21.

20. Coogan, *End of Neutrality*, 194–205. Other important overviews of the American reaction to Britain's unfolding "blockade" include Doenecke, *Nothing Less*, 45–49; Robert W. Tucker, *Woodrow Wilson and the Great War: Reconsidering America's Neutrality, 1914–1917*

(Charlottesville, Va., 2007), 55–87; and Ross A. Kennedy, *The Will to Believe: Woodrow Wilson, World War I and America's Strategy for Peace and Security* (Kent, Ohio, 2009), 65–71.

21. For a somewhat more detailed discussion of these efforts, see Hannigan, *New World Power*, 225–29.

22. Originally published in New York, it is available at Project Gutenberg, http://www.gutenberg.org/etext/6711. See especially chaps. 28, 48, 50, and 52. A good discussion of the novel can be found in Hodgson, *Wilson's Right Hand*, 47–53. Also see Neu, *Colonel House*, 70–74.

23. Indeed, the Wilson administration would eventually come back to this approach in China itself.

24. Address at Christiania, Norway, May 5, 1910, in Hermann Hagedorn, ed., *The Works of Theodore Roosevelt*, 20 vols. (New York, 1926), 16:308–9; Taft to Otis, June 10, 1910, William Howard Taft Papers (Library of Congress, Washington, D.C.).

25. Charles Seymour, ed., *The Intimate Papers of Colonel House: Arranged as a Narrative*, 4 vols. (Boston, 1926–28), 1:240.

26. Seymour, *Intimate Papers*, 1:239–40, 246; "From the Diary of Colonel House," December 2, 1913, *PWW*, 29:12–13; Burton J. Hendrick, *The Life and Letters of Walter H. Page*, 2 vols. (Garden City, N.Y., 1922), 1:281.

27. Seymour, *Intimate Papers*, 1:255–56.

28. House to Wilson, May 29, 1914, *PWW*, 30:109.

29. Ernest R. May, *The World War and American Isolation, 1914–1917* (Chicago, 1959, 1966), 73–76.

30. House to Wilson, August 22, 1914, *PWW*, 30:432–33; Wilson to House, August 25, 1914, *PWW*, 30:450. A month later, Wilson urged House to convey this concern about Germany's destruction leaving no check on Russia to the British. See Doenecke, *Nothing Less*, 22.

31. "From the Diary of Colonel House," August 30, 1914, *PWW*, 30:461–62.

32. House to Wilson, September 6, 1914, *PWW*, 31:5–6; House to Wilson, September 18, 1914, *PWW*, 31:45; Wilson to House, September 19, 1914, *PWW*, 31:55; "From the Diary of Colonel House," September 28, 1914, *PWW*, 31:94–95.

33. House to Wilson, October 8, 1914, *PWW*, 31:137; "From the Diary of Colonel House," December 3, 1914, *PWW*, 31:385.

34. Seymour, *Intimate Papers*, 1:340; "From the Diary of Colonel House," December 18, 1914, *PWW*, 31:490.

35. Fritz Fischer, *Germany's Aims in the First World War* (New York, 1967), 110–13; David Stevenson, *The First World War and International Politics* (Oxford, 1991), 91–94; Stevenson, *Cataclysm*, 104–6.

36. V. H. Rothwell, *British War Aims and Peace Diplomacy, 1914–1918* (Oxford, 1971), 18–24; Stevenson, *International Politics*, 106–10; Stevenson, *Cataclysm*, 117–21; May, *World War*, 77; Bryce to Wilson, September 24, 1914, *PWW*, 31:82.

37. For a more detailed discussion of his trip, see Hannigan, *New World Power*, 237–40.

38. House to Wilson, February 9, 1915, *PWW*, 32:204–7; Arthur S. Link, *Wilson: The Struggle for Neutrality, 1914–1915* (Princeton, N.J., 1960), 219.

39. House to Page, October 3, 1914, in Hendrick, *Life and Letters*, 1:414–15; Edward H. Buehrig, *Woodrow Wilson and the Balance of Power* (Bloomington, Ind., 1955), 193–94; House

to Wilson, February 9, 1915, *PWW*, 32:205; House to Wilson, February 11, 1915, *PWW*, 32:220–21; Seymour, *Intimate Papers*, 1:368–69. Alsace and Lorraine were territories surrendered by France to Germany at the end of the Franco-Prussian War in 1871. Historian Derek Heater writes that "[i]n Britain, Asquith, Grey and Churchill . . . were all by 1915 commending ethnography as a necessary foundation for a secure peace [presumably in Europe]." See his *National Self-Determination: Woodrow Wilson and His Legacy* (New York, 1994), 30.

40. House to Wilson, February 15, 1915, *PWW*, 32:237–38.

41. Seymour, *Intimate Papers*, 1:369–70; House to Wilson, February 23, 1915, *PWW*, 32:278; House to Wilson, March 20, 1915, *PWW*, 32:402–3; House to Wilson, March 26, 1915, *PWW*, 32:438–39; House to Wilson, March 27, 1915, *PWW*, 32:441–43; House to Wilson, March 29, 1915, *PWW*, 32:455–56; House to Wilson, April 11, 1915, *PWW*, 32:504–7.

42. House to Wilson, March 20, 1915, *PWW*, 32:402–3.

43. Savage, *Policy*, 2:265–66; Hodgson, *Wilson's Right Hand*, 107. Washington did complain of the flag ruse. But, as Doenecke notes, the protest was "innocuous" and "contained no threat of retaliation." See *Nothing Less*, 60. For valuable accounts of the course of the war to this point, see Gilbert, *First World War*, 35–145; Stevenson, *Cataclysm*, 37–78; Strachan, *First World War*, 67–145.

44. Joseph P. Tumulty, *Woodrow Wilson as I Know Him* (New York, 1921), 230–31.

45. Bryan to Gerard, February 10, 1915, in Savage, *Policy*, 2:267–69; Tucker, *Woodrow Wilson*, 94–97.

46. Bryan to Gerard, February 10, 1915, in Savage, *Policy*, 2:267–69.

47. Memorandum dated February 15, 1915, *FR: The Lansing Papers, 1914–1920*, 2 vols., 1:367–68.

48. Bryan to Wilson, February 15, 1915, *PWW*, 32:235–36.

49. Quoted in Coogan, *End of Neutrality*, 229; Devlin, *Too Proud*, 202, 207–9; Siney, *Allied Blockade*, 64–65; A. C. Bell, *A History of the Blockade of Germany and of the Countries Associated with Her in the Great War, Austria-Hungary, Bulgaria, and Turkey* (London, 1937), 221, 232, 237–38. Lord Chancellor Richard Haldane commented, "The submarine business is annoying but that is all." See Doenecke, *Nothing Less*, 59–60.

50. Bell, *Blockade*, 233; Siney, *Allied Blockade*, 66–68; Thomas Fleming, *The Illusion of Victory: America in World War I* (New York, 2004), 67.

51. Tucker, *Woodrow Wilson*, 105.

52. Coogan, *End of Neutrality*, 228–35.

53. One American had died when the British liner *Falaba* was torpedoed on March 28. A month later, the *Cushing*, an American ship, was hit by a bomb from a German plane. On May 1, three Americans died when the American *Gulflight* was torpedoed. Both of the American ships were mistaken for British vessels. Damage was slight in the case of the *Cushing*; compensation was eventually offered in the case of the *Gulflight*. No course of action had been decided upon in the *Falaba* case when the *Lusitania* was struck, but an extremely important exchange over the incident had taken place between Anderson and Lansing. Anderson's view, as stated in his diary, was that the case did "not involve an affront to the United States, as [the American] Thrasher's death was not the specific purpose of the attack by the submarine. . . . The attack on the ship of course was unlawful in the opinion of the United States, but inasmuch as we came in contact with the case only through one of its indirect results, it seems to me that we might place the matter on the plane of a claim for pecuniary damages."

Anderson told Lansing that such an approach would "keep us out of trouble." As evidenced in the *Lusitania* case, the administration instead persisted in making an issue of the safety of Americans traveling on Allied steamers. See Buehrig, *Woodrow Wilson*, 24–27.

54. Doenecke, *Nothing Less*, 71–75. The classic study is Thomas A. Bailey and Paul B. Ryan's riveting *The Lusitania Disaster* (New York, 1975).

55. Bryan to Gerard, May 13, 1915, in Savage, *Policy*, 2:315–18.

56. Karl E. Birnbaum, *Peace Moves and U-Boat Warfare: A Study of Imperial Germany's Policy Toward the United States, April 18, 1916–January 9, 1917* (Stockholm, 1958), 41.

57. Bryan to Wilson, May 9, 1915, *PWW*, 33:135; Paolo E. Coletta, *William Jennings Bryan*, 3 vols. (Lincoln, Neb., 1964–69), 2:301–20; Kendrick A. Clements, *William Jennings Bryan: Missionary Isolationist* (Knoxville, Tenn., 1982), 106–9; Michael Kazin, *A Godly Hero: The Life of William Jennings Bryan* (New York, 2006), 235–37.

58. Tucker, *Woodrow Wilson*, 114.

59. House to Wilson, May 9, 1915, *PWW*, 33:134.

60. Page to Wilson, May 8, 1915, *PWW*, 33:130.

61. Wilson to Bryan, May 10, 1915, *PWW*, 33:139.

62. House to Wilson, May 13, 1915, *PWW*, 33:190.

63. Wilson to House, May 16, 1915, *PWW*, 33:205; House to Wilson, May 13, 1915, *PWW*, 33:189–90; Bernstorff to Bethmann Hollweg, May 29, 1915, *PWW*, 33:283; Tucker, *Woodrow Wilson*, 125.

64. Wilson to House, May 18, 1915, *PWW*, 33:217.

65. House to Wilson, May 25, 1915, *PWW*, 33:254.

66. Borchard and Lage, *Neutrality*, 207–9.

67. Gerard to Bryan, May 29, 1915, in Savage, *Policy*, 2:327–30.

68. Lansing to Gerard, June 9, 1915, in Savage, *Policy*, 2:340–43; Coletta, *Bryan*, 2:329–44; Clements, *Bryan*, 109–11; Kazin, *Godly Hero*, 237–40.

69. Gerard to Lansing, July 8, 1915, in Savage, *Policy*, 2:351–55.

70. House to Wilson, July 10, 1915, *PWW*, 33:490–91.

71. Wilson to House, July 14, 1915, *PWW*, 33:505–6; Lansing to Gerard, July 21, 1915, in Savage, *Policy*, 2:361–63.

72. Devlin, *Too Proud*, 307–8.

73. Wilson to Galt, August 19, 1915, *PWW*, 34:257–61; Wilson to House, August 21, 1915, *PWW*, 34:271; Wilson to Galt, August 27, 1915, *PWW*, 34:304.

74. Wilson to Galt, August 9, 1915, *PWW*, 34:151.

75. Wilson to Galt, August 19, 1915, *PWW*, 34:258.

76. House to Wilson, August 22, 1915, *PWW*, 34:298–99; Lansing to Wilson, August 20, 1915, *PWW*, 34:264–66.

77. Gerard to Lansing, August 24, 1915, *PWW*, 34:320; Bernstorff to Lansing, September 1, 1915, in Savage, *Policy*, 2:378; Birnbaum, *Peace Moves*, 34–35.

78. Devlin, *Too Proud*, 327–34; Link, *Struggle*, 653–81; Birnbaum, *Peace Moves*, 35–37.

79. House to Wilson, June 16, 1915, *PWW*, 33:406. This was sent from Long Island, N.Y., shortly after his return.

80. Gilbert, *First World War*, 146–223; Stevenson, *Cataclysm*, 81–102, 123–31; Strachan, *First World War*, 115–23, 151–56, 178–82.

81. "From the Diary of Colonel House," September 22, 1915, *PWW*, 34:506.

82. Seymour, *Intimate Papers*, 2:82.

83. "From the Diary of Colonel House," October 8, 1915, *PWW*, 35:42–44.

84. House to Grey, October 17, 1915, *PWW*, 35:81–82. The word "probably" was added by the president. He told House, "I do not want to make it inevitable quite that we should take part to force terms on Germany, because the exact circumstances of such a crisis are impossible to determine. The letter is altogether right. I pray God it may bring results." See Wilson to House, October 18, 1915, *PWW*, 35:80.

85. Grey to House, November 9, 1915, *PWW*, 35:186.

86. House to Wilson, November 10, 1915, *PWW*, 35:186; Wilson to House, November 11, 1915, *PWW*, 35:187.

Chapter 3. Pursuing a Seat at the Table

1. Seymour, *Intimate Papers*, 2:72.

2. Ibid., 2:98.

3. House to Wilson, January 7, 1916, *PWW*, 35:454.

4. Seymour, *Intimate Papers*, 2:129.

5. House to Wilson, January 11, 1916, *PWW*, 35:465.

6. House to Wilson, January 15, 1916, *PWW*, 35:485–86.

7. Seymour, *Intimate Papers*, 2:130.

8. Ibid., 2:142.

9. House to Wilson, January 30, 1916, *PWW*, 36:52.

10. House to Wilson, February 3, 1916, *PWW*, 36:125.

11. Seymour, *Intimate Papers*, 2:168; House to Wilson, February 9, 1916, *PWW*, 36:150.

12. Seymour, *Intimate Papers*, 2:201–2.

13. Ibid., 2:195. When they met in Washington, according to his diary, House "spoke of the pride I would feel if the plan could be realized and I could see him [the president] sitting at the head of the counsel table at the Hague."

14. "From the Diary of Colonel House," March 6, 1916, *PWW*: 36:262; House to Grey, March 7, 1916, *PWW* 36:266; House to Wilson, March 12, 1916, *PWW*: 36:294. For other discussions, see Devlin, *Too Proud*, 450–54; Tucker, *Woodrow Wilson*, 167–70; and Hodgson, *Wilson's Right Hand*, 119–21.

15. Seymour, *Intimate Papers*, 1:298.

16. "An Annual Message to Congress," December 8, 1914, *PWW*, 31:414–24.

17. Abrahamson, *America Arms*, 151–76; O'Brien, *Naval Power*, 113–19; Doenecke, *Nothing Less*, 145–54; House to Wilson, August 8, 1915, *PWW*, 133–35.

18. Arthur S. Link, *Wilson: Confusions and Crises, 1915–1916* (Princeton, N.J., 1964), 15–45; John Milton Cooper, Jr., *The Vanity of Power: American Isolationism and World War I, 1914–1917* (Westport, Conn., 1969), 90–96; Johnson, *Peace Progressives*, 43–59.

19. Quoted in Cooper, Jr., *Vanity*, 93.

20. "An Address in Milwaukee on Preparedness," January 31, 1916, *PWW*, 36:57; "An Address in Pittsburgh on Preparedness," January 29, 1916, *PWW*, 36:28; "Address in New York on Preparedness," January 27, 1916, *PWW*, 36:10–11; Link, *Confusions*, 45–49.

21. Link, *Confusions*, 50–54, 327–33; Mary Klachko, with David Trask, *Admiral William Shepherd Benson: First Chief of Naval Operations* (Annapolis, Md., 1987), 46–49.

22. Lansing to Wilson, January 2, 1916, *PWW*, 35:420–22.

23. On these policies, see Tucker, *Woodrow Wilson*, 136–37.

24. Lansing to Wilson, January 7, 1916, *PWW*, 35:448; Devlin, *Too Proud*, 373.

25. Wilson to Lansing, January 10, 1916, *PWW*, 35:457.

26. Link, *Confusions*, 145–63.

27. For the ensuing struggle, see ibid., 163–94; Cooper, Jr., *Vanity*, 106–17; Johnson, *Peace Progressives*, 45–62; Doenecke, *Nothing Less*, 155–66.

28. Wilson to Stone, February 24, 1916, *PWW*, 36:213–14.

29. Birnbaum, *Peace Moves*, 63–64.

30. For overviews of the crisis, see Devlin, *Too Proud*, 473–82; Link, *Confusions*, 222–79; Birnbaum, *Peace Moves*, 70–92; and Tucker, *Woodrow Wilson*, 131–32.

31. House to Grey, April 6, 1916, *PWW*, 36:421 (signed by House but composed jointly).

32. Quoted in Link, *Confusions*, 238.

33. "From the Diary of Colonel House," March 30, 1916, *PWW*, 36:388.

34. Lansing to Gerard, April 18, 1916, in Savage, *Policy*, 2:476–80.

35. Savage, *Policy*, 2:494–95; Birnbaum, *Peace Moves*, 88–92; Stevenson, *International Politics*, 71–72.

36. "An Address in Washington to the League to Enforce Peace," May 27, 1916, *PWW*, 37:113–16; "From the Diary of Colonel House," May 3, 1916, *PWW*, 36:596–602; House to Grey, May 7, 1916, *PWW*, 36:652 (dispatched on May 10, 1916); House to Wilson, May 7, 1916, *PWW*, 36:631–32; Wilson to House, May 8, 1916, *PWW*, 36:652; House to Grey, May 11, 1916, *PWW*, 37:21. Background on the League to Enforce Peace to mid-1916 is contained in Ruhl J. Bartlett, *The League to Enforce Peace* (Chapel Hill, N.C., 1944), 3–56; and Warren F. Kuehl, *Seeking World Order: The United States and International Organization to 1920* (Nashville, Tenn., 1969), 184–92. Background on the speech is included in Knock, *End*, 75–81; and in Tucker, *Woodrow Wilson*, 179–83.

37. Grey to House, May 29, 1916. Also see Grey to House, May 12, 1916, *PWW*, 37:43–44; House to Wilson, with enclosure, May 17, 1916, *PWW*, 37:62–64; Wilson to House, May 18, 1916, *PWW*, 37:68; House to Grey, May 23, 1916, *PWW*, 37:100. On the British government's outlook, see C. M. Mason, "Anglo-American Relations: Mediation and 'Permanent Peace,'" in F. H. Hinsley, ed., *British Foreign Policy Under Sir Edward Grey* (Cambridge, 1977), 477–80; Rothwell, *British War Aims*, 33–36; Paul Guinn, *British Strategy and Politics, 1914–1918* (Oxford, 1965), 124–25; Stevenson, *International Politics*, 81; David R. Woodward, *Trial by Friendship: Anglo-American Relations, 1917–1918* (Lexington, Ky., 1993), 14–22.

38. House to Wilson, May 14, 1916, *PWW*, 37:42.

39. House to Grey, June 8, 1916, *PWW*, 37:178–80.

40. Wilson to House, June 22, 1916, *PWW*, 37:280–81.

41. As early as the spring of 1915, Wilson had noted that "we are more and more becoming, by the force of circumstances, the mediating nation of the world in respect to its finance." The president referred again to this leverage in an article, "America's Opportunity," that he wrote but did not publish in the summer of 1916. See "Remarks to the Associated Press in New York," April 20, 1915, *PWW*, 33:38; and "An Unpublished Article," July 30, 1916, *PWW*, 37:500–502.

42. "From the Diary of Colonel House," May 3, 1916, *PWW*, 36:596–602; House to Wilson, July 30, 1916, *PWW*, 37:502.

43. Seymour, *Intimate Papers*, 2:284.

44. Lansing to Wilson, June 23, 1916, *PWW*, 37:287–88; Gerd Hardach, *The First World War* (Berkeley, Calif., 1977), 238–40; Siney, *Allied Blockade*, 177–79; Carl P. Parrini, *Heir to*

Empire: United States Economic Diplomacy, 1916–1923 (Pittsburgh, 1969), 15–16; Jeffrey Safford, *Wilsonian Maritime Diplomacy, 1913–1921* (New Brunswick, N.J., 1978), 89.

45. Wilson to House, July 23, 1916, *PWW*, 37:467. Also see Lansing to Jusserand, May 24, 1916, in Savage, *Policy*, 2:498–504; Polk to Page, July 26, 1916, in Savage, *Policy*, 2:505–7; Siney, *Allied Blockade*, 146, 148–55, 181–85; Kathleen Burk, *Britain, America and the Sinews of War, 1914–1918* (Boston, 1985), 41; Devlin, *Too Proud*, 505–14; Safford, *Maritime*, 90.

46. Seymour, *Intimate Papers*, 2:319.

47. Quoted in Ross Gregory, *The Origins of American Intervention in the First World War* (New York, 1971), 110.

48. Devlin, *Too Proud*, 518.

49. "From the Diary of Colonel House," September 24, 1916, *PWW*, 38:258–59. Also see House to Wilson, May 17, 1916, *PWW*, 37:64; House to Wilson, June 1, 1916, *PWW*, 37:134; House to Wilson, June 18, 1916, *PWW*, 37:265; House to Wilson, June 25, 1916, *PWW*, 37:295; Harold and Margeret Sprout, *The Rise of American Naval Power, 1776–1918* (Princeton, N.J., 1966), 334–46; Klachko, *Benson*, 49; O'Brien, *Naval Power*, 115–19.

50. Arthur S. Link, *Wilson: Campaigns for Progressivism and Peace, 1916–1917* (Princeton, N.J., 1965), 1–48, 93–164; David Sarasohn, *The Party of Reform: Democrats in the Progressive Era* (Jackson, Miss., 1989), 192–238; Kazin, *Godly Hero*, 250–52; John Milton Cooper, Jr., *The Warrior and the Priest: Woodrow Wilson and Theodore Roosevelt* (Cambridge, Mass., 1983), 304–8; Doenecke, *Nothing Less*, 213.

51. House to Wilson, with enclosures, October 20, 1916, *PWW*, 38:494–96; Birnbaum, *Peace Moves*, 124–99.

52. "From the Diary of Colonel House," November 14, 1916, *PWW*, 38:646.

53. House to Wilson, November 6, 1916, *PWW*, 38:619.

54. "From the Diary of Colonel House," November 15, 1916, *PWW*, 38:658.

55. "From the Diary of Colonel House," November 14, 1916, *PWW*, 38:647.

56. House to Wilson, November 20, 1916, *PWW*, 40:4–6.

57. "A Draft of a Peace Note," ca. November 25, 1916, *PWW*, 40:70–74; Tumulty to Wilson, ca. November 21, 1916, *PWW*, 40:24.

58. Wilson to House, December 3, 1916, *PWW*, 40:131.

59. Bryan to J. P. Morgan and Co., August 15, 1916, in Savage, *Policy*, 1:194.

60. "News Report," November 21, 1916, *PWW*, 40:19–20; Davison to Wilson, November 25, 1916, *PWW*, 40:75–76; Wilson to Harding, with enclosure, November 26, 1916, *PWW*, 40:77–80; Burk, *Sinews*, 75–88; Hew Strachan, *Financing the First World War* (Oxford, 2004), 161–201.

61. Spring Rice to Foreign Office, December 3, 1916, *PWW*, 40:136–37.

62. The note is enclosed in Wilson to Lansing, December 9, 1916, *PWW*, 40:197–200.

63. Enclosed in Lansing to Wilson, December 14, 1916, *PWW*, 40:231–32.

64. "An Appeal for a Statement of War Aims," December 18, 1916, *PWW*, 40:273–76; "From the Diary of Colonel House," December 14, 1916, *PWW*, 40:238; Wilson to Lansing, with enclosure, December 15, 1916, *PWW*, 40:241–43; Wilson to Lansing, December 17, 1916, *PWW*, 40:256; Wilson to House, December 19, 1916, *PWW*, 40:276.

65. Gerard to Lansing, December 26, 1918, *PWW*, 40:331.

66. Wilson to House, with enclosures, November 21, 1916, *PWW*, 40:20–24; Lansing to Wilson, with enclosure, December 4, 1916, *PWW*, 40:141–46; House to Wilson, with enclosure, December 5, 1916, *PWW*, 40:160–61.

67. Devlin, *Too Proud*, 544–51.

68. Ibid., 551.

69. Guinn, *British Strategy*, 174–76, 191–95; Rothwell, *British War Aims*, 39–55, 59, 60–61, 66; Stevenson, *International Politics*, 110–11; Anne Orde, *The Eclipse of Great Britain: The United States and British Imperial Decline, 1895–1956* (New York, 1996), 47–48; Sterling J. Kernek, "Distractions of Peace During War: The Lloyd George Government's Reactions to Woodrow Wilson, December 1916—November 1918," *Transactions of the American Philosophical Society* 65 (April 1975): 7–27; Woodward, *Trial*, 22–29; Page to Wilson, December 29, 1916, *PWW*, 40:355–58.

70. Sharp to Lansing, January 10, 1917, *PWW*, 40:439–41.

71. Link, *Campaigns*, 238; Balfour to Spring Rice, January 13, 1917, *PWW*, 40:500–503.

72. "From the Diary of Colonel House," January 3, 1917, *PWW*, 40:403–5.

73. "An Address to the Senate," January 22, 1917, *PWW*, 40:533–39. Also see "From the Diary of Colonel House," January 11, 1917, *PWW*, 40:445–46; "From the Diary of Colonel House," January 12, 1917, *PWW*, 40:462–63; Link, *Campaigns*, 254–55.

74. Wilson to House, January 24, 1917, *PWW*, 41:3.

75. House to Wilson, January 25, 1917, *PWW*, 41:17.

76. House to Wilson, January 26, 1917, *PWW*, 41:25.

77. See enclosure with Lansing to Wilson, January 31, 1917, *PWW*, 41:71–79. Also see Birnbaum, *Peace Moves*, 199–339; Fritz Fischer, *Germany's Aims*, 285–324; Stevenson, *International Politics*, 104–6; Stevenson, *Cataclysm*, 108–11, 212–14.

78. Kazin, *Godly Hero*, 252–53; Cooper, Jr., *Vanity*, 168; Doenecke, *Nothing Less*, 254.

79. "From the Diary of Colonel House," February 1, 1916, *PWW*, 41:87.

80. "A Memorandum by Robert Lansing," February 4, 1916, *PWW*, 41:120. "We are the only one of the great White nations that is free from war today," he told House a month earlier, "and it would be a crime against civilization for us to go in." "From the Diary of Colonel House," January 4, 1917, *PWW*, 40:409.

81. Link, *Campaigns*, 296.

82. Lansing to Wilson, with enclosure, February 2, 1917, *PWW*, 41:96–99; Lansing to Wilson, February 2, 1917, *PWW*, 41:99–100; "A Memorandum by Robert Lansing," February 4, 1917, *PWW*, 41:118–25; "From the Diary of Colonel House," February 1, 1917, *PWW*, 41:87; "An Address to a Joint Session of Congress," February 3, 1917, *PWW*, 41:108–12; Link, *Campaigns*, 298–99.

83. House to Wilson, February 10, 1917, *PWW*, 41:190. On this last point, see House's comments as reported in Hohler to Hardinge, March 23, 1917, *PWW*, 41:460.

84. Devlin, *Too Proud*, 642.

85. House to Wilson, January 27, 1917, *PWW*, 41:39–40; "From the Diary of Colonel House," February 1, 1917, *PWW*, 41:88–89; Penfield to Lansing, February 5, 1917, *PWW*, 41:129–30; Lansing to Page, February 8, 1917, *PWW*, 41:158–59; Page to Lansing, February 11, 1917, *PWW*, 41:211–14; Page to Lansing, February 20, 1917, *PWW*, 41:260; Lansing to Wilson, with enclosure, February 21, 1917, *PWW*, 41:267–68; Penfield to Lansing, February 27, 1917, *PWW*, 41:297–300; Wilson to Lansing, with enclosure, March 3, 1917, *PWW*, 41:313; Link, *Campaigns*, 314–17; Kernek, "Distractions," 38–40.

86. Link, *Campaigns*, 378–79; Devlin, *Too Proud*, 646.

87. Lansing to Wilson, with enclosure, February 21, 1917, *PWW*, 41:266.

88. "An Address to a Joint Session of Congress," February 26, 1917, *PWW* 41:283–87.

89. "A Statement," March 4, 1917, *PWW*, 41:320.

90. Burk, *Sinews*, 310–13; 340–41; Devlin, *Too Proud*, 643–45, 652–63; Link, *Campaigns*, 347–67, 372–77; Cooper, Jr., *Vanity*, 158–60, 175–89; Johnson, *Peace Progressives*, 66–67; David P. Thelen, *Robert M. La Follette and the Insurgent Spirit* (Boston, 1976), 132–34.

91. The quote reflects his views as rendered by Secretary of the Navy Josephus Daniels. See Daniels to Wilson, March 9, 1917, *PWW*, 41:370. Also see Klachko, *Benson*, 56.

92. Page to Wilson, February 24, 1917, *PWW*, 41:281.

93. "A News Report," ca. February 28, 1917, *PWW*, 41:302–5; Friedrich Katz, *The Secret War in Mexico: Europe, the United States, and the Mexican Revolution* (Chicago, 1981), 350–67; Mark T. Gilderhus, *Diplomacy and Revolution: U.S.-Mexican Relations Under Wilson and Carranza* (Tucson, Ariz., 1977), 59–64; Arthur S. Link, *Woodrow Wilson and the Progressive Era, 1910–1917* (New York, 1963), 272–73; Cooper, Jr., *Warrior*, 318.

94. "A News Report," ca. February 28, 1917, *PWW*, 41:302–5.

95. Included in Jusserand to Briand, March 3, 1917, *PWW*, 41:315–17. Bergson reported as well that the Federal Reserve Board would soon be reversing its policy on loans to the Allies. Indeed, on March 8, after consultation with the administration, the Fed issued a statement meant to nullify the warning it had issued in November. Asserting that it had been misunderstood, the board now declared foreign loans "a very important, natural and proper means of settling the balances created in our favor by our large export trade." Devlin, *Too Proud*, 661; Burk, *Sinews*, 93–95; Strachan, *Financing*, 201.

96. Lansing to House, March 19, 1917, *PWW*, 41:429–30; Lansing to Wilson, March 19, 1917, *PWW*, 41:425–27.

97. "A Proclamation," March 21, 1917, *PWW*, 41:446; "A Memorandum by Robert Lansing," March 20, 1917, *PWW*, 41:436–44.

Chapter 4. China and Latin America

1. Ian Nish, *Japanese Foreign Policy, 1869–1942: Kasumigaseki to Miyakezaka* (London, 1977), 93–96; Peter Lowe, *Britain in the Far East: A Survey from 1819 to the Present* (New York, 1981), 100–102; W. G. Beasley, *Japanese Imperialism, 1894–1945* (Oxford, 1987), 109–10; Walter LaFeber, *The Clash: A History of U.S.-Japanese Relations* (New York, 1997), 106–8; Frederick R. Dickinson, *War and National Reinvention: Japan in the Great War* (Cambridge, Mass., 1999), 34–85; Noriko Kawamura, *Turbulence in the Pacific: Japanese-U.S. Relations During World War I* (Westport, Conn., 2000), 11–18; Stevenson, *Cataclysm*, 88–89.

2. That leasehold had been forcibly acquired by Germany in 1898. The islands in question were the Mariana, Caroline, and Marshall groups. See Imanuel Geiss, *German Foreign Policy, 1871–1914* (London, 1976), 70, 84–85, 90.

3. Nish, *Japanese Foreign Policy*, 96–99; Beasley, *Japanese Imperialism*, 112–14; Dickinson, *Reinvention*, 92; Stevenson, *Cataclysm*, 121.

4. "From the Diary of Colonel House," January 25, 1915, *PWW*, 32:120.

5. As witnessed in Bryan to Chinda, March 13, 1915, *FR 1915*, 105–11. Also see Burton F. Beers, *Vain Endeavor: Robert Lansing's Attempts to End the American-Japanese Rivalry* (Durham, N.C., 1962), 37–41. On Reinsch and the crisis, see Noel H. Pugach, *Paul S. Reinsch: Open Door Diplomat in Action* (New York, 1979), 143–56.

6. Bryan to Guthrie, May 11, 1915, *FR 1915*, 146; Wilson to Bryan, May 10, 1915, *PWW*, 33:140–41; Nish, *Japanese Foreign Policy*, 99–103; Beasley, *Japanese Imperialism*, 114–15;

Beers, *Vain Endeavor*, 45–47; LaFeber, *Clash*, 111–12; Roy W. Curry, *Woodrow Wilson and Far Eastern Policy, 1913–1921* (New York, 1957), 122–27; Kawamura, *Turbulence*, 28–57.

7. Reinsch to Wilson, July 25, 1915, *PWW*, 34:25–26; Pugach, *Reinsch*, 165–214; Nish, *Japanese Foreign Policy*, 92; Lowe, *Britain in the Far East*, 92–97; Curry, *Far Eastern Policy*, 154; Beers, *Vain Endeavor*, 72–92; Daniel M. Crane and Thomas A. Breslin, *An Ordinary Relationship: American Opposition to Republican Revolution in China* (Miami, 1986), 146–57.

8. Nish, *Japanese Foreign Policy*, 106–15; Beasley, *Japanese Imperialism*, 117, 163; Beers, *Vain Endeavor*, 79–80, 108, 111–12.

9. Frederick Dickinson meanwhile insists that the shift from Okuma to Terauchi "signaled less a change of substance than of form" for Japanese policy. See *Reinvention*, 158. For the text of the agreement, concluded on November 2, see *FR 1917*, 264–65. American interests were further protected, for the duration of the war, by a secret protocol in which both governments promised not to take advantage of the conflict "to seek special rights or privileges which would abridge the rights of subjects of other nations." See LaFeber, *Clash*, 112–16. Also see Nish, *Japanese Foreign Policy*, 115–18; Beasley, *Japanese Imperialism*, 163–64; Beers, *Vain Endeavor*, 100–16; Kawamura, *Turbulence*, 77–103.

10. Donald A. Yerxa, *Admirals and Empire: The United States Navy and the Caribbean, 1898–1945* (Columbia, S.C., 1991), 35–36.

11. "An Address in New York to the National League of Commission Merchants," January 11, 1912, *PWW*, 24:33.

12. Healy, *Drive to Hegemony*.

13. Yerxa, *Admirals and Empire*, 1–2, 32.

14. Much of this discussion of the involvement of the Taft and Wilson administrations in Nicaragua draws on Hannigan, *New World Power*, 41–45, 47–48.

15. Quoted in Arthur S. Link, *Wilson: The New Freedom* (Princeton, N.J., 1956), 335.

16. Quoted in Dana G. Munro, *Intervention and Dollar Diplomacy in the Caribbean, 1900–1921* (Princeton, N.J., 1964), 398.

17. For a more extended treatment of administration policy in this period toward Haiti and the Dominican Republic, see Hannigan, *New World Power*, 48–50.

18. Wilson to Edith Bolling Galt, August 15, 1915, *PWW*, 34:208–9.

19. Caperton is quoted in Healy, *Drive to Hegemony*, 197.

20. Healy, *Drive to Hegemony*, 174.

21. See Wilson to Bryan, April 8, 1913, *PWW*, 27:272.

22. Healy, *Drive to Hegemony*, 230–31. Historian Walter LaFeber notes that American pressure on Tinoco increased during the war as a result of his conclusion of a deal for exploration with a British, rather than American, oil group. See his *Inevitable Revolutions: The United States in Central America* (New York, 1993), 58–59.

23. Healy, *Drive to Hegemony*, 198; Munro, *Intervention*, 492.

24. "An Address to the Senate," January 22, 1917, *PWW*, 40:536–37.

25. "From the Diary of Colonel House," November 25, 1914, *PWW*, 31:354–55; "From the Diary of Colonel House," December 16, 1914, *PWW*, 31:469–70.

26. "From the Diary of Colonel House," December 17, 1914, *PWW*, 31:481; "From the Diary of Colonel House," December 19, 1914, *PWW*, 31:497–98. The subsequent negotiations are detailed at greater length in Hannigan, *New World Power*, 85–86. See also Gilderhus, *Pan*

American Visions, 52–77; Mark T. Gilderhus, *The Second Century: U.S.-Latin American Relations Since 1889* (Wilmington, Del., 2000), 46–52; David Sheinin, *Searching for Authority: Pan-Americanism, Diplomacy and Politics in U.S.-Argentine Relations, 1910–1930* (New Orleans, 1998), 49–52.

27. "Annual Message on the State of the Union," December 7, 1915, *PWW*, 35:296.

28. "An Address to the Pan American Scientific Congress," January 6, 1916, *PWW*, 35:444–45.

29. Quoted in Gilderhus, *Pan American Visions*, 69. Wilson's first inclination was to try to move forward even if he did not have the agreement of the bigger states. But it was pointed out that such a course was likely to work in opposition to the fundamental purposes of the pact.

30. Joseph Smith, *Unequal Giants: Diplomatic Relations Between the United States and Brazil, 1889–1930* (Pittsburgh, 1991), 101.

31. Gilderhus, *Second Century*, 46.

32. This section draws on Hannigan, *New World Power*, 86–88. On the war's economic impact, also see Bill Albert, *South America and the First World War: The Impact of the War on Brazil, Argentina, Peru, and Chile* (Cambridge, 1988), 1–115. Other important studies of U.S. economic expansion in Latin America after 1914 include Burton I. Kaufman, *Efficiency and Expansion: Foreign Trade Organization in the Wilson Administration, 1913–1921* (Westport, Conn., 1974), 91–147; Gilderhus, *Pan American Visions*, 37–45, 56–62, 70–74, 77–80; Emily S. Rosenberg, *World War I and the Growth of United States Predominance in Latin America* (New York, 1987); and Joseph S. Tulchin, *The Aftermath of War: World War I and U.S. Policy Toward Latin America* (New York, 1971).

33. "Annual Message on the State of the Union," December 7, 1915, *PWW*, 35:302.

34. Quoted in P. Edward Haley, *Revolution and Intervention: The Diplomacy of Taft and Wilson in Mexico* (Cambridge, Mass., 1970), 163.

35. The above draws on Hannigan, *New World Power*, 165–83. On Wilson, Carranza, and Villa, also see Gilderhus, *Diplomacy and Revolution*; Larry D. Hill, *Emissaries to a Revolution: Woodrow Wilson's Executive Agents in Mexico* (Baton Rouge, La., 1973); John Mason Hart, *Revolutionary Mexico: The Coming and Process of the Mexican Revolution* (Berkeley, Calif., 1987), 270–326; Alan Knight, *The Mexican Revolution*, 2 vols. (Lincoln, Neb., 1990), 2:172–354; and three important works by Friedrich Katz: *Secret War*, 253–383; *The Life and Times of Pancho Villa* (Stanford, Calif., 1998); and "From Alliance to Dependency: The Formation and Deformation of an Alliance Between Francisco Villa and the United States," in Daniel Nugent, ed., *Rural Revolt in Mexico and U.S. Intervention* (San Diego, 1988), 229–49.

Part III. Military Intervention (1917– 1918)

Epigraphs, in sequence: *PWW*, 44:132; quotation from Stephen Vaughn, *Holding Fast the Inner Lines: Democracy, Nationalism, and the Committee on Public Information* (Chapel Hill, N.C., 1980), 4; "Address to the Gridiron Club," *PWW*, 45:240; "Memorandum by Franklin Knight Lane," *PWW*, 51:605.

Chapter 5. "The Whole Force of the Nation"

1. Lansing to Wilson, March 19, 1917, *PWW*, 41:425–27; "A Memorandum by Robert Lansing," March 20, 1917, *PWW*, 41:436–44.

2. Lansing paraphrasing Wilson in memorandum, "A Memorandum by Robert Lansing," March 20, 1917, *PWW*, 41: ibid., 441.

3. The president spoke to his cabinet on March 20 "of the situation in this country, of the indignation and bitterness in the East and the apparent apathy of the Middle West." Ibid., 438.

4. On this issue of framing the war address around the "democracy" vs. "autocracy" theme, see also the discussions in Buehrig, *Woodrow Wilson*, 135–50; and Tucker, *Woodrow Wilson*, 194–98. Congressman Thomas Hardwick (D-Ga.) would in fact continue to argue that the administration should be prepared to make peace if Berlin altered its submarine campaign. See Johnson, *Peace Progressives*, 71.

5. "An Address to a Joint Session of Congress," *PWW*, 41:519–27.

6. *Congressional Record*, 65th Cong., 1st Sess., 223–36. La Follette and Bryan had been working prior to this to get Congress to endorse a referendum. See Thelen, *La Follette*, 131.

7. Eighty-two senators voted in favor, as did three hundred seventy-three congressmen. Virtually all the no votes were from outside the Northeast. Doenecke argues that sentiments like the need to demonstrate "national unity" and "patriotism in a time of crisis," as well as "party loyalty" on the part of southern Democrats—as opposed to support for Wilson's course—accounted for a large number of the yes votes. On the debates and subsequent votes, see Doenecke, *Nothing Less*, 289–97; Cooper, Jr., *Vanity*, 196–208, 220–38; David M. Kennedy, *Over Here: The First World War and American Society* (New York, 1982), 20–23; and Fleming, *Illusion*, 24–27, 30–42.

8. "From the Diary of Colonel House," March 27, 1917, *PWW*, 41:482. Also see Neu, *Colonel House*, 297.

9. Quoted in Vaughn, *Holding Fast*, 4.

10. This is an argument made in David M. Kennedy, "American Political Culture in a Time of Crisis: Mobilization in World War I," in Schröder, *Confrontation*, 213–27.

11. In late May 1917 the president's secretary, Joseph Tumulty, described most Americans as "indifferent" to the war. On the country's mood going into belligerency, see Doenecke, *Nothing Less*, 297.

12. Kennedy, *Over Here*, 59.

13. Jackson A. Giddens, "American Foreign Propaganda in World War I" (PhD diss., Fletcher School of Law and Diplomacy, Tufts University, 1966), 11.

14. Quoted in Vaughn, *Holding Fast*, 141. Indeed, as Vaughn notes, the CPI "enlisted some of the best advertising men in America." It also, in turn, had an impact on American advertising itself, and on the field of public relations, as can be seen most dramatically in the subsequent career of CPI official Edward L. Bernays.

15. Quoted in Vaughn, *Holding Fast*, 206.

16. Quoted in Ronald Schaffer, *America in the Great War: The Rise of the War Welfare State* (New York, 1991), 5. For contemporary critiques of such a definition of patriotism, see Jonathan M. Hansen, *The Lost Promise of Patriotism: Debating American Identity, 1890–1920* (Chicago, 2003). On immigrant communities as a target of concern, see Vaughn, *Holding Fast*, 39–60; Kennedy, *Over Here*, 63–64.

17. Kennedy, "American Political Culture," 225.

18. Vaughn, *Holding Fast*, 17.

19. As Kennedy is aware. See *Over Here*, 25–27, 75–86.

20. "Address to the Gridiron Club," December 8, 1917, *PWW*, 45:240.

21. Paul L. Murphy, *World War I and the Origin of Civil Liberties in the United States* (New York, 1979), 76–85.

22. Schaffer, *America*, 14; Murphy, *Civil Liberties*, 80, 98–103. Interference with the foreign-language press was facilitated by the Trading with the Enemy Act, passed in October 1917.

23. Schaffer, *America*, 15; Murphy, *Civil Liberties*, 79–80; Nick Salvatore, *Eugene V. Debs, Citizen and Socialist* (Urbana, Ill., 1982), 291–96.

24. Schaffer, *America*, 17; Kennedy, *Over Here*, 81–83; Nancy Gentile Ford, *The Great War and America: Civil-Military Relations During World War I* (Westport, Conn., 2008), 60.

25. Schaffer, *America*, 18–30; Kennedy, *Over Here*, 66–69.

26. Jordan A. Schwarz, *The Speculator: Bernard M. Baruch in Washington, 1917–1965* (Chapel Hill, N.C., 1981), 59; Kennedy, *Over Here*, 123–24; Daniel R. Beaver, *Newton D. Baker and the American War Effort, 1917–1919* (Lincoln, Neb., 1966), 99–108; Robert D. Cuff, *The War Industries Board: Business-Government Relations During World War I* (Baltimore, 1973), 115.

27. Schwarz, *Speculator*, 56–57.

28. Jennifer D. Keene, *The United States and the First World War* (Harlow, 2000), 27; Schaffer, *America*, 35; Kennedy, *Over Here*, 117–23; Joan Hoff Wilson, *Herbert Hoover: Forgotten Progressive* (Boston, 1975), 44–47.

29. Safford, *Maritime*, 21–139; Schaffer, *America*, 37. On shipping bottlenecks in late 1917 to early 1918, see Beaver, *Baker*, 84–87.

30. Schwarz, *Speculator*, 50–98; Cuff, *War Industries Board*, 111, 219–20; Kennedy, *Over Here*, 134, 139–40; Schaffer, *America*, 40–61; Mark R. Wilson, "Economic Mobilization," in Ross A. Kennedy, ed., *A Companion to Woodrow Wilson* (Malden, Mass., 2013), 289–307.

31. Kennedy, *Over Here*, 258–78; Schaffer, *America*, 64–74; Valerie Jean Conner, *The National War Labor Board: Stability, Social Justice, and the Voluntary State in World War I* (Chapel Hill, N.C., 1983); Melvyn Dubofsky, *Industrialism and the American Worker, 1865–1920* (Wheeling, Ill., 1996), 127–54; Ronald Radosh, *American Labor and United States Foreign Policy* (New York, 1969), 150–84.

32. Charles Gilbert, *American Financing of World War I* (Westport, Conn., 1970), 75–76, 82, 84, 117, 120–21, 126–28, 135–38, 163–70; Kennedy, *Over Here*, 99–112; Keene, *First World War*, 32–33, 98; Hugh Rockoff, "Until It's Over, Over There: The U.S. Economy in World War I," in Stephen Broadberry and Mark Harrison, eds., *The Economics of World War I* (Cambridge, 2005), 315–27.

33. Wilson to House, July 21, 1917, *PWW*, 43:237–38; Burk, *Sinews*, 127–77; Kennedy, *Over Here*, 319–24; Keene, *First World War*, 32; Strachan, *Financing*, 202–23.

34. Edward M. Coffman, *The War to End All Wars: The American Military Experience in World War I* (New York, 1968), 93–97; Gilbert, *First World War*, 329.

35. William J. Williams, "Josephus Daniels and the U.S. Navy's Shipbuilding Program During World War I," *Journal of Military History* 60 (January 1996): 7–38; Klachko, *Benson*, 64–75; Hagan, *This People's Navy*, 255; Stevenson, *Cataclysm*, 296.

36. Stevenson, *Cataclysm*, 370; Coffman, *War*, 99; Fleming, *Illusion*, 194; W. B. Fowler, *British-American Relations, 1917–1918: The Role of William Wiseman* (Princeton, N.J., 1969), 86–88; Maartje M. Abbenhuis, *The Art of Staying Neutral: The Netherlands in the First World War, 1914–1918* (Amsterdam, 2006), 132–33.

37. Coffman, *War*, 42; Beaver, *Baker*, 39–40; Woodward, *Trial*, 37, 43.

38. Woodward, *Trial*, 47.

39. Coffman, *War*, 8–9; Woodward, *Trial*, 47–60; Beaver, *Baker*, 40–41. On the spring British-French offensive, see especially Stevenson, *Cataclysm*, 140–43; and Strachan, *First World War*, 242–48.

40. Beaver, *Baker*, 28–32; Kennedy, *Over Here*, 18, 144, 147; Thelen, *La Follette*, 135–36; Keene, *First World War*, 30; Christopher Capozzola, *Uncle Sam Wants You: World War I and the Making of the Modern American Citizen* (New York, 2008), 26–27; Ford, *Great War*, 28.

41. Schaffer, *America*, 175; Capozzola, *Uncle Sam*, 7. For an insightful discussion of this poster, see Elliot Shore, "The *Kultur* Club," in Schröder, *Confrontation*, 127–33.

42. Schaffer, *America*, 176–77; Beaver, *Baker*, 33–37; Coffman, *War*, 25–29; Capozzola, *Uncle Sam*, 9–10, 18, 28; Ford, *Great War*, 29–30; Kennedy, *Over Here*, 166–67.

43. Coffman, *War*, 8–9, 29–31, 43–49, 122–25.

44. Susan Kingsley Kent, *The Influenza Pandemic of 1918–1919: A Brief History with Documents* (Boston, 2013), 7–8.

45. Schaffer, *America*, 96–103; Ford, *Great War*, 39–42. Daniels had already banned liquor from naval bases and ships.

46. Schaffer, *America*, 177–79.

47. Kennedy, *Over Here*, 24; Ford, *Great War*, 42–46; Keene, *First World War*, 61.

48. Many white southerners were uneasy with the thought of African Americans being trained militarily, while some African American leaders thought that greater equality might flow from support for, and participation in, the war. Some African American troops would see combat in Europe. See Ford, *Great War*, 46–50; Capozzola, *Uncle Sam*, 33–36; Schaffer, *America*, 75–90; Keene, *First World War*, 61–63.

49. Ford, *Great War*, 37–38; Schaffer, *America*, 133–39; Keene, *First World War*, 30–32; Stephen Jay Gould, *The Mismeasure of Man* (New York, 1981), 192–233.

50. Coffman, *War*, 64–68.

51. Ibid., 121–58; Woodward, *Trial*, 132, 158–59; Beaver, *Baker*, 116–50; Stevenson, *Cataclysm*, 328–29.

Chapter 6. To the Fourteen Points Address

1. These developments, and their impact, were first examined in depth in Arno J. Mayer, *Political Origins of the New Diplomacy, 1917–1918* (New York, 1970).

2. With Wilson's help, the CPI eventually established its primacy in these efforts. See Giddens, "Foreign Propaganda," 32–48.

3. "An Address to a Joint Session of Congress," January 8, 1918, *PWW*, 45:534–39.

4. See here especially the important study by Erez Manela, *The Wilsonian Moment: Self-Determination and the International Origins of Anticolonial Nationalism* (New York, 2007), 3–53.

5. House to Wilson, March 17, 1917, *PWW*, 41:422–23; House to Wilson, May 6, 1917, *PWW*, 41:233–34; Tumulty to Wilson, May 21, 1917, *PWW*, 42:360–61; "To the Provisional Government of Russia," May 22, 1917, *PWW*, 42:365–67; Stevenson, *International Politics*, 148–50; Mayer, *Political Origins*, 71–83; Georg Schild, *Between Ideology and Realpolitik: Woodrow Wilson and the Russian Revolution, 1917–1921* (Westport, Conn., 1995), 17–27. On the general subject of Wilson and Russia, see also Lloyd C. Gardner, *Safe for Democracy: The Anglo-American Response to Revolution, 1913–1923* (New York, 1984).

6. House to Wilson, April 10, 1917, *PWW*, 42:29–31; Lansing to Wilson, April 10, 1917, *PWW*, 42:36; Wilson to Lansing, May 22, 1917, *PWW*, 42:368–69; Wilson to Polk, ca. August 10, 1917, *PWW*, 43:416; Schild, *Ideology*, 29–34.

7. Gilderhus, *Pan American Visions*, 85–101.

8. David Kirby, "International Socialism and the Question of Peace: The Stockholm Conference of 1917," *Historical Journal* 25 (September 1982): 709–16; Stevenson, *International Politics*, 156–58; Mayer, *Political Origins*, 192–228.

9. House to Wilson, June 5, 1917, *PWW*, 42:456. For subsequent efforts aimed at Germany, see Giddens, "Foreign Propaganda," 139–50.

10. "Flag Day Address," June 14, 1917, *PWW*, 42:498–504.

11. Lansing to Wilson," August 13, 1917, *PWW*, 43:438–39; Page to Lansing, August 15, 1917, *PWW*, 43:482–85; Stevenson, *International Politics*, 162–63.

12. House to Wilson, July 19, 1917, *PWW*, 43:219–21; House to Wilson, August 15, 1917, *PWW*, 43:471–72; House to Wilson, August 17, 1917, *PWW*, 43:508–9; Mayer, *Political Origins*, 234.

13. "From the Diary of Colonel House," August 15, 1917, *PWW*, 43:486; Wilson to House, August 16, 1917, *PWW*, 43:488–89; "From the Diary of Colonel House," August 18, 1917, *PWW*, 43:521; House to Wilson, August 19, 1917, *PWW*, 43:522–23.

14. Wilson to Page, August 27, 1917, *PWW*, 44:57–59. For Lansing's views, see Lansing to Wilson, August 20, 1917, *PWW*, 43:523–25; Lansing to Wilson, August 21, 1917, *PWW*, 44:18–22.

15. Stevenson, *International Politics*, 164–69; Woodward, *Trial*, 99–104.

16. "Wilson Sees End of War Only When Enemy Is Beaten," October 8, 1917 (published in the *New York Times* the next day), *PWW*, 44:325–27. Also see Wilson to David Lawrence, October 5, 1917, *PWW*, 44:309. "The Germans," the president wrote, "have in effect realized their programme of Hamburg to Bagdad, could afford to negotiate as to all the territorial fringes, and, if they could bring about a discussion of peace now, would insist upon discussing it upon terms which would leave them in possession of all that they ever expected to get."

17. "An Address in Buffalo," November 12, 1917, *PWW*, 45:11–17. Wilson discussed these themes and his desire to make such an address with House in mid-October. See "From the Diary of Colonel House," October 13, 1917, *PWW*, 44:379.

18. Stevenson, *Cataclysm*, 308–11; Gilbert, *First World War*, 369, 375–76.

19. The above draws heavily on Daniela Rossini's fine *Woodrow Wilson and the American Myth in Italy: Culture, Diplomacy, and War Propaganda* (Cambridge, Mass., 2008), 82–136. Wilson's involvement in these activities and his emphasis on their importance is a theme developed throughout Giddens, "Foreign Propaganda."

20. This quote is from Martin Gilbert, *Atlas of the First World War* (New York, 1984), 103.

21. Firstworldwar.com, http://www.firstworldwar.com/source/decreeonpeace.htm; Stevenson, *International Politics*, 183–85; Mayer, *Political Origins*, 262. The secret treaties provided for the partition of Turkey, for Italy to be rewarded with territory at the expense of Austria-Hungary and outside Europe in exchange for entering the war, and for territorial rearrangements along the Rhine and on Germany's eastern border to the advantage respectively of France and Russia.

22. Seymour, *Intimate Papers*, 3:233, 277–83; House to Wilson, November 30, 1917, *PWW*, 45:166; Wilson to House, December 1, 1917, *PWW*, 45:176; House to Wilson, December 2, 1917, *PWW*, 45:184–85; House to Wilson, December 3, 1917, *PWW*, 45:188–89; Mayer,

Political Origins, 267, 272–77, 286–90; Fowler, *British-American Relations*, 96–108; Stevenson, *International Politics*, 190.

23. "From the Diary of Colonel House," December 18, 1917, *PWW*, 45:323–24.

24. Wilson to House, September 2, 1917, *PWW*, 44:120–21; Lawrence E. Gelfand, *The Inquiry: American Preparations for Peace, 1917–1919* (New Haven, Conn., 1963), 24–78; Hodgson, *Wilson's Right Hand*, 157–61; Neil Smith, *American Empire: Roosevelt's Geographer and the Prelude to Globalization* (Berkeley, Calif., 2003), 119–22; Neu, *Colonel House*, 318.

25. "Memorandum by Sidney Edward Mezes, David Hunter Miller, and Walter Lippmann, 'The Present Situation: The War Aims and Peace Terms It Suggests,'" ca. December 22, 1917 (incorporating subsequent revisions), *PWW*, 45:459–74; Seymour, *Intimate Papers*, 3:319–21; Hodgson, *Wilson's Right Hand*, 162–65.

26. Originally published on November 29, the text of Lansdowne's letter was reprinted in the *New York Times*, November 30, 1917. Wilson's immediate response came four days later in his annual address. "Our present and immediate task," the president insisted, "is to win the war." "Those who desire to bring peace about before that purpose is achieved I counsel to carry their advice elsewhere." "Annual Message on the State of the Union," December 4, 1917, *PWW*, 45:194–202. On the impact of the letter, also see Mayer, *Political Origins*, 282–86.

27. "An Address to a Joint Session of Congress," January 8, 1918, *PWW*, 45:534–39. Particularly useful discussions of the speech as a whole, its purposes, and impact are included in Stevenson, *International Politics*, 193–96 and Mayer, *Political Origins*, 329–67. Also see "From the Diary of Colonel House," January 9, 1918, *PWW*, 45:550–59.

28. Included in Francis to Lansing, December 31, 1917, *PWW*, 45:411–14. Also see Manela, *Wilsonian Moment*, 40–41; and Heater, *National Self-Determination*, 36–37.

29. Of Trotsky's ideas about self-determination, Lansing opined to Wilson, "If the Bolsheviks intend to suggest that every community . . . can determine its allegiance to this or that political state or to become independent, the present political organization of the world would be shattered." See Lansing to Wilson, January 2, 1918, *PWW*, 45:427–30.

30. "An Address to a Joint Session of Congress," February 11, 1918, *PWW*, 46:318–24.

31. Here also see Schild, *Ideology*, 55–57.

32. See, in particular, the discussions in the Mezes memorandum and in House's diary (entry of January 9, 1918) above.

33. Daniel M. Smith, *The Great Departure: The United States and World War I, 1914–1920* (New York, 1965), 96–97. According to Richard L. Hughes, "by the armistice, the CPI boasted of offices in virtually every major city in the world outside the Central Powers." See his "Wilson and the Committee on Public Information," in Kennedy, *Companion*, 309.

34. David Stevenson argues that "Brest-Litovsk and the German offensives did more than Wilson to reintegrate the [Western European] labour and socialist movements into the pro-war consensus." For his useful discussion of the impact of the address, see *Cataclysm*, 320.

Chapter 7. Casting Every Selfish Dominion Down in the Dust

1. Woodward, *Trial*, 130.

2. Baker to Wilson, October 11, 1917, *PWW*, 44:361; March to Baker, with enclosure, June 24, 1918, *PWW*, 48:418–21; Woodward, *Trial*, 142.

3. Lansing to Wilson, December 10, 1917, *PWW*, 45:263–65; Wilson to Lansing, with enclosures, December 12, 1917, *PWW*, 274–75; David S. Foglesong, *America's Secret War Against Bolshevism: U.S. Intervention in the Russian Civil War, 1917–1920* (Chapel Hill, N.C., 1995), 87–102; Donald E. Davis and Eugene P. Trani, *The First Cold War: The Legacy of Woodrow Wilson in U.S.-Soviet Relations* (Columbia, Mo., 2002), 91–99.

4. David W. McFadden, *Alternative Paths: Soviets and Americans, 1917–1920* (New York, 1993), 52–107; Davis and Trani, *First Cold War*, 68–69, 83–98.

5. See "To the Fourth All-Russia Congress of Soviets," March 11, 1918, *PWW*, 46:598; Stevenson, *Cataclysm*, 315; Fischer, *Germany's Aims*, 477–94; Gilbert, *First World War*, 386–401; Strachan, *First World War*, 286; Sheila Fitzpatrick, *The Russian Revolution, 1917–1932* (Oxford, 1982), 66; Adam Tooze, *The Deluge: The Great War and the Remaking of Global Order, 1916–1931* (London, 2014), 108–40.

6. Polk to Wilson, with enclosure, January 29, 1918, *PWW*, 46:153–55; Richard H. Ullman, *Anglo-Soviet Relations, 1917–1921*, 3 vols. (Princeton, N.J., 1968–1972), 1:93–96.

7. House to Wilson, March 3, 1918, *PWW*, 46:518–19.

8. Betty Miller Unterberger, *America's Siberian Expedition, 1918–1920: A Study of National Policy* (Durham, N.C., 1956), 25–35; Davis and Trani, *First Cold War*, 115–27; Foglesong, *Secret War*, 143–54; Fowler, *British-American Relations*, 166–68. Japan had reasons of its own for wanting to move at least into eastern Siberia. With the Russian Empire in collapse, it hoped to secure a buffer zone that would secure its interests and influence in northern China. See Michael A. Barnhart, *Japan and the World Since 1868* (London, 1995), 57–65.

9. Reported in Reading to Drummond, March 27, 1918, *PWW*, 47:170.

10. Unterberger, *Siberian Expedition*, 52; Davis and Trani, *First Cold War*, 128–40.

11. The "shadow" of this plan can be seen emerging in Wilson to Lansing, June 17, 1918, *PWW*, 48:335–36; and Lansing to Wilson, June 23, 1918, *PWW*, 48:398–99. It quickly began to eclipse a more roundabout idea that members of the administration had been considering in which a U.S. relief mission led by Herbert Hoover would go to Russia, armed intervention to follow upon a request by him to the effect that he needed military protection to do his work. See Lansing to Wilson, June 13, 1918, *PWW*, 48:305. Also see Unterberger, *Siberian Expedition*, 54–88; Davis and Trani, *First Cold War*, 141–48; Schild, *Ideology*, 77–84; Foglesong, *Secret War*, 154–60.

12. As recounted by Lansing; quoted in Unterberger, *Siberian Expedition*, 64.

13. Stevenson, *Cataclysm*, 324–45; Strachan, *First World War*, 290–98; Gilbert, *First World War*, 406–43; Kent, *Influenza*, 4.

14. Quoted in Beaver, *Baker*, 125.

15. "An Address," April 6, 1918, *PWW*, 47:270.

16. "We won the war at Chateau Thierry," Wilson said in May 1919. See Kennedy, *Will to Believe*, xi. On this aspect of the war, see Stevenson, *Cataclysm*, 341–51, 358–60, 368–70; Strachan, *First World War*, 310–11; Woodward, *Trial*, 161–63; Beaver, *Baker*, 116–18, 137, 148.

17. Stevenson, *Cataclysm*, 346–51; Strachan, *First World War*, 315–20; Gilbert, *First World War*, 443–71.

18. In April 1918, the Allies sponsored a Congress of Oppressed Peoples, held in Rome, to encourage nationalist independence movements in Austria-Hungary. See Gilbert, *First World War*, 413. For Wilson's new tack, a shift, reluctantly, from the Fourteen Points, see

Wiseman to Drummond, May 30, 1918, *PWW*, 48:205–6 and Wilson to Lansing, June 26, 1918, *PWW*, 48:435–38. On Austria, the Ottomans, the Salonica Front, and Bulgaria, see Stevenson, *Cataclysm*, 129–30, 220, 273, 354–57, 375–76, 380–81; Strachan, *First World War*, 159–60, 318, 321–23.

19. Stevenson, *Cataclysm*, 381–83; Oederlin to Wilson, with enclosure, October 6, 1918, *PWW*, 51:252–53.

20. Woodward, *Trial*, 185; Fowler, *British-American Relations*, 209–15; Bullitt Lowry, *Armistice 1918* (Kent, Ohio, 1996), 15–16, 43; Klachko, *Benson*, 116 (on American suspicions of the British trade mission, under Sir Maurice de Bunsen, to Latin America in 1918); Stevenson, *Cataclysm*, 359 (on British irritation with the Americans using much-needed merchant ships for the development of hemispheric and Pacific trade). On the general tenor of wartime positioning and economic competition, I am also indebted to Robert H. Van Meter, Jr., "Anglo-American Economic Rivalry, 1914–1925: An Overview," 11–18 (paper, Pacific Coast Branch, American Historical Association meeting, Honolulu, August 9, 1979).

21. House to Wilson, September 3, 1918, *PWW*, 49:428.

22. "Address in the Metropolitan Opera House," September 27, 1918, *PWW*, 51:127–33. Also see Fowler, *British-American Relations*, 216.

23. The French had intercepted Germany's request to Wilson. Lowry, *Armistice*, 10–11, 33–34.

24. Lansing to Oederlin, October 8, 1918, *PWW*, 51:268–69; "From the Diary of Colonel House," October 9, 1918, *PWW*, 51:275–80; Arthur Walworth, *America's Moment: 1918—American Diplomacy at the End of World War I* (New York, 1977), 19–24; Inga Floto, *Colonel House in Paris: A Study of American Policy at the Paris Peace Conference, 1919* (Princeton, N.J., 1973), 35–37; Lowry, *Armistice*, 23–24.

25. *PWW*, 51:317.

26. Lansing to Oederlin, October 14, 1918, *FR 1918*, suppl. I, *The World War*, V.I (1918), 358–59; Walworth, *America's Moment*, 25; Lowry, *Armistice*, 34–36; Floto, *House*, 37–38; Hodgson, *Wilson's Right Hand*, 182–83.

27. Oederlin to Lansing, October 22, 1918, *FR 1918*, suppl. I, *The World War*, V.I (1918), 379–81; Stevenson, *Cataclysm*, 385–86.

28. Lansing to Oederlin, October 23, 1918, *FR 1918*, suppl. I, *The World War*, V.I (1918), 381–83; "Memorandum by Franklin Knight Lane," October 23, 1918, *PWW*, 51:413–15; Stevenson, *Cataclysm*, 385; Lowry, *Armistice*, 39–40.

29. Lowry, *Armistice*, 44, 51, 53, 60. The attitude of Clemenceau and Lloyd George was impacted by their concern that the Allies would give up momentum and morale if a cease-fire took place; it would indeed be hard to start up the fighting again. All the more reason, as they saw it, to insist on whatever they could in the armistice terms. See ibid., 17; Stevenson, *Cataclysm*, 388.

30. It would only be then that the Fourteen Points would be given precise definition. On this point, see Wilson's response to House in connection with the so-called Cobb-Lippmann memorandum. Drawn up at House's request to help provide guidance, the document still left the meaning of many points vague, and that clearly suited the president (as well as House). Asked to comment, Wilson cabled, "Analysis . . . satisfactory interpretation . . . but details of application mentioned should be regarded as merely illustrative suggestions and reserved for peace conference." See House to Wilson, October 29, 1918, *PWW*, 51:495–504; Wilson to House, October 30, 1918, *PWW*, 51:511; Lowry, *Armistice*, 80–82.

31. House and Lloyd George quoted in Lowry, *Armistice*, 87.

32. Stevenson, *Cataclysm*, 391; Lowry, *Armistice*, 91. House was at pains to tell Wilson that Clemenceau promised this would not lead to annexation. See ibid., 93.

33. Lowry, *Armistice*, 82–84.

34. "From the Diary of Colonel House," October 13, 1918, *PWW*, 51:315–16. Also see Fowler, *British-American Relations*, 218–20; Floto, *House*, 58; Klachko, *Benson*, 119. In a memorandum he drew up after the Paris armistice negotiations, Geddes opined that Wilson was pursuing the "'Balance of Power' theory" in regard to naval strength. "I am convinced," he wrote, "that by the methods I have set out above, it is the aim and purpose of the President to reduce comparatively the preponderance in sea power of the British Empire." "Memorandum by Sir Eric Geddes," November 7, 1918, *PWW*, 51:633–34.

35. Fowler, *British-American Relations*, 223–24; Lowry, *Armistice*, 127.

36. Wilson to House, October 29, 1918, *PWW*, 51:504–5.

37. House to Wilson, November 3, 1918, *PWW*, 51:569–70; Lowry, *Armistice*, 124–30.

38. House to Wilson, November 5, 1918, *PWW*, 51:594–95.

39. Lansing to Sulzer, November 5, 1918, *FR 1918*, suppl. I, *The World War*, V.I (1918), 468–69.

40. Stevenson, *Cataclysm*, 391; Lowry, *Armistice*, 53, 72–73, 139–48, 157, 161.

41. Lowry, *Armistice*, 120, 150.

42. Stevenson, *Cataclysm*, 391–404.

43. A sitting president's party normally lost seats in midterm elections. And more American voters in this era identified themselves as Republicans than Democrats, Wilson's presidential victories being the products of unusual circumstances. By accepting exceptionally high wartime prices on cotton, produced in the South, but opposing higher prices on wheat, the president had meanwhile helped position the Democrats for a poor showing in 1918 on the American Plains. In his appeal, Wilson had said that a Republican victory would be "interpreted on the other side of the water as a repudiation" of his leadership. "An Appeal for a Democratic Congress," October 19, 1918 (released on October 25), *PWW*, 51:381–82; Kennedy, *Over There*, 232–45; Seward W. Livermore, *Woodrow Wilson and the War Congress* (Seattle, 1968), 123–247; Walworth, *America's Moment*, 110–13; John Milton Cooper, Jr., *Pivotal Decades: The United States, 1900–1920* (New York, 1990), 312–14; William C. Widenor, *Henry Cabot Lodge and the Search for an American Foreign Policy* (Berkeley, Calif., 1980), 287.

Part IV. The Paris Settlement (1919–1920)

Epigraphs, in sequence: "President Wilson's Address to Congress," in Albert Shaw, ed., *The Messages and Papers of Woodrow Wilson*, 2 vols. (New York, 1924), 1:475; "From the Diary of Ray Stannard Baker," March 8, 1919, *PWW*, 55:464; quotation from Lloyd E. Ambrosius, *Woodrow Wilson and the American Diplomatic Tradition: The Treaty Fight in Perspective* (New York, 1987), 58; "From the Diary of Colonel House," May 31, 1919, *PWW*, 59:644.

Chapter 8. The Future of Europe—and the World

1. There were many, on both sides of the Atlantic, who had misgivings about this move. Some argued that the president would lose the leverage that he might have were he more aloof. See, for example, the views expressed in "Memorandum by Lansing," November 12,

1918, *PWW*, 53:65–66 (though the editors suggest the possibility that this was written ex post facto); House to Wilson, November 14, 1918, *PWW*, 53:71–72; Pittman to Wilson, November 15, 1918, *PWW*, 53:93–94. But Wilson would not be deterred. See Wilson to House, November 16, 1918, *PWW*, 53:96–97 and the discussions of this question in Hodgson, *Wilson's Right Hand*, 193–94; and Walworth, *America's Moment*, 113–19.

2. See the discussion in William R. Keylor, "Versailles and International Diplomacy," in Manfred G. Boemeke, Gerald D. Feldman, and Elisabeth Glaser, eds., *The Treaty of Versailles: A Reassessment After 75 Years* (Cambridge, 2006), 477–78; Orde, *Eclipse*, 62. "I intend to carry as many weapons to the peace table as I can conceal on my person," Wilson quipped. "From the Diary of Josephus Daniels," November 6, 1918, *PWW*, 51:615.

3. See Manela, *Wilsonian Moment.*

4. See, for example, Wilson's remarks to the Swiss president: "Translation of a Memorandum," January 23, 1919, *PWW*, 54:233–34.

5. At Paris, House even urged Wilson to use this situation as leverage with Lloyd George: "I suggested that he [the president] tell them that the Covenant for the League of Nations would either be written into the Treaty of Peace or we would have none of it; that the only excuse we could give for meddling in European or world affairs was a league of nations through which we hope to prevent wars." "From the Diary of Colonel House," March 24, 1919, *PWW*, 56:207.

6. Lansing to Wilson, with enclosure, November 9, 1918, *PWW*, 53:6–9.

7. Hoover to Wilson, November 9, 1918, *PWW*, 53:16.

8. House to Wilson, November 10, 1918, *PWW*, 53:25.

9. "Address to a Joint Session of Congress," November 11, 1918, *PWW*, 53:42.

10. See, for example, Hoover to Wilson, December 20, 1918, *PWW*, 53:454.

11. Herbert Hoover, *The Ordeal of Woodrow Wilson* (New York, 1958), 87–113, 152–72; Walworth, *America's Moment*, 213–30; Arthur Walworth, *Wilson and His Peacemakers: American Diplomacy at the Paris Peace Conference, 1919* (New York, 1986), 82–90; Arno J. Mayer, *Politics and Diplomacy of Peacemaking: Containment and Counterrevolution at Versailles, 1918–1919* (New York, 1967), 265–83; Robert H. Van Meter, Jr., "The United States and European Recovery, 1918–1923: A Study of Public Policy and Private Finance" (PhD diss., University of Wisconsin, 1971), 21, 70–71; Anne Orde, *British Policy and European Reconstruction After the First World War* (Cambridge, 2002), 26–29, 108–10; Frank Costigliola, *Awkward Dominion: American Political, Economic, and Cultural Relations with Europe, 1919–1933* (Ithaca, N.Y., 1987), 40–50.

12. Page to Wilson, November 5, 1918, *PWW*, 51:601.

13. "From the Diary of William C. Bullitt," December 9/10, 1918, *PWW*, 53:351; Gelfand, *Inquiry*, 171–74; Zara Steiner, *The Lights That Failed: European International History, 1919–1933* (Oxford, 2005), 34. For the initial reception and then changing view of Wilson in France, see Georges-Henri Soutou, "The French Peacemakers and Their Home Front," in Boemeke, Feldman, and Glaser, *Treaty of Versailles*, 181–82; For Italy, see Rossini, *Italy*, 179–80. On Wilson's limited grasp of the situation, see Jan Willem Schulte Nordholt, *Woodrow Wilson: A Life for World Peace* (Berkeley, Calif., 1991), 287.

14. Walworth, *Peacemakers*, 13; George W. Egerton, *Great Britain and the Creation of the League of Nations: Strategy, Politics, and International Organization, 1914–1919* (Chapel Hill,

N.C., 1978), 85; Steiner, *Lights*, 21, 28; A. Lentin, *Lloyd George, Woodrow Wilson and the Guilt of Germany* (Baton Rouge, La., 1985), 32. Writes Godfrey Hodgson of Wilson's reception, "There was something poignant in the outpouring of affection and expectation with which the peoples of Europe greeted Wilson. They saw him as a savior whose country had won a war that many in Britain and France had feared they could never win. . . . For a brief historical moment, people in many countries . . . were united in seeing the American president as their symbol of a better life in the future. They did not know much about him, and it did not take long for normal life to be resumed. There was nothing surprising about the fact that politicians . . . who had hung on grimly for victory continued to battle dourly for what they had promised their people: peace, prosperity, national glory." See his *Wilson's Right Hand*, 195–96.

15. Walworth, *America's Moment*, 153–55; James T. Shotwell, *At the Paris Peace Conference* (New York, 1937), 99–100; Margaret MacMillan, *Paris 1919: Six Months That Changed the World* (New York, 2002), 23.

16. "From the Diary of Colonel House," January 1, 1919, *PWW*, 53:586.

17. "From the Diary of Colonel House," December 31, 1918, *PWW*, 53:577.

18. Van Meter, "European Recovery," 18–21, 23; Orde, *British Policy*, 26–31.

19. "Annual Message on the State of the Union," December 2, 1918, *PWW*, 53:282.

20. "From the Diary of Edith Benham," December 5, 1918, *PWW*, 53:321; O'Brien, *Naval Power*, 132–38.

21. Walworth, *America's Moment*, 220; Egerton, *League*, 85.

22. House to Wilson, December 25, 1918, *PWW*, 53:507; "From the Diary of Edith Benham," January 21, 1919, *PWW*, 54:198; "News Report of a Press Conference," February 14, 1919, *PWW*, 55:162; Egerton, *League*, 83–109; Woodward, *Trial*, 212. Also see Peter J. Yearwood, *Guarantee of Peace: The League of Nations in British Policy, 1914–1925* (Oxford, 2009), 7–128.

23. Derby to Balfour, January 6, 1919, *PWW*, 53:634.

24. Alan Sharp, *The Versailles Settlement: Peacemaking After the First World War, 1919–1923* (New York, 2008), 24–25; "Hankey's Notes," January 12, 1919, *PWW*, 54:12–26.

25. Walworth, *Peacemakers*, 16–17. Wilson vetoed participation for Costa Rica, even though it had declared war against Germany, this as an extension of his policy to isolate and overthrow the government there via nonrecognition. See "Hankey's Notes," January 13, 1919, *PWW*, 54:45–47.

26. Gilderhus, *Second Century*, 54.

27. Walworth, *Peacemakers*, 16–19; "Hankey's Notes," January 13, 1919, *PWW*, 54:43–45.

28. Walworth, *Peacemakers*, 17–18; MacMillan, *Paris 1919*, 46. Canada, South Africa, and Australia each got two seats, as did India.

29. The French government provided Wilson with a private home. See Walworth, *America's Moment*, 121–26; Hodgson, *Wilson's Right Hand*, 192–95; MacMillan, *Paris 1919*, 24–25; also House to Wilson, November 23, 1918, *PWW*, 53:181–82.

30. "Hankey's Notes," January 15, 1919, *PWW*, 54:68, 70–74; "Minutes of a Meeting of the Imperial War Cabinet," December 30, 1918, CAB 23/42/19, 5–6, available at www.nationalarchives.gov.uk/cabinetpapers/; MacMillan, *Paris 1919*, 55–56; Erik Goldstein, *The First World War Peace Settlements, 1919–1925* (London, 2002), 10–11.

31. "From the Diary of Colonel House," January 28, 1919, *PWW*, 54:333–34; MacMillan, *Paris 1919*, 56–57; Goldstein, *Peace Settlements*, 10; Sharp, *Versailles*, 25; Walworth, *Peacemakers*, 23–30. Wilson's first press conference did not come until February 14, the day of his departure for a brief trip home.

32. "Hankey's Notes," January 22, 1919, *PWW*, 54:208–9; Walworth, *Peacemakers*, 44–45. The "smaller" states were still less than pleased. In protesting their limited role, representatives from Belgium, Serbia, Greece, and Brazil made an impression on Wilson's private physician, who was an observer at the second plenary. See "From the Diary of Dr. Grayson," January 25, 1919, *PWW*, 54:262–63. Later, despite the opposition of Wilson and Cecil, the ranks of the "smaller" nations on the commission were expanded, but this still left the great powers dominant. See "Minutes of a Meeting of the Commission on the League of Nations," February 4, 1919, *PWW*, 54:432; Sharp, *Versailles*, 56.

33. Steiner, *Lights*, 41.

34. "Minutes of a Meeting of the Commission on the League of Nations," February 4, 1919, *PWW*, 54:483; Egerton, *League*, 126–31. This was not a change without some meaning, perhaps especially insofar as the view that most decisions had to be unanimously agreed to by all members had already been accepted (majorities would prevail on procedural questions, which by Article V included "the appointment of Committees to investigate particular matters"). See Cromwell A. Riches, *The Unanimity Rule and the League of Nations* (Baltimore, 1933), 1–41.

35. "From the Diary of Colonel House," January 7, 1919, *PWW*, 53:652–53.

36. Egerton, *League*, 134–36; David Stevenson, "French War Aims and Peace Planning," in Boemeke, Feldman, and Glaser, *Treaty of Versailles*, 93; Patrick O. Cohrs, *The Unfinished Peace After World War I: America, Britain and the Stabilization of Europe, 1919–1932* (Cambridge, 2008), 54.

37. See "Minutes of a Meeting of the Commission on the League of Nations," February 11, 1919, *PWW*, 55:75–76; "From the Diary of Lord Robert Cecil, February 11, 1919, *PWW*, 55:80; "From the Diary of David Hunter Miller," February 12, 1919, *PWW*, 55:118; Egerton, *League*, 134–36.

38. "Minutes . . . Commission on the League of Nations," February 13, 1919, *PWW*, 55:138–40; "Minutes of a Meeting of the League of Nations Commission," April 11, 1919, *PWW*, 57:256–65; "From the Diary of Colonel House," February 4, 5, 13, and April 12, 1919, *PWW*, 54:485, 500, 55:155, and 57:285; MacMillan, *Paris 1919*, 316–21; Walworth, *Peacemakers*, 38, 119, 309–11. According to House, Wilson initially felt that the phrase suggested in April for the preamble was unproblematic, but accepted his (House's) view that to go along with it would be dangerous. An illuminating discussion of Asian exclusion around the Pacific Rim in the late nineteenth century to early twentieth is contained in Offer, *First World War*, 164–214.

39. The court provision had been removed by Wilson from a draft charter prepared for him by House and Miller in the summer of 1918. It was restored in early 1919 in the British-American "Hurst-Miller" draft. See Walworth, *Peacemakers*, 117.

40. "An Address to the Third Plenary Session of the Peace Conference," February 14, 1919, *PWW*, 55:164–73.

41. While acknowledging these antecedents, historians who admire Wilson insist that what he was about was nevertheless entirely different. The lines of this argument parallel older

claims that a Wilsonian "missionary diplomacy" marked a rejection of the "dollar diplomacy," etc., of his predecessors. The problem is that what is adduced as evidence of a difference, captured by the phrases "conservative internationalism" and "liberal internationalism," is for all practical purposes just Wilson's rhetoric. See here, for example, Knock, *End*, 55–58.

42. "An Address to the Senate," January 22, 1917, *PWW*, 40:533–39; "Memorandum by Isaiah Bowman," December 10, 1918, *PWW*, 53:354.

43. Wilson to Lansing, April 12, 1917, *PWW*, 41:44; Moncheur to de Broqueville, August 14, 1917, *PWW*, 43:468.

44. "Address at Guildhall," December 28, 1918, *PWW*, 53:532.

45. And indeed had taken that position in 1917. See Moncheur to de Broqueville, August 14, 1917, *PWW*, 43:468; House to Wilson, July 14, 1918, *PWW*, 48:608; "From the Diary of Colonel House," August 15, 1918, *PWW*, 49:265–68.

46. By contrast, he thought the British were generally a force for good in their extensive holdings, and he certainly felt this way about the United States in the Philippines. See, for example, Manela, *Wilsonian Moment*, 28–31.

47. See, for example, his interview with Salomon Frederik van Oss, June 7, 1919, *PWW*, 60:254–55.

48. "Memorandum by Wiseman," October 16, 1918, *PWW*, 51:347–52; Fowler, *British-American Relations*, 203–4.

49. Egerton, *League*, 115–32; Wiseman to Reading, August 16, 1918, *PWW*, 49:273; Yearwood, *Guarantee*, 75–82.

50. House to Wilson, January 25, 1919, *PWW*, 54:263–64; "Protocol of a Plenary Session of the Inter-Allied Conference for the Preliminaries of Peace," January 25, 1919, *PWW*, 54:266.

Chapter 9. The Treaty of Versailles

1. Steiner, *Lights*, 22.

2. Van Meter, "European Recovery," 66–69; Costigliola, *Awkward Dominion*, 36.

3. Cecil still thought this gave the United States considerable leverage. See "From the Diary of Lord Robert Cecil," March 26, 1919, *PWW*, 56:297. But see Van Meter, "European Recovery," 64–65. Also see Orde, *British Policy*, 44; Orde, *Eclipse*, 69; Keylor, "Versailles," 477–78.

4. See, for example, Glass to Wilson, April 5, 1919, *PWW*, 56:42.

5. For a recent analysis of the distance that developed between the two, see Hodgson, *Wilson's Right Hand*, 215–34.

6. Good overviews of French objectives are contained in Stevenson, "French War Aims," 87–109; Steiner, *Lights*, 20–26; and Cohrs, *Unfinished*, 48–51. On Britain and the question of the relationship between the debt and reparations, see Cohrs, *Unfinished*, 44; and Orde, *British Policy*, 33. Churchill, at this point secretary of state for war, remarked in an Imperial War Cabinet meeting on December 30, 1918, that "the only point of substance was to induce the United States to let us off the debt we had contracted with them, and return us the bullion and script we had paid over, on the understanding that we should do the same to the Allies to whom we had made advances. If President Wilson were prepared to do that, we might go some way towards meeting his views in the matter of indemnity." See "Minutes of a Meeting of the Imperial War Cabinet," December 30, 1918, CAB 23/42/19, 7, available at www.nation

alarchives.gov.uk/cabinetpapers/; "Memorandum," December 30, 1918, *PWW*, 53:567. The House entry, dated January 4, 1919, is in Seymour, *Intimate Papers*, 4:268.

7. For an overview, see Steiner, *Lights*, 26–34; and Cohrs, *Unfinished*, 37–45. The impact of British politics are the particular concern of Erik Goldstein, "Great Britain: The Home Front," in Boemeke, Feldman, and Glaser, *Treaty of Versailles*, 147–66; and Lentin, *Lloyd George*, 1–29.

8. Wiseman to Reading, August 16, 1918, *PWW*, 49:273–74; "From the Diary of Colonel House," October 15, 1918, *PWW*, 51:340–41; "From the Diary of Dr. Grayson," December 8, 1918, *PWW*, 53:336–40; Van Meter, "European Recovery," 58–59; Steiner, *Lights*, 34–38.

9. In June, the president told the U.S. delegates that "the most fatal thing that could happen . . . in the world, would be that sharp lines of division should be drawn among the Allied and Associated Powers." See "A Discussion with the American Delegation," June 3, 1919, *PWW*, 60:68–69.

10. "From the Minutes of a Plenary Session," May 31, 1919, *PWW*, 59:628.

11. See, for example, "Hankey's Notes," March 17, 1919, *PWW*, 56:26.

12. Walworth, *Peacemakers*, 217–20, 258–65, 286–87, 453; Sharp, *Versailles*, 127–32, 203. On Austria, see the "Memorandum by Franklin K. Lane," November 1, 1918, *PWW*, 51:548; "From the Diary of Dr. Grayson," December 8, 1918, *PWW*, 53:339. On Danzig, see below.

13. Taking the Rhineland "away from Germany," the president told his doctor, "would simply give a cause for hatred and a determination for renewal of the war throughout Germany that would always be equal to the bitterness felt by France against Germany over the 'lost provinces.'" "From the Diary of Dr. Grayson," March 12, 1919, *PWW*, 55:480. House told an aide to Tardieu in early February "that it would be bad for France, as well as for England and the United States, to impose a wrong upon Germany, and it would react against us as the German wrong to France in '71 had reacted upon her." Seymour, *Intimate Papers*, 4:346.

14. See, for example, "An Address at the University of Paris," December 21, 1918, *PWW*, 53:462; and "Address to the Third Plenary Session of the Peace Conference," February 14, 1919, *PWW*, 55:164–78.

15. See, for example, Wilson's "Address to the French Chamber of Deputies," February 3, 1919, *PWW*, 54:464–67.

16. The following discussion of the negotiations surrounding the Rhineland (and Saarland) at the conference draws heavily on Sharp, *Versailles*, 32–34; Steiner, *Lights*, 46–50; Stevenson, *Cataclysm*, 422–25; Melvyn Leffler, *The Elusive Quest: America's Pursuit of European Stability and French Security, 1919–1933* (Chapel Hill, N.C., 1979), 5–11; and Stephen A. Schuker, "The Rhineland Question: West European Security at the Paris Peace Conference of 1919," in Boemeke, Feldman, and Glaser, *Treaty of Versailles*, 275–312.

17. Good overviews of French objectives are contained in Stevenson, "French War Aims," 87–109; Steiner, *Lights*, 20–26; and Cohrs, *Unfinished*, 48–51.

18. Seymour, *Intimate Papers*, 4:345.

19. "From the Diary of Colonel House," February 14, 1919, *PWW*, 55:193–96.

20. Seymour, *Intimate Papers*, 4:362.

21. House to Wilson, March 7, 1919, *PWW*, 55:458.

22. Wilson to House, March 10, 1919, *PWW*, 55:472.

23. "Memorandum by Lloyd George," March 25, 1919, *PWW*, 56:259–70; MacMillan, *Paris 1919*, 196–98.

24. "Mantoux's Notes," March 27, 1919, *PWW*, 56:316.

25. "Mantoux's Notes," March 27, 1919, *PWW*, 56:319.

26. On the Rhineland and Saar, see Sharp, *Versailles*, 32–34; Stevenson, *Cataclysm*, 422–25; Schuker, "Rhineland Question," 275–312; Steiner, *Lights*, 46–50.

27. House to Wilson, October 29, 1918, *PWW*, 51:500; Seymour, *Intimate Papers*, 4:268; "Principles of Reparation," February 8, 1919, *PWW*, 55:29–34; Lansing, House, Baruch, Davis, McCormick to Wilson, February 19, 1919, *PWW*, 55:210–11; Wilson to Lansing, February 23, 1919, *PWW*, 55:231. This discussion of the negotiations surrounding reparations draws heavily on Sharp, *Versailles*, 81–108; Steiner, *Lights*, 26, 31–32, 37–39, 55–61; Lentin, *Lloyd George*, 11–12, 31; A. Lentin, "A Comment," in Boemeke, Feldman, and Glaser, *Treaty of Versailles*, 224–27; Sally Marks, "Smoke and Mirrors: In Smoke-Filled Rooms and the Galerie des Glaces," in Boemeke, Feldman, and Glaser, *Treaty of Versailles*, 340–47; and MacMillan, *Paris 1919*, 180–93.

28. Quoted in MacMillan, *Paris 1919*, 180.

29. Lentin, "A Comment," 225–27.

30. U.S. Department of State, *The Treaty of Versailles and After: Annotations of the Text of the Treaty* (Washington, D.C., 1947), 413, 425.

31. House to Wilson, March 7, 1919, *PWW*, 55:458; "Memorandum by John Foster Dulles," April 1, 1919, *PWW*, 56:498–501; "From the Diary of Vance McCormick, April 1, 1919, *PWW*, 56:501–2; Lentin, *Lloyd George*, 58.

32. Though that amount, in House's view, seemed "perfectly absurd." See Seymour, *Intimate Papers*, 4:343–44; "From the Diary of Colonel House," March 17, 1919, *PWW*, 56:4–6; "From the Diary of Colonel House," March 24, 1919, *PWW*, 56:206–8; "Mantoux's Notes," March 25, 1919, *PWW*, 56:249–52.

33. "From the Diary of Vance McCormick," March 31, 1919, *PWW*, 56:444; Seymour, *Intimate Papers*, 4:397–405.

34. Lansing had written the president on April 12, "There is undoubtedly a wide-spread irritation among the lesser belligerent states as to the way that they have been ignored and generally excluded from the deliberations as to the terms of the treaty. If this exclusion is carried up to the day when the treaty is laid before the German representatives there will be great irritation and possibly actual rebellion against the dictatorship by the Five Powers." See *PWW*, 57:292–93.

35. Initially fifteen days, the deadline was later extended to May 29. The following discussion of the presentation of the treaty draft and Germany's reaction relies heavily on MacMillan, *Paris 1919*, 459–67; Steiner, *Lights*, 61–63; Sharp, *Versailles*, 105–38; Walworth, *Peacemakers*, 387–93; Klaus Schwabe, "Germany's Peace Aims and the Domestic and International Constraints," in Boemeke, Feldman, and Glaser, *Treaty of Versailles*, 37–68.

36. In the end, Germany would lose about 13 percent of its prewar European territory. See Sharp, *Versailles*, 136.

37. Quoted in MacMillan, *Paris 1919*, 459–60.

38. Wilson to Herron, April 28, 1919, *PWW*, 58:204–5; Walworth, *Peacemakers*, 394–95; MacMillan, *Paris 1919*, 467; Van Meter, "European Recovery," 97.

39. Hoover, *Ordeal*, 234. On Hoover, but also on the American commission as a whole, see "From the Diary of Ray Stannard Baker," May 23, 1919, *PWW*, 59:447–48.

40. "From the Diary of Ray Stannard Baker," May 19, 1919, *PWW*, 59:285–86; MacMillan, *Paris 1919*, 467.

41. Quoted in Walworth, *Peacemakers*, 394–95.

42. "From the Diary of Colonel House," May 30, 1919, *PWW*, 59:623–24; Walworth, *Peacemakers*, 395. By the end of May, House was aware that he was not playing the role he had hitherto with Wilson. He told his diary, on May 30, that Wilson was "influenced by his constant association with Clemenceau and George. I seldom or never have a chance to talk with him seriously and, for the moment, he is practically out from under my influence. When we meet, it is to settle some pressing problem and not to take inventory of things in general or plan for the future. This is what we used to do."

43. Steiner, *Lights*, 67–68. The modern historiography of reparations is usefully summarized in Sharp, *Versailles*, 105–8. The "Carthaginian peace" characterization had its origins within the British delegation, particularly with people like Smuts and John Maynard Keynes. See Lentin, *Lloyd George*, 132–33.

44. On Clemenceau, see for example his exchange with Wilson (and Lloyd George) at a meeting of the Council of Four on March 27. "[O]ur greatest error," the president told him, "would be to give her [Germany] powerful reasons for taking revenge." The French premier rejoined that what the three of them found fair would not necessarily be seen as such by the Germans. They were "a servile people who need force to sustain an argument. . . . I believe we can do something to spare the world from German aggression for a long time; but the German spirit will not change so quickly." "Mantoux's Notes," *PWW*, 56:316–18.

45. "From the Diary of Dr. Grayson," May 2, 1919, *PWW*, 58:332; Walworth, *Peacemakers*, 415–16.

46. Schwabe, "Germany's Peace Aims," 40–49. Also see Peter Kruger, "German Disappointment and Anti-Western Resentment," in Schröder, *Confrontation*, 325–27; and MacMillan, *Paris 1919*, 461.

47. MacMillan, *Paris 1919*, 464–66.

48. Brockdorff-Rantzau to Clemenceau, May 29, 1919, *PWW*, 59:579–84; Stevenson, *Cataclysm*, 425–26; Steiner, *Lights*, 63.

49. Steiner, *Lights*, 63–64; MacMillan, *Paris 1919*, 469–70.

50. "From the Diary of Dr. Grayson," June 1, 1919, *PWW*, 60:3–4.

51. "From the Diary of Dr. Grayson," June 3, 1919, *PWW*, 60:43.

52. "A Discussion with the American Delegation," June 3, 1919, *PWW*, 60:68–69. "He hopes and expects that the League, once started to functioning, will gradually and so to speak automatically correct the shortcomings of the peace project," recorded Salomon Frederik van Oss later that week. See "An Interview," June 7, 1919, *PWW*, 60:253. The Germans were "waiting for a split" among the victorious powers, Wilson told a number of his advisers the following week. See "From the Diary of Vance McCormick," June 13, 1919, *PWW*, 60:492.

53. "A Discussion with the American Delegation," June 3, 1919, *PWW*, 60:46–48. Also see "Memorandum by Norman Davis," June 1, 1919, *PWW*, 60:4–8.

54. Walworth, *Peacemakers*, 417–23; MacMillan, *Paris 1919*, 470–71; Steiner, *Lights*, 64–66.

55. Under orders from the fleet's commander, Admiral Ludwig von Reuter, apparently fulfilling standing orders from his superiors not to allow the fleet ever to be turned over to the Allies. See Holger H. Herwig, *"Luxury" Fleet: The Imperial German Navy, 1888–1918* (London, 1987), 254–57. Also see MacMillan, *Paris 1919*, 471–72.

56. MacMillan, *Paris 1919*, 472–74, Steiner, *Lights*, 66.

57. The event is described in MacMillan, *Paris 1919*, 474–77. From House's standpoint, the ceremony ran counter to American objectives: "The whole affair was elaborately staged and made as humiliating to the enemy as it well could be." That morning, the guarantee treaties, between Britain and France and between the United States and France, were also signed.

Chapter 10. Americans in Paris: The Russian Revolution, the Royal Navy, Power in the Western Hemisphere

1. MacMillan, *Paris 1919*, 66–72.

2. Baker to Wilson, November 27, 1918, *PWW*, 53:227–28; "Memorandum," December 30, 1918, *PWW*, 53:560; Baker to Wilson, January 1, 1919, *PWW*, 53:582; "Hankey's Notes," January 16, 1919, *PWW*, 54:101–4; McFadden, *Alternative Paths*, 172–74, 197, 214; Davis and Trani, *First Cold War*, 158–59.

3. McFadden, *Alternative Paths*, 175.

4. As reported by Lloyd George to the Imperial War Cabinet, see "Memorandum," December 30, 1918, *PWW*, 53:561; McFadden, *Alternative Paths*, 168–69, 175–81.

5. Buckler to Lansing, January 18, 1919, *PWW*, 54:136–37; McFadden, *Alternative Paths*, 181–87.

6. "Hankey's Notes," January 22, 1919, *PWW*, 54:205–6; McFadden, *Alternative Paths*, 195–201; Davis and Trani, *First Cold War*, 160. Originally the thought had been that Paris might be the location for such a meeting, but Clemenceau did not want Bolsheviks in the French capital.

7. McFadden, *Alternative Paths*, 201–17; Davis and Trani, *First Cold War*, 160–62.

8. "Hankey's Notes," February 14, 1919, *PWW*, 55:181; McFadden, *Alternative Paths*, 209–12; Davis and Trani, *First Cold War*, 163–65.

9. A very good and detailed discussion of the Bullitt Mission can be found in McFadden, *Alternative Paths*, 218–43.

10. The quote is from Christian Herter, who was a secretary to Joseph Grew, secretary of the commissioners. See McFadden, *Alternative Paths*, 225.

11. Bullitt to Wilson, March 16, 1919, *PWW*, 55:540–45. The proposal the Soviets agreed to is printed in *FR 1919, Russia*, 78–80.

12. "From the Diary of Colonel House," March 26, 1919, *PWW*, 56:309.

13. In addition to the chapter in McFadden, cited above, see Davis and Trani, *First Cold War*, 169–73; and Robert K. Murray, *Red Scare: A Study in National Hysteria, 1919–1920* (New York, 1955). Bullitt wrote Wilson a fiery letter on the day of his resignation, predicting that the legacy of Paris would be "a new century of war." See Bullitt to Wilson, May 17, 1919, *PWW*, 59:232–33.

14. Davis and Trani, *First Cold War*, 170–74; McFadden, *Alternative Paths*, 239–56; MacMillan, *Paris 1919*, 80–81.

15. Ullman, *Anglo-Soviet Relations*, 2:33–34, 114, 161–70; McFadden, *Alternative Paths*, 253–54.

16. Particularly useful sources on the "naval battle of Paris" are Klachko, *Benson*, 130–52; and O'Brien, *Naval Power*, 131–44. Also see John R. Ferris, "The Symbol and the Substance of Seapower: Great Britain, the United States and the One-Power Standard, 1919–21," in B. J. C. McKercher, ed., *Anglo-American Relations in the 1920s: The Struggle for Supremacy* (Edmonton, 1990), 55–68.

17. Even Tirpitz had never publicly articulated as his wish a "navy second to none," comments Paul M. Kennedy in his *Rise and Fall of British Naval Mastery* (London, 1983), 263. "Here," he writes, "was the greatest naval challenge to the Royal Navy's mastery yet seen—and launched at the worst possible time, when Britain was heavily in debt to the United States, physically and psychologically exhausted by the war, and desperate to reduce her enormous defence expenditures." Further context is provided in Carolyn Kitching, *Britain and the Problem of International Disarmament, 1919–1934* (London, 1999), 42–43.

18. See, for example, Benson to Wilson, February 7, 1919, *PWW*, 54:552–54. For the prime minister's brief effort to connect this issue to the fate of the German navy, see Mac-Millan, *Paris 1919*, 178. On this question, also see Ferris, "Symbol," 65–66. Benson continued to worry about this throughout the spring, presumably right up until the time the German fleet was scuttled at Scapa Flow. See Benson to Wilson, April 28, 1919, *PWW*, 58:206; Benson to Wilson, May 5, 1919, *PWW*, 58:456–57.

19. Egerton, *League*, 161–62.

20. Klachko, *Benson*, 145–50; O'Brien, *Naval Power*, 139–42.

21. "United States Naval Policy," April 7, 1919, enclosed in Benson to Wilson, April 9, 1919, *PWW*, 57:180.

22. "From the Diary of Lord Robert Cecil," April 8–10, 1919, *PWW*, 57:142.

23. Cecil to House, April 8, 1919, *PWW*, 57:144.

24. House to Cecil, April 9, 1919, *PWW*, 57:179.

25. "From the Diary of Colonel House," April 9, 1919, *PWW*, 57:179.

26. "From the Diary of Lord Robert Cecil," April 8–10, 1919, *PWW*, 57:142; "From the Diary of Colonel House," April 10, 1919, *PWW*, 57:215; Memorandum of April 10, 1919, enclosed in Cecil to House of that date, *PWW*, 57:216–17.

27. This aspect of the trip home is described in Cooper, Jr., *Breaking*, 55–71; Knock, *End*, 239–42; Widenor, *Lodge*, 314–16.

28. Quoted in Widenor, *Lodge*, 315.

29. "An Address at the Metropolitan Opera House," March 4, 1919, *PWW*, 55:413–21.

30. "From the Diary of Colonel House," March 16, 1919, *PWW*, 55:538; "From the Diary of Lord Robert Cecil," March 16, 1919, *PWW*, 55:539.

31. Hitchcock to Wilson, March 4, 1919, *PWW*, 55:437; Taft to Wilson, March 18, 1919, *PWW*, 56:83; Taft to Wilson, March 21, 1919, *PWW*, 56:157–59; Walworth, *Peacemakers*, 191–92.

32. "From the Diary of Colonel House," March 18, 1919, *PWW*, 56:82–83; "From the Diary of David Hunter Miller," March 18, 1919, *PWW*, 56:75–81; Walworth, *Peacemakers*, 193.

33. See in particular the discussion with regard to a proposed French amendment to Article 9. Designed to provide greater speed to a League response in a crisis, it focused on the creation of machinery for contingency planning, especially with regard to credits, mobilization, and coordination. "Minutes of a Meeting of the Commission on the League of Nations," March 24, 1919, *PWW*, 56:223–26.

34. "Minutes of a Meeting of the Commission on the League of Nations," April 10, 1919, *PWW*, 57:221–26.

35. "Minutes of a Meeting of the Commission on the League of Nations," March 24, 1919, *PWW*, 56:229.

36. "Minutes of a Meeting of the Commission on the League of Nations," March 26, 1919, *PWW*, 56:301–3.

37. Sharp, *Versailles*, 61.

38. "Minutes of a Meeting of the Commission on the League of Nations," April 10, 1919, *PWW*, 57:226.

39. "Minutes of a Meeting of the Commission on the League of Nations," April 10, 1919, *PWW*, 57:227–32; "Minutes of a Meeting of the Commission on the League of Nations," April 11, 1919, *PWW*, 57:254–57.

40. "From the Diary of Colonel House," April 12, 1919, *PWW*, 57:285. The revised Covenant can be found in *PWW*, 58:188–99.

41. See Walworth, *Peacemakers*, 281, 313.

42. Cable of April 18, 1919, quoted in ibid., 302n3.

Chapter 11. Americans in Paris: The Colonial World

1. Jan Smuts, *The League of Nations: A Practical Suggestion* (London, 1918), 12, 15–30.

2. He wanted, for example, South Africa to annex what had been German Southwest Africa. See "Hankey's Notes," January 24, 1919, *PWW*, 54:248–54.

3. See, for example, the Cobb-Lippmann memo included with House to Wilson, October 29, 1918, *PWW*, 51:502–3; Seymour, *Intimate Papers*, 4:284–85; and Barclay to Foreign Office, November 3, 1918, *PWW*, 51:574–75. George Louis Beer, of the Inquiry, had used the term "international mandate" in connection with German territory in Central Africa at the end of 1917. See Brian Digre, *Imperialism's New Clothes: The Repartition of Tropical Africa, 1914–1919* (New York, 1990), 135. Wilson told Wiseman that he opposed the return of Germany's colonies in a conversation held in mid-October 1918; instead he suggested that they be administered "in trust" for the League. See "Memorandum by Wiseman," October 16, 1918, *PWW*, 51:350.

4. Indeed, one pro-administration newspaper made precisely this point; see the *New York World*, May 24, 1919.

5. Derby to Balfour, December 22, 1918, *PWW*, 53:470.

6. "Memorandum by Isaiah Bowman," December 10, 1918, *PWW*, 53:355; Digre, *Imperialism's New Clothes*, 141.

7. Three categories were ultimately agreed upon: A, B, and C mandates. As Egerton notes, Wilson "accepted the thinly veiled annexation" that was implied in the C-type mandates. See his *League*, 113.

8. The evolution of the general outlines of the mandate system in late 1918 to early 1919 can be followed in Seymour, *Intimate Papers*, 4:293–99; Barclay to Foreign Office, November 3, 1918, *PWW*, 51:574–75; "From the Diary of William C. Bullitt," December 9/10, 1918, *PWW*, 53:351; Derby to Balfour, December 22, 1918, *PWW*, 53:470–71; "Hankey's Notes," January 24, 1919, *PWW*, 54:249–50; "Hankey's Notes," January 27, 1919, *PWW*, 54:293–301; "Hankey's Notes," January 30, 1919, *PWW*, 54:350–61 and 361–78 (morning and late afternoon meetings of the Council of Ten).

9. Walworth, *Peacemakers*, 69, 70, 70n31, 73, 77; Kawamura, *Turbulence*, 142; Edward S. Miller, *War Plan Orange: The U.S. Strategy to Defeat Japan, 1897–1945* (Annapolis, Md., 1991), 112. In 1917, London had promised to support the transfer of these islands to Japan in exchange for Tokyo agreeing that Germany's islands further south would be turned over to the British Empire. Although Africa, per se, did not receive great emphasis by the United

States at the Paris Peace Conference, Wilson's naval advisers had something to say about this area as well. In a memo passed on to him through Secretary of the Navy Daniels in early December, the president was urged to try for the internationalization of all of the continent with the exception of Egypt, South Africa, and Algeria, this to be accomplished, essentially, via League mandates. This would reduce great power friction and "place all the nations on an equal footing for the trade of an immense area." See Daniels to Wilson, December 3, 1918, Woodrow Wilson Papers (Library of Congress, Washington, D.C.).

10. Barclay to Foreign Office, November 3, 1918, *PWW*, 51:574–75; Close to Lansing, June 24, 1919, *PWW*, 61:127–29.

11. "From the Diary of Colonel House," April 30, 1917, *PWW*, 42:172.

12. "From the Diary of Colonel House," April 28, 1917, *PWW*, 42:155–57. Also see "From the Diary of Colonel House," April 26, 1917, *PWW*, 42:143; and Hodgson, *Wilson's Right Hand*, 145. European great power machinations with regard to the Middle East to this point in the war are related in Paul C. Helmreich, *From Paris to Sèvres: The Partition of the Ottoman Empire at the Peace Conference of 1919–1920* (Columbus, Ohio, 1974), 3–7; Laurence Evans, *United States Policy and the Partition of Turkey, 1914–1924* (Baltimore, 1965), 108–10.

13. Helmreich, *From Paris to Sèvres*, 7–31; Sharp, *Versailles*, 186–90. On the Wilson administration's response to the Balfour Declaration, see Evans, *Partition*, 45–48.

14. "Hankey's Notes," March 20, 1919, *PWW*, 56:112–16.

15. Harry N. Howard, *The King-Crane Commission: An American Inquiry in the Middle East* (Beirut, 1963), 36–86. King was the president of Oberlin College. Crane was a prominent American businessman with international experience. It would appear that both were already in Europe.

16. Crane to Wilson, July 10, 1919, *PWW*, 61:442–24. The United States would be the preferred mandatory, they wrote, because it was felt that it had no territorial ambitions. See also Howard, *King-Crane*, 133–34; and Evans, *Partition*, 153.

17. Crane to Wilson, August 31, 1919, *PWW*, 62:607–8; Howard, *King-Crane*, 209–37.

18. Evans, *Partition*, 153–54.

19. Summarized in Sharp, *Versailles*, 193–95.

20. Quoted in William Roger Louis, "Great Britain and the African Peace Settlement of 1919," *American Historical Review* 71 (April 1966): 877.

21. "Hankey's Notes," May 13, 1919, *PWW*, 59:89. Earlier he had expressed interest in the United States taking the mandate for German East Africa. See Michael D. Callahan, *Mandates and Empire: The League of Nations and Africa, 1914–1931* (Brighton, 1999), 22, 28, 32.

22. Quote, from Beer diary entry, in William Roger Louis, "The United States and the African Peace Settlement of 1919: The Pilgrimage of George Louis Beer," *Journal of African History* 4 (1963): 418.

23. "Mantoux's Notes," June 26, 1919, *PWW*, 61:215–16.

24. "From the Diary of Dr. Grayson," June 27, 1919, *PWW*, 61:235–39.

25. Wilson to Lansing, August 4, 1919, *PWW*, 62:149.

26. "Address at Mount Vernon," July 4, 1918, *PWW*, 48:514–17. Also see the discussion in Manela, *Wilsonian Moment*, 43–44.

27. Manela, *Wilsonian Moment*, 10–11, 22.

28. Ibid., 5.

29. William J. Duiker, *Ho Chi Minh* (New York, 2000), 54–61; Manela, *Wilsonian Moment*, 3–4, 60.

30. Manela, *Wilsonian Moment*, 119–35, 197–213.

31. These paragraphs draw on ibid., 77–97, 159–75.

32. Quoted in ibid., 96.

33. The quotations in this paragraph are from ibid., 163, 166.

34. The above is chronicled in ibid., 63–75, 141–57. The U.S. announcement is quoted on p. 147. Also see Wiseman to House, April 18, 1919, *PWW*, 57:464–65; House to Balfour, April 19, 1919, *PWW*, 57:499; and Zagloul to Wilson, June 18, 1919, *PWW*, 61:8. Wiseman told House that the alternative might be a holy war and that the Egyptian nationalists were "chiefly paid agents of the revolutionary party in Turkey and the Bolshevists."

35. Bernadette Whelan, *United States Foreign Policy and Ireland: From Empire to Independence, 1913–29* (Dublin, 2006), 57, 136; Tumulty, *Woodrow Wilson*, 392–97. Also see Wilson to Lansing, April 10, 1917, *PWW*, 42:24–25.

36. Walsh to Wilson, December 2, 1918, *PWW*, 53:299; Wilson to Walsh, December 3, 1918, *PWW*, 53:306.

37. Wiseman to Drummond and Balfour, February 4, 1918, *PWW*, 46:247–50.

38. Whelan, *Ireland*, 197–200.

39. Ibid., 205–12; Conner, *War Labor Board*, 29.

40. Whelan, *Ireland*, 190–91, 197, 212–14.

41. Cyrus Veeser, "Caribbean, Central America, and Mexico, Interventions in, 1903–34," entry in Michael Kazin, ed., *The Princeton Encyclopedia of American Political History*, 2 vols. (Princeton, N.J., 2009), 1:69; Priscilla Roberts, "Wilson, Europe's Colonial Empires, and the Issue of Imperialism," in Kennedy, *Companion*, 504.

42. Herbert Aptheker, ed., *Selections from The Crisis, 1911–1925* (Millwood, N.Y., 1983), 159; Mark Robert Schneider, *"We Return Fighting": The Civil Rights Movement in the Jazz Age* (Boston, 2002), 8–9; Kennedy, *Over Here*, 199–200; Schaffer, *America*, 75–90; Hansen, *Lost Promise*, 173–75, 181–84; "From the Diary of Dr. Grayson," March 10, 1919, *PWW*, 55:471. Wilson, wrote Grayson, "said the American negro returning from abroad would be our greatest medium in conveying bolshevism to America. For example, a friend recently related the experience of a lady friend wanting to employ a negro laundress offering to pay the usual wage in that community. The negress demands that she be given more money than was offered for the reason that 'money is as much mine as it is yours.' Furthermore, he called attention to the fact that the French people have placed the negro soldier in France on an equality with the white man, and 'it has gone to their heads.'"

43. Clarence G. Contee, "Du Bois, the NAACP, and the Pan-African Congress of 1919," *Journal of Negro History* 57 (January 1972): 14–23; David Levering Lewis, *W.E.B. Du Bois: Biography of a Race, 1868–1919* (New York, 1993), 561–75.

44. Aptheker, *Selections*, 167–68; Lewis, *Biography*, 562; Contee, "Du Bois," 15; Schneider, *"We Return,"* 11; Geiss, *German Foreign Policy*, 155.

45. Aptheker, *Selections*, 191.

46. Ibid., 178–79, 182–85; Contee, "Du Bois," 19–24; Lewis, *Biography*, 574–76; Schneider, *"We Return,"* 11.

47. Aptheker, *Selections*, 168. Du Bois was able to gain an audience with House, the latter playing a familiar role. He evinced sympathy, but was noncommittal, telling Du Bois that he would be able to lay his resolution before the peace conference only if Clemenceau approved. Nothing came of that, and Du Bois failed to gain entrée to Wilson. See Contee, "Du Bois," 26.

48. Quoted in Lloyd E. Ambrosius, *Wilsonian Statecraft: Theory and Practice of Liberal Internationalism During World War I* (Wilmington, Del., 1991), 112.

49. Kennedy, *Over Here*, 281–83; "From the Diary of Raymond Blaine Fosdick," December 8, 1918, *PWW*, 53:340–41; "From the Diary of Ray Stannard Baker, March 13, 1919, *PWW*, 55:489; "From the Diary of Dr. Grayson," June 11, 1919, *PWW*, 60:381–82.

50. For his reactions, see David Levering Lewis, *W.E.B. Du Bois: The Fight for Equality and the American Century, 1919–1963* (New York, 2000), 13–19.

Chapter 12. Americans in Paris: The Adriatic and Shandong Controversies

1. Sterling J. Kernek, "Woodrow Wilson and National Self-Determination Along Italy's Frontier: A Study of the Manipulation of Principles in the Pursuit of Political Interests," *Proceedings of the American Philosophical Society* 126 (August 1982): 274–75.

2. "An Address to a Joint Session of Congress," January 8, 1918, *PWW*, 45:537; M. B. B. Biskupski, "Wilson's Policies Toward Eastern and Southeastern Europe, 1917–1919," in Kennedy, *Companion*, 406–25.

3. Sharp, *Versailles*, 144–45; Lowry, *Armistice*, 101.

4. Kernek, "Italy's Frontier," 258; Walworth, *Peacemakers*, 337; H. C. Darby and Harold Fullard, eds., *The New Cambridge Modern History Atlas* (Cambridge, 1970), 147.

5. "An Address to a Joint Session of Congress," January 8, 1918, *PWW*, 45:537.

6. Sharp, *Versailles*, 148.

7. "From the Diary of Edith Benham," January 18, 1919, *PWW*, 54:149.

8. Wilson to House, November 1, 1918, *PWW*, 51:541.

9. "From the Diary of Dr. Grayson," December 8, 1918, *PWW*, 53:338–39. Rossini, *Italy*, 137, 139.

10. "From the Diary of Dr. Grayson," January 9, 1919, *PWW*, 53:696–97; Mark Thompson, *The White War: Life and Death on the Italian Front, 1915–1919* (New York, 2008), 5, 26–28; Rossini, *Italy*, 159–60.

11. Wilson to Orlando, January 13, 1919, *PWW*, 54:50–51.

12. Thompson, *White War*, 373; MacMillan, *Paris 1919*, 281, 289, 293–94. MacMillan notes, "In Fiume itself, Italians were in a slight majority but, if its suburbs of Susak were added in, the Croats were."

13. "Memorandum Concerning the Question of Italian Claims on the Adriatic," April 14, 1919, *PWW*, 57:343–45.

14. "Hankey's Notes," April 19, 1919, *PWW*, 57:484–87.

15. Wilson to Norman Davis, April 19, 1919, *PWW*, 57:495; Walworth, *Peacemakers*, 341, 348.

16. "Mantoux's Notes," April 21, 1919, *PWW*, 57:536–41.

17. "From the Diary of Colonel House," April 21, 1919, *PWW*, 57:534; "Hankey's and Mantoux's Notes," April 21, 1919, *PWW*, 57:545–53.

18. "Hankey's and Mantoux's Notes," April 22, 1919, *PWW*, 57:610–14; "Hankey's and Mantoux's Notes," April 23, 1919, *PWW*, 58:15.

19. "A Statement on the Adriatic Question," April 23, 1919, *PWW*, 58:5–8.

20. MacMillan, *Paris 1919*, 299–300.

21. Evans, *Partition*, 165–66.

22. To British discomfort. See "Hankey's Notes," May 13, 1919, *PWW*, 59:84–94; "Mantoux's Notes," May 13, 1919, *PWW*, 59:94–103; Helmreich, *From Paris to Sèvres*, 91–101, 114.

23. "Hankey's Notes," May 17, 1919, *PWW*, 59:208–12; "Hankey's Notes," May 17, 1919, *PWW*, 59:223–26; Helmreich, *From Paris to Sèvres*, 117.

24. "Hankey's Notes," May 19, 1919, *PWW*, 59:258–65; Helmreich, *From Paris to Sèvres*, 126.

25. MacMillan, *Paris 1919*, 302–3.

26. "Mantoux's Notes," June 28, 1919, *PWW*, 61:309. Also see Wilson to Lansing, June 28, 1919, *PWW*, 61:306–7.

27. "Hankey's and Mantoux's Notes," June 25, 1919, *PWW*, 61:156–57. "For the peace of the world, I believe that Italy must remain outside Asia Minor," he told Clemenceau and Lloyd George at the end of May. See "Mantoux's Notes of a Conversation," May 26, 1919, *PWW*, 59:492–95.

28. Helmreich, *From Paris to Sèvres*, 120–26; Sharp, *Versailles*, 179–85.

29. Wilson to Lansing, September 17, 1918, *PWW*, 51:25–26. As to Wilson's miscalculation, see Kawamura, *Turbulence*, 110–28. The administration's apprehension is captured in an exchange that House had with Ishii in the summer of 1918. As he later recounted in a letter to the president, House told the ambassador "that many thought Japan stood at the parting of the ways, and had not determined whether she would follow the German or American civilization." House "pointed out the advantage to his country of following the international ideals set forth by" Wilson. House to Wilson, July 6, 1918, *PWW*, 48:540–41. Also see Polk to Lansing, December 21, 1918, *PWW*, 53:463–65.

30. Xu Guoqi, *China and the Great War: China's Pursuit of a New National Identity and Internationalization* (Cambridge, 2005), 78–187.

31. Manela, *Wilsonian Moment*, 100–103; Hans Schmidt, "Democracy for China: American Propaganda and the May Fourth Movement," *Diplomatic History* 22 (Winter 1998): 1–28.

32. Xu, *China and the Great War*, 244–45, 250–57; MacMillan, *Paris 1919*, 331–32.

33. "From the Diary of Dr. Grayson," January 28, 1919, *PWW*, 54:308–9; "Hankey's Notes," January 28, 1919, *PWW*, 54:318; MacMillan, *Paris 1919*, 333–34; Xu, *China and the Great War*, 248; Manela, *Wilsonian Moment*, 115, 177–78; Stephen G. Craft, *V.K. Wellington Koo and the Emergence of Modern China* (Lexington, Ky., 2004), 51–53.

34. Kawamura, *Turbulence*, 140–46; Dickinson, *Reinvention*, 43–63, 84–85, 140–42, 208.

35. "Mantoux's Notes," April 15, 1919, *PWW*, 57:358–59. Also see Manela, *Wilsonian Moment*, 179–82; Lansing to Wilson, April 12, 1919, *PWW*, 57:298–301.

36. "Mantoux's Notes," April 18, 1919, *PWW*, 57:453–54.

37. "Hankey's and Mantoux's Notes of a Meeting of the Council of Four," April 21, 1919, *PWW*, 57:553–56; Walworth, *Peacemakers*, 367. The next day, during a meeting of the Council, Lloyd George took note of London's "engagement with Japan" over the issue dating back to 1917. He said to Makino that "[t]he only doubt he felt was as to whether the ultimate destination of Kiauchau [the German leased territory in Shandong] was a matter for inclusion in the Treaty with Germany." See "Hankey's and Mantoux's Notes of a Meeting of the Council of Four," April 22, 1919, *PWW*, 57:602–3.

38. "Hankey's and Mantoux's Notes," April 22, 1919, *PWW*, 57:599–610, 615–26; Xu, *China and the Great War*, 259–61; MacMillan, *Paris 1919*, 335–36.

39. "From the Diary of Colonel House," April 26, 1919, *PWW*, 58:153; "Memorandum by Lansing," April 28, 1919, *PWW*, 58:185; Bliss to Wilson, April 29, 1919, *PWW*, 58:232–34; Williams to Wilson, April 24, 1919, *PWW*, 58:70–72; Manela, *Wilsonian Moment*, 183–85; Walworth, *Peacemakers*, 368–72.

40. "From the Diary of Ray Stannard Baker," April 30, 1919, *PWW*, 58:270–71. These are not direct quotes, but Baker's recollections.

41. Tumulty to Wilson, April 24, 1919 (two telegrams this date), *PWW*, 58:105; Tumulty to Wilson, April 26, 1919, *PWW*, 58:170.

42. Wilson to Tumulty, April 30, 1919, *PWW*, 58:272–73; Tumulty to Grayson, April 30, 1919, *PWW*, 58:273.

43. Quoted in Manela, *Wilsonian Moment*, 184.

44. Ibid., 184–93; MacMillan, *Paris 1919*, 338–41; Xu, *China and the Great War*, 262–69.

Chapter 13. The Campaigns for Treaty Ratification

1. Cooper, Jr., *Breaking*, 85–86, 97–98; Knock, *End*, 236–39. The *New Republic* had used the "peace without victory" phrase as the title of an editorial in December 1916. See Charles Forcey, *The Crossroads of Liberalism: Croly, Weyl, Lippmann and the Progressive Era, 1900–1925* (New York, 1967), 266, 288–91.

2. Cooper, Jr., *Breaking*, 99–100; Herbert F. Margulies, *The Mild Reservationists and the League of Nations Controversy in the Senate* (Columbia, Mo., 1989), 31; Ralph Stone, *The Irreconcilables: The Fight Against the League of Nations* (New York, 1973), 105.

3. Margulies, *Mild Reservationists*, 99–100.

4. Early leadership strategy can be traced via ibid., 10, 27, 31–33; Stone, *Irreconcilables*, 70–74, 90–98, 110–15; Ambrosius, *Diplomatic Tradition*, 94, 148, 151; Cooper, Jr., *Breaking*, 113.

5. W. Stull Holt, *Treaties Defeated by the Senate* (Baltimore, 1933), 179, 258–60; Widenor, *Lodge*, 302–4.

6. Margaret Leech, *In the Days of McKinley* (New York, 1959), 329–30.

7. Quoted in Widenor, *Lodge*, 173.

8. Such antipathy was certainly evident in TR, who passed away at the beginning of 1919. It was also present in Philander C. Knox, William E. Borah, Frank Brandegee, Warren G. Harding, and Hiram Johnson, among other figures important in the "treaty fight." The best overviews of the debate that took place over the treaty are Cooper, Jr., *Breaking*; Stone, *Irreconcilables*; Margulies, *Mild Reservationists*; and Ambrosius, *Diplomatic Tradition*.

9. Stone, *Irreconcilables*, 131–33; Johnson, *Peace Progressives*, 71–102; Robert James Maddox, *William E. Borah and American Foreign Policy* (Baton Rouge, 1969), 57–68; Thelen, *La Follette*, 150–54.

10. U.S. Department of State, *Treaty of Versailles*, 83.

11. Wiseman to Reading, August 16, 1918, *PWW*, 49:273; "A Report of a Press Conference," July 10, 1919, *PWW*, 61:421; Wilson to Lansing, May 24, 1919, *PWW*, 59:470–71.

12. See Wilson's emphasis on this during his dinner with House and Senate members as reported in the *New York Times*, February 27, 1919, *PWW*, 55:268–76.

13. Root to House, August 16, 1918, *PWW*, 49:272.

14. Quoted in Cooper, Jr., *Breaking*, 41.

15. Ambrosius, *Diplomatic Tradition*, 88; Cooper, Jr., *Breaking*, 69, 114–15, 132–33; Margulies, *Mild Reservationists*, 33, 58, 153.

16. Root to Lodge, April 4, 1919, Henry Cabot Lodge Papers, Massachusetts Historical Society, Boston (hereafter HCLP); Root to Lodge, July 24, 1919, HCLP; U.S. Congress, Senate, *Letters of the Honorable Elihu Root Relative to the League of Nations*, S. Doc. 41, 66th Cong.,

1st sess., 1919; Jessup, *Elihu Root*, 2:376–400; Richard W. Leopold, *Elihu Root and the Conservative Tradition* (Boston, 1954), 130–39.

17. Its deterrent value was a theme of his "Remarks to Members of the Democratic National Committee" on February 28, 1919. See *PWW*, 55:317–19. On his belief in its significance to France, see "From the Diary of David Hunter Miller," March 18, 1919, *PWW*, 56:77. On the League and American international leadership, see Wilson to Tumulty, June 23, 1919, *PWW*, 61:115–16.

18. "A Report of a Press Conference," July 10, 1919, *PWW*, 61:423.

19. Thus, as he had in his remarks in Boston, upon his return to America following the completion of the first draft of the Covenant, and again in New York, just before his return to Paris, so too did Wilson on July 10 (before the Senate) ask Americans to accept what he termed their "duty" to the "world." See "An Address in Boston," February 24, 1919, *PWW*, 55:238–45; "An Address at the Metropolitan Opera House," March 4, 1919, *PWW*, 55:413–21; and "An Address to the Senate," July 10, 1919, *PWW*, 61:426–36.

20. Stone, *Irreconcilables*, 100–18; Ambrosius, *Diplomatic Tradition*, 144–49.

21. Tumulty to Wilson, July 18, 1919, *PWW*, 61:534; Ambrosius, *Diplomatic Tradition*, 150–51.

22. See *New York Times*, August 2, 1919, *PWW*, 62:92–93, on what the president was telling senators in private sessions with them in this period. "All the world is waiting . . . to know when it shall have peace," he said in his "Address to a Joint Session of Congress," August 8, 1919, *PWW*, 62:210, on American economic conversion to peace. See also Ambrosius, *Diplomatic Tradition*, 151–58.

23. "Wilson Continues Firm," July 23, 1919, *PWW*, 61:601.

24. Ambrosius, *Diplomatic Tradition*, 158–67; Cooper, Jr., *Breaking*, 121, 141–46. For a record of the August 19 meeting at the White House, see "A Conversation with Members of the Senate Foreign Relations Committee," August 19, 1919, *PWW*, 62:339–411.

25. See Lewis L. Gould, *The Presidency of William McKinley* (Lawrence, Kans., 1980), 143.

26. Hannigan, *New World Power*, 220–24.

27. J. Michael Hogan, *Woodrow Wilson's Western Tour: Rhetoric, Public Opinion, and the League of Nations* (College Station, Tex., 2006), 19–20, 67–68; Cooper, Jr., *Breaking*, 152–53.

28. "A Memorandum by Robert Lansing," August 11, 1919, *PWW*, 62:258–59; Margulies, *Mild Reservationists*, 71, 87; Ambrosius, *Diplomatic Tradition*, 181–82.

29. As I read the memorandum he gave to Senator Gilbert M. Hitchcock (D-Neb.), who was handling the treaty for the president in the Senate, Wilson on his departure was still unwilling to envision any but interpretive reservations, and then only if he had to. See "A Memorandum," September 3, 1919, *PWW*, 62:621.

30. The issues of leadership and exemptions were central to "An Address in the Seattle Area," September 13, 1919, *PWW*, 63:254–64. "The only thing that causes me uneasiness, my fellow countrymen," said Wilson in Seattle (255), "is not the ultimate outcome, but the impressions that may be created . . . by the perplexed delay. The rest of the world believes absolutely in America and is ready to follow it anywhere, and it is now a little chilled. It now asks: 'Is America hesitating to lead? We are ready to give ourselves to her leadership here. Will she not accept the gift?'"

31. Hogan, *Western Tour*, 23–25, 60–71, 99–134. For a list of the reporters taken along, see "From the Diary of Dr. Grayson," September 3, 1919, *PWW*, 62:626–27.

32. Hogan, *Western Tour*, 62.

33. "Address to the Columbus Chamber of Commerce," September 4, 1919, *PWW*, 63:8–10, 12; "Remarks on Board the Presidential Train, Richmond, Indiana," September 4, 1919, *PWW*, 63:18–19; "Address in the Spokane Armory," September 12, 1919, *PWW*, 63:228; "Address in the Portland Auditorium," September 15, 1919, *PWW*, 63:285; "Address in the San Diego Stadium," September 19, 1919, *PWW*, 63:374–76. In an "Address in the Tacoma Armory," on September 13, 1919, Wilson said, "[I]t is of particular importance to remember . . . at this moment, when some men have dared to introduce party passion into this question, that some of the leading spirits, perhaps I may say the leading spirits, in the conception of this great idea were the leading figures of the great Republican party." See *PWW*, 63:247.

34. "An Address in the Indianapolis Coliseum," September 4, 1919, *PWW*, 63:22–23; "A Luncheon Address to the St. Louis Chamber of Commerce," September 5, 1919, *PWW*, 63:38–39.

35. "An Address in the Indianapolis Coliseum," September 4, 1919, *PWW*, 63:27. As historian Thomas A. Bailey notes, this constituted a "tactical error," for a "logical inference was that if we could mind other people's business those people could start minding ours." See his *Woodrow Wilson and the Great Betrayal* (Chicago, 1963), 118.

36. "Address in the Tacoma Armory," September 13, 1919, *PWW*, 63:247–48; "Address in the Tabernacle in Salt Lake City," September 23, 1919, *PWW*, 63:449–63. "Instead of wishing to ask to stand aside, get the benefits of the League, but share none of its burdens or responsibilities, I for my part want to go in and accept what is offered to us—the leadership of the world," said Wilson (455).

37. See his comments at the beginning of his "Address in the St. Louis Coliseum," September 5, 1919, *PWW*, 63:43.

38. "An Address in the Indianapolis Coliseum," September 4, 1919, *PWW*, 63:29.

39. "A Luncheon Address to the St. Louis Chamber of Commerce," September 5, 1919, *PWW*, 63:35–36. The same theme recurs in his speeches in Indianapolis, Des Moines, Helena, and Coeur d'Alene. Often he spoke of the Bremen to Baghdad route, at other times of Russia. For example, at Coeur d'Alene, Wilson said that "[a]t this moment the only people who are dealing with the Bolshevik government are the Germans. . . . They are making all their plans that . . . the development of Russia shall as soon as possible be in the hands of Germans. And just so soon as she can command that great power, that is also her road to the East and to the domination of the world. If you do not guarantee the titles that you are setting up in these treaties, you leave the whole ground fallow in which again to sow the dragon's teeth with the harvest of armed men."

40. "An Address at Coeur d'Alene," September 12, 1919, *PWW*, 63:214. A week later, Assistant Secretary of State William Phillips informed the president that "Kolchak's forces have resumed the offensive and are driving the Bolsheviki back towards the Urals." Wilson responded by okaying the dispatch of additional supplies to Kolchak's army. See Phillips to Wilson, September 19, 1919, *PWW*, 63:394; and Wilson to Phillips, September 20, 1919, *PWW*, 63:421.

41. "Address in the St. Louis Coliseum," September 5, 1919, *PWW*, 63:46.

42. "An Address at Coeur d'Alene," September 12, 1919, *PWW*, 63:218.

43. "Address in the St. Louis Coliseum," September 5, 1919, *PWW*, 63:44–47.

44. "Address in the Marlow Theater in Helena," September 11, 1919, *PWW*, 63:189.

45. "Address in the Shrine Auditorium in Los Angeles," September 20, 1919, *PWW*, 63:416.

46. "Address in the St. Paul Auditorium," September 9, 1919, *PWW*, 63:143, 148.

47. "Address in Convention Hall in Kansas City," September 6, 1919, *PWW*, 63:72; Stone, *Irreconcilables*, 129.

48. "An Address in the Des Moines Coliseum," September 6, 1919, *PWW*, 63:77.

49. "Address in the Seattle Arena," September 13, 1919, *PWW*, 63:254.

50. Hogan, *Western Tour*, 25. For a different assessment, see Cooper, Jr., *Breaking*, 186–87, 190–91; and John Milton Cooper, Jr., *Woodrow Wilson: A Biography* (New York, 2009), 531–32.

51. For the most recent analysis of what transpired in connection with Wilson's health, see Cooper, Jr., *Woodrow Wilson*, 530–31, 533–40.

52. Stone, *Irreconcilables*, 39–40, 131–33.

53. Ambrosius, *Diplomatic Tradition*, 183, 188; Cooper, Jr., *Breaking*, 168–71. For Lansing's effort to explain himself to the president, see Lansing to Wilson, September 17, 1919, *PWW*, 63:337–40. In this telegram, the secretary of state also assured the president that he wished "to do everything I can to help in the ratification of the treaty."

54. Margulies, *Mild Reservationists*, 103; Ambrosius, *Diplomatic Tradition*, 185; Cooper, Jr., *Breaking*, 194–95. Wilson was informed on September 22 that agreement had been reached between the "mild reservationists" and Lodge on a reservation with regard to Article 10. He condemned the development in his speech at Salt Lake City the following day. See Phillips to Wilson, September 22, 1919, *PWW*, 63:444; "Address in the Tabernacle in Salt Lake City," September 23, 1919, *PWW*, 63:453–54. Wilson said that the reservation was "an absolute withdrawal from the moral obligations of Article X." It "would be a rejection of the Covenant."

55. See Cooper, Jr., *Breaking*, 225–26; Ambrosius, *Diplomatic Tradition*, 189–208.

56. Hitchcock to E. G. B. Wilson, November 13, 1919, *PWW*, 64:28–30; Hitchcock to E. B. G. Wilson, November 15, 1919, *PWW*, 64:37–41; "Memorandum by Grayson," November 17, 1919, *PWW*, 64:43–45; Ambrosius, *Diplomatic Tradition*, 206–8; Margulies, *Mild Reservationists*, 149, 164.

57. Two votes were taken on the treaty with the "Lodge reservations." It was defeated by 39–55 and 41–50. The treaty by itself was defeated 38–55. See Ambrosius, *Diplomatic Tradition*, 208.

58. "News Report [printed in the *New York Times*, December 6, 1919]," *PWW*, 64:126; E. B. G. Wilson to Hitchcock, December 19, 1919, *PWW*, 64:206; Stone, *Irreconcilables*, 149.

59. Margulies, *Mild Reservationists*, 198; Cooper, Jr., *Breaking*, 290.

60. These included Senators Lodge, Harry New, of Indiana, Irvine L. Lenroot, of Wisconsin, and Frank B. Kellogg, of Minnesota, for the Republicans and Hitchcock, Robert L. Owen, of Oklahoma, Kenneth S. McKellar, of Tennessee, Furnifold M. Simmons, of North Carolina, and Thomas J. Walsh, of Montana, for the Democrats. No "irreconcilables" were included. Cooper, Jr., *Breaking*, 303–9; Ambrosius, *Diplomatic Tradition*, 228–30; Margulies, *Mild Reservationists*, 199–206.

61. "News Report [printed in the *New York Times*, January 23, 1920]," *PWW*, 64:311–12; Margulies, *Mild Reservationists*, 207; Stone, *Irreconcilables*, 156–57; Cooper, Jr., *Breaking*, 310–11; Maddox, *Borah*, 70. J. P. Morgan partners, particularly Thomas W. Lamont, were

strong advocates of the League. See, for example, Bailey, *Great Betrayal*, 226. There were also some prominent corporate and financial figures who were critics.

62. Stone, *Irreconcilables*, 158; Ambrosius, *Diplomatic Tradition*, 242.

63. Ambrosius, *Diplomatic Tradition*, 241; Stone, *Irreconcilables*, 160.

64. Cover letter to Mrs. Wilson, dated November 24, 1919, enclosing letter, elaborating on these ideas, addressed to the president, *PWW*, 64:88–90. Also see House's follow-up of November 27, *PWW*, 64:95–96.

65. Davis to Tumulty, December 1, 1919, *PWW*, 64:104–5; Ambrosius, *Diplomatic Tradition*, 216–17, 219; Margulies, *Mild Reservationists*, 217.

66. "Draft of a Public Letter," ca. December 17, 1919, *PWW*, 64:199–202; Cooper, Jr., *Breaking*, 289–90.

67. "A Jackson Day Message," January 8, 1920, *PWW*, 64:257–59; Ambrosius, *Diplomatic Tradition*, 227; Cooper, Jr., *Breaking*, 297–99.

68. "From the Diary of Ray Stannard Baker," January 23, 1920, *PWW*, 64:320–21; Bert E. Park, "Aftermath of Wilson's Stroke," in *PWW*, 64:525–28 (appendix).

69. Stone, *Irreconcilables*, 153; Ambrosius, *Diplomatic Tradition*, 227, 242; Cooper, Jr., *Breaking*, 322–28, 326; Keynes, *Economic Consequences of the Peace*, originally published in the United States in 1920, it is available online at http://www.gutenberg.org/files/15776/15776 -h/15776-h.htm.

70. Hitchcock to Wilson, February 24, 1920, *PWW*, 64:466. It seems Hitchcock himself may have preferred Wilson accept the treaty with reservations.

71. Wilson to Hitchcock, March 8, 1920, *PWW*, 65:67–71.

72. The last stages of this act in the treaty fight are chronicled in detail in Stone, *Irreconcilables*, 160–70; Margulies, *Mild Reservationists*, 215–60; Ambrosius, *Diplomatic Tradition*, 240–50; Cooper, Jr., *Breaking*, 314–70.

73. See http://www.presidency.ucsb.edu/ws/?pid = 29635; Margulies, *Mild Reservationists*, 261–71; Ambrosius, *Diplomatic Tradition*, 251–64; Cooper, Jr., *Breaking*, 376–84; Wesley M. Bagby, *The Road to Normalcy: The Presidential Campaign and Election of 1920* (Baltimore, 1962), 80–81.

74. Ambrosius, *Diplomatic Tradition*, 265–89; Cooper, Jr., *Breaking*, 385–95; Stone, *Irreconcilables*, 271–77; Warren F. Kuehl and Lynne K. Dunn, *Keeping the Covenant: American Internationalists and the League of Nations* (Kent, Ohio, 1997), 1–18; Bagby, *Road to Normalcy*, 160–67; Paul F. Boller, Jr., *Presidential Campaigns* (Oxford, 1984, 2004), 212; Allan J. Lichtman, "The Election of 1920," in Kennedy, *Companion*, 551–65. Wilson did not finally relinquish thoughts of running for a third term until the Democrats' San Francisco convention.

75. A report by Stephen T. Early to Franklin Roosevelt, Cox's running mate, quoted in Cooper, Jr., *Breaking*, 388.

Part V. The Republicans Try Their Hands (1921–24)

Epigraphs, in sequence: Harding to Henry Cabot Lodge, Warren G. Harding Papers (Ohio Historical Society, Columbus), hereafter WGHP; CAB 23/30/20, pp. 14–15, accessible at www.nationalarchives.gov.uk/cabinetpapers/; Logan to Herbert Hoover, quoted in Peter H. Buckingham, *International Normalcy: The Open Door Peace with the Former Central Powers, 1921–29* (Wilmington, Del., 1983), 119–20.

Chapter 14. Latin America and China

1. For overviews of the Republican Party and of the Harding administration, see Eugene P. Trani and David L. Wilson, *The Presidency of Warren G. Harding* (Lawrence, Kans., 1977); and John D. Hicks, *Republican Ascendancy, 1921–1933* (New York, 1960). Also see chap. 2, "The Domestic Roots of Republican Foreign Policy," in Costigliola, *Awkward Dominion*, 56–75. The Democratic descent meanwhile is surveyed in David Burner, *The Politics of Provincialism: The Democratic Party in Transition, 1918–1932* (New York, 1970), 41–102. Harding referred to the political challenges he faced in a letter to Lodge written shortly after his election. He told him that "I am pursuing the most tactful course I know with the thought of finding some common ground on which we ourselves may unite before attempting to fix a definite policy in dealing with the remainder of the world. I am sure you will agree that it is perfectly hopeless to think of a program in dealing with other nations until we have some assurance concerning what we may agree upon among ourselves." Harding to Lodge, December 29, 1920, WGHP.

2. Trani and Wilson, *Harding*, 109–10.

3. Leopold, *Root*, 147.

4. Harding to Lodge, December 29, 1920, WGHP; Trani and Wilson, *Harding*, 141.

5. Charles DeBenedetti, *The Peace Reform in American History* (Bloomington, Ind., 1980), 108–20.

6. Johnson, *Peace Progressives*, 106–99.

7. Still of some use for its survey of this mood is Adler's arch-Wilsonian *Isolationist Impulse*, 7–150.

8. Warren I. Cohen, *Empire Without Tears: America's Foreign Relations, 1921–1933* (New York, 1987), xii.

9. "Annual Message on the State of the Union," December 7, 1915, PWW, 35:302.

10. See above, Chapter 4; also Hannigan, *New World Power*, 86–88; Tulchin, *Aftermath*, 3–37; Rosenberg, *World War I*, 31–110.

11. Tulchin, *Aftermath*, 38–117.

12. Ibid., 157–65.

13. Ibid., 206–33; Emily S. Rosenberg, *Spreading the American Dream: American Economic and Cultural Expansion, 1890–1945* (New York, 1982), 90–97. The quote is from the latter work, p. 95. It is by Owen Young, formerly of GE, who became the first president of RCA and was also destined to play a major role in U.S. foreign economic policy in the following years.

14. Tulchin, *Aftermath*, 118–54; Rosenberg, *American Dream*, 128–32; Daniel Yergin, *The Prize: The Epic Quest for Oil, Money and Power* (New York, 1992), 234–37, 258; LaFeber, *Inevitable Revolutions*, 77. On British-American relations in the postwar Middle East, see William Stivers, *Supremacy and Oil: Iraq, Turkey, and the Anglo-American World Order, 1918–1930* (Ithaca, N.Y., 1982).

15. Elisabeth Glaser-Schmidt, "The Guggenheims and the Coming of the Great Depression in Chile, 1923–1934," *Business and Economic History* 24 (Fall 1995): 176–85; Cohen, *Empire*, 39; Albert, *South America*, 308.

16. Joan Hoff Wilson, *American Business and Foreign Policy, 1920–1933* (Boston, 1973), 169; Robert Freeman Smith, "Latin America, the United States and the European Powers,

1830–1930," in Leslie Bethell, ed., *Cambridge History of Latin America*, 12 vols. (Cambridge, 1986), 4:112; Rosemary Thorp, "Latin America and the International Economy from the First World War to the World Depression," in Bethell, *Cambridge History*, 4:63–64. The quotation is from the latter source.

17. Thorp, "Latin America," 65–66; Rosenberg, *American Dream*, 123; Gilderhus, *Second Century*, 60; Cohen, *Empire*, 22, 41; Joseph S. Tulchin, *Argentina and the United States: A Conflicted Relationship* (Boston, 1990), 48; Albert, *South America*, 308.

18. Wilson, *American Business*, 169; Rosenberg, *World War I*, 65; Thorp, "Latin America," 66.

19. Hannigan, *New World Power*, 40–50.

20. Robert N. Seidel, "American Reformers Abroad: The Kemmerer Missions in South America, 1923–1931," in Paul W. Drake, ed., *Money Doctors, Foreign Debts, and Economic Reforms in Latin America from the 1890s to the Present* (Wilmington, Del., 1994), 86–109; Barry Eichengreen, "House Calls of the Money Doctor: The Kemmerer Missions to Latin America, 1917–1931," in Drake, *Money Doctors*, 110–32; Emily S. Rosenberg, *Financial Missionaries to the World: The Politics and Culture of Dollar Diplomacy, 1900–1930* (Cambridge, Mass., 1999), 103–5, 151–65.

21. Eichengreen, "House Calls," 112–13; Rosenberg, *Financial Missionaries*, 152; Daniel Díaz Fuentes, "Latin America During the Interwar Period: The Rise and Fall of the Gold Standard in Argentina, Brazil, and Mexico," in John Coatsworth and Alan M. Taylor, eds., *Latin America and the World Economy Since 1800* (Cambridge, Mass., 1998), 443–69; Drake, *Money Doctors*, xxviii.

22. What follows draws heavily on Tulchin, *Aftermath*, 83, 94; Dana G. Munro, *The United States and the Caribbean Republics, 1921–1933* (Princeton, N.J., 1974), 3–214; Louis A. Pérez, Jr., *Cuba and the United States: Ties of Singular Intimacy* (Athens, Ga., 1990), 166–69; LaFeber, *Inevitable Revolutions*, 56–67; John H. Coatsworth, *Central America and the United States: The Clients and the Colossus* (New York, 1994), 39–41; and Lars Schoultz, *Beneath the United States: A History of U.S. Policy Toward Latin America* (Cambridge, Mass., 1998), 253–71.

23. See Chapters 1 and 4 above; also Hannigan, *New World Power*, 39–50.

24. Munro, *Caribbean Republics*, 9.

25. Hannigan, *New World Power*, 34–39.

26. On Cuban precedents, see Lester D. Langley, *The Banana Wars: United States Intervention in the Caribbean, 1898–1934* (Wilmington, Del., 2002), 42–43.

27. Munro, *Caribbean Republics*, 123.

28. Smith, *Unequal Giants*, 138–39, 168.

29. Gilderhus, *Second Century*, 65; Smith, "Latin America," 118.

30. Wilson, *American Business*, 163; Smith, "Latin America," 115.

31. What follows draws heavily on Robert Freeman Smith's classic account, *The United States and Revolutionary Nationalism in Mexico, 1916–1932* (Chicago, 1972), 1–228.

32. Article 27 is printed in the appendix of Smith, *Revolutionary Nationalism*, 267–70; this quotation appears on p. 268. Additional useful characterizations of the constitution may be found in Knight, *Mexican Revolution*, 469–72; and Hart, *Revolutionary Mexico*, 327–33. Also see Cohen, *Empire*, 63–67.

33. On this, see also Clifford W. Trow, "Woodrow Wilson and the Mexican Interventionist Movement of 1919," *Journal of American History* 58 (June 1971): 46–72.

34. LaFeber, *Clash*, 80–134; William D. O'Neil, *Interwar U.S. and Japanese National Product and Defense Expenditure* (June 2003), 6, available at http://www.analysis.william doneil.com/CIM_D0007249.A1.pdf; Akira Iriye, *After Imperialism: The Search for a New Order in the Far East, 1921–1931* (New York, 1969), 9–10; Roger Dingman, *Power in the Pacific: The Origins of Naval Arms Limitation, 1914–1922* (Chicago, 1976), 53; Barnhart, *Japan*, 68–70; Thomas H. Buckley, "The Icarus Factor: the American Pursuit of Myth in Naval Arms Control, 1921–36," in Erik Goldstein and John Maurer, eds., *The Washington Conference, 1921–22: Naval Rivalry, East Asian Stability and the Road to Pearl Harbor* (Portland, Ore., 1994), 127.

35. Warren I. Cohen, "America and the May 4th Movement: The Response to Chinese Nationalism, 1917–1921," *Pacific Historical Review* 35 (February 1966): 83–100; Brian T. George, "The State Department and Sun Yat-sen: American Policy and the Revolutionary Disintegration of China, 1920–1924," *Pacific Historical Review* 46 (August 1977): 387–408.

36. Roberta Allbert Dayer, *Bankers and Diplomats in China, 1917–1925* (London, 1981), 39–92; Warren I. Cohen, *The Chinese Connection: Roger S. Greene, Thomas W. Lamont, George E. Sokolsky and American-East Asian Relations* (New York, 1978), 51–70.

37. Stephen J. Valone, *"A Policy Calculated to Benefit China": The United States and the China Arms Embargo, 1919–1929* (Westport, Conn., 1991), 41–82.

38. See Chapter 10 above. For background on postwar naval matters, see Dingman, *Power*, 107–11; Christopher Hall, *Britain, America and Arms Control, 1921–1937* (New York, 1987), 1–35; Malcolm H. Murfett, "Look Back in Anger: The Western Powers and the Washington Conference of 1921–1922," in B. J. C. McKercher, ed., *Arms Limitation and Disarmament: Restraints on War, 1899–1939* (Westport, Conn., 1992), 83–103; Richard W. Fanning, *Peace and Disarmament: Naval Rivalry and Arms Control, 1922–1933* (Lexington, Ky., 1995), 1–11; O'Brien, *Naval Power*, 135–74.

39. John Chalmers Vinson, *The Parchment Peace: The United States Senate and the Washington Conference, 1921–1922* (Athens, Ga., 1955), 51–96; Maddox, *Borah*, 86–94; Dingman, *Power*, 143–52; Trani and Wilson, *Harding*, 149–52.

40. Robert H. Van Meter, Jr., "The Washington Conference of 1921–1922: A New Look," *Pacific Historical Review* 46 (November 1977): 603–24.

41. Harding to Lodge, February 20, 1921, WGHP.

42. Vinson, *Parchment*, 82.

43. Quoted in ibid., 104. Also see Dingman, *Power*, 152.

44. LaFeber, *Clash*, 130–36; Buckley, "Icarus Factor," 128–31; Vinson, *Parchment*, 101–9; Dingman, *Power*, 154–57.

45. For the texts of these treaties, see FR 1922, 1–288. Very good essays on the United States and the other major participants at the conference are contained in Goldstein and Maurer, *Washington Conference*. Also see LaFeber, *Clash*, 136–42; Dingman, *Power*, 196–214; and, on the Nine Power Pact, Shizhang Hu, *Stanley K. Hornbeck and the Open Door Policy, 1919–1937* (Westport, Conn., 1995), 52–56.

46. Here see especially David Armstrong, "China's Place in the New Pacific Order," in Goldstein and Maurer, *Washington Conference*, 249–66.

47. On the dealings between the United States and Japan at the conference, see especially LaFeber, *Clash*, 139–43.

48. Vinson, *Parchment*, 175–212.

49. George, "State Department," 396.

50. Ibid., 396–404.

51. Dayer, *Bankers*, 123–212 (the MacMurray quote is on p. 174); Cohen, *Chinese Connection*, 97–119.

Chapter 15. Europe

1. Michael Dunne, *The United States and the World Court, 1920–1935* (New York, 1988); Cohen, *Empire*, 57–59. On the theme of a law-bound world order, see Robert Freeman Smith, "Republican Policy and the Pax Americana, 1921–1932," in William Appleman Williams, ed., *From Colony to Empire: Essays in the History of American Foreign Relations* (New York, 1972), 253–92.

2. All this is nicely summarized in Stephen V. O. Clarke, *Central Bank Cooperation: 1924–31* (New York, 1967), 18–20. Also see Kathleen Burk, "The House of Morgan in Financial Diplomacy, 1920–1930," in McKercher, *Anglo-American Relations*, 125; Steiner, *Lights*, 182.

3. Noteworthy studies centering on Strong and his interactions with American bankers and European central bankers, on the restoration of the gold standard, and on efforts at monetary stabilization in the 1920s include Richard H. Meyer, *Bankers' Diplomacy: Monetary Stabilization in the Twenties* (New York, 1970); Clarke, *Cooperation*; Stephen V. O. Clarke, *The Reconstruction of the International Monetary System: The Attempts of 1922 and 1933* (Princeton, N.J., 1973); Barry Eichengreen, *Golden Fetters: The Gold Standard and the Great Depression, 1919–1939* (New York, 1992), especially 67–186; Rosenberg, *Financial Missionaries*; Harold James, *The End of Globalization: Lessons from the Great Depression* (Cambridge, Mass., 2001), particularly chap. 2; and Liaquat Ahamed, *Lords of Finance: The Bankers Who Broke the World* (New York, 2009). On Hoover's ideas and role, see especially Robert H. Van Meter, "Herbert Hoover and the Struggle for European Economic Recovery in the 1920s," in Lee Nash, ed., *Herbert Hoover and World Peace* (Lanham, Md., 2010). On the theme of continuity from the Wilson into the Harding administrations, see Parrini, *Heir to Empire*.

4. Davis and Trani, *First Cold War*, 191–99.

5. Joan Hoff Wilson, *Ideology and Economics: U.S. Relations with the Soviet Union, 1918–1933* (Columbia, Mo., 1974), 28–29; Katherine A. S. Siegel, *Loans and Legitimacy: The Evolution of Soviet-American Relations, 1919–1933* (Lexington, Ky., 1996), 50.

6. Trani and Wilson, *Harding*, 124; Siegel, *Loans*, 90.

7. Davis and Trani, *First Cold War*, 199. In late 1918, House had advocated that Russia be broken up, arguing that it was too big for "the safety of the world." But Lansing and Wilson disagreed, the former arguing that that would provide less of a check to Japanese or German expansion. See Schild, *Ideology*, 118–21; and Neal Pease, *Poland, the United States, and the Stabilization of Europe, 1919–1933* (New York, 1986), 9. That policy was then sustained by Colby and then Hughes.

8. Wilson, *Ideology*, 42–43; Siegel, *Loans*, 99.

9. Christine A. White, *British and American Commercial Relations with Soviet Russia, 1918–1924* (Chapel Hill, N.C., 1992), 171.

10. Trani and Wilson, *Harding*, 119–23; Costigliola, *Awkward Dominion*, 88–92; Siegel, *Loans*, 55–61.

11. White, *Commercial Relations*, 111–38, 196, 206. American exports to Russia doubled between 1921 and 1922.

12. Orde, *British Policy*, 161–207; Steiner, *Lights*, 153–69, 209–10; Trani and Wilson, *Harding*, 123; Van Meter, "European Recovery," 338–39; Cohrs, *Unfinished*, 87.

13. Quoted in White, *Commercial Relations*, 195.

14. *FR 1923*, vii–xxiv.

15. White, *Commercial Relations*, 206.

16. Ibid., 206–24; Siegel, *Loans*, 65–88.

17. Wilson, *Ideology*, 32; Steiner, *Lights*, 172–75.

18. Cohrs, *Unfinished*, 69–70; Buckingham, *International Normalcy*, 10; Steiner, *Lights*, 208–11.

19. Van Meter, "European Recovery," 66–69; Orde, *British Policy*, 88, 160; Benjamin D. Rhodes, "The Image of Britain in the United States, 1919–1929: A Contentious Relative and Rival," in McKercher, *Anglo-American Relations*, 194; Stephen A. Schuker, "Origins of American Stabilization Policy in Europe: The Financial Dimension, 1918–1924," in Schröder, *Confrontation*, 385–86.

20. Wilson to Lloyd George, November 3, 1920, *PWW*, 66:309–11; Orde, *British Policy*, 103–4; Van Meter, "European Recovery," 237–38.

21. Keith L. Nelson, *Victors Divided: America and the Allies in Germany, 1918–1923* (Berkeley, Calif., 1975), 1–181; Sharp, *Versailles*, 100.

22. Manfred Jonas, *The United States and Germany: A Diplomatic History* (Ithaca, N.Y., 1984), 158–61; Buckingham, *International Normalcy*, 7, 22–33.

23. On this issue, for 1921–23, see especially Orde, *British Policy*, 153–60, 208–37; Leffler, *Elusive*, 64–70; Van Meter, "Herbert Hoover," 82–84.

24. CAB 23/30/20, p. 16, accessible at www.nationalarchives.gov.uk/cabinetpapers/.

25. For the text, see the *Federal Reserve Bulletin* for September 1922, 1047–48, at fraser .stlouis/docs/publications/FRB/pages/1920–1924/27269_1920–1924.pdf.

26. Steiner, *Lights*, 197–201.

27. Buckingham, *International Normalcy*, 108–11.

28. Ibid., 117–20. Logan's letter is quoted on p. 119.

29. Quoted in ibid., 124; Nelson, *Victors Divided*, 244–45; Buckingham, *International Normalcy*, 121–25.

30. Nelson, *Victors Divided*, 246–49.

31. Steiner, *Lights*, 201–37.

32. Buckingham, *International Normalcy*, 133, 138.

33. Ibid., 133–45. Hughes is quoted on p. 139.

34. A very good recent discussion is Cohrs's, *Unfinished*, 107–96. Also see Steiner, *Lights*, 240–50; Costigliola, *Awkward Dominion*, 123; and Rosenberg, *Financial Missionaries*, 171.

Conclusion

1. Key texts include Charles C. Tansill, *America Goes to War* (Boston, 1938); Harry Elmer Barnes, *The Genesis of the World War* (New York, 1929); Charles A. Beard, *The Devil Theory of War* (New York, 1936); C. Hartley Grattan, *Preface to Chaos* (New York, 1936); H. C. Petersen, *Propaganda for War: The Campaign Against American Neutrality, 1914–1917* (Norman, Okla., 1939); Paul Birdsall, "Neutrality and Economic Pressures, 1914–1917," *Science and Society* 3 (Spring 1939): 217–28. The revisionists are discussed as a group in Warren I. Cohen, *The American Revisionists: The Lessons of Intervention in World War I* (Chicago, 1967).

2. There is a vast literature. The main outlines can be appreciated via the following: John Gallagher and Ronald Robinson, "The Imperialism of Free Trade," *Economic History Review*, n.s. 6 (1953): 1–15; Paul Kennedy, *The Realities Behind Diplomacy: Background Influences on British External Policy, 1865–1980* (London, 1981); P. J. Cain and A. G. Hopkins, *British Imperialism, 1688–2000* (Harlow, 2002); and John Darwin, *The Empire Project: The Rise and Fall of the British World-System, 1830–1970* (Cambridge, 2011).

3. See Kennedy, *Rise and Fall*, 202.

4. "From the Diary of Colonel House," April 30, 1917, *PWW*, 42:172.

INDEX

ACKNOWLEDGMENTS

I have been on the receiving end of much kindness writing this book. A number of colleagues and friends have shared with me their expertise or served as sounding boards for my ideas. These include Feroz Ahmad, Herb Bix, Matteo Casini, John Cavanagh, Lester Lee, Pat Reeve, Stacy Stein, Ron Suleski, Leonid Trofimov, and Cyrus Veeser.

Tom Baker, a friend of long standing, going back to our days in graduate school, kindly gave a close reading to the first complete draft of the manuscript. I benefited enormously from his comments.

As with previous projects, I gained immeasurably from the encouragement and feedback of Walter LaFeber—a great scholar, the finest teacher I have ever had, and, since those Cornell days, a dearly prized adviser and friend.

There is perhaps no historian with a more encyclopedic grasp of the Wilson years and the 1920s than Bob Van Meter. I cannot begin to calculate the number of hours we have spoken by phone or in person about that period. He very generously shared with me many documents and leads, as well as his reactions to the entire manuscript in its penultimate form. Bob is an exceptional historian, as well as a treasured friend.

To my great good fortune, Princeton University was a hotbed of Wilson and World War I studies when I was a graduate student in the history department there many years ago. It brought me into contact with some of the major figures in the field, such as Richard Challener, Arthur Link, and Arno Mayer, as well as with a number of fellow students interested in the lively debates surrounding that crucial period. These were the years when the project to publish the sixty-nine-volume *Papers of Woodrow Wilson* there, overseen by Professor Link, was beginning to reach its stride as well. No historian can write a book like this without pausing to comment on the utility of that extraordinarily comprehensive and well-edited collection of materials.

The foreign policy seminar referred to in my dedication has been a central part of my life as a historian. Amazingly, it has met four times a year now for more than three decades, generally at the University of Connecticut. Initially guided by Tom Paterson and Garry Clifford, now no less ably coordinated by Frank Costigliola, it has regularly brought together historians from New England, New York, and beyond to discuss cutting-edge papers and, more generally, to talk over new developments in our field. I know I am not alone in appreciating the stimulating and constructive environment the seminar has created. Garry epitomized its spirit. Over the years, he read my work, always asked after my progress, and unfailingly provided me with useful tips or questions to think about. Above all, Garry was an exemplary human being. He is missed.

Once again, it is a pleasure to note the exceptional virtues, care, and assistance of my editor, Peter Agree, as well as the high professionalism of the people at the University of Pennsylvania Press. I would also like to thank its outside readers for their many useful and constructive suggestions.

Last, but not least, my wife, Irene, and son, Ted, have, as always, sustained me with their encouragement, love, and support.